A SENTENCE DIC

A Sentence
DICTIONARY

Compiled by

ERIC NEAL

HULTON EDUCATIONAL PUBLICATIONS

©
HULTON EDUCATIONAL PUBLICATIONS
1965
Reprinted 1967
Reprinted and revised 1973
Reprinted 1974
Reprinted 1978
Reprinted 1983
Reprinted 1985

ISBN 0 7175 0194 9

First published 1965 by Hulton Educational Publications Ltd,
Raans Road, Amersham, Bucks.
Printed in Great Britain by
Richard Clay (The Chaucer Press) Ltd,
Bungay, Suffolk

PREFACE

THE selection of the 10,000+ words in this dictionary is based on investigations into the words most used by children between the ages of 9 and 13 in their school work. The words include the names of days, months, important cities and countries, numbers, fractions and abbreviations. Many common words such as dog, cat, boy, it, etc., are not included since it is unlikely that a child capable of using a dictionary would have any need to look them up. Some simple words are included because of some special feature, e.g. a secondary meaning, or spelling that is not obvious from the pronunciation. Words derived from those in the dictionary are not included if they merely require the application of a simple spelling rule such as the addition of *-ed* or *-ing*. Exceptions have been made, however, for words known to be common sources of error.

All words, including derivations, are listed alphabetically, since not all users of a dictionary of this kind can be expected to know, for example, that to find the spelling of *bought* one has to look up *buy*.

The author is a teacher who has been dealing with pupils' written work in a variety of subjects for many years and has carried out a number of investigations into children's vocabularies and their spelling difficulties. Also, he has observed how often children look up a word in their school dictionary and then have to ask the teacher what the explanation means.

Tests made with girls and boys in the junior half of a Secondary School showed that children understand many words better by seeing them used in appropriate sentences, than by looking up the meanings in a dictionary. One cannot presume that a word has been made clear to a child when all that has been given is a synonym that is even less well known to him than the original word. Where, however, a synonym simpler than a word is available, this will usually be the best means of explaining the word. All too often a child is perfectly capable of understanding the meaning of a word, but is baffled by the explanation. In such circumstances, a sentence will be a better way of making the meaning clear. A sentence is also better than a definition for a word where the meaning is known but there are doubts about its spelling. It is hoped that teachers will find that the sentences also provide useful material for a variety of English exercises.

To many children, the guides to pronunciation in dictionaries are incomprehensible if they are phonetic, or confusing if they look like simplified spellings. As all the words in this dictionary are those constantly heard or used by the children, guides to pronunciation would be superfluous. Pronunciations are therefore indicated only in special cases, e.g. where they are necessary to explain a difference in meaning.

The symbol ■ is used to separate the different meanings of a word. It also serves to separate uses of a word as different parts of speech, for merely labelling a word *noun*, *verb*, or *adj.*, etc., is unlikely to help the child for whom this dictionary is intended.

IMPORTANT NOTE

The mark ■ shows that a word has
another meaning, or that it can be used
as a different part of speech.

abandon At the shout, '*Abandon ship*!' all the sailors jumped overboard.

abashed To be *abashed* is to feel shy and ashamed.

abbess the chief nun in an abbey.

abbey an ancient church once used by monks.

abbey

abbot the head of the monks in an abbey.

abbreviation The *abbreviation* for mister is Mr.

abdomen the lower part of the body, between the chest and the thighs. Young children call a pain in the *abdomen* a tummy-ache.

abide to stay or dwell.

ability To have *ability* is to be able to do something.

ablaze The dry old house was *ablaze* from top to bottom before the firemen could arrive.

able After his accident John was *able* to walk only with crutches.

abnormal not normal, e.g. There was an *abnormal* amount of rain last summer.

aboard When all the passengers were *aboard*, the ship set sail.

abode The place in which anyone lives is his *abode*.

abolish do away with, e.g. Many schoolboys would like to *abolish* homework.

abolition doing away with, e.g. Many schoolgirls would be in favour of the *abolition* of homework.

abominable very unpleasant and hateful.

aborigines The people who first lived in a country are called the *aborigines*.

abound To say that rivers *abound* in fish means that they are full of fish.

about At *about* sunset ■ you can see bats flying *about*.

above We saw the moon in the sky *above* us.

abrasion a sore place caused by scraping off the skin.

abreast Two *abreast* is two side by side.

abroad When we go *abroad* to France or Italy, we need a passport.

abrupt His going was so *abrupt* that we had no time to say goodbye.

abscess a large and painful sore.

abscond The prisoners tried to *abscond* during the night, but they were soon caught.

absence being absent.

absent not present, e.g. He was *absent* from school because he was ill.

absolute An *absolute* ruler is in complete command of his country. ■ An *absolute* victory means that all resistance was crushed.

absolutely completely.

absorb He watched the blotting-paper *absorb* the ink from the blot.

abstain Many people *abstain* from meat on Fridays and eat fish instead.

abstract An *abstract* noun names something which cannot be seen or touched, e.g. ambition.

absurd silly or ridiculous.

abundance plentiful supply.

abundant As the explorers had an *abundant* water supply, they could drink as much as they liked.

abuse *Abuse*, when it rhymes with 'juice', means insulting language; ■ when it rhymes with 'news', it means to use wrongly.

abusive To be *abusive* is to say insulting things.

abyss a deep crack or hole in the earth.

acacia The *acacia* tree is grown in England chiefly because its feathery leaves are so decorative.

acacia

academy a place where students go to study.

accede The boys did not expect the headmaster to *accede* to their request, but they asked him just the same.

accelerate John's new car can *accelerate* from 10 m.p.h. to 60 m.p.h. in a few seconds.

acceleration The car's *acceleration* is so good that it can increase its speed from 10 m.p.h. to 60 m.p.h. in a few seconds.

accelerator If you want a car to accelerate, you press your foot on a pedal called the *accelerator*.

accent Ivan speaks English with a Russian *accent* (pron. ák-sent). ■ (pron. ak-sént) The dash over *cént* means that you *accént* that part of the word.

accept I am always pleased to *accept* presents, especially on my birthday.

access We were refused *access* to the house by the policeman who stood at the door.

accessary someone who helps to do something—usually something criminal.

accessible The cave was not *accessible* because it was so high up the cliff face.

accessory an additional piece of equipment.

accident an unexpected or unintentional happening.

accidentally As I reached for the butter, I *accidentally* knocked over a tea-cup.

acclimatized Visitors from India find our weather very cold until they become *acclimatized*.

accommodate The landlady could not *accommodate* us because all her rooms were booked.

accommodation We had to seek *accommodation* in a hotel because our friends had no spare beds in their house.

accompaniment Jane sang while John played the piano *accompaniment* for her.

accompanist While Jane sang, John, her *accompanist*, played the piano.

accompany 'If I sing, will you *accompany* me on the piano?' ■ 'I would rather *accompany* you home,' replied John.

accomplice someone who helps in doing something wrong.

accomplish to finish doing something.

accomplished An *accomplished* person is one who is especially clever at something.

accomplishment To have passed the examination with so many distinctions was a great *accomplishment*.

according *According* to John we have a holiday tomorrow, but *according* to Peter we haven't.

accordion An *accordion* is like a small organ, pumped by the player squeezing it between his hands.

accost To *accost* someone means to go up to him and start a conversation.

account Tom's story did not agree with Fred's *account* of the incident.

accountant When the *accountant* checked the office books, he found an error of 50p in the total.

accumulate Dust will soon begin to *accumulate* on furniture left unused.

accumulation There was such an *accumulation* of newspapers when we returned from holiday,

that we could scarcely open the door.

accumulator a large battery in which electricity is stored.

accuracy He threw the dart with great *accuracy* into the bull's-eye, but showed less *accuracy* in adding up the score.

accurate exactly correct.

accusation Fred said that Jim had stolen his purse, but Jim denied the *accusation*.

accuse You must not *accuse* Jim of the crime unless you know that he did it.

accustomed Jane was not *accustomed* to being shouted at; people had always spoken quietly to her at home.

ace the playing-card that is highest in value, having on it only one spade, heart, diamond or club. ■ An outstanding sportsman is called an *ace*. ■ In tennis an *ace* is a first service that beats the opponent.

accordion   ace

acetylene a gas which gives a very hot flame when burnt with oxygen.

ache a continuous pain.

achieve To *achieve* something is to succeed in doing or completing it.

achievement An important undertaking which has been successfully done or completed can be called an *achievement*.

acid *Acids* are sour substances, many of which are poisonous.

acidity sourness or bitterness.

acknowledge To *acknowledge* something is to admit having received it, or ■ to admit that it is true.

acknowledgement, acknowledgment I shall not know that you have received my letter if you do not send me an *acknowledgement.* ■ The queen waved in *acknowledgement* of the crowd's cheers.

acorn The fruit of the oak tree is a little nut, called an *acorn.*

acorn   acrobat

acquaintance I do not know George very well; he is not a friend, only an *acquaintance.*

acquire If you did not steal the watch, you had better explain how you did *acquire* it.

acquisition An *acquisition* is something that one has obtained.

acquit The judge will *acquit* a prisoner if there is no evidence against him.

acre an area about the size of a school football pitch. 2·5 acres = 1 hectare.

acreage The amount of fertilizer required depends upon the *acreage* of the field; you need 254 kg. per acre.

acrobat The *acrobat* turned a series of backward somersaults.

across It is dangerous to run *across* a road without looking.

act In the first *act* of the play, ■ Henry had to *act* the part of a duke.

action An *action* is something done or a movement made.

active Uncle John took no *active* part in the game, but sat and shouted advice to the players.

activity I'm bored with sitting still; I'd like some *activity* such as dancing or playing table tennis.

actor Henry was the *actor* who had to pretend to be a duke in the play.

actress Julia was the *actress* who had to pretend to be an old lady in the play.

actual Her *actual* age was 50, but she always said she was only 30.

actually He called himself Mr. Jones, but *actually* he was Lord Gedny.

acute An *acute* angle is less than a right angle. ■ An *acute* person is quick to notice things.

adapt We hadn't a proper hutch for our rabbit so we had to *adapt* an orange-box for the purpose.

add If you *add* two and three, the total is five.

adder a small poisonous snake.

adder

addition 'Two and three are five' is an *addition* sum.

address My *address* is where I live, i.e. the number of the house and the name of the street, town, and country, etc.

adenoids growths at the back of the nose and throat, which sometimes make breathing difficult.

adept Anyone who is especially expert at something could be described as *adept*.

adequate The water supply was *adequate* for our needs, so while no one went thirsty, we had none to spare.

adhere stick fast – to a thing, a person, or an opinion.

adhesive Glue is an *adhesive*. ■ *Adhesive* tape is sticky.

adieu good-bye or farewell.

adjacent next to. The fox squeezed through our garden fence into the *adjacent* field and escaped.

adjective a word added to the name of something in order to describe it, e.g. 'new' in 'new bicycle'.

adjoin When two houses *adjoin*, they usually share the same middle wall.

adjust Billy's bicycle brakes were not working properly, so he had to *adjust* them.

administer You can *administer* punishment with a cane, *administer* medicine in a spoon, ■ and *administer* a theatre by managing its affairs.

admirable It was such an *admirable* idea that we all agreed enthusiastically.

admiral The officer of highest rank in the navy is an *admiral*.

admire George stopped to *admire* the new car. 'Isn't she a beauty!' he exclaimed.

admission After being forced into the *admission* that we were not players, ■ we had to pay for *admission* to the cricket ground.

admit I *admit* that I broke into the house through a window, ■ and then opened the front door to *admit* my friends.

admonish to give warning and advice, especially to someone who has done something wrong or foolish.

ado She made such an *ado* about the spider that we thought she was being attacked by wild beasts.

adolescence the period in life between childhood and manhood or womanhood.

adolescent Another word for *adolescent* is teenager.

adopt A married couple will sometimes *adopt* someone else's baby and bring it up as their own.

adorable Sheila thought the puppy so *adorable* that she had to pick it up and cuddle it.

adore Sheila cuddled the puppy in her arms. 'I *adore* puppies,' she said.

adorn To *adorn* something, you decorate it or add beauty in some other way.

adrift The anchor rope snapped and soon the boat was *adrift* and at the mercy of wind and waves.

adult grown up.

advance   To *advance* is to go forward, ■ or to move something forward.

advantage   An *advantage* of being tall is that you can see over other people's heads.

advent   Trees bursting into leaf are a sign of the *advent* of spring. ■ The Church calls the period before Christmas *Advent*.

adventure   An *adventure* story is one about exciting events.

adventurous   Tom was an *adventurous* boy who always liked doing something exciting.

adverb   An *adverb* adds to the meaning of a verb, an adjective, or another adverb, e.g. 'bravely' in 'He fought bravely.'

advertise   A good way of letting people know that you have a car for sale is to *advertise* in the newspaper.

advertisement   The television film was followed by an *advertisement* for a washing powder.

advice   My *advice* is, 'Never borrow money from your school-friends.'

advisable   It is *advisable* never to borrow money from your school-friends.

advise   I *advise* you not to borrow money from your school-friends.

advocate   To *advocate* something is to recommend it, or to speak in favour of it.

aerial   Radio and television broadcasts are picked up by the *aerial* of the receiving set.

aerodrome   As a train stops at a station, so an aircraft lands at an *aerodrome*.

aeroplane   An *aeroplane* often travels above the clouds.

aeroplane

afar   We could see *afar* the snow-covered tips of the mountains, low on the horizon.

affable   The man had been quite *affable*, but when we mentioned money he suddenly became angry.

affair   'Why did you go to see her?' asked Joan. 'That's my *affair*,' snapped Jill.

affect   I dropped the baton in the relay race, but this did not *affect* the result, for we would have lost anyway.

affected   A girl is said to be *affected* when she puts on airs and behaves unnaturally.

affection   Far from showing *affection* for her chick, the old hen constantly pecked the poor little thing.

afflicted   The unfortunate man was *afflicted* with a horrible disease.

affliction   Deafness is a very serious *affliction*.

afford   I cannot *afford* to buy a watch because I spent so much money on my summer holiday.

affront   an insult. ■ To *affront* someone is to insult him.

afloat   The flood water rose till all the boxes in the grocer's shop were *afloat*.

afoot Hearing the commotion, a policeman came to see what was *afoot*.

afraid People who are *afraid* of heights may feel no such fear in an aircraft.

Africa a large continent, halfway between the North Pole and the South Pole.

African Things from Africa are described as *African*. ■ *Africans* are people whose home is Africa.

aft at or near the stern (i.e. back) of a ship.

after Will you walk home with me *after* the party?

afternoon We worked until midday and then played games all the *afternoon*.

afterwards You may borrow my football boots for the match if you promise to clean them *afterwards*.

again I first saw the strange bird on Sunday and saw it *again* on Tuesday.

against 'I refuse to play *against* that team,' said Fred, ■ and rested his bat *against* a tree.

age At the *age* of 10 years we learnt about ■ the Bronze *Age* people, who lived 3,000 years ago.

aged Grandad has *aged* (grown old) since we last saw him. ■ The winner was a boy *aged* 5 years. ■ (pron. a-jed). Uncle has to look after his *aged* (old) mother.

agency the means by which something is done; ■ the place in which an agent works.

agent Insurance companies employ *agents* to collect payments for them. The owners of newspapers have news *agents* to sell the papers for them.

aggravate to make worse, e.g. That bang on the head will *aggravate* your head-ache.

aggression the starting of a quarrel or an attack.

aggressive acting in a manner likely to start a quarrel or a fight.

aggressor The one who starts a quarrel, a fight, or a war, is the *aggressor*.

aggrieved The *aggrieved* passenger shouted and swore that he would report his complaint to the inspector.

aghast Susan was *aghast* at the thought that she had been the cause of such a terrible accident.

agile The small boy, *agile* as a monkey, clambered up the tree in a moment.

agitate Workers *agitate* for better conditions by making speeches, organizing processions, etc.

agitated Mary was no longer hysterical but still very *agitated* and far from being calm.

aglow The fire had died down, but the logs were still *aglow* with friendly warmth.

ago The Roman Empire came to an end a long time *ago*.

agog The children were all *agog* to see the important visitor.

agonizing The pain was so *agonizing* that he could not bear it.

agony The injured man screamed in *agony* as the rescuers tried to pull him from his wrecked car.

agree When two people have the same opinion or thoughts about something, they *agree* about it.

agreeable There is nothing so *agreeable* as a hot bath when you are tired.

agreed I thought it was time to go home, and Dick *agreed* with me (i.e. he thought so too).

agriculture the growing of crops on farms.

aground The ship ran *aground* and tugs had to be used to pull her back into deep water.

ahead People who always look behind will be unable to see the dangers that lie *ahead*.

aid help. ■ To *aid* someone is to help him.

ailment an illness.

aim He took careful *aim* and threw the dart straight into the bull's-eye.

aimlessly He wandered *aimlessly* round the streets, neither knowing nor caring where he was going.

air a song; ■ also the name given to the mixture of gases that we breathe.

airborne An aircraft is *airborne* when it has risen off the ground.

aircraft *Aircraft* are aeroplanes. An *aircraft* is an aeroplane.

airport The aircraft left London *Airport* this morning.

airtight An *airtight* tin or jar is one that air cannot get into (or out of).

aisle (pron. I'll). The gangway between the seats in a church is called the *aisle*.

ajar The door was *ajar* and a light push swung it wide open.

akin like or related to.

alarm A fire *alarm* makes a loud noise to warn people of the danger from fire. ■ An *alarm* clock tells people when it is time to get up.

alas We had looked forward to a lovely week by the sea, but *alas*, it rained every day.

Albania a small country to the east of the Adriatic Sea.

Albanian a citizen of Albania. ■ Things from Albania are described as *Albanian*.

albatross a large sea-bird, very beautiful in flight.

albatross   alcove

album a book especially made for keeping collections of photographs, stamps, autographs, etc.

alcohol It is the *alcohol* in drink which makes people drunk.

alcove Hollowed out of one wall of the room was an *alcove*, big enough to contain some shelves.

alderman someone on a town council elected from among the more experienced councillors. *Aldermen* are next in importance to the mayor.

ale a kind of beer.

alert The sentries were on the *alert*, so they were not surprised by the enemy attack.

algebra Calculations in *algebra* require letters as well as figures, e.g.: $3x^2 + 2xy = 8z$.

Algeria a country in north Africa.

Algerian People or things of Algeria are described as *Algerian*.

Algiers the chief city of Algeria.

alias Fred Smith, *alias* Harry Green, *alias* James Forsythe, etc., always invented a new false name for each new crime he committed.

alibi a claim by an accused person that he was somewhere else when the crime of which he is accused was committed.

alien a foreigner.

alight We saw him *alight* from the train. ■ Uncle puffed at his pipe to make sure that it was *alight*.

alike The twins were as *alike* as two peas in a pod.

alive A large reward was offered for the capture of the outlaw, dead or *alive*.

allay We tried to *allay* her fears by assuring her that George was safe and with friends.

allegation a statement which has not been proved.

allege So you *allege* that you are late because you lost your way to school! A most unlikely story!

alley a narrow street or passage.

alliance a uniting of friends or allies.

alligator an American reptile, like a crocodile.

alligator

allocate As it was John's job to *allocate* the seats, everyone was expected to sit where John told him.

allotment Uncle's garden is next to his house, but the *allotment* on which he grows his fruit and vegetables is some distance away.

allow We do not *allow* smoking in schools.

allowed People are not *allowed* to smoke in this theatre.

alloy Bronze is not a single metal; it is an *alloy* of copper and tin.

all right It is quite *all right*; you have nothing to worry about.

ally To unite for some special purpose is to *ally*.

almanac If I require such information as the date, or time of sunrise, I look at an *almanac*.

almighty God is often described as *almighty*, which means all-powerful.

almond *Almond* nuts grow on *almond* trees, which look very like peach trees.

almost Start putting on your coat, for it is *almost* time for us to go.

alms money or gifts given to needy people.

aloft The sailors were up *aloft* in the rigging, while far below them the waves swept over the bows of the ship.

alone All the others went, leaving Jack *alone*.

along We walked *along* the promenade.

aloof Susan stood *aloof*; she did not feel like joining in the fun and games that her friends were enjoying.

aloud You ought not to talk *aloud* during the service in church.

alphabet Our *alphabet* begins with the letters A, B, C.

Alps Holidaymakers ski on the *Alps* in Switzerland.

already I was going to ask you to wash up the cups and saucers, but I see you have *already* done it.

also When you go for a day by the sea you should take your swimming trunks and *also* a mackintosh.

altar An *altar* is a flat-topped stone, table, etc., on which offerings are made to God. There is one at the east end of most churches.

alter If you do not like the arrangements we have made, we will *alter* them for you.

alternate Two things are said to *alternate* (pron. ál-ter-nate) when they continue to come in turn, like day and night. ■ If you put pictures on *alternate* (pron. al-tér-nate) pages of a book, each page of pictures is followed by a page without pictures.

alternative one or the other of two things.

although The boys went skating *although* they knew that the ice was thin.

altitude The aircraft was at an *altitude* of 5,000 metres when it began to descend.

alto The men with the highest voices sing *alto*; other men sing tenor or bass.

altogether If you go 4 miles, 2 miles and 6 miles, that is 12 miles *altogether*.

aluminium a metal which does not rust and which is light in weight and in colour.

always It is *always* cold at the North Pole.

amass I wonder how a man can *amass* such great riches in so short a time without being dishonest.

amateur An *amateur* does a job or plays a game just for the pleasure it gives him and not in order to earn money.

amaze to surprise very much.

ambassador An *ambassador* lives in a foreign country as his own country's official representative there.

amber a yellowish colour, seen in traffic lights.

ambiguous having two meanings, e.g. You see this nail? When I nod my head, you hit it with the hammer.

ambition It is my *ambition* to be a great scientist when I grow up.

ambitious Fred is not *ambitious*; he neither knows nor cares what he wants to do when he grows up.

amble I like to walk briskly, not *amble* along at this slow pace.

ambulance The injured boy was taken to hospital in an *ambulance*.

ambulance   anchor

ambush We made an *ambush* in the woods and surprised the girls when we jumped out on them. ■ 'We will *ambush* you next time,' they declared.

amen The last word of many hymns and prayers is *Amen*, which means, 'so be it'.

amends Jane was very late home but she made *amends* by getting up first the next morning.

amenities In the town where I live, we have no such *amenities* as libraries, parks or swimming-baths.

America U.S.A. is short for the United States of *America*.

American a citizen of America. ■ Things belonging to America are *American*.

amiable As my father was feeling so *amiable*, I took the opportunity to ask him for the money I wanted.

amicable friendly, e.g. We did not quarrel; it was a perfectly *amicable* conversation.

amicably The quarrel was forgotten and the boys played *amicably* together.

amid, amidst in the middle of.

amiss Hearing the complaints, an official came along to see what was *amiss* (i.e. what was the matter).

ammonia The strong-smelling gas which makes your eyes water when you sniff smelling-salts is *ammonia*.

ammunition The soldiers had no *ammunition* for their guns, so they could not fire.

amok To run *amok* is to rush madly about, in a wild urge to injure people (also spelt *amuck*).

among, amongst I saw Susan *among* (*amongst*) the crowds at the horse show.

amount If I add up all the items, they will *amount* to £5. ■ This is a greater *amount* than you can pay.

amp *Amp* (short for *ampère*) is the unit in which electric current is measured, e.g. This battery supplies a current of half an *amp*.

amphibian an animal, such as the frog, which lives both on land and in water.

amphibious The frog is an *amphibious* animal, equally at home in water or on land.

ample We have *ample* food for the picnic, so you need not bring any.

amplify If the radio is not loud enough you can *amplify* the sound by turning a knob.

amputate To *amputate* a leg or arm is to cut it off from the body.

amuck To run *amuck* is to rush madly about, in a wild urge to injure people (also spelt *amok*).

amuse The children had games, books and toys to *amuse* them during the holidays.

anaesthetic I hope the dentist will give me an *anaesthetic* so that I shall not feel the pain of his drill.

anatomy In *anatomy* lessons we cut up such creatures as frogs to find out how their bodies are made up.

ancestor The *ancestor* of whom I am proudest is my great-grandfather.

anchor When a captain wants to *anchor* his ship, ■ he drops an *anchor* which hooks into the sea-bed.

B

anchorage The bay did not provide a good *anchorage* for ships as there was insufficient shelter from storms.

ancient The *Ancient* Britons lived in Britain before the Romans came.

anemone (pron. a-nem-on-ee) a spring flower, found in woodlands.

anemone   ankle

angel Hymn 225 begins, 'Ye holy *angels* bright, Who wait at God's right hand.'

angelic A voice, a face, or a disposition is described as *angelic* when it is considered to be like that of an angel.

anger Joe showed his *anger* by banging his fist on the table.

angle a corner, or the space between two lines where they meet. ■ To *angle* is to try to catch fish with a hook and bait

angler An *angler* is a fisherman who uses a rod, hook and bait.

angry If you tease the animal, he may become *angry* and bite you.

anguish a very severe pain or very deep anxiety.

angular An object is described as *angular* if it has sharp corners or angles.

animal Which *animal* do you like best, a dog, a cat, or a horse?

animated An *animated* discussion is one that is lively. ■ *Animated* drawings move as if the characters were alive.

Ankara the capital city of Turkey.

ankle The joint between the foot and the leg is called the *ankle*.

annex an extra part added to a building. ■ To *annex* land, estates, etc., is to take possession of them.

annihilate To *annihilate* something means to blot it completely out of existence.

anniversary The 25th *anniversary* of a wedding is known as a Silver Wedding, when couples celebrate twenty-five years of married life.

announce After assembly, the headmaster will *announce* the names of the boys who have been elected prefects.

announcer A television *announcer* has to speak clearly as well as look pleasant.

annoy to worry, irritate or tease.

annoyance To Mother's *annoyance*, the dog put his dirty paws on her new coat.

annual An *annual* event is one which occurs once each year. ■ A plant is an *annual* if it lives only one year. ■ A book is an *annual* if new issues are printed each year.

anoint to put on oil or ointment, especially in a religious ceremony.

anonymous As the gift was *anonymous*, we did not know whom we had to thank for it.

another If you don't like this book, try *another* one.

answer I cannot *answer* your

question. ■ I do not know the *answer* to your question.

answerable The boys know that if they damage the books they will be *answerable* to the headmaster.

ant a tiny insect.

Antarctic the region of the South Pole. ■ An *Antarctic* explorer is one who explores this region.

antelope an African animal very like a deer.

antelope   anvil

anthem The church choir sang an *anthem* in place of the first hymn.

anthology a collection of selected short poems or pieces of prose.

anthracite a hard, shiny, smokeless coal.

anticipate A good footballer will *anticipate* a pass and so be in the correct position for receiving the ball when it comes.

anticipation Mother prepared two large plates of bread and butter in *anticipation* of the return of the hungry boys.

antics Fred was trying to dance a war-dance, but we thought by his *antics* that a bee had got inside his shirt.

anticyclone an area of high pressure, in which the weather is usually dry and settled.

antidote The baby did not die after swallowing the poison because the doctor was able to give him the correct *antidote* immediately.

antique I like *antique* furniture better than much of the modern stuff. ■ The dingy-looking chair was valuable because it was an *antique*.

antiquity Carol-singing is a custom of great *antiquity*, going back at least a thousand years.

antiseptic We put *antiseptic* cream on the wound to prevent it from becoming poisoned.

antlers A stag has horns with many branches, called *antlers*.

anvil A blacksmith beats the hot iron into shape on a specially-made block of iron called an *anvil*.

anxiety a feeling of concern and worry.

anxious John was so *anxious* to make a good impression that he put on his best suit and even had a special haircut for the occasion.

anybody Is there *anybody* at home?

anyhow We tried all the doors and the windows, but we could not get into the house *anyhow*.

anyone Is there *anyone* at home?

anything I ought to write him a letter, but I can't think of *anything* to say. Joe will do *anything* that you ask him.

anywhere 'Where shall I put this book?' 'It doesn't matter; put it *anywhere*.'

apart I keep these books *apart* from the rest because they are my school prizes.

apartments lodgings, especially those in seaside boarding-houses.

ape a tailless monkey. ■ To *ape* someone is to imitate him as a monkey might do.

ape   apple

apiece Uncle disposed of the two pounds by giving the four boys 50p *apiece.*

apologize If you have been rude you should at least *apologize* to the person you have offended.

apology I owe you an *apology* for my rudeness last night.

apostles The twelve *apostles* were the twelve disciples whom Jesus sent out to preach the Gospel.

apostrophe (pron. a-póss-tro-fee) a comma put above a word to show possession, or to show that letters have been left out, e.g. Fred's toe, and can't (meaning cannot).

appalling The results of the explosion were *appalling*; there were injured people lying all over the street.

apparatus The *apparatus* brought by the photographer included a camera, an exposure meter and a flash.

apparent The car had suffered no *apparent* damage, but as soon as we tried to drive away, we realized that a wheel was loose.

apparently The car was *apparently* undamaged, but when we tried to drive away, we realized that a wheel was loose.

appeal Classical music does not *appeal* to Fred; he prefers 'pop'. ■ The headmaster made an *appeal* to the boys to help the blind.

appear When we saw the man *appear* from behind the hut, we hid, ■ lest we should *appear* to be spying on him.

appearance Sally made an *appearance* on television. ■ You will never see Jim dirty or untidy; he takes a pride in his *appearance.*

appease To *appease* is to do something intended to soothe someone who is angry.

appendix A small addition to a book is called the *appendix*. ■ A small off-shoot from the intestine is also called the *appendix.*

appetite When I am ill I have no *appetite* for food. ■ My brother has an enormous *appetite* for detective stories.

applaud However much you like the song you should not *applaud* before the singer has finished it.

apple Eve pulled an *apple* from the tree and ate it.

appliance My first pocket-knife included an *appliance* for removing stones from horses' hoofs.

applicant Every *applicant* for the job had to fill in a form and attend an interview.

application All applicants for the job must fill in an *application* form. ■ The makers recommend the *application* of three coats of paint.

apply The conditions *apply* to all children under 14 ■ who *apply* for membership of the club.

appoint When does the headmaster *appoint* next term's prefects?

appointment I have an *appointment* with the dentist at 3 p.m. today.

appreciate John has a keen sense of humour; he can *appreciate* a good joke. ■ I must write and tell Auntie how much I *appreciate* the gift she sent me.

apprehend to understand. ■ To *apprehend* a thief is to arrest him.

apprentice someone who is learning a trade by working at it.

approach We could not *approach* the burning house because of the intense heat.

appropriate Our fishmonger has a most *appropriate* name; it is I. Salmon.

approval Dad indicated his *approval* with a nod of the head.

approve If you do not *approve* of the plan, you must vote against it.

approximate An *approximate* answer is one that is not absolutely accurate.

apricot An *apricot* is a fruit quite like a peach or a plum, but orange-coloured.

April the fourth month of the year.

apron Our butcher wears a white *apron* to protect the front of his clothes.

apt Grandad is quite willing to do the shopping, but unfortunately he is *apt* to forget what he has to buy.

aquarium In our classroom we have an *aquarium* containing water plants and several little fish.

aquarium

arable Land that is suited to the growing of crops is called *arable* land.

arc part of a curve. ■ An *arc* lamp produces a very bright light by making electricity jump across a gap.

arcade An *arcade* is made by covering over the passage between two rows of shops.

arch a curved structure that supports the roof of a church, etc. ■ *Arch* also means chief, e.g. in *arch*bishop, *arch*criminal.

archbishop The *Archbishop* of Canterbury is the chief bishop of the Church of England.

archer The *archer* fired his arrows with such power that he broke his bow.

apricot   archer

architect The *architect* who designed St. Paul's Cathedral was Sir Christopher Wren.

architecture Norman *architecture* can be recognized by heavy semicircular arches in churches, etc.

Arctic the region around the North Pole. ■ An *Arctic* explorer is one who explores the North Polar area.

area The *area* of a room 3 m long and 4 m wide is 12 m².

arena the centre part of a circus ring or stadium where the performance takes place.

Argentina, Argentine a large country in South America.

argue A good sportsman does not *argue* with the referee; he accepts every decision.

argument After a long *argument* the boys agreed to Jane's proposal.

arise Should any trouble *arise*, you are to let me know immediately.

aristocrat a person of noble birth.

arithmetic I like *arithmetic* lessons only when I get all my sums right.

ark a large wooden ship in which Noah and his animals were saved from the Flood.

ark

arm We will *arm* our soldiers with swords and pistols. ■ The cricketer could not bowl because he had hurt his *arm*.

armada The Spanish *Armada* was the most powerful fleet of warships that had ever sailed against England.

armful Jane grabbed an *armful* of blankets and staggered along to the bedroom.

armfuls Jane took four *armfuls* of blankets from the cupboard.

armour In olden times, knights wore steel *armour* to protect themselves against the swords and arrows of their enemies.

arms weapons, such as guns or swords; ■ also the two limbs of the body to which the hands are attached.

army Join the *army* and fight for your country!

arose When the alarm sounded, Jane *arose* and staggered towards the door, still half asleep.

around All *around* the house were beautiful lawns and gardens.

arouse It is not easy to *arouse* John when he is asleep.

arrange We will *arrange* to meet you at the station. ■ The books will look tidier if you *arrange* them in order of size.

arrangements Jill made all the *arrangements* for the outing, so it was a great success.

arrest We saw the policeman *arrest* the thief and take him away to the police-station.

arresting We saw a policeman *arresting* a thief. ■ Once an avalanche has started to move down a mountain, there is little hope of *arresting* its progress.

arrival We waited on the platform for the *arrival* of the train bringing our friends.

arrive Our train leaves London at 8 a.m., so we expect to *arrive* at Dover before 10.

arrogant John is so *arrogant* that he thinks he is better than everyone else.

arrow The Indian fitted an *arrow* to his bow and took aim at the buffalo.

arrow

arterial An *arterial* road is an important main road.

artery a blood vessel through which blood is pumped from the heart.

artful The fox is so *artful* that he often outwits the people hunting him.

article There was not a single *article* in our lost property cupboard. ■ I always read the leading *article* in our daily paper.

artificial A person who seems drowned may be brought to life by *artificial* respiration. The captain had an *artificial* leg, made of wood.

artillery big guns and cannon.

artist The picture was painted by a famous *artist*.

asbestos The mineral *asbestos* consists of fibres that will not burn, so it is useful for weaving fireproof materials.

ascend We saw him *ascend* the stairs on his way to the flat above us.

ascent The *ascent* of the mountain was difficult so it was evening before they reached the top.

ash The bark of the *ash* tree is a silvery-grey colour. ■ The *ash* from his cigarette dropped into my tea.

ashamed Jane was so *ashamed* of herself for being rude that she hid in her room until she thought the incident had been forgotten.

ashore As soon as the ship's gangways were in place, the passengers hurried *ashore*, eager to be on land again.

aside Pushing *aside* the people in his way, Dick plunged into the blazing building.

ask I will *ask* some questions and you must write down the answers.

askew The wind has blown your hat *askew*; put it straight again.

asleep We always know when Grandfather is *asleep*, for he snores very loudly.

aspect a particular view of something.

aspen The leaves of the *aspen* tree tremble in the slightest breeze.

asphalt a mixture of pitch and sand, put on roads and paths to give them a smooth, hard surface.

aspire I do not *aspire* to be a space explorer, but I would like an air trip round the world.

aspirin a small, white tablet that some people take when they wish to cure a headache.

assassin He was killed by an *assassin* who had mixed with the crowds of admirers.

assault To *assault* someone is to attack him violently by actions or by words, e.g. Joe was the victim of an *assault*; hence his black eye.

assemble The children were told to *assemble* in the school hall at 4 p.m.

assembly We have our morning service in the *assembly* hall. ■ The morning *assembly* at our school is at 9 o'clock.

assent A bill passed by Parliament does not become law until the Queen has given her *assent* (i.e. her approval).

assert You must *assert* yourself or they will continue to bully you. ■ Although no one believed him, Jim continued to *assert* that he had found gold.

assess We could not accurately *assess* the amount of damage done by the fire, but it was certainly over £1,000.

assist Betty was asked to *assist* the conjurer by holding his top hat.

assistance Seeing the policeman in trouble, the boys rushed to his *assistance* and the thieves were soon handcuffed.

assistant The conjurer's *assistant* held his top hat for him.

association Three examples are: The Football *Association*, the Automobile *Association* and our Old Boys' *Association*.

assortment a mixture of different kinds – especially of sweets or chocolates.

assume It is unwise to *assume* that your friend will enjoy a practical joke; he might be angry instead.

assumption We will order tea for twelve people on the *assumption* that all twelve will come.

assurance The headmaster gave his *assurance* that no one would be punished for speaking the truth.

assured Billy would not jump into the water though we *assured* him that it was only one metre deep.

aster a common garden flower, like a very large and colourful daisy.

aster

asterisk the sign * used by printers to mark a special word.

astern at the rear of a ship.

asthma a disease which causes a person to have difficulty in breathing.

astonish to surprise very much, e.g. It will *astonish* you to hear what I paid for this ring.

astray We lost our way because we were led *astray* by a misprint on the map.

astrologer a person who tells fortunes by means of the stars.

astrology the art of connecting fortune-telling with the positions of the stars.

astronomer a scientist whose special study is the stars.

astronomy the scientific study of stars, planets and their satellites.

astute No one is likely to outwit Tom; he is such an *astute* boy.

asylum a place of refuge or shelter. ■ Mental homes used to be called *asylums*.

Athenian A citizen of Athens is called an *Athenian*.

Athens the capital city of Greece.

athlete This great *athlete* has broken world records for both running and jumping.

athletic John was not an *athletic* boy; he was better at reading than running. Our school won the *athletic* sports because we have so many good runners.

atlas My school *atlas* contains maps of all the countries in the world.

atmosphere The *atmosphere* usually means the air round the earth, ■ but we also talk of the *atmosphere* in a room.

atom An *atom* was thought to be the tiniest possible particle of matter; but *atoms* can now be split. ■ 'We hadn't an *atom* of food' means that we hadn't the tiniest bit of food.

atomic *Atomic* bombs, *atomic* power-stations, ships, etc., all get their power by the splitting of atoms.

atrocious Billy's writing was bad enough, but Fred's was *atrocious*.

attach You are supposed to *attach* a rope to the anchor before throwing it overboard!

attached The sailor *attached* a rope to the anchor and threw it overboard.

attack We made our *attack* on the enemy as soon as it was light.

attempt We shall *attempt* to break the record for the relay race. ■ The *attempt* will be made tomorrow.

attend I shall *attend* evening classes when I leave school. ■ Nurses *attend* to sick people.

attendance Brown is sure to win the prize for the best *attendance*; he is never absent.

attendant As the duke appeared, one *attendant* stepped forward to open the door, while another took his hat and coat.

attention Pay *attention*, children! ■ The soldiers stood at *attention*.

attentive The pupils were most *attentive* and didn't miss a single word of the lesson.

attic a room in the roof of a house.

attire to dress or clothe. ■ Clothing is sometimes called *attire*.

attitude The priest stood with his head bowed in an *attitude* of prayer. ■ You have the wrong *attitude* to your school work.

attract Fred will do anything to *attract* attention. The salesman banged a drum to *attract* a crowd.

attraction Seeing the crowd, we pushed to the front to find out what the *attraction* was.

attractive Sally is a most *attractive* girl; all the boys fall in love with her.

auction At an *auction* goods are sold to the person who bids the highest price.

auctioneer a person who sells goods by auction.

audible loud enough to be heard.

audience At the end of the concert the *audience* applauded loudly.

audition Before employing a performer, the B.B.C. gives him an *audition* in order to hear what he can do.

August the eighth month of the year.

aunt My *aunt* Mary is my mother's sister.

aurora the spectacular area of coloured light in the sky above the earth's poles.

Australia a large island on the opposite side of the globe from Britain.

Australian someone whose home is Australia. ■ The kangaroo is an *Australian* animal.

Austria a country in the centre of Europe; its capital city is Vienna.

Austrian Mozart was a famous *Austrian* composer.

author The *author* of the book 'Oliver Twist' was Charles Dickens.

authority Policemen have *authority* to arrest lawbreakers. ■ Fathers should assert their *authority* and not let children do as they like.

autograph *Autograph* albums are books in which people collect signatures.

automatic A thing is described as *automatic* if it acts by itself without human aid.

automobile a motor-car or lorry.

autumn the season that comes between summer and winter.

available at hand and ready for use.

avalanche An *avalanche* crashed down the mountainside and covered a whole village with snow and rocks.

avenge to pay back someone for an evil he has done to another.

avenue a road or street, but especially one lined with trees.

average ordinary, not outstanding, e.g. Tom is an *average* player. ■ The *average* mark of a class is found by adding all the marks together, and dividing by the number of pupils in the class.

aversion I have an *aversion* to getting my feet wet so I wear rubber boots whenever it rains.

avert The sight was so terrifying that the boys had to *avert* their gaze.

aviary a special place in which to keep birds.

aviary

aviation the art of flying.

avoid Jim swerved to *avoid* the cat and fell off his bicycle.

await We finished our exams last week and we now *await* the results.

awake My baby sister pulls open Daddy's eyes to see if he is *awake*.

award I shall *award* a prize of £5 for the best essay.

aware conscious, knowing about, e.g. I am *aware* of the danger.

awash The deck of a ship is *awash* when water is just lapping over it.

away The grocer is giving *away* balloons today. ■ Go *away*!

awe fear, reverence or wonder, or a mixture of these feelings, e.g. Joan gazed in *awe* at the judge.

awful Jane felt *awful* when she realized that she had been the cause of her friend Susan getting into trouble.

awhile You must wait here *awhile* and rest before continuing your journey.

awkward An *awkward* person is one who is clumsy. ■ A thing is *awkward* if it is of unsuitable size or shape for its purpose.

awoke The noise of breaking glass *awoke* the sleeper.

awry crooked or out of place.

axe He felled the tree with a dozen blows of his *axe*.

axe   axle

axis The *axis* of the earth is an imaginary line which goes from the North Pole to the South Pole.

axle The rod on which a wheel revolves is called the *axle*.

azure blue, e.g. the *azure* sky of a summer day.

babble meaningless chatter. ■ A brook is said to *babble* when the water makes a noise as it flows.

babe A baby is sometimes called a *babe*.

babies Mothers wheel their *babies* to the baby show in their prams.

baboon large African monkey.

baboon   backbone

baby Mother was nursing her *baby*. ■ A *baby* lion is called a cub.

bachelor a man who is not married.

back Always carry a red light on the *back* of your bicycle. ■ Give me *back* the book I lent you. ■ If he does not believe you, I will *back* you up.

backbone The bone that runs right from the top of your back to the bottom is called the *backbone*.

backwards Dad put the car into reverse by mistake, so it went *backwards* instead of forwards.

bacon cured meat from the back and sides of pigs. We love eggs and *bacon*.

bacteria extremely tiny living things, some of which cause illnesses.

badge There is a *badge* embroidered on the pocket of your school blazer.

badger an English wild animal which hunts at night. ■ To *badger* is to worry or tease.

badger

badly Jeff wrote the exercise so *badly* that he had to do it again.

baffle To *baffle* someone is to deceive or bewilder him completely.

baggage A porter carried our *baggage* to the train.

bail the money paid to obtain the release of an accused person from prison; ■ one of two small bars put on the top of cricket stumps.

bailiff A *bailiff* may be a law officer ■ or a landowner's agent.

bait When I go fishing I use a worm on my hook for *bait*.

bake Bakers *bake* bread in huge ovens.

baker The *baker* makes bread and cakes which he sells in his shop.

bakery The baker makes his bread and cakes in the *bakery*.

balance The dancer could *balance* on one toe. ■ A *balance* is a weighing machine.

balcony an upper floor in a theatre or cinema. ■ A platform outside an upper door or window of any building is called a *balcony*.

bald A *bald* man has no hair on his head.

bale a large bundle. ■ To *bale* (or *bail*) out a boat is to throw out water with cans, etc. ■ An airman is said to *bale* out when he jumps by parachute.

balk to hinder or thwart. ■ A *balk* is a roughly squared lump of timber (also spelt *baulk*).

ballad a simple song or a poem that tells a story.

ballast When a ship has no cargo it may be necessary to put heavy material, called *ballast*, in the hold to steady it.

ballet a stage performance consisting of music and dancing only.

balloon Bob blew up the *balloon* until it burst.

bamboo The stems of the tropical grass called *bamboo* are thick enough to be used as sticks.

ban to forbid, e.g. We will *ban* all smoking in our club. ■ We have put a *ban* on smoking.

banana The *banana* is a curious fruit; it hangs in the shop in bunches like thick, yellow fingers.

band There is an elastic *band* round my diary. ■ The *band* played while we danced. ■ We were set upon by a *band* of robbers.

bandage The nurse wrapped a *bandage* round the wound. ■ Do you know how to *bandage* an injured arm?

bandit This *bandit* is one of the gang that robbed the travellers.

bang The tyre burst with a *bang* like the noise of a gun.

bangle My sister wears a gold *bangle* on her arm.

banish When a king *banished* people they had to go and live elsewhere. ■ To *banish* a thought is to dismiss it from your mind.

banisters *Banisters* are put beside stairways for people to hold, not so that small boys can slide down them.

banjo   barometer

banjo a musical instrument played like a guitar but shaped like a frying pan.

bank We stand on the river *bank* to fish. ■ We keep our money in a *bank* for safety.

banknotes I have three *banknotes*; two of them are £1 notes and one is a £5 note.

banner The two boys carried poles between which was a *banner* bearing the words, 'Down with School'.

banquet At the mayor's *banquet* there were so many good things to eat that some of the guests felt ill afterwards.

baptism a religious ceremony in which a person is sprinkled with water, or immersed in water.

baptize To *baptize* the baby, the priest will sprinkle water on its head.

barbarian an uncivilized person, usually of a backward race.

barber Men and boys go to a *barber* when they require a haircut.

bard A *bard* was a wandering poet and musician.

bare A person is said to be *bare* if he has no clothes on. ■ A cupboard is *bare* if it is empty – like Mother Hubbard's.

barefaced shameless or impudent.

barely only just.

bargain I bought a coat for only 50p at the sales; it was a real *bargain*.

barge a flat-bottomed boat, used for carrying goods on canals and rivers.

baritone a man singer whose voice is higher than a bass but lower than a tenor.

bark The *bark* is the outer covering of a tree. ■ Dogs *bark* loudly when they are excited.

barley *Barley* looks like wheat with hairs growing from the ends of the grains.

barn A farmer stores his crops in a *barn*.

barnacle a very small shell-fish which fixes itself firmly to rocks, ships' bottoms, etc.

barometer Weather forecasters measure the air pressure with a *barometer*.

baron a nobleman entitled to be addressed as 'Lord'.

barracks a special building in which soldiers live.

barrel Beer is stored in a specially-made wooden tub called a *barrel*. ■ The metal tube of a gun is called the *barrel*.

barren Land unable to produce crops is described as *barren*. A woman unable to have children is described as *barren*.

barricade a barrier across a road.

barrier a fence for keeping people from moving forward.

barrow The man was wheeling a *barrow* piled high with fruit.

barrow   bassoon

barter To *barter* is to exchange goods for other goods, not for money.

base The *base* of anything is the part on which it stands. ■ A *base* action is one that is cowardly or mean.

basement A floor below the ground level of a building is called the *basement*.

bash to hit hard so as to smash in.

bashful shy.

basin We cook puddings in a pudding *basin*. ■ We wash in a wash-*basin*. ■ A river *basin* is the area drained by a river.

bask to lie and enjoy the warmth of a fire or of the sun.

basket My dad hates carrying the shopping *basket*.

bass (pron. base) the lowest part in a piece of music; ■ (pron. *bass*) a kind of fish.

bassoon A *bassoon* is a musical instrument which produces very low notes when it is blown.

batch A number of things together, or treated as a set, may be called a *batch*, e.g. Mother took a *batch* of mince pies out of the oven.

bath Mother had to *bath* the baby in the sink ■ because the *bath* in the ■ *bath*-room was broken.

bathe Some people like to *bathe* in the sea; others prefer to sun-*bathe* on the beach.

baton Orchestra conductors beat time with a short stick called a *baton*. ■ The stick passed on in a relay race is called a *baton*.

batsman The cricket match ended with a *batsman* hitting the ball into the crowd.

batter to hit again and again. ■ *Batter* is flour, milk, egg, etc., beaten up into a paste. ■ This paste when cooked is called *batter* pudding.

battery My torch gives a poor light because it needs a new *battery*. ■ A group of big guns is called a *battery*.

battle William the Conqueror won the *Battle* of Hastings in 1066. ■ We watched the swimmer *battle* against the waves.

battleship The largest and most powerful type of warship was the *battleship*.

baulk to hinder or thwart. ■ A *baulk* is a roughly squared beam of wood (also spelt *balk*).

bawl to shout loudly.

bay a wide inlet filled by the sea; ■ also an evergreen bush. ■ A *bay* window curves outwards from a house. ■ Dogs bark; hounds and wolves are said to *bay*.

bazaar an eastern market; ■ a fête or fair in which the stalls are set out in the fancy style of an eastern market.

beach What I like best about the seaside is playing in the sand on the *beach*.

beacon a signal fire, or light.

beads Jane likes to wear a long string of *beads* round her neck.

beak The bird flew off with a worm in its *beak*.

beaker I take a plastic *beaker* to drink from when we go on a picnic.

beam The roof was supported by a great oak *beam* over a foot thick. ■ The *beam* of light from the car's headlamp could be seen for miles.

bean There are many kinds of *beans*, including the runner *bean*, broad *bean*, kidney *bean* and coffee *bean*; but baked *beans* are what I like best.

bear The polar *bear* has a thick white fur coat. ■ I cannot *bear* the pain. ■ Never *bear* a grudge.

bearable I had to put my sore finger into water so hot that it was hardly *bearable*.

beard No one would recognize Father Christmas if he took off his big white *beard*.

beast a four-footed animal. ■ 'You *beast* !' is what you might say to a brutal man, or to anyone whom you dislike.

beastly nasty.

beat to hit repeatedly. ■ Jim *beat* Tom by a yard and won the race. ■ A policeman's round is called his *beat*.

beautiful lovely to look at. Helen of Troy was so *beautiful* that men fought a war over her.

beauty 'The Sleeping *Beauty*' is a story about a beautiful princess who slept for a hundred years.

beaver a fur-covered animal which lives in water and on land.

beak   beaver

became After eating all those rich cakes the children *became* ill.

because The children were ill *because* they had eaten too much.

beckon She couldn't hear me so I had to *beckon* her with my finger to come closer.

become You will *become* ill if you eat too much.

becoming Jill is *becoming* very beautiful as she grows up.

bedlam There was *bedlam* in the room when the teacher went out, means that there was uproar, noise and disorder.

bedraggled (pron. be-drag-'ld) wet and limp.

bee The *bee* lives in a hive and makes honey.

beech a tree which is often found in English woods.

beef The flesh of cattle is called *beef*.

beehive Bees are kept in a *beehive*, which is where they make their honey.

beeline To make a *beeline* for a place means to go straight there, by the shortest route.

been Where have you *been*? ■ I have *been* looking for you.

beer a drink made from malt, hops, etc.

beet There are two kinds of *beet*root: red *beet* which is used in salads, and white *beet*, from which sugar is made.

beetle A *beetle* is an insect whose upper wings have become hard wing-cases, covering the delicate wings with which it flies.

befall happen; e.g. Whatever may *befall*, you may rely on me to help you.

before Look carefully *before* you cross the road.

beforehand It is no use your telling me of the danger after the accident has happened; you should have told me *beforehand*.

befriend Everyone has a friend except Jimmy; I hope someone will *befriend* him.

began It *began* to rain, so we all put on our macintoshes.

beggar A *beggar* in the street asked for money from passers-by.

begin Lessons *begin* at 9 a.m. and end at 4 p.m.

beginner As we went to the baths, Jane said, 'I am only a *beginner*; I cannot swim at all yet.'

beginning The place to start a book is at the *beginning*, that is, on the first page.

begun Jim had *begun* the sum correctly, but he didn't know how to finish it.

behalf On *behalf* of all the boys in 3A, I would like to thank Mr. Green for his kindness.

behave Remember that we have visitors here this evening, so you must *behave* especially well.

behaviour We have visitors here this evening, so I expect your *behaviour* to be better than usual.

behead To *behead* a man is to cut off his head.

beheld saw, e.g. On turning the corner, we *beheld* a sight that made us rub our eyes.

behind Turn round and look *behind* you. ■ We ran ahead and left the others far *behind*. ■ While skating Tom fell backwards on to his *behind*.

behindhand We were *behindhand* with the payments on the television set, so a man came and took it away.

behold see, take notice or look upon.

beige material made of undyed wool. ■ The colour called *beige* is the colour of undyed wool.

being Behave like a human *being*. ■ You are *being* unkind to the animal.

Belfast a big city in Northern Ireland, famous for shipbuilding.

belfry We climbed up to the *belfry* to see the huge bells hanging there.

Belgian a citizen of Belgium. ■ We travelled in a *Belgian* aircraft.

Belgium a small country on the North Sea coast between Holland and France.

Belgrade the capital city of Jugoslavia.

belief It is my *belief* that the man is a Frenchman, as he speaks with a strange accent.

believe To *believe* something is to accept it as true.

believing It is said that seeing is *believing*, but I do not believe all I see.

belittle Whatever we do, Mary tries to *belittle* the achievement by saying that it was easy, or that anyone could have done it.

bell Nobody remembered to ring the school *bell* so we were all late home.

bellow A punch on the nose would make George *bellow* like a bull with pain and fury.

bellows The blacksmith uses a *bellows* to blow air into his furnace.

belly the front of the body between the chest and legs.

belong Does this purse *belong* to you?

belongings Take all your *belongings* with you when you go; I do not want any of your possessions left here.

beloved darling, or dearly loved.

below From the tower, the people in the street *below* looked like ants. ■ Jane is in the form *below* mine.

belt A scout carries all kinds of equipment attached to the *belt* round his waist.

bench A *bench* is a long seat, ■ or the table at which a carpenter works.

bend The car took the *bend* in the road too fast and crashed. ■ The blacksmith tried to *bend* the iron bar into a ring.

beneath below, under, or underneath.

benefactor a person who does good to others, e.g. Mr. Jones is the *benefactor* who gave the money for the building of our hospital.

beneficial I knew that the treatment had been *beneficial* for I felt better after it.

benefit a gain or an advantage. ■ To *benefit* is to gain by something. ■ A *benefit* (cricket) match is one from which the profits go to a particular player.

bent The crash *bent* the frame of my cycle so badly that I could not straighten it.

bequeath If you make a will leaving property to someone when you die, you are said to *bequeath* the property to him.

bereaved A person is said to have been *bereaved* when he has been left sad and lonely as a result of the death of a relative or close friend.

beret (pron. beh-ray) a small, round, flat hat.

bellows   beret

Berlin Before the war *Berlin* was the capital of a united Germany.

berry a small fruit, such as a black*berry*, a goose*berry* or a rasp*berry*.

berth a sleeping place, especially in a ship. ■ To *berth* a ship is to moor it in a suitable place, ■ often called a *berth*.

beseech to ask earnestly for something.

beset I am *beset* with worries.

beside Janet hurried along with little Fred *beside* her, holding her hand.

besides *Besides* Eric and George, there will be Freda, Sally and Jane, making five altogether.

besiege To *besiege* a city an attacking army had to surround it.

best The *best* runner in the class is John. ■ At a wedding, the bridegroom's special companion is called the *best* man.

betray To *betray* one's friends is to reveal things about them to an enemy.

better This is good chocolate, but that is *better*. ■ I have been ill in bed but I am now *better* and able to get up.

between The pirate gripped the knife *between* his teeth. ■ Divide this money *between* the two of you. ■ I will meet you *between* 8 and 9 o'clock.

beverage At this café you can buy any kind of *beverage*, including tea, coffee, lemonade and minerals.

beware A notice on the gate saying, '*Beware* of the dog,' warns visitors that the dog may bite them.

bewilder To *bewilder* anyone is to confuse, puzzle or mislead him.

bewitch In fairy stories, to *bewitch* anyone is to put a spell on him. ■ Nowadays, to *bewitch* means to charm or delight.

beyond This was *beyond* a joke so no one was amused. ■ The sun sets *beyond* the distant hills.

Bible the great religious book which tells the stories of Jesus and the ancient Hebrew prophets.

biblical to do with the Bible.

biceps a special kind of muscle; there is one in your upper arm.

biceps   bicycle

bicycle You ought not to ride your *bicycle* on the road until you have passed a test.

bid to say, e.g. to *bid* good-bye, to *bid* good night; ■ to offer a price, e.g. At the sale Dad *bid* £1 for an old lamp.

bide to wait or endure. 'I'll *bide* my time' means 'I'll await the best opportunity'.

bier a stand on which a coffin can be carried to the grave.

bigger A horse is a big animal, but the camel is a *bigger* one.

biggest The horse, camel and elephant are all big animals, but the *biggest* of the three is the elephant.

bilberry a small bush that grows on heaths; its fruit is a small blue berry called a *bilberry*. It is also called blaeberry and whortleberry.

bilious After feeling *bilious* all the evening, Sally finally had to rush out of the room to be sick.

bill The bird held a worm in its *bill.* ■ We received a *bill* from the shopkeeper for the six tins of fruit he had sent us.

billiards a game played with ivory balls on a table covered in green cloth.

billion In Britain, a *billion* is a million millions (1,000,000,000,000). In the U.S.A., a *billion* is a thousand millions.

billy-goat male goat.

bin We put our rubbish in the dust *bin,* our coal in the coal *bin* and our flour in the flour *bin.*

bind to fasten with a band or cord. ■ To *bind* a book you fix its pages between the covers.

binoculars *Binoculars,* also called field-glasses or opera-glasses, consist of two little telescopes, one for each eye, to help people to see distant objects clearly.

biography A written account by someone of another person's life.

biology In *biology* lessons we learn about living things – plants and animals.

biplane an aircraft with two planes (i.e. wings) on each side instead of the usual one.

biplane

birch a tree with smooth bark and thin branches ; ■ or a bundle of *birch* twigs used for flogging wrong-doers. ■ To *birch* is to flog with a birch.

bird The *bird* that flew off the nest was a robin.

Birmingham a large manufacturing town in the English Midlands.

birth The *birth* of a baby is often called a happy event.

birthday On my next *birthday* I shall be 14 years old. ■ Will you come to my *birthday* party ?

biscuit a small, flat cake, usually hard and dry.

bisect to cut into two equal parts.

bishop a clergyman of high rank. ■ In chess, a *bishop* is a piece shaped like a bishop's head-dress.

bite This is tasty. Have a *bite* of it. ■ Do not be afraid of the dog; it will not *bite* you. ■ This itchy spot is an insect *bite.*

bitter I prefer *bitter* marmalade to the sweet kind.

bitterly It was so *bitterly* cold that our fingers were frozen. ■ Susan wept *bitterly* as if her heart were broken.

black The floor was as *black* as coal. ■ At funerals many people wear *black.*

blackberry a fruit consisting of a mass of tiny soft black berries, each with a seed in the middle. ■ A *blackberry* bush or bramble is usually very tough and prickly.

blackbird My favourite song-bird is the *blackbird.*

blackguard (pron. bla-gard) someone whose behaviour and language are low and vulgar.

blacking The black polish used when cleaning shoes is called *blacking.*

blacklead used in pencils and for blacking stoves.

blackmail To *blackmail* anyone is to extract money from him by threatening to tell a secret about him to somebody else.

blacksmith Our village *blacksmith* has few horses to shoe nowadays, so he makes iron gates instead.

bladder a bag made of thin skin, rubber, etc., e.g. There is an air *bladder* inside the football. The *bladder* in the human body holds the waste water until it is passed out.

blade The big *blade* on my knife is very sharp. ■ You are meant to hit the ball with the *blade* of the bat, not with the handle.

blame To *blame* someone is to accuse him of being responsible for doing wrong. ■ Don't put the *blame* on me; I didn't break the window.

blancmange (pron. bla-monj) A *blancmange* sets like a jelly, but is like coloured custard.

blank The paper was quite *blank*; nothing had been written on it.

blanket I have a *blanket* on my bed to keep me warm.

blaring The radio was *blaring* so loudly that we could not even understand what was being said.

blast The *blast* of air from the explosion knocked us flat.

blaze A fire is said to *blaze* when it burns with a bright flame. ■ To *blaze* a trail is to mark a path by chipping the bark of trees.

blazer Our school *blazer* is a blue and yellow jacket with the school badge on the pocket.

bleach If you want dark hair to become light, you *bleach* it.

bleak The island was a *bleak* place, cold, bare and wind-swept.

bleat to make a noise like a sheep, goat or calf.

bled The wound *bled* for a time but very little blood was lost.

bleed The man may *bleed* to death if you do not stop the flow of blood.

blemish The only *blemish* on the beautiful carpet was an ink stain.

blend to mix together, e.g. A tobacconist may *blend* different kinds of tobacco, a tea merchant may *blend* different kinds of tea and an artist may *blend* different colours.

bless Good-bye and may God *bless* you.

blew The wind *blew* very hard. The draught *blew* out the candle.

blight a disease that affects plants. ■ To *blight* a thing is to make it diseased.

blind Samson was *blind* because the Philistines had put out his eyes.

blindfold In this game we *blindfold* the players by tying a scarf round their eyes.

blazer

blink to open and close the eyes quickly.

bliss perfect happiness.

blister a bubble of skin containing a colourless liquid, and caused by a burn, a tight shoe, etc., e.g. After that long walk I had a *blister* on my toe.

blithe a word used chiefly by poets, meaning 'happy'.

blithely happily or gaily.

blizzard a blinding snowstorm with strong, icy winds.

bloater a herring which has been salted and smoked.

blob a drop or spot, e.g. a *blob* of ink or paint.

block A group of buildings may be called a *block*. ■ To *block* means to put an obstacle in the way. ■ The lump of wood on which people had to place their heads in order to be beheaded was called the *block*.

blockade To *blockade* an enemy is to prevent supplies reaching him.

blockhead A stupid person is sometimes called a *blockhead*.

blond having fair hair and skin, e.g. The boy has a *blond* complexion. My dad is a *blond* man.

blonde A fair-haired woman is called a *blonde*.

blood The *blood* from my cut finger made a red patch on my clean handkerchief.

bloodshed the shedding of blood, fighting.

bloodthirsty A *bloodthirsty* person is one who is eager for the shedding of blood.

bloom a flower. ■ To *bloom* is to come into flower.

blossom A tree grows its *blossom* before the fruit. ■ To *blossom* is to come into flower.

blot A drop of ink fell from my pen and made a *blot* on my book. ■ *Blot* up the ink with this blotting-paper.

blotter a pad containing blotting-paper.

blouse Every girl in our school wears a blue skirt and a white *blouse*.

blow This strong wind will *blow* your hat off. ■ Jim swung his axe and with the first *blow* cut the rope.

blue The sky is *blue*. ■ A person may be said to be *blue* if he is miserable.

bluebell My favourite woodland spring flower is the *bluebell*.

bluebell   bluebottle

bluebottle an unpleasant fat fly which lays eggs on meat.

bluff to deceive people by appearing to be very confident; ■ such deceit is called *bluff*. ■ A *bluff* person is one who is blunt and hearty.

blunder a stupid mistake. ■ To *blunder* is to make a stupid mistake. ■ To *blunder* can also mean to move blindly or to stumble.

blunt You cannot cut meat with a *blunt* knife. I cannot draw a thin line because my pencil is *blunt*.

blur to smudge or make indistinct.

blurred An object is said to look *blurred* when you cannot see it distinctly.

blurt To *blurt* out a remark is to come out with it suddenly and thoughtlessly.

blush People who become red in the face through shame or embarrassment are said to *blush*.

boar The male pig is called a *boar*.

boar   bobbin

board a plank of wood; ■ a committee. ■ To *board* a ship, train or bus is to go on it. ■ To *board* a person is to supply him with daily meals.

boast Tom loved to *boast* about his father's expensive car, his uncle's motor-boat, his sister's good looks and his own cleverness.

boat We stepped into the little *boat* and rowed round the lake.

bobbin The thread was wound on a *bobbin* before being put in the sewing-machine.

bodice the part of a woman's dress above the waist.

bodily If you have any *bodily* ail-ment you should see a doctor. ■ The crane lifted the engine *bodily* (i.e. the whole thing) off the rails.

body When I had measles my whole *body* was covered with little spots. ■ 'At last the people in a *body* to the town hall came flocking.'

bog The man sank into a *bog* and was soon waist-deep in black mud.

bogey, bogy a child's name for the devil or for some imaginary goblin whom he fears.

boil You must let the water *boil* before making the tea.

boiler container in which things are boiled, or in which steam is made for steam engines, etc. ■ The hot water for all the radiators and wash-basins in the building comes from a *boiler* in the basement.

boisterous rough, wild and noisy. Rugby is a *boisterous* game.

bold Drake was a *bold* seaman who feared no one. ■ Print it in *bold* letters which are easily read.

boldness All admired Drake's *boldness* in sailing into an enemy harbour to attack their ships.

bolster I like a *bolster* under my pillow to make it higher. ■ To *bolster* anything up is to give it support or assistance.

bolt A horse is said to *bolt* when it rushes off out of control. ■ The steel plates were fastened together with a nut and *bolt*.

bomb An atomic *bomb* does fearful damage when it explodes. ■ To *bomb* something is to drop bombs on it.

bomber an aircraft made to carry and drop bombs.

bond something that binds; ■ a legal document.

bone Our bodies consist of a framework of *bone*, covered with flesh. ■ To *bone* meat is to take out the bone.

bonfire On November the 5th we light an enormous *bonfire* which burns all night.

bonfire   boomerang

bonnet a hat tied on with ribbons, e.g. a baby's *bonnet* or a Salvation [Army *bonnet*. ■ The covering over the engine of a car is called the *bonnet*.

bonny Such a *bonny* baby would take a prize in any baby-show.

bonus At Christmas all the workers are given a *bonus* of £5 in addition to their wages.

book The *book* I had from the library was called 'Treasure Island'.

boom a sudden increase in trade. ■ The sound of '*boom*' describes the noise of a distant explosion. ■ To *boom* is to make a deep sound.

boomerang an Australian weapon, consisting of a curved piece of wood, which returns to the person who throws it.

boot We put the luggage into the *boot* of the car. ■ Jack took off his *boot* because it was hurting his foot.

booth A *booth* is a light, temporary structure, such as a stall at a fair or a place in which to vote.

booty The pirates buried the *booty* which they had captured, on Treasure Island.

border The Cheviot Hills are on the *border* between England and Scotland.

bore *Bore* a hole in this plank. ■ Will it *bore* you to hear the story again? ■ A small-*bore* rifle has a narrow barrel. ■ He *bore* the pain bravely.

bored Sam *bored* a hole in the plank. ■ We were so *bored* that we couldn't help yawning.

boring The lesson was so *boring* that we couldn't help yawning. ■ Sam is still *boring* that hole in the plank.

born Christ was *born* on the first Christmas Day.

borne I could not have *borne* the pain as bravely as Joan did.

borough a town which is governed by a council or sends a member to Parliament.

borrow May I *borrow* a 5p piece from you and repay it tomorrow?

bosom a word used, chiefly by poets, to mean 'breast'; as in 'The father clasped the boy to his *bosom*.'

boss the person who is in charge; ■ (slang) to order people about.

botany In our *botany* lessons we learn about plants, seeds and flowers.

both I know *both* Jack and Jill.

bother Do not *bother* me with unimportant things when I am busy. ■ I never mind looking after Jill; she is no *bother*.

bottle The doctor gave me a *bottle* of medicine. ■ We saw the factory where they *bottle* the milk that we drink.

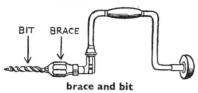

BIT BRACE

brace and bit

bottom We turned it upside-down and saw a name on the *bottom*. ■ There is a pond at the *bottom* of the garden.

bough Jack was climbing the tree when a big *bough* broke off and he fell to the ground.

bought I went to the shop and *bought* a slab of chocolate for 20p.

boulder a large, rounded stone.

bounce If you drop a rubber ball it will *bounce* up again.

bound We *bound* up the cut with a bandage. ■ Mother is *bound* to find out. ■ We are *bound* for the seaside. ■ A mountain goat will *bound* from rock to rock.

boundary This wall marks the *boundary* of the school grounds. ■ The batsman hit a *boundary* right into the crowd.

bouquet The bride carried a lovely *bouquet* of roses and carnations.

bout At the boxing tournament the first *bout* was between Basher Brown and Slogger White.

bow [when it rhymes with 'low'] a weapon for shooting arrows ■ or the stick with which a violin is played. ■ The ribbon was tied in a *bow*.

bow [when it rhymes with 'cow'] to bend the body or head forward. ■ The front part of a ship is called the *bow*.

bowels part of the body consisting of yards of tubing inside the abdomen.

bowl a basin; ■ a big, heavy, wooden ball used in playing the game of bowls. ■ To *bowl* in cricket is to throw the ball smoothly towards the stumps.

bowls a game in which heavy wooden balls are rolled towards a smaller white ball. Drake played *bowls* while awaiting the Armada.

box He gave her a *box* of chocolates. ■ She gave him a *box* on the ear. ■ The boxer did not *box* fairly. ■ There is a shrub called *box*.

boxer someone specially trained to fight with his fists.

brace a support, e.g. to hold teeth in place. ■ A *brace* is the tool which holds the bit with which a carpenter drills holes. ■ A *brace* of pheasants is two pheasants.

bracelet My aunt wears a beautiful gold *bracelet* on her wrist.

bouquet   **bracelet**

braces Some boys use *braces* to hold up their trousers; Tom uses a belt.

bracken tall fern that grows on heathland.

bracket The shelf was supported by a *bracket* which was screwed to the wall. ■ Each of the following three figures is in *brackets* (1), [2], {3}.

bradawl A *bradawl* looks like a small, sharp screwdriver and is used to make holes in wood.

bradawl   bracket

brag to boast.

braid to interweave or plait hair, thread, etc.; ■ a cord or band made by weaving or plaiting.

braille a system of printing in raised dots, which blind people can read by touch.

brain Inside your head is your *brain*, with which you think.

brakes The car could not stop soon enough because its *brakes* were faulty.

bramble The *bramble*, or blackberry, is usually a prickly bush, but its fruit is delicious.

bran *Bran* consists of the husks from grain.

branch We cut the broken *branch* off the tree. ■ There is a *branch* of Woolworth's in almost every town.

brand a trade mark. ■ You *brand* cattle by stamping them with a hot iron. ■ The *brand* mark on

goods or cattle is made with a hot iron.

brandish To *brandish* a sword is to wave it about before beginning a fight.

brandy a strong drink made from wine. The sick man was given *brandy* to revive him.

brass an alloy of copper and zinc. ■ A *brass* instrument is a trumpet, horn, trombone or tuba.

brave Only a *brave* man would dare to travel unarmed in that dangerous country.

bravery I admire the *bravery* of a man who would dare to travel unarmed in that dangerous country.

brawl a noisy quarrel. ■ To *brawl* is to quarrel noisily.

bray The donkey began to *bray*, 'Ee-orr! Ee-orr!'

brazen made of brass ■ or sounding like brass. ■ A *brazen* person is one who is shameless. ■ To '*brazen* it out' is to bluff one's way out of a situation, though in the wrong.

brazier a bucket-shaped iron basket for holding a fire.

Brazil a large country in South America.

bread The boys eat three loaves of *bread* each day.

breadth The length of the carpet was 6m and its *breadth*, 4m.

break If you drop the glass it will *break* into pieces. ■ At our school the morning *break* lasts for only ten minutes.

breaker A big wave which breaks into foam on the beach is called a *breaker*.

breakfast The first meal of the day is *breakfast*.

breast A baby sucks milk from his mother's *breast*. ■ James always has a white handkerchief in the *breast* pocket of his jacket.

breath I was out of *breath* when I arrived at school, because I had run all the way.

breathe When we *breathe* we draw air into our lungs.

breathing The animal was still *breathing*, so we knew it was still alive.

breed What *breed* of dog is that? A poodle? ■ If you want to buy a puppy, go to someone who *breeds* dogs.

breeze The *breeze* was so gentle that it didn't even move the leaves on the trees.

brew We *brew* tea by pouring boiling water on to tea-leaves in a teapot, and then leaving it for a few minutes.

brewery Beer is brewed, or prepared in a *brewery*.

bribe In return for a *bribe* of £5, the guard let the prisoner go. ■ If you *bribe* the guard with a £5 note he will let the prisoner go.

brick A house *brick* is about 230mm long and made of baked clay. ■ That *brick* wall contains thousands of bricks.

bridal My mother kept her *bridal* veil for many years after her wedding.

bride The woman being married is called the *bride*.

bridegroom The man being married is called the *bridegroom*.

bridge The road goes over the river on a *bridge*. ■ We shall *bridge* the river here. ■ *Bridge* is a card-game like whist. ■ You'll

find the captain of the ship on the *bridge*.

bridle The *bridle* is the part of a horse's harness that goes on his head.

bridle

brief I haven't time to hear a long story, so be *brief*. I have only come for a *brief* stay; I must go back tomorrow.

brigade a large group of soldiers. ■ Tony belongs to the Boys' *Brigade*.

brigand A *brigand* held up the travellers at pistol-point and robbed them.

bright The light was so *bright* that we could not look at it. ■ Sue isn't very *bright*; she doesn't understand things as well as other children do.

brilliant The flash of the explosion was the most *brilliant* light that I have ever seen; it almost blinded me.

brim I couldn't get another drop in the glass; it was full to the *brim*. ■ He pulled the *brim* of his hat down over his eyes.

brine salt water.

bring *Bring* me my horse. ■ David had no mother so his father paid a nurse to *bring* him up.

brink The boys stood shivering on the *brink* of the river, hesitating to dive into the icy water below them.

brisk active and full of life. He went for a *brisk* walk before breakfast.

bristle Hair is said to *bristle* when it stands upright. ■ A person may *bristle* when he is angry.

bristles the stiff hairs on a pig's back. Short, stiff hairs on other animals or on man are also called *bristles*.

Britain Great *Britain* consists of England, Scotland, and Wales.

British The *British* people live in Britain. My nationality is *British*. I am *British*.

Briton A British person is called a *Briton*. ■ The Ancient *Britons* lived in Britain long ago.

brittle Egg-shells are so *brittle* that the slightest tap will break them.

broad The river was too *broad* for us to swim across. ■ We expect to see bats in the evening, not in *broad* daylight.

broadcast Radio and television programmes are *broadcast* from London. ■ To sow seeds *broadcast* means not to plant them in rows, but to scatter them about.

broccoli, brocoli a green vegetable like a cauliflower.

broke The glass *broke* when I dropped it. ■ A person who has spent all his money is said to be *broke*.

broken You have *broken* the glass. ■ Pick up the pieces of *broken* glass. ■ You have *broken* your promise, so it will be difficult for me ever to believe you again.

bronze an alloy of copper and tin; ■ the colour *bronze*.

brooch Aunt Mary had a lovely gold *brooch* pinned to her blouse.

brood I love to see a hen with her *brood* of chicks. ■ A person is said to *brood* over a problem when he ponders on it very earnestly.

brook a small stream.

broom For sweeping a floor you need a *broom*. ■ *Broom* is a wild bush which has yellow flowers.

broth thin soup.

brother My father's other son is my *brother*.

brought I have *brought* my sister to see you.

brow The forehead is sometimes called the brow, as in 'He wiped the sweat off his *brow*.' ■ The *brow* of a hill is the top.

brown I like *brown* bread better than white.

bruise This dark patch on my leg is the *bruise* I received when the cricket ball hit me. ■ If you drop an apple you will *bruise* it.

brunt full force, e.g. The *brunt* of the attack fell on Jack, so the other defenders had little to do.

brush I paint with a *brush*. ■ I *brush* my coat to remove dust from it.

Brussels the capital city of Belgium.

brutal A *brutal* person is one who is cruel or savage.

brute a savage beast; ■ also a person who is cruel or savage.

bubble A soap *bubble* is made by blowing air into soapy water. ■ Water can be seen to *bubble* when it boils.

buccaneer a pirate.

Bucharest the capital city of Roumania.

buck The male of a deer, rabbit, etc. is called a *buck*. ■ '*Buck* up!' means 'Hurry up!' or 'Cheer up!' ■ A horse is said to *buck* when it leaps upwards.

bucket Jack and Jill went up the hill and fetched a *bucket* of water.

buckle I cannot fasten my belt because the *buckle* has broken. ■ I saw my bicycle wheel *buckle* as it hit the lamp-post.

bud The little green *bud* on the tree will soon open into leaves or flowers.

Budapest the capital city of Hungary.

budge We pulled with all our might, but the rock would not *budge* one inch from its place.

budgerigar A *budgerigar* looks like a pretty little parrot.

buffalo a kind of ox much used for farm work in the East.

buffers *Buffers* are fitted to the ends of railway engines and coaches to lessen the force of collisions.

bug a small blood-sucking insect which has an unpleasant smell.

bugle A *bugle* is like a small trumpet without valves.

build We *build* houses with bricks. ■ John has the same sturdy *build* as Tom though he is not as strong as Tom.

building The men were *building* a block of flats. ■ That new *building* is a block of flats.

built The house was *built* in ten weeks.

bulb A daffodil grew from one *bulb* and a hyacinth from the other. ■ The electric light *bulb* broke and left us in darkness.

Bulgaria a country to the north of Greece and Turkey.

Bulgarian A native of Bulgaria is called a *Bulgarian*. ■ I knew that I was in Bulgaria when I saw the *Bulgarian* flag.

bulge We knew that he had our ball because we could see the *bulge* in his pocket.

bulky The parcel was so *bulky* that we could not get it in through the doorway.

bull The male of cattle is called a *bull*. ■ There are also *bull* elephants, *bull* whales, etc.

bulldozer a powerful tractor which pushes before it a broad steel plate to level land and remove obstacles.

bullet The *bullet* fired from the rifle went clean through the door.

bulletin I always listen to the news *bulletin* on the radio.

bullock a kind of male of the cattle family especially produced to provide us with meat.

bull's-eye The centre of a target is called the *bull's-eye*.

bully someone who ill-treats weaker people. ■ To *bully* is to ill-treat weaker people.

bulrush a tall reed which grows beside rivers.

bumble-bee A large furry bee, called a *bumble-bee*, buzzed round the room.

bulrush

bumble-bee

bump I received this *bump* on the head by walking into a lamp-post. ■ If you walk into a lamp-post you will *bump* your head.

bumper A car has a springy *bumper* front and back to take the shock of a collision.

bun I like a *bun* for tea. On Good Fridays I have a hot cross *bun*. I have also had a Chelsea *bun*, a cream *bun* and a coconut *bun*.

bunch When Jane was in hospital, we took her a *bunch* of flowers and a *bunch* of grapes. ■ It is dangerous for cyclists to *bunch* together.

bundle The tramp carried his belongings in an untidy *bundle* wrapped in an old sheet.

bungalow a house with only a ground floor.

bungle To *bungle* a job is to do it badly and clumsily.

bunk a shelf-like bed in a ship. ■ To talk *bunk* is to talk nonsense. ■ To do a *bunk* is to run away (slang).

buoy (pron. boy) The edge of the sand-bank is marked by a brightly-coloured *buoy* floating in the water.

buoy

bush

burden The porter was glad to lower the heavy *burden* from his back and rest awhile. ■ I will not *burden* you with my troubles.

burglar A *burglar* broke into the house and stole Mother's imitation jewellery.

burial After the funeral service in church came the *burial* in the cemetery.

burly A *burly* man is one who is big and strong and rather fat.

burn *Burn* this letter on the fire. ■ That *burn* on her hand was caused by a hot cinder. ■ In Scotland, a small stream is called a *burn*.

burrow Animals like foxes and rabbits *burrow* into the ground. ■ They burrow into the ground to make a hole called their *burrow*.

burst The balloon *burst* with a pop when Dick pricked it, ■ and Jean *burst* into tears.

bury It was the custom of pirates to *bury* their treasure in the ground.

bus (short for) omnibus. ■ It is a fivepenny *bus*-ride to school.

bush Dad planted a gooseberry *bush* in the garden.

bushel a measure of corn, etc., equal to 8 gallons (= 36·32 litres).

busily Mother was *busily* cutting sandwiches (i.e. she was working hard at the job).

business My *business* is selling cars; yours is studying at school. ■ 'Mind your own *business*' means 'Do not interest yourself in my affairs.'

bust a model of someone's head and shoulders. ■ A woman's *bust* is her bosom.

busy I am too *busy* to talk to you now; come back later when I have nothing to do.

butcher We buy our meat from the *butcher*. ■ To *butcher* people is to slaughter them cruelly.

butler The chief servant in a household is called the *butler*; his special duty is to see to the wines, etc.

butt a barrel, e.g. a water-*butt*.

butter *Butter* is made by shaking up cream in a churn. I like jam on my bread and *butter*.

buttercup The yellow *buttercup* and the white daisy both grow wild in English meadows.

buttercup   **butterfly**

butterfly The ugly caterpillar will eventually turn into a beautiful *butterfly* and fly away.

button '*Button* up your coat!' ■ 'I cannot because the *button* has come off.' ■ If you press that *button* a bell will ring.

buttress a structure built to support or strengthen a wall.

buy Go to the shop and *buy* a fivepenny packet of sweets.

buzz the noise made by a bee. ■ To *buzz* is to make a humming noise. ■ '*Buzz* off!' means 'Go away!' (slang).

buzzer The noise of the electric *buzzer* indicates that the doctor is ready for the next patient.

cabbage We eat *cabbage* more often than any other green vegetable.

cabin a room in a ship; ■ a little hut.

cabinet a piece of furniture containing drawers and shelves.

cable a strong thick rope; ■ a wire rope; ■ a wire covered with insulating material and intended for conducting electricity.

cackle A hen will often *cackle* when she has laid an egg.

cactus a prickly plant that grows in deserts.

cad A boy who tells tales about his friends is a *cad*.

caddy Many people keep their tea in a small box or tin, called a *caddy*.

cadet a young man training for the army, navy, air force, or police force.

cadge To *cadge* something is to get it by begging.

café (pron. cáff-ay) a place where people can buy and consume food and drink.

cafeteria A café in which the customers collect their own food and drink is called a *cafeteria*.

cage It is cruel to imprison a wild bird in a *cage*.

Cairo the chief city of Egypt.

cake We always have *cake* for tea on Sundays. ■ I lost the *cake* of soap in the bath.

calamity a very serious and unpleasant event.

calculate To *calculate* the area of a room you multiply the length by the breadth.

calendar When I want to know the date, I look at a *calendar*.

calf A cow's baby is called a *calf*. ■ The muscle on the back of a person's leg is called the *calf*.

call You can *call* out, but no one will hear you. ■ *Call* for me in the car at 8 o'clock. ■ There is a phone *call* for you. ■ We *call* the baby Pat.

called When I *called* at my friend's house, ■ he *called* out, 'Just coming'.

caller anyone who pays a call or visit.

calling Go at once; your mother is *calling* you. ■ You should become a clergyman only if you have a *calling* for such work.

callous A *callous* person is one who can be cruel or witness cruelty, and not care.

calm The sea was as *calm* and smooth as a duck pond. ■ In spite of the danger, John did not panic, but remained *calm*.

calves more than one calf.

camel an animal that has one or two large humps on its back.

camera My new *camera* takes very good photographs.

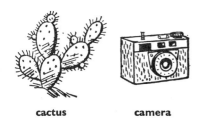

cactus   camera

camouflage To *camouflage* something is to disguise it so that it looks like its surroundings.

camp We will put up our tents and *camp* here for the night. ■ Our school *camp* consists of tents and huts in a meadow by the sea.

campaign the part of a war which takes place in a single area or for part of the time, e.g. Julius Caesar's *campaign* in Britain.

Canada the northern part of the American continent.

Canadian I like *Canadian* cheese, *Canadian* butter and ■ every *Canadian* that I have met.

canal The Panama *canal* was dug so that ships might sail straight from the Atlantic to the Pacific Ocean through central America.

canary In the cage was a pretty yellow song-bird called a *canary*.

cancel If you *cancel* a football match you arrange for it not to be played. ■ If you *cancel* in arithmetic, you cross out figures like

this: $\dfrac{\cancel{12}^{3^1}}{\cancel{15}_{3_1}} \times \dfrac{\cancel{5}^1}{\cancel{8}_2}$

cancer *Cancer* is a disease. ■ The Tropic of *Cancer* is $23\frac{1}{2}°$ north of the equator.

candid Don't just say what you think will please me; be *candid* and tell me what you really think of my idea.

candidate At the last election, Mother voted for the Labour *candidate* and Father voted for the Conservative *candidate*.

candle The baby blew out the *candle* too hard and sent the hot wax on to her birthday cake.

cane a thick stick. ■ The headmaster will *cane* those who disobey. ■ Sugar is extracted from sugar-*cane*.

caned The boy was *caned* for being disobedient.

caning The boy was given a *caning* for being disobedient.

canned We have brought *canned* soup, *canned* meat and *canned* fruit but no can-opener. ■ Fruit is *canned* by being cooked and sealed into tins.

cannibal The *cannibal* cooked and ate the policeman sent to arrest him.

cannon The gunners fired a *cannon*-ball ■ from the *cannon*. ■ All ten *cannon* were fired at once. (The word 'gun' is used nowadays in place of *cannon*).

cannot I'm sorry I *cannot* come today; please ask me some other time.

canoe We get very wet paddling our *canoe* on the rough water of the river.

canoe

capstan

canon a clergyman who has special duties connected with a cathedral.

canopy In addition to the hood for keeping off the rain, the pram had a pretty fringed *canopy* for keeping the sun off the baby's face.

can't cannot. I *can't* come to school today because I have a cold.

canteen The *canteen* at school provides lunches for 300 children each day.

canter A horse is said to *canter* when it goes along at an easy gallop.

canvas Tents and sails are made of a tough cloth called *canvas*.

canvass Before an election people come to our houses to *canvass* for votes for the various candidates.

canyon a very deep and steep-sided river valley.

capable I would not have thought Jane *capable* of such a nasty trick. ■ George is a *capable* boy; he'll tackle almost any job and do it well.

capacity This jug has a *capacity* of half a litre. The sports ground has a *capacity* of 20,000 people.

cape a kind of overcoat without sleeves; ■ land jutting out into the sea, e.g. *Cape* Horn.

Cape Town a port at the southern tip of Africa.

capital London is the *capital* of England. ■ *Capital* punishment is punishment by death. ■ THIS SENTENCE IS IN CAPITAL LETTERS.

capsize A sudden gust of wind caused the yacht to *capsize* and the men aboard were flung into the water.

capstan a giant reel which is turned by men or by machinery in order to wind in ropes on ships, etc.

capsule A *capsule* containing a dose of cod-liver oil looks like a transparent pill. ■ The first space man travelled in a *capsule* mounted on the tip of a rocket.

captain The man in charge of an aircraft or a ship is the *captain*. Jim is our school *captain* and *captain* of the football team.

captivate to charm and delight.

captive No *captive* has ever escaped from this prison.

captivity After five years in *captivity* the prisoner was set free.

capture The hunters set out to *capture* wild animals for the zoo.

caramel a toffee-like sweet.

carat the measure of the purity of gold, pure gold being 24 carat. A 10-*carat*-gold article is $\frac{10}{24}$ths gold.

caravan We live in a *caravan* which we tow behind our car. ■ In eastern countries a *caravan* is a company of traders, travelling together for safety.

caravan

carcase, carcass After killing the antelope, the lion left the *carcase* to be devoured by vultures.

card The playing *card* missing from this pack is the ten of hearts. ■ I sent you a birthday *card* and a Christmas *card*.

cardboard Shoes are often packed in *cardboard* boxes.

Cardiff an important town in South Wales.

cardigan a knitted woollen waistcoat or jacket.

cardinal an important official of the Church, e.g. *Cardinal* Wolsey.

care Take *care* of your new watch. ■ I don't *care* what you do. ■ The poor child was an orphan who had no one to *care* for her.

career To *career* along is to go fast or wildly. ■ A person's *career* is his way of earning a living, such as teaching or engineering.

careful Be *careful* when crossing roads.

careless Many accidents are caused by *careless* drivers.

caress a friendly touch or a kiss. ■ To *caress* a person or animal is to pet or stroke him.

caretaker The *caretaker* looks after the school building.

cargo The ship carried a *cargo* of iron ore.

carnation a red or white garden flower with a strong perfume.

carnival a festival in which there may be music and dancing in the street and a ■ *carnival* queen.

carol The *carol* singers sang ■ my favourite *carol*, 'The holly and the ivy.'

carpenter The *carpenter* was sawing wood to make doors for the new house.

carpet I love to step out of bed on to a warm, woolly *carpet*. ■ Ground covered with a carpet of flowers is said to be *carpeted* with flowers.

carriage Every compartment of the railway *carriage* was full of passengers. ■ *Carriage* is also the cost of carrying something by rail or road.

a

carrot an orange-red root vegetable. A donkey loves a *carrot*.

carrot   cask

carry Please *carry* my bag for me. ■ These pipes *carry* water to the town.

carrying Mother is *carrying* the shopping; Father is *carrying* the baby.

cart The horse pulled a *cart* loaded with potatoes. ■ In P.E. lessons we turn *cart*wheels. ■ We have to *cart* all those boxes to the shed.

carton Our breakfast cornflakes are packed in a cardboard *carton*.

cartoon A newspaper *cartoon* is an amusing drawing, usually about some event in the news.

cartridge The gamekeeper put a *cartridge* in his gun and fired. ■ The stiff white paper on which we draw is called *cartridge* paper.

carve At the dinner-table, Father's job is to *carve* the meat.

carving Father carves the meat with a *carving* knife.

case I carry my books in a leather *case*. ■ Take your mac. in *case* it rains. ■ The jury who tried the *case* found the prisoner guilty.

cash money. ■ To *cash* a cheque is to obtain money in return for it.

cashier The person who has charge of the money in a bank or a shop, etc. is called the *cashier*.

cask a wooden barrel.

casket a small box, often beautifully decorated, in which jewels, love letters, etc., may be kept.

casserole an earthenware or oven-glass dish and lid, in which food can be cooked in an oven and brought on to the table.

cassock A choirboy wears a black *cassock* under his white surplice.

cast The rainwater pipes are made of *cast* iron. ■ The *cast* of the play lined up on the front of the stage.

castaway someone who has been shipwrecked on a desert island, like Robinson Crusoe.

caste In India people of the lowest *caste* were sometimes called untouchables. They did the dirtiest work. The highest *caste* were the Brahmins, who were the priests.

castle The baron lived in a strong *castle* so as to be safe from attack. ■ A *castle* is a chess piece that looks like a castle.

castle

castor *Castor* sugar consists of very fine grains. ■ The small wheels on the legs of chairs, beds, etc., are called *castors* (also spelt *caster*).

castor oil *Castor oil* is a nasty medicine; it makes me feel sick.

casual unplanned or accidental. A *casual* labourer is one who hasn't a steady job, but works when there is work for him.

casualty When the aircraft crashed, the only *casualty* was a man who had broken his ankle; the other passengers walked away uninjured.

catalogue a complete list of goods, books, etc., usually in alphabetical order. ■ To *catalogue* goods, etc., is to make such a list.

catapult A boy makes a *catapult* from a forked stick and a piece of elastic. ■ A powerful catapult is used to *catapult* aircraft into the air from a carrier.

catapult

catarrh Simon was always having to blow his nose because he suffered from *catarrh*.

catastrophe (pron. cat-ass-tro-fee) a disastrous end to something.

catch How do you *catch* fish? ■ *Catch* this ball. ■ That paper is too wet to *catch* fire. ■ Wet feet may make you *catch* cold. ■ You'll *catch* it if your dad hears about this.

category If we divide the boys in our form into workers, sportsmen and talkers, most of us would be in the third *category*.

cater The restaurant manager told us he did not *cater* for school parties, so he wouldn't serve us.

caterpillar The ugly green *caterpillar* will eventually turn into a beautiful butterfly.

caterpillar   catkins

cathedral a bishop's headquarters and the chief church of its district.

catholic wide, including all men or all things; hence *Catholic* Church which includes all Christians everywhere. The head of the Roman *Catholic* Church is the Pope.

catkins the flowers of hazel or willow trees, which are soft and fluffy and appear early in the spring.

cattle The herd of *cattle* included several cows, a bull and some bullocks.

caught The paper *caught* fire. ■ The policeman *caught* the thief. ■ Jim *caught* the ball. ■ Jane *caught* cold.

cauldron We boiled the soup in a great *cauldron* hung over the camp fire.

cauldron   cauliflower

cauliflower a vegetable like a cabbage with a big white centre called the flower.

cause   The *cause* of the fire was a cigarette-end. ■ A cigarette-end may *cause* a forest fire.

causeway   a road raised above low or wet ground.

caution   *Caution*: Dangerous hill. We had to walk with *caution* on that dangerous, icy slope. ■ I must *caution* you against swimming in this rough sea.

cautious   My mother is a *cautious* motorist; she never does any dangerous driving.

cavalier   a horseman, especially one of those who fought for King Charles I against Parliament.

cavalry   horse soldiers.

cave   a hollow in a hillside, or in the ground. ■ A *cave*man was one who lived in a cave.

cavern   an underground hollow.

cavity   The dentist found a *cavity* in my back tooth and put some filling in it.

cease   *Cease* this noise at once! The battle ended with the order, '*Cease* fire.'

ceaseless   We did not sleep all night because of the *ceaseless* roar of the traffic passing the house.

cedar   an evergreen tree which has cones like those of a pine tree.

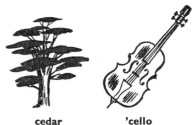

cedar   'cello

ceiling   The electric light hangs from the *ceiling* above you.

celebrate   We had a party to *celebrate* Mother's silver wedding.

celebration   The party was in *celebration* of Mother's silver wedding. ■ We held the *celebration* in the church hall.

celebrity   a well-known person.

celery   a plant whose crisp white stalks are eaten as salad or vegetable.

celestial   A *celestial* object is something in the sky, e.g. a planet.

cell   The prisoner was locked in a *cell*. ■ My torch battery is made up of three *cells*.

cellar   Under our house is a *cellar* in which the coal was kept.

'cello   (pron. chello) short for violon*cello*, an instrument like a very large violin.

Celsius   Temperatures are measured in degrees *Celsius*, e.g. water boils at 100°C.

cement   fine powder which is mixed with sand, etc., to make concrete. ■ Any soft substance used for sticking things together is a *cement*. ■ To *cement* is to join.

cemetery   Auntie goes to the *cemetery* each week to put flowers on Uncle's grave.

census   When there is a *census*, the names of all the people in the country are written on forms so that we may find out how many people there are.

cent   a hundredth part of a dollar, an American coin.

centenary   Our school was founded in 1880, so our *centenary* will be celebrated in 1980.

Centigrade   The boiling-point of water is 100° *Centigrade*, which is now called 100° Celsius (100°C.).

centime   a hundredth part of a franc, a French coin.

centimetre a hundredth part of a metre; 10mm.

centipede a tiny creature that lives in the soil and has very many legs.

centipede   chaffinch

central The *central* station is in the middle of the town. ■ A building is said to have *central* heating when it has radiators all heated from one boiler.

centre The bull's-eye is in the *centre* of the target.

centurion a Roman officer in charge of a hundred soldiers.

century a hundred runs at cricket or ■ a hundred years of time.

cereal For our breakfast *cereal* we have wheat, corn or rice. Barley, oats and rye are also *cereals*.

ceremony The wedding *ceremony* took place in St. John's Church.

certain If you poke your finger into the fire, you are *certain* to get burnt.

certainly If you poke your finger into the fire, you'll *certainly* get burnt.

certainty It is a *certainty* that you'll get your finger burnt if you poke it into the fire.

certificate Your birth *certificate* is a large sheet of paper which states where and when you were born.

certify This swimming certificate is to *certify* that I can swim one hundred metres.

chafe That rough collar will *chafe* your neck and make it sore.

chaff to tease someone good-humouredly; ■ such teasing is called *chaff*. ■ *Chaff* is also chopped hay or straw or husks off grain.

chaffinch a bird about the size of a sparrow, but much prettier in appearance and in voice.

chain The anchor was attached to a *chain*. ■ *Chain* up that dog; he's dangerous.

chair Baby sits in a high *chair*, the invalid in a bath *chair*, the holiday maker in a deck *chair* and grandad in an easy *chair*.

chairman The person in charge of a meeting, conference, etc., is called the *chairman*.

chalet (pron. shall-ay) A Swiss wooden house is called a *chalet*. ■ A seaside hut built in similar style is also called a *chalet*.

chalet

chalk a white rock, common in English hills. ■ Blackboard *chalk* is a chemical substance, specially made for writing on blackboards.

challenge We shall *challenge* King's School to a chess match. ■ We heard the sentry's *challenge*: 'Who goes there?'

champion The *champion* racing driver is the one who has won most races. ■ The dog that wins most prizes at the show is the *champion*.

championship If our team wins the final match, we shall have won the Schools' Football League *championship*.

chance opportunity, e.g. If you get a *chance* to go abroad, take it. ■ A game of *chance* is one that does not depend on skill, e.g. Snakes and Ladders.

chancel In church, the congregation sit in the nave, while the choir and clergy occupy the *chancel*.

chancellor The *Chancellor* of the Exchequer is the minister of the government who has charge of the country's finances.

change The shopkeeper gave me 5p *change*. ■ I'm tired of jam for tea; let's have paste for a *change*. ■ *Change* your clothes before you go out.

changeable The weather was very *changeable*, sometimes wet, sometimes sunny.

changing We cannot decide where to go because people keep *changing* their minds. ■ Dick is *changing* out of his wet clothes.

channel *Channel* swimmers try to swim from England to France ■ across the English *Channel*.

chant to sing; ■ a short tune which is repeated for each verse of a psalm.

chaos (pron. kay-oss) complete confusion, e.g. There was *chaos* in the town after the hurricane had struck.

chap These icy winds *chap* my hands so that they are a mass of sore cracks. ■ Your brother is a jolly good *chap* (slang).

chapel The residents of a royal palace, or college, etc., often have their own *chapel* in which to worship.

chaplain a clergyman attached to a private chapel, or to a ship, regiment, prison, etc.

chapter My sister always reads the last *chapter* of a book first.

character No one would trust Sam, for he had a bad *character*. ■ Sam was a bad *character*. ■ Fagin is a *character* in the Dickens novel, 'Oliver Twist'.

charade (pron. sha-ráhd) a party game in which people have to guess a word from acted clues.

charcoal a black substance made by partly burning wood, bone, etc. We sometimes draw with sticks of *charcoal*.

charge How much does he *charge* for a drink? ■ Who is in *charge* of this child? ■ The cavalry made a *charge* at the enemy.

chariot In London there is a statue of Queen Boadicea riding in her *chariot*. ■ The Romans loved *chariot* racing, though it was dangerous to both horses and men.

chariot

charity Among his gifts to *charity* were £50 to the blind and £50 to a hospital.

charm Simon wore a lucky *charm* on a chain round his neck. ■ Mary had such *charm* that everyone loved her.

charming Everyone loved Mary; she was such a *charming* girl.

chart The captain's *chart* showed the exact position of Treasure Island.

charter a document giving special rights to someone, e.g. the *charter* that gives a town the right to become a borough.

chase My dog loves to *chase* cats.

chasing My dog loves *chasing* cats.

chasm The explorers were stopped by a great *chasm* in the ground, too deep and steep to climb down and too wide to jump.

chat I stayed with the gardener and had a friendly *chat* about the weeds and the weather.

chatter Stop your useless *chatter* and listen to what Roy is saying. ■ Betty is an awful *chatter*-box – she never stops talking.

chauffeur (pron. sho-fer) a man paid to drive a car.

cheap These apples were very *cheap*, only 5p a pound.

cheat That man is a *cheat*; he deliberately gave me too little change. ■ Dishonest people *cheat* at cards.

check *Check* your bicycle brakes before you ride. ■ A *check* is a squared pattern, on material usually.

cheek Uncle Tom kissed Mary on the *cheek*. ■ You've got a *cheek* to ask for your ball back after it has broken my window.

cheeky That *cheeky* boy actually asked for his ball back after it had broken my window.

cheer We gave the winner a *cheer* as he crossed the finishing line. ■ Don't be sad; *cheer* up!

cheerful Billy was a *cheerful* lad who had a smile and a joke for everyone.

cheerfully Sally *cheerfully* set about the washing up, humming a little tune as she did so.

cheese I love bread and *cheese*. I like Cheshire *cheese* and Cheddar *cheese* best. We bait the mousetrap with *cheese*.

chef (pron. sheff) The man who is head cook in a restaurant, hotel, etc., is called the *chef*.

chemical a substance made or used by chemists.

chemist a man who sells medicines, pills, ointments, etc. Another kind of *chemist* works in a laboratory doing experiments with metals, liquids, gases, etc.

chemistry In *chemistry* lessons we do experiments to discover what happens when various substances are mixed together, heated, etc.

cheque If you take this *cheque* to the bank, they will pay you the amount of money written on it.

cherry a small stone fruit which grows in clusters.

cherry

cherub an innocent and beautiful child, sometimes with wings, as painted by some artists.

    cherub   **chicken**

chess a game like a battle, played on a squared board and using pieces called knights, castles, kings, queens, etc.

chest My heart and lungs are in my *chest*. ■ The miser kept his money in an old oak *chest*.

chestnut A *chestnut* tree produces sweet brown nuts in a prickly case. ■ A horse-*chestnut* tree has similar-looking nuts, called conkers.

chew If I *chew* a toffee it may pull the filling out of my tooth.

chicken The *chicken* laid no eggs, so we killed it and had it for our Sunday dinner.

chief The *chief* meal of the day is dinner. ■ The Red Indian *chief* had a feathered head-dress.

chiefly The audience consisted *chiefly* of children, but there were a few parents present as well.

chieftain head man, usually of an uncivilized tribe.

chilblain a very itchy red swelling on the hand or foot, caused by cold weather.

child The *child* was hurrying to school.

childish *Childish* behaviour is that expected from a child.

children All *children* are expected to attend a school.

chill I knew I had a *chill* because I was sneezing and shivering. ■ I like the sun to take the *chill* off the water before I bathe.

chilly I felt cold after the bathe because the water was too *chilly*.

chime We lay awake and heard the clock bells *chime* every hour and half-hour throughout the night.

chimney The smoke wouldn't go up the *chimney* because of a bird's nest there.

chimpanzee an African ape that looks rather like a man.

chin Father Christmas's *chin* is hidden by his big beard.

china Mother's best tea cups are made of beautiful thin *china*.

China a huge, thickly populated country in east Asia.

Chinese The *Chinese* are the people of China. ■ I went to a *Chinese* restaurant in London.

chink Through a *chink* in the shutters, the prisoner could see a narrow strip of the street outside. ■ We heard the *chink* of money.

chip A *chip* is a small piece. ■ To *chip* is to break off a small piece.

chipped A small piece had been *chipped* off the ornament. ■ I like *chipped* potatoes with my fried fish.

chips We have fish and *chips* for dinner on Fridays.

chirp The birds sit in the trees and *chirp* gaily but untunefully.

chisel In the woodwork lesson we were taught how to cut with a *chisel*.

chisel

chivalrous A *chivalrous* man is one who is gentlemanly, honourable and courteous, especially to ladies.

chivalry (pron. shiv-al-ry) was the whole system of knighthood in the Middle Ages, involving duties to Church, king, the weak, etc.

chloroform The vapour from *chloroform* puts people to sleep.

chocolate I shall eat my bar of *chocolate* at break.

choice Choose a book and when you've made your *choice*, let me see it. ■ We put all the *choice* apples on one side for the hospital, and ate the poorer ones ourselves.

choir (pron. kwire) Jimmy sings in the church *choir*.

choke A fishbone stuck in Janet's throat and made her *choke*. ■ In autumn, leaves get into the drains and *choke* them.

choose Here are all the books; come and *choose* the one you would like.

chop Lumberjacks *chop* down trees with axes. ■ I love a pork *chop* for dinner.

chord (pron. kord) A group of notes sounding together harmoniously is called a *chord*.

chorus Susan sang the verse and the rest of us joined with her in singing the *chorus*.

chose Sandra went to the library yesterday and *chose* a book about ponies.

chosen I was told I could have whichever book I liked, so I have *chosen* this one.

christen To *christen* someone is to baptize him. ■ But 'to *christen*' may simply mean 'to name', e.g. The girls *christened* her Cyn; her real name is Cynthia.

Christian A *Christian* is someone who believes in the religion of Christ. ■ Joan Smith's *Christian* name is Joan.

Christianity The Christian religion is called *Christianity*.

Christmas I love to receive *Christmas* presents from Father *Christmas* on *Christmas* Day.

chromium The bumpers on our new car are so shiny because they are covered with a metal called *chromium*.

chrysalis The *chrysalis* into which a caterpillar changes seems hard and lifeless, but a butterfly will come from it.

chrysalis   chrysanthemum

chrysanthemum a beautiful autumn flower like an enormous double daisy.

chubby round-faced and plump.

chuckle We dared not laugh aloud, but we enjoyed a quiet *chuckle* to ourselves.

chum a boy's special friend.

chunk A *chunk* of bread means a thick lump. People also talk of a *chunk* of wood or a *chunk* of cheese, etc.

church A place where Christians worship.

churn Cream is made into butter by being shaken about in a *churn*. ■ To *churn* something is to stir it up vigorously.

chute I love to slide down the *chute* into the water at the swimming baths.

chutney Have some of this *chutney* with your meat; we made it ourselves from tomatoes, apples, sugar, spices and vinegar.

cider a popular drink made from apples.

cigar a roll of tobacco leaves prepared for smoking.

cigar

cigarette Many people have stopped *cigarette* smoking because it can cause serious illness.

cinder Mother left the cake in the oven all day and it was burnt to a *cinder*.

cinema We went to a *cinema* and saw an exciting film about cowboys and Indians.

circle This o is a *circle*. ■ The space-craft will *circle* the moon twice. ■ In a theatre, the *circle* is the tier between the gallery and the floor.

circuit The rocket did one *circuit* of the earth and returned to base. ■ A short *circuit* in the electric motor put the train out of action.

circular A wheel is *circular* in shape. ■ We all knew about the fair because a printed *circular* about it had been sent to every house.

circulate The pumping of the heart makes the blood *circulate* round the body.

circulation Tight clothing interferes with the *circulation* of the blood. ■ The School Magazine has a *circulation* of 500 copies.

circumference The *circumference* of a circle is the distance round it.

circumstances When Jill arrived with Jimmy, it was tea time, so under the *circumstances*, we had to ask them both to tea.

circus We went to the *circus* to see the clowns and the performing animals.

cistern Water is stored in a big iron *cistern* in the roof of the house.

cities London, Paris and York are all large *cities*.

citizen A *citizen* of London is called a Londoner.

city A *city* is a specially important town, such as London, Paris or York.

civic having to do with a city or citizens, e.g. It's my *civic* duty to vote at borough elections.

civil not connected with the armed forces. ■ A *civil* war is one between people of the same country ■ A *civil* answer is a polite one.

civilian someone who is not in the army, navy or air force.

civility politeness.

civilization An atomic war could destroy all our cities, colleges, factories, etc., and this would mean the end of our *civilization*.

civilize It was necessary to *civilize* the savages for they were warlike and ignorant.

claim Mabel stepped forward to *claim* the prize she had won.

clamber Our hands and feet were bruised and torn through having to *clamber* up the cliff to safety.

clammy A *clammy* hand is cool and damp.

clamour There was such a *clamour* from the angry crowd that the speaker could not make himself heard.

clamp a kind of portable vice, for holding things together.

clan a Scottish tribe, all descended from the same man. Examples are: the MacDonalds, the Campbells, etc.

clang The bell sounded with a loud *clang*. ■ Don't *clang* the bell or you'll wake the baby.

clap Ask the audience not to *clap* until the end of the performance. ■ We were awakened by a loud *clap* of thunder.

clapped At the end of the concert we all *clapped* our hands until they were sore.

clapping At the end of the concert the *clapping* went on for a long time.

clarinet a wood-wind musical instrument in which the sound is produced by the vibration of a single reed.

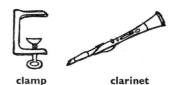

clamp clarinet

clash You can't wear orange with purple; the colours *clash*. ■ The music ended with a *clash* (banging against each other) of cymbals.

clasp Jill's necklace fell off because the *clasp* had broken. ■ To *clasp* is to hold firmly.

class There are thirty children in my *class* at school.

classical Jazz and pop music are very different from the *classical* music of Bach.

classify To *classify* things is to arrange them into groups or kinds.

clatter I could hear by the *clatter* of plates that someone had started the washing up.

clause part of a sentence; ■ one of the parts of a legal agreement.

claw That scratch was made by the *claws* of my cat. ■ The cat might *claw* the dog's eyes.

clay a stiff, sticky kind of earth used in modelling and for making pottery, bricks, etc.

clean If your hands are not *clean*, go and wash them. ■ The prisoner got *clean* away and was never seen again.

cleanliness is being clean, e.g. schoolboys are not usually noted for their *cleanliness*.

cleanse make clean: used when a more impressive word than 'clean' is required.

clear The water was so *clear* that we could see the sea bottom. ■ It is *clear* to me that we're lost. ■ The road ahead was *clear* of traffic.

clearance There was a *clearance* of only 150 mm between the top of the bus and the underside of the bridge. ■ Our plane awaited a *clearance* of the fog.

clearly When the mist blew away we could see the wreck *clearly*. ■ The men advanced with smiles and outstretched hands; *clearly* they were friends.

cleft He *cleft* the post from top to bottom with a blow of his axe. ■ We hid the paper in a *cleft* in the tree-trunk.

clench To *clench* your teeth is to shut them tightly together. ■ You *clench* your fist in order to punch someone.

clergy The *clergy* present at the wedding included the Bishop, the vicar, the curate and the Rev. Mr. Bates.

clergyman The *clergyman* I know best is our vicar, the Rev. J. Jones.

clerical A clerk is a man who does *clerical* work. ■ A clergyman wears a *clerical* collar, which fastens at the back.

clerk (pron. clark) a man who works in an office writing letters, keeping accounts, etc.

clever I am not *clever* enough to come first in the class.

cleverly Joe *cleverly* eluded the bandits by dodging down a side-street and then coming out again behind them.

cleverness When young John made a television set which worked, all the family admired his *cleverness*.

click There was a *click* as the key turned in the lock.

client Lawyers, private detectives, bankers, etc., call a person they work for their *client*.

cliff We looked over the edge of the *cliff* and saw the sea far below us.

climate The *climate* of the Congo is hot and wet, but the English *climate* is cooler and drier.

climax The *climax* of a story is the most exciting part in which the outcome is decided.

climb To *climb* a mountain you have to use your hands and feet.

climber someone who climbs. ■ A plant which climbs up a support is called a *climber*.

clinch To *clinch* an argument or a bargain is to settle it finally. ■ *Clinch* is also another way of spelling *clench*, which means to shut together tightly.

cling Limpets *cling* to rocks so tightly that you cannot get them off. We shall get separated in the crowd if you don't *cling* to my arm.

clinic We go to the school *clinic* to have cuts and bruises treated.

clip The pages were held together with a paper-*clip*. ■ To *clip* is to cut with scissors.

cloak A *cloak* is like an overcoat without sleeves. ■ To *cloak* something is to conceal or hide it.

clock   We were all late for school because the school *clock* was ten minutes fast.

clockwise   A thing is said to go round *clockwise* when it revolves in the same direction as the hands of a clock.

clockwork   A *clockwork* motor is one worked by a spring.

clog   If you *clog* the drain the water will not be able to run away.

clogs   wooden shoes.

       clogs   **clown**

close   'To *close*' (rhymes with 'nose') means 'to shut'. ■ *Close* (rhymes with 'dose' [of medicine]) means 'near' or 'stuffy', e.g. We are *close* to my house. ■ It is *close* in this room.

clot   A *clot* of blood formed in the wound and stopped the bleeding.

cloth   Coats are made of woollen *cloth*. ■ Put on the table*cloth*; it is dinner-time.

clothe   (pron. to rhyme with 'loathe' [hate]) They *clothe* the beauty queen in a beautiful gold dress and put a crown on her head.

clothes   The boys couldn't dress after their swim because someone had hidden their *clothes*.

clothing   I cannot dress until I find my *clothing*.

cloud   The rain is falling from that big grey *cloud* overhead.

clout   She gave the boy a *clout* on the head which hurt her knuckles.

clover   a field flower which has three little round leaves to each leaf-stalk.

clown   The *clown* is in the circus to make everyone laugh.

club   Betty belongs to the swimming *club*. ■ Father plays golf with a golf *club*. ■ In cards the ace of *clubs* looks like a black clover-leaf.

clue   The *clue* which led the detectives to the solution of the mystery was an old bus ticket.

clump   We hid behind a *clump* of bushes. ■ We heard Mac in his heavy boots *clump* across the floor.

clumsiness   Dick is noted for his *clumsiness*; he spills or drops almost everything he touches.

clumsy   Eric is too *clumsy* to make a dancer; he would trample on his partner's feet or push her over.

cluster   You boys are not to *cluster* round the notice-board and block the corridor. ■ There is a large *cluster* of daffodils in the garden.

clutch   A drowning man will *clutch* at anything near enough to support him. ■ The bird was sitting on a *clutch* of eggs. ■ Most cars have a *clutch* pedal.

coach   Travelling by road is much pleasanter in a motor *coach* than it used to be in a stage *coach*. ■ The guard travels in the last *coach* of the train. ■ Most football teams have a *coach* who directs their training. ■ The trainer is there to *coach* the team.

coal   We burn *coal* on the fire. ■ My uncle was a *coal* miner.

coarse   rough in texture. ■ *Coarse* language is vulgar or rough talk.

coast We went down to the *coast* for a day by the sea. ■ A *coast*guard saw the wreck and sent for help.

coaster a vessel which does not go overseas, but trades up and down the coast.

coat Put on your *coat*; it's raining. ■ I must put a *coat* of paint on that door.

coax Mother has to *coax* the baby to drink milk because he doesn't like it.

cobbler someone who mends shoes.

cobra a poisonous snake.

cobweb The spider made a big *cobweb* across the corner of my room.

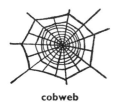

cobweb   **cockle**

cock The hen bird lays the eggs; the *cock* bird crows.

cockerel a young male chicken.

cockle We found lots of *cockle* shells on the beach, ■ but none contained a *cockle*.

cockney a Londoner.

cockpit The fighter pilot sat in the *cockpit* of his aircraft awaiting the signal to take off.

cockroach a large black beetle which lives in houses and comes out at night to feed.

cock-sure Jim had been so *cock-sure* about winning the race that he looked a complete fool when John beat him by yards.

cocoa I like *cocoa* better than tea or coffee because it tastes like chocolate.

coconut a big, brown hairy nut containing a milky liquid.

cocoon The larva of a silkworm spins a *cocoon* of silky thread round itself for protection.

cod a large sea fish.

code The message was in a secret *code* so that the enemy could not read it.

coffee I drink *coffee* at breakfast. ■ Coffee is made from *coffee* beans which have been roasted and ground into tiny pieces.

coffin The body of a dead person is put in a *coffin* before being buried.

cog A *cog* wheel has ■ little projections round its edge called *cogs*; these fit into another cog wheel, so one wheel turns the other.

cog wheels   **coil**

coil A *coil* of rope is a length arranged in rings, one on top of the other. ■ To *coil* rope is to arrange it in a coil.

coin A penny is a copper *coin*; a tenpence piece is a silver *coin*.

coinage In some countries metal *coinage* is being replaced by paper money.

coincidence I was at the Post Office posting a letter to Betty, when by a strange *coincidence* I met Betty posting a letter to me.

coke a smokeless fuel, made from coal.

colander We strain the vegetables through a *colander*.

cold If you keep sneezing and have a running nose, you probably have a *cold*. ■ It was so *cold* that there was ice on the pond.

coldness We were having such fun bathing that we didn't notice the *coldness* of the water.

collapse If the walls of the trench *collapse*, the men digging it will be buried.

collar Your *collar* is too tight round your neck. ■ You *collar* the thief and hold on to him until the police arrive.

collect (pron. col-léct) You are to *collect* a penny from each boy. ■ (pron. cól-lect) a short prayer.

collected We *collected* all our belongings and set off for home.

collection We passed round a hat for the *collection* and collected 4p. ■ Come and see my stamp *collection*.

college I hope that when I leave school, I shall be able to continue my education at *college*.

collide If two cars *collide*, the drivers are likely to be seriously hurt.

collie a large, long-haired Scottish sheep-dog.

colliery a coal mine.

collision As a result of the *collision* between the two cars, both drivers had to be taken to the hospital.

colon two little dots, like this (:). ■ The *colon* is the end piece of the intestine.

colonel (pron. kér-nel) The officer in charge of a regiment of soldiers is the *colonel*.

colonial A *colonial* is a person from one of the colonies. ■ The *Colonial* Office is the government department concerned with the colonies.

colonist A settler in a colony is called a *colonist*.

colony Australia became a British *colony* through British people settling there.

colossal St. Peter's church is a *colossal* building, bigger even than St. Paul's Cathedral.

colour Red is the *colour* of blood; the *colour* of the sky is blue. ■ Take your paints and *colour* this picture.

colt a young male horse; ■ also an inexperienced person.

column One *column* in the newspaper was headed, 'Big fire in School'. ■ A long, upright cylinder, usually of stone, is called a *column*.

comb You ought to *comb* your hair; it is very untidy. ■ I need a *comb* so that I can tidy my hair.

combat a contest, a struggle or a fight.

combination a combining of things together, e.g. my brother has a motorcycle and sidecar *combination*.

combine The two old schools are to *combine* to form one big new school. ■ A *combine* (harvester) both cuts the corn and extracts the grain from it.

combustion burning. The internal *combustion* engine is so called because petrol is burnt inside it.

come *Come* here! I have *come* home from school.

comedian Next on the programme was a *comedian,* who made us all laugh.

comedy a stage play intended to amuse and usually with a happy ending.

comet A *comet* looks like a star with a tail.

comet

comfort To *comfort* anyone is to cheer him up when he is sad. ■ If a house is cold and cheerless, there is said to be no *comfort* in it.

comfortable If I am not *comfortable* in bed, I cannot sleep. ■ These shoes are not *comfortable*: they're too small.

comic a funny magazine. ■ A *comic* song is one that is meant to be funny.

coming I shall be *coming* home to tea. ■ The *coming* week is an important one.

comma a punctuation mark, like this (,)—but I must not end my sentence with it.

command A royal *command* must be obeyed. ■ I *command* you to leave this house. ■ An officer is in *command* of soldiers.

commandment The Bible lists ten *commandments.* The sixth *commandment* is: 'Thou shalt not kill.'

commemorate to remember and do honour to a person or event in a special ceremony.

commence to begin.

commend To *commend* someone is to speak well of him.

comment The only *comment* Dad made after the accident was, 'Thank God you weren't killed.'

commentary The broadcast *commentary* on the football match described every movement in the game.

commentator someone who broadcasts a commentary.

commercial having to do with buying and selling goods, e.g. *Commercial* television or ■ a *commercial* in a TV. show.

commit We should punish people who *commit* crimes. ■ I could not find out from Jim whether he wants to come or not; he would not *commit* himself.

committee Jim is a member of the school Road Safety *Committee.* Jim's dad is on the factory strike *committee.*

common usual, or often met with. ■ A *common* is a publicly-owned piece of ground. ■ 3 is a *common* factor of 6, 9 and 12.

commonwealth The British Empire is now known as the British *Commonwealth* of Nations.

commotion a noisy disturbance —in a crowd, for example.

communicate When I wish to *communicate* with you, I will telephone, write a letter or perhaps come and talk to you.

communications There was no news from the island because *communications* had been cut by the severe storms.

community a group of people with similar interests, ■ who meet, e.g. at the *Community* Centre.

companion Your *companion* is the person (or animal) you are with. ■ A lady's *companion* is a woman who is paid to live with her.

company I don't like being alone; stay and keep me *company*. ■ Dad had a letter from the Insurance *Company* about the damage to the car.

comparatively Our school is *comparatively* small when compared with a skyscraper.

compare If you *compare* your bag with Jean's, you will see that hers is a little bigger and darker in colour.

comparison In *comparison* with that oil tanker, the car ferry is a tiny boat.

compartment The train had only one empty carriage and the eight of us filled one *compartment* of it.

compass A *compass* needle always points north, so travellers use one when they need to know in which direction they are going.

compass   compasses

compasses We use *compasses* for drawing circles.

compel To *compel* is to use force, e.g. I will not go unless you *compel* me.

compensation a gift of money, or something done to make up for an injury inflicted on someone.

compete Alan could not *compete* in the race because he had twisted his ankle.

competent A *competent* person is one who is properly qualified and able to do a job.

competition My sister won a prize in a beauty *competition* at the seaside last year.

competitor one who takes part in a competition.

complain A neighbour called to *complain* about the noise we were making. Joe had to work while we were at the party, but he didn't *complain* (grumble).

complaint Jane has a serious *complaint*, so we've called in the doctor. ■ We had a *complaint* from the neighbours about the noise we made.

complete We were one player short, so our opponents had to give us a man to *complete* our team.

completely The enemy army was *completely* destroyed; not even one soldier escaped.

complexion the colour and condition of a person's skin, especially the skin on the face.

complicated These instructions are too *complicated* for us to follow; make them simpler.

compliment The headmaster stopped to *compliment* Bob on his success in the examination.

component part of a machine or some other device.

compose I wish I could *compose* music like Beethoven's.

composer Handel was a famous *composer* of music. Benjamin Britten is a famous modern *composer*.

composition 'Messiah' is a (musical) *composition* by Handel. ■ For our English homework we have to write a *composition* entitled 'Holidays'.

compound This cough mixture is a *compound* of honey, glycerine and orange juice.

comprehensive A *comprehensive* school caters for children of all grades of ability.

compress (pron. com-préss) to squeeze together. ■ A *compress* (pron. cóm-press) is a pad put on bruises or severe cuts.

compulsory School attendance is *compulsory* for children (i.e. children are forced to attend school).

comrade The soldier stayed with his wounded *comrade*. ■ Some people, especially Russians, call a man *Comrade* instead of Mr.

conceal The spy tried to *conceal* the message inside his tie.

concede To *concede* victory to one's opponents is to admit that they have won.

conceit The worst thing about Alan is his *conceit*; he is so sure that he can do everything better than anyone else.

conceited Alan is so *conceited* that he is convinced that he can do everything better than anyone else.

concentrate If you *concentrate* on your work, you will not notice other things.

concern That's my *concern*, so I'll do as I like about it. ■ Do not *concern* yourself with my affairs; mind your own business.

concert At our school *concert* there was singing, dancing, and music by the orchestra.

concession something permitted, e.g. As a special *concession*, you may stay at the party till midnight.

conclude We will *conclude* our concert with the National Anthem. ■ I *conclude* from your remarks that you do not like our dog.

conclusion After considering the matter, Dad came to the *conclusion* that David was to blame. ■ At the *conclusion* of the concert, we sang the National Anthem.

conclusive The result of the election was not *conclusive*, for Ted received the same number of votes as Ann.

concrete a mixture of cement, sand, stones and water which sets hard.

concussion injury to the head caused by a heavy fall or a hard knock.

condemn If the jury find the prisoner guilty, the judge will *condemn* him to a year's imprisonment.

condense The story you have written is too long; can you *condense* it to half that length?

condescend To *condescend* is to behave as if granting a favour, e.g. Laura is so proud that she will not *condescend* to speak to us.

condition You may go on *condition* that you are home by ten o'clock. ■ Your cycle is in such a bad *condition* that you must not ride it.

conduct (pron. cón-duct) behaviour; ■ (pron. con-dúct) to lead.

conductor I asked the bus *conductor* for a fivepenny ticket. ■ The *conductor* of an orchestra stands in front of it. ■ Copper wire is used in electrical apparatus because copper is a good *conductor* of electricity.

cone   pine cone

cone A church steeple is *cone* shaped, i.e. it has a circular base and a pointed top. ■ A pine *cone* is the fruit of a pine tree.

confectioner a person whose business is making or selling sweets or cakes.

confectionery sweets and cakes.

conference An organization calls a *conference* so that its members may come together to discuss matters that interest them.

confess I *confess* that I like noisy parties. Some people go to a priest to *confess* their sins.

confession I have to make a *confession*; it was I who broke your window.

confetti At a wedding we throw bits of coloured paper, called *confetti*, at the bride and bridegroom.

confide You can safely *confide* in Jane; she can be relied upon to keep any secret.

confidence I have no *confidence* in this car; it has broken down twice already.

confident absolutely sure, e.g. I am *confident* that Dad will help us.

confidentially If you are told something *confidentially*, you are expected not to pass on the information to anyone else.

confirm Unless someone can *confirm* Jim's story that we have a holiday tomorrow, I shall go to school as usual.

confirmation I cannot believe Jim's story without some *confirmation* of it. ■ At a *Confirmation* Service, the bishop admits people to full membership of the Church.

confiscate A thing is *confiscated* if it is taken away as a punishment, e.g. I shall *confiscate* your ball if you play with it in school.

confuse I always *confuse* Australia with Austria. Which is which? ■ If you give people too many instructions at once, you *confuse* them.

confusion In the *confusion* following the fire alarm, boys put on each other's clothes.

congestion On Bank Holiday, the *congestion* on the road was such that vehicles hardly moved at all.

congratulate We would like to *congratulate* Pat on winning the Sports Trophy.

congratulations We offered our *congratulations* to Pat on winning the Sports Trophy.

congregate People began to *congregate* round the speaker in such crowds that the traffic was stopped.

congregation The *congregation* in church stood for the singing of a hymn.

congress The parliament of the United States is called *Congress*.

conjunction a word, such as 'and', which is used to join two words or two groups of words.

conjurer, conjuror The *conjurer* entertained the children by producing a rabbit out of a hat.

conker

conker a horse-chestnut. Boys play conkers with a *conker* dried and threaded on a string.

connect. We must have a wire to *connect* the battery to the bell. *Connect* the hose to the tap and turn on the water.

connection Some people say the moon shows when we may expect rain; others can see no *connection* between the moon and our weather.

conquer to win a victory over. William the Conqueror set out to *conquer* the English. Man is now trying to *conquer* the dangers of pollution.

conqueror William I, who conquered the English at the Battle of Hastings, became known as William the *Conqueror*.

conquest The Norman victory over the English at the Battle of Hastings is known as the Norman *Conquest* or just 'The *Conquest*'.

conscience A person has a guilty *conscience* when he feels unhappy as a result of doing something wrong.

conscientious A *conscientious* person is one who works as hard as he can, even when no one else is likely to know about it.

conscious Jack was put to sleep for the operation and was not *conscious* again for hours. ■ We were *conscious* of someone else in the room with us.

consent Before Jack can marry Jill he has to have her father's *consent*. ■ Will you *consent* to your daughter's marriage to me?

consequence Betty was sick as a *consequence* of eating too many cream buns.

consequently as a result.

conservative A *conservative* person is one who prefers to keep things as they are. ■ Many famous British politicians belonged to the *Conservative* Party.

consider Before you decide, *consider* carefully what may happen. ■ I do not *consider* that Jones would make a good prefect.

considerable The house was not cheap; we paid a *considerable* sum of money for it.

considerate A *considerate* man is one who takes account of the wishes and feelings of others.

consideration Before punishing the boy you should take into *consideration* his good work for the school orchestra.

consist The mess on the baby's plate seemed to *consist* of fruit, custard, jam, cake and fish paste.

consistency The *consistency* of the mixture must be just right, neither too stiff nor too watery.

consolation When you have just missed a bus, it is a great *consolation* to discover that it wasn't the bus you needed.

console Nothing we could do would *console* Janet; she just cried and cried.

consonant Every letter of the alphabet is a *consonant* except the five vowels a, e, i, o, u.

conspicuous Jones's house is very *conspicuous* because it is the only one in the neighbourhood that is painted yellow.

conspiracy Guy Fawkes was executed for his part in a *conspiracy* to blow up the British Houses of Parliament.

constable A police *constable* is sometimes called simply *constable*.

constellation

constantly I *constantly* chase that cat off our garden, but it always comes back again.

constellation The Pole Star is near a *constellation* which forms the shape of a plough.

consternation We were just pitching our tents, when to our *consternation* we saw an angry bull charging towards us.

construct to make.

consult I shall have to *consult* my father before I can say whether or not I may come on holiday with you.

consume It didn't take the hungry boys long to *consume* the loaf of bread. ■ Fire can *consume* whole forests.

consumer A producer is someone who makes something; a *consumer* is someone who buys it, e.g. My dad is a *consumer* of electricity.

contact Billy has measles and if you have been in *contact* with him you may have caught it. ■ You can *contact* me on the telephone.

contagious A *contagious* disease is one caught through contact with someone who has the disease.

contain The box was meant to *contain* pills. ■ Joe could *contain* his anger no longer and he hit out with his fists.

container Goods are loaded on to *container*-ships already packed in huge *containers* (boxes).

contemplate To *contemplate* anything is to study it with eye or mind; ■ so, to *contemplate* may be to look thoughtfully or to consider carefully.

contemporary Nelson was a *contemporary* of Haydn (i.e. they lived at the same time). ■ Often used nowadays to mean present-day, or modern, e.g. *contemporary* designs, furniture, etc.

contempt I show *contempt* for something because I despise it.

contemptuous showing contempt, e.g. She dismissed his advice with a *contemptuous* toss of her head.

content Harry was *content* to lie in the sun while the others bathed.

contents The *contents* of anything, e.g. a jug, are whatever is in it.

contest The English Civil War was a *contest* between King Charles and Parliament.

contestant One *contestant* in the English Civil War was King Charles and the other was Parliament.

continent The *continent* of Asia lies to the east of the *continent* of Europe.

continually We never have any peace because the baby is *continually* screaming.

continue I shall *continue* shouting until you let me out of this room.

continuous going on all the time.

contours outlines, especially the lines on a map which show the shape and height of high ground.

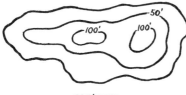

contours

contract (pron. cón-tract) a business agreement. ■ (pron. con-tráct) become smaller, e.g. Most things expand when they are heated and *contract* again on cooling.

contractor someone who agrees to do certain work, e.g. a building *contractor*, a haulage *contractor*.

contradict These newspapers *contradict* each other; one says the minister is to retire, and the other says he isn't.

contrary The book is not a dull story; on the *contrary*, it is an exciting adventure in space.

contrast There was a striking *contrast* between the two girls, one of them tall, fair and slender, the other short, plump and dark.

contribute We would like everyone to *contribute* 5p to the Famine Relief Fund.

contribution Everyone gave fivepence as a *contribution* to the Famine Relief Fund.

contrive Even if unexpected visitors arrive, Mother can always *contrive* something tasty for dinner.

control Fred lost *control* of his cycle on the hill and ran into a tree.

controversy argument, e.g. There was much *controversy* before the family would agree to my suggestion.

convalescence After recovering from his illness Dad needed a period of *convalescence* before returning to work.

convalescent A *convalescent* is a person recovering from an illness. ■ A *convalescent* home is a residence for people recovering their health.

convenience 'At your *convenience*' means 'At a time that suits you'. ■ A public *convenience* is a lavatory for the use of the public.

convenient It is not *convenient* for you to see Dad now because he is having a bath.

convent a place where nuns live and attend to their religious duties.

converge Lines which come to a point from different directions are said to *converge*.

conversation We had a long *conversation*, talking late into the night.

conversion the changing of one thing into another, e.g. pounds into pence, sinners into saints, coal gas fires to burn North Sea gas.

convert (pron. con-vért) to change, e.g. pence into pounds, heathen into Christians, etc. ■ (pron. cón-vert) a person who has been converted to a new religion (or political faith, etc.).

convey to carry.

convict (pron. cón-vict) The *convict* escaped from prison. ■ (pron. con-víct) To *convict* someone is to prove him guilty.

convince We had to look under the beds and in every room of the house to *convince* Martha that there were no burglars about.

convoy a group of ships travelling together for safety in wartime. ■ To *convoy* ships is to act as guard-ship to a convoy.

cook Mary is such a bad *cook* that ■ she cannot even *cook* an egg.

cookery In *cookery* lessons girls learn how to cook.

cool It was a *cool* day, neither hot nor cold. ■ Amid all the excitement Fred remained *cool* and calm. ■ Let that hot soup *cool* before you taste it.

coolly While the others rushed away in terror, the sergeant *coolly* picked up the bomb, walked to a water tank and dropped it in.

coolness After such a hot day we enjoyed the *coolness* of the evening breeze.

co-operate To *co-operate* is to work together.

co-operation A driver cannot win a motor race without the *co-operation* of his mechanics and other assistants.

cope Can you *cope* with all this work? ■ Many clergymen wear a *cope* when they walk round the church in procession.

Copenhagen the capital city of Denmark.

copper Two p, one p, and ½p pieces are called *coppers*; ■ they contain *copper*, a reddish metal. ■ Grandma boils the washing and the Christmas pudding in her *copper*.

copy It is dishonest to *copy* your neighbour's answers. ■ This is not the original picture, but just a *copy* of it.

copying You should make no mistakes when just *copying* from the blackboard.

coral a hard, usually pink, rock formed in tropical seas.

cord thin rope or thick string.

cordial a strongly - flavoured drink. ■ A *cordial* welcome is one that is sincere and friendly.

cordon There was a *cordon* of policemen round the building so that no one could escape from it.

corduroy a thick tough cloth with a ridged, velvety surface.

core In the middle of the apple is a tough, uneatable part called the *core*.

cork Pull the *cork* out of the bottle. ■ We have a *cork* bath mat.

corn *Corn* includes such grains as wheat, barley and oats. ■ In the U.S.A. *corn* is maize. ■ The tight shoe caused a painful *corn* on my toe.

corner place where walls, sides or edges meet, e.g. *corner* of a street, room or page. ■ If you *corner* a rat, he may fly at you.

cornet a brass instrument very like a trumpet. ■ An ice-cream *cornet* is a cone-shaped biscuit containing ice-cream.

cornet   **ice-cream cornet**

cornflour *Cornflour* is made by grinding maize.

cornflower a pretty blue flower which grows among corn.

coronation At the Queen's *coronation* in Westminster Abbey, a crown was placed on her head.

coroner If the reason for someone's death is not known, a *coroner* holds an inquest, which is an inquiry into the cause of death.

corporal *Corporal* punishment is caning, birching, etc. ■ An army *corporal* has charge of a small number of men; he wears two stripes on his sleeve.

corporation A town or city is governed by its mayor and *corporation*. The B.B.C. means the British Broadcasting *Corporation*.

corps (pron. kor) a body of soldiers. ■ The chorus in a ballet is known as the *corps* de ballet.

corpse (pron. korps) a dead body.

correct If a sum is *correct* it is marked with a tick (√). ■ If we get sums wrong we have to *correct* them.

correction After our books have been marked we have to write out our *corrections*.

correspond You *correspond* with someone when the two of you write letters to each other. ■ Your story does not *correspond* with the tale Pat told me.

correspondence I had lots of *correspondence* this morning, four letters and nine cards.

corridor a passage from which doors open into rooms, especially in a train or a large building.

corrode Rain and chemicals in the air had caused the metal to *corrode* so that it crumbled to pieces in my hand.

corrugated *Corrugated* iron, like *corrugated* cardboard, has a crinkled surface.

corset a tight-fitting undergarment, worn to support the body.

cosmetics used, chiefly by girls and women, to beautify themselves – powder, lipstick, skin-cream, etc.

cost What is the *cost* of a visit to the circus? ■ It will *cost* you 25p to go to the circus.

coster, costermonger a trader who sells his goods from a barrow in the street.

costermonger

costly I can afford quite an expensive bracelet, but not one as *costly* as this.

costume Joyce has a new bathing *costume*. ■ Mother has a new *costume* to wear at my sister's wedding.

cosy Put the *cosy* on the tea-pot to keep it warm. ■ It was so warm and *cosy* in bed that Simon didn't want to get out.

cot The baby sleeps in a *cot*.

cot

cottage My aunt lives in a pretty thatched *cottage* in the country. ■ A *cottage* loaf is like a little bread roll baked on top of a big one.

cotton A girl wearing a pretty *cotton* dress ■ bought a reel of *cotton* ■ and a packet of *cotton*-wool.

couch Mary was not well so she was lying on the *couch* in the living room.

cough Cover your mouth when you *cough*. ■ John had a bad *cough* which kept everyone in the house awake.

could I *could* run as fast as you if I wished.

couldn't could not. I *couldn't* lift the box so Dad picked it up for me.

council A borough *council* consists of people who have been elected to direct the affairs of the borough.

councillor A member of a council is called a *councillor*.

counsel to advise, e.g. I would *counsel* you to say nothing about the affair. ■ *Counsel* for the Defence made a speech defending the prisoner.

counsellor an adviser.

count My little sister can *count* up to ten. ■ The title of a foreign nobleman, e.g. the *Count* of Monte Cristo.

counter The shopkeeper put my groceries on the *counter*. ■ In *counter*-attack, *counter*-clockwise, etc., *counter* means 'against' or 'in return'.

counterpane the top covering of a bed.

countess the wife of a count or an earl.

counties The eastern *counties* of England include Norfolk, Suffolk and Essex.

countless There were *countless* numbers of locusts passing overhead like a great dark cloud.

countries England and France are two of the *countries* of Europe.

country England is a small *country*; Brazil is a very large *country*.

county Yorkshire is a large *county*. ■ A county is governed by its *county* council.

couple two of something.

coupling The train split into two because the *coupling* between the carriages broke.

coupon a ticket torn from a package, magazine, etc. which can be exchanged for goods or money.

courage The explorer showed

great *courage* in tackling the lion which was mauling his comrade.

courageous Tackling that angry lion was a *courageous* action.

course Of *course* I shall come to your party. ■ The race *course* is oval in shape. ■ I didn't like the last *course* of the meal.

court Sir Walter Raleigh was well known at the *court* of Queen Elizabeth I. ■ The prisoner was brought into *court* for his trial.

courteous A *courteous* person is one who is polite and considerate in the way he speaks or behaves.

courtesy We show *courtesy* to people by being polite and considerate to them.

courtier someone who is constantly in attendance at a royal court.

cousin *Cousin* Sally is Aunt Mabel's daughter. Any son or daughter of one of my parents' brothers or sisters will be my *cousin*.

cove a small bay. Lulworth *Cove* is near Weymouth.

covenant an agreement.

cover *Cover* the table with a cloth. ■ If we *cover* the entrance to the cave with bracken, no one will find it.

covered They *covered* the body with a sheet.

covet to want passionately something belonging to someone else. The 10th commandment begins: 'Thou shalt not *covet* . . .'.

covetous A *covetous* person is someone who is desperately anxious to have something belonging to someone else.

cow the female of the ox family; she provides milk for us. Female

elephants, whales, etc., are also called *cows*.

coward Eric is such a *coward* that at the first sign of danger he runs away.

cowardice the opposite of bravery.

cowardly To run away at the first sign of danger is a *cowardly* action.

cowslip The *cowslip* is a pretty yellow wild flower having lots of small flowers on one stalk.

coxswain (*cox* for short) the person responsible for steering a boat.

coy A girl who is *coy* is shy or modest.

crab a shell-fish with ten legs and two strong nippers. ■ A *crab-apple* is a small, very sour wild apple.

crab   cracker

crack The plate you dropped didn't break, but there's a *crack* in it. ■ *Crack* me a nut, please. ■ There was a loud *crack* as the ice broke.

cracker At the party I pulled a *cracker* with Father Christmas.

crackling There was a *crackling* sound as the dry sticks began to blaze. ■ The crisp brown skin on roasted pork is called *crackling*.

cradle Mother put the baby in its *cradle* and rocked it to sleep.

craft A strange *craft* sailed into the harbour and dropped anchor. ■ In *craft* lessons we make things with our hands.

craftsman someone who has special skill in a craft such as carving, cabinet-making, etc.

crafty sly and cunning.

crag a steep and rugged rock.

crag   crane

cram The greedy boy tried to *cram* a whole cake into his mouth. The bag seems full, but I could perhaps *cram* in one more article.

cramp a sudden and very painful tightening of a muscle; ■ a metal device for pressing things together.

crane used for lifting heavy loads; ■ a bird with long legs, neck and beak. ■ We had to *crane* our necks to see over the crowd.

crank a bent rod, like the starting handle of a car. ■ Dad had to *crank* the car to start it. ■ A *crank* is an odd person.

cranny Though we searched in every nook and *cranny*, we couldn't find the lost 5p piece.

crash We saw the aircraft *crash* and burst into flames. ■ Winnie dropped the tray of cups and saucers with a *crash*.

crate a big wooden packing case.

crater Smoke, flames and lava poured from the *crater* of the volcano.

crave To *crave* something is to long for it very much.

crawl Most babies learn to *crawl* before learning to walk. ■ My fastest swimming stroke is the *crawl*.

crayon a coloured pencil.

craze The latest *craze* among girls is to have pictures painted on their nails.

crazy My sister is *crazy* about pop singers. ■ I helped Dad to lay the *crazy* paving along the garden path.

creak We heard the door *creak* and knew that someone had come into the room.

cream We'll skim the *cream* off the milk and have it with our fruit. ■ Things are described as *cream* when they are the colour of cream, i.e. yellowish.

crease A *crease* is made if you fold a piece of paper and press along the fold. ■ Similarly, you *crease* clothes if you press folds into them.

create Do not *create* a disturbance in the classroom. ■ Experts *create* new dress styles for ladies every season.

creation The Bible story of The *Creation* describes how plants, animals and man were created.

creator The *Creator* is God, who made everything. ■ The *creator*

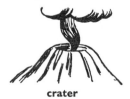

crater

of this new ladies' fashion is a Frenchman.

creature The explorers didn't know whether the strange *creature* was human or animal.

credit It isn't fair; Pat does the work and Jane gets the *credit* for it. ■ You wouldn't *credit* it, but Tim says he's seen a man from Mars.

credulous Only a *credulous* person would believe such an unlikely story about flying saucers.

creed a set of beliefs, e.g. The *Creed* is a statement of the beliefs of a Christian.

creek a narrow inlet on a sea coast.

creep No one will see us if we *creep* along with our bodies close to the ground.

creeper a plant such as ivy, that creeps along the ground or up a wall.

creeping After *creeping* as close as possible, the cat suddenly leapt on the mouse.

cremate To burn. When their captain dies, they will *cremate* his body and scatter the ashes over the sea.

crematorium a place where bodies are solemnly burnt.

creosote a dark oily liquid obtained from tar. ■ To *creosote* wood is to paint it with creosote to preserve it.

crept The boys *crept* along with their bodies close to the ground,

crescent moon

hoping to get near without being noticed.

crescent A new moon is *crescent*-shaped.

cress We use two kinds of *cress* in salads, water*cress* and garden *cress*.

crest The bird has a *crest* of red feathers on his head. ■ When I bathe in the sea, I love being carried along on the *crest* of a wave.

crestfallen Robin was so *crestfallen* when nobody arrived for his party that he began to cry.

crevice a narrow crack or gap, usually in a rock.

crew The *crew* are paid to do all the work on a ship.

crib The baby was put to bed in his *crib*. ■ You are supposed to work out the answers for yourself and not *crib* them from Joan.

cricket We won the *cricket* match by 10 runs. ■ A *cricket* is an insect like a grasshopper or a locust.

cried Ellen *cried* when she hurt herself. ■ The beggar *cried* out to the passers-by, 'Please take pity on the blind!'

crime a wrong deed such as stealing, which is punishable by law.

criminal The *criminal* responsible for all the bank robberies was at last arrested.

crimson Pink is light red, scarlet is bright red and *crimson* is dark red.

cringe to shrink back from someone, in fear.

crinkle To *crinkle* or wrinkle is to fold or bend into uneven ridges.

cripple For a month after the

accident Jim was a *cripple* and couldn't walk without crutches.

crippled The old lady was so *crippled* with rheumatism that she couldn't walk.

crisis the turning-point in an illness; ■ a moment of special danger in politics, etc.

crisp I like my cornflakes *crisp* and hard, not soft and squashy. ■ Let's have a packet of potato *crisps* with our lunch.

critic anyone who finds fault; ■ also a person whose job it is to say what is good and bad in a book, a play, or a concert, etc.

critical A *critical* person is one who finds fault. ■ An invalid's condition is described as *critical* when it is at danger point.

criticism Your *criticism* of my work shows how I can do better next time.

criticize You have a cheek to *criticize* Betty's painting, when you yourself cannot paint at all.

croak The *croak* of a frog is not a musical sound.

crochet to knit with a single hooked needle.

crockery We packed all the *crockery*, including plates, cups, saucers, basins and jugs.

crocodile The travellers mistook the *crocodile* for a floating log until he opened his enormous mouth.

crocus One of the first flowers to appear in the garden each spring is the *crocus*.

crocus   crook

crook a hooked stick, especially that used by a shepherd or a bishop. ■ *Crook* is also a slang word for a criminal.

crooked not straight.

croon to sing softly. A mother may be said to *croon* to her baby. Pop singers *croon* sentimental songs.

crop We had a good *crop* of apples from the tree in our garden this year.

cross A *cross* is shaped like this: +. ■ Be careful how you *cross* the road. ■ Jimmy made me so *cross* that I hit him.

crotchet the musical note that looks like a black oval on a stick.

crotchet   crow

crouch The travellers saw the lion *crouch* down in the grass ready to spring.

crow I woke up at cock-*crow*. ■ That big black bird is a *crow*. ■ Now that we have won the cup, we have something to *crow* about.

crowd There was a *crowd* of 20,000 people at the football match. ■ We can't all *crowd* into that little room.

crown At the coronation, the archbishop put a *crown* on the queen's head. ■ We saw the archbishop *crown* the queen.

crucifix a model of Jesus on the cross.

crucifixion killing by nailing to a cross, e.g. the *crucifixion* of Jesus.

crucify To *crucify* someone is to put him to death by fastening him to a cross.

crude A *crude* drawing or carving is one that is roughly made. ■ *Crude* oil is oil just as it comes from the ground, before it is refined.

cruel It is *cruel* to keep a dog on a short chain, to cut horses' tails or to put wild birds in cages.

cruelly As we pushed our way through the bushes, the thorns tore our legs *cruelly*.

cruelty the causing of needless pain, or having no pity. *Cruelty* to children or animals is a crime in Britain.

cruet a special holder for the little pots of salt, pepper and mustard, used at meal times.

crumble *Crumble* some bread for the birds. ■ The ancient beams will *crumble* to fragments as soon as you touch them.

crumbling The ancient woodwork was *crumbling* to pieces as the workmen tried to move it.

crumple Jennifer wouldn't sit down because she didn't want to *crumple* her new dress.

crunch You should hear our dog *crunch* up a bone !

crusade King Richard the Lion Heart went on a *crusade* to drive the Mohammedans out of the Holy Land.

crush Don't *crush* the primroses as you walk across the grass. ■ There was such a *crush* in the room that no one could move.

crust I love the crisp *crust* on new bread.

crutch The lame man had a *crutch* to support him when he walked.

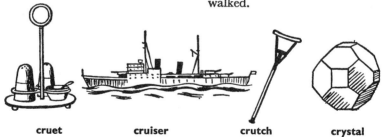

cruet   cruiser   crutch   crystal

cruise a tour by ship. ■ A car, ship or aircraft is said to *cruise* when travelling at a speed which it can easily keep up for a long time.

cruiser a fast warship.

crumb The birds pecked away at the bread till not a *crumb* was left.

cry All babies can *cry*, even if they can make no other noise. ■ We heard the sentry *cry*, 'Halt !'

crying Betty is *crying* because she has toothache.

crystal a piece of mineral, clear and shiny like ice and with surfaces which are evenly shaped and smooth.

cub   The baby of a fox or a bear is called a *cub*. ■ A Wolf-*Cub* is a junior Boy Scout.

cube   a block of something, having six equal square surfaces. Please get me an ice-*cube* out of the fridge.

the growing of crops. ■ You should *cultivate* the habit of listening to what you are told.

culture   'I am learning about the *culture* of tomatoes' means that I am learning how to grow tomatoes successfully.

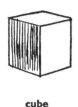

cube

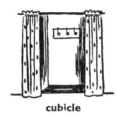

cubicle

cucumber

cubic   cube-shaped. ■ A container 2m × 3m × 4m has a volume of 24 *cubic* metres (m³).

cubicle   At the swimming baths we each have a separate *cubicle* in which to undress.

cuckoo   the bird that sings, 'Cuck-oo, cuck-oo'.

cucumber   a long, green, juicy vegetable, which is cut into thin slices and eaten as salad.

cuddle   If I pick up the baby in my arms and give him a *cuddle*, he stops crying. ■ My brother likes to sit and *cuddle* his girl-friend.

cue   In the school play, my *cue* for coming on to the stage was the remark, 'But here is cousin Bob.'

cuff   I put my hand so far into the water that I wet my shirt-*cuff*. ■ The angry man gave Willy a *cuff* on the head, which hurt.

culprit   Some one has broken my window. Who is the *culprit*?

cultivate   to prepare ground for

cumbersome   The armour was so *cumbersome* that David could not move about with it on.

cunning   The fox is so *cunning* that often he outwits the hounds trying to catch him.

cup   I would like a *cup* of tea, please.

cupboard   Put the books back into the *cupboard* and shut the doors.

curable   If you have a *curable* disease, you can be made well again.

curate   The *curate* assists the vicar or parish priest in his church duties.

curator   The *curator* is the person who is in charge of a museum, picture gallery, etc.

curb   If you don't learn to *curb* your temper, you may do something you'll regret.

curdle   Milk is said to *curdle* when it turns sour and lumpy.

cure   The doctor's job is to *cure* people who are ill. ■ To *cure* bacon, herrings, etc., the meat is treated with salt and smoked or dried.

curio an object that is curious and unusual.

curiosity Maureen's *curiosity* was aroused by the mysterious parcel so that she couldn't rest until she had opened it.

curious Maureen was so *curious* to know what was in the mysterious parcel that she couldn't rest till she had opened it.

curl I wish my hair would *curl* like Rosemary's. ■ When Mary's hair was cut off, we kept one *curl* as a souvenir.

curly Bill's hair is straight, but Ian's is *curly*.

currant There's only one *currant* ■ in this *currant* bun. ■ We have a black*currant* bush in our garden.

current The swimmer was carried along by the strong *current* in the river. ■ The electric *current* was cut off, so we had no lights.

curse To *curse* someone is to wish him harm. ■ To *curse* is to use bad language.

curt short and rather impolite, e.g. I sent him a *curt* note. She gave me a *curt* answer.

curtail 'I shall have to *curtail* my holiday' means that I shall have to cut my holiday short.

curtain Draw the *curtain* so that people cannot see us through the window. At the end of the play the stage *curtain* is lowered.

curtsey, curtsy The ladies had to learn how to *curtsey* to the queen.

curve a smooth bend.

cushion After riding his bicycle all day, Dick was glad of a *cushion* to sit on because it was soft.

custard We always have *custard* with our pudding or stewed fruit.

custody If a policeman takes a man into *custody* he arrests him. ■ When Uncle went abroad, Dad had the *custody* of his children.

custom something that is usually done, e.g. It is our *custom* to give a party for the school leavers each Christmas.

customer The *customer* paid the shopkeeper with a pound note.

cutlass Seamen used to fight with a short curved sword called a *cutlass*.

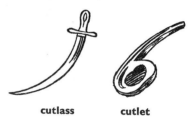

cutlass   cutlet

cutlery knives, forks, spoons, etc., used for preparing or eating food, e.g. We can't eat our dinner properly because we have no *cutlery*.

cutlet a chop from a neck of mutton.

cutting The railway ran through a *cutting* with high banks on each side. ■ Father is *cutting* the grass.

cycle Will you *cycle* to school today? ■ My *cycle* (or bicycle) is broken, so I shall have to walk.

cyclone a big mass of low pressure air, which brings stormy weather to the areas it passes over.

cygnet a young swan.

cygnet · cylinder

cylinder A *cylinder* is the shape of a roller. A tin of fruit is a *cylinder*.

cymbals musical instruments like brass plates, which are usually sounded by being clashed together.

cymbals cypress

cypress a dark evergreen tree, which is usually tall and grows to a point.

cyst (pron. sist) a small, hard, painless lump which forms under the skin.

Czech (pron. chek) a citizen of Czechoslovakia.

Czechoslovakia *Czechoslovakia* is a country in the middle of Europe, whose neighbours include Germany, Poland, Hungary and Austria.

dabble To *dabble* in something is to take only a slight part in it, e.g. Uncle Joe used to *dabble* in politics.

dachshund (pron. daks-hoont) a dog with a long body and short legs. *Dachshund* is German for badger-dog.

daffodil a yellow, trumpet-shaped spring flower, which grows from a bulb.

daffodil dagger

dagger The prisoner stabbed the guard with a *dagger*.

dahlia a garden flower, usually like a large and colourful double daisy.

daily every day, e.g. We milk the cows twice *daily*. ■ My father reads the *daily* paper at breakfast each morning.

daintily Mary picked her way *daintily* through the mud so as not to dirty her new shoes.

dainty To encourage the invalid to eat we offered her a *dainty* morsel of chicken.

dairy place where milk is stored, and cream and butter produced. ■ *Dairy* produce is milk, cream, butter and cheese. ■ A shop that sells dairy produce is called a *dairy*.

D

dais a low platform.

daisy small white flower with a yellow centre, common in fields. Children love to pick *daisies*  and link them together into *daisy* chains.

dale a valley.

dalmatian a large, spotted dog.

dam a wall or barrier which stops the flow of a stream. ■ To *dam* a stream is to hold back its waters by putting a dam across it.

damage The only *damage* to our car was a bent bumper. ■ How did you *damage* your car?

damages The judge ordered the motorist to pay £1,000 *damages* to the cyclist whom he had injured.

dame 'Dame' used to mean 'lady'; nowadays it is a title given to ladies whom the British wish to honour, e.g. *Dame* Ethel Smyth, the musician.

damn To *damn* anyone is to wish him ill.

damp Although the grass wasn't wet, it was too *damp* for Mother to sit on.

damsel a young girl.

damson a small plum which is very dark in colour.

dance Dad likes to *dance* a waltz, but we children would rather jive. ■ Dad's favourite *dance* is the waltz.

dancing I would love *dancing* to jazz music if only I knew the right steps. ■ John goes to *dancing* lessons to learn how to dance.

dandelion a field plant with jagged leaves and a yellow flower. ■ A *dandelion* clock is the ball of soft, feathery material round *dandelion* seeds.

Danes The people of Denmark are called *Danes*.

danger *Danger*: Road Repairs. The firemen were in *danger* from the flames and from the falling building.

dangerous You may get hurt if you get too near the tiger; he's a *dangerous* animal.

dangle It must be exciting to *dangle* on cords underneath a parachute, high in the sky.

Danish (pron. Dane-ish). The language spoken by the Danes is called *Danish*. ■ *Danish* butter, *Danish* bacon, etc., come from Denmark.

dare I *dare* not jump into the river because I cannot swim. ■ I *dare* you to ask the headmaster for a holiday.

daring bold, e.g. A *daring* workman walked along a narrow steel girder high above the street.

dark When it is *dark* we switch on the light. ■ *Dark* brown is almost black.

darken We can *darken* a room by covering the windows with blinds or shutters.

darkness The boys, unable to see in the *darkness*, walked right into the fishpond.

darling My brother calls his girlfriend 'My *darling*'.

darn If you have a hole in your sock, *darn* it neatly, so that ■ the *darn* doesn't show.

dandelion   **darn**

dart Making a sudden *dart*, the bird grabbed the worm. ■ Tom threw the *dart* ■ into the *dart*-board.

dart

dash We made a *dash* through the rain to the bus shelter. ■ We had to *dash* or we should have missed the bus. ■ A *dash* is a line like this: —.

dashing daring and gay, e.g. Joyce fell in love with a *dashing* young soldier.

date a fruit with a long-shaped stone. ■ Dates grow on *date*-palms. ■ If you want to know the *date*, look at a calendar.

daub To *daub* anything is to coat it thickly or badly. Why do you *daub* that wall with mud?

daughter A girl is the *daughter* of her parents; a boy is their son.

daunted discouraged, e.g. Our team were not *daunted* by the injury to their best player, and went on to win the match.

dawdle As we *dawdle* along to school, all the other children walk past us.

dawn We got out of bed at *dawn* to see the sun rise.

daybreak when the sun begins to rise.

daylight Colours do not look the same under artificial light as they do in *daylight*.

daytime Bats sleep in the *daytime* and come out to hunt for food at night.

dazed After falling on his head, Roy staggered about in a *dazed* condition, not quite knowing what he was doing or saying.

dazzle When the headlights of an approaching car *dazzle* a motorist, he cannot see where he is going.

dazzling I cannot see because the light is *dazzling* me. ■ The prince was enchanted by the *dazzling* beauty of the princess.

deacon a clergyman lower in rank than a priest. ■ In some churches, a *deacon* is not a clergyman, but a church official.

dead Julius Caesar is *dead*; he was murdered. Dad cut the *dead* branches out of the tree.

deaden The doctor gave the patient medicine to *deaden* the pain. Cars are fitted with silencers to *deaden* the noise of their exhausts.

deadlock There is said to be a *deadlock* in talks, etc., when no progress is being made towards agreement.

deadly able to cause death, e.g. *Deadly* nightshade is a poisonous plant.

deaf *Deaf* people cannot hear.

deafen To *deafen* someone is to make him unable to hear.

deafened We could not hear what was said because we were *deafened* by the noise of the aircraft.

deafness Grandad cannot hear what you say because he suffers from *deafness*.

deal Mother does not *deal* with that grocer. ■ You *deal* the cards. ■ *Deal* is a piece of fir or pine wood. ■ We had a good *deal* of trouble with the car.

dealer a shopkeeper or trader; ■ the player who deals the cards.

dean the clergyman next in rank below a bishop.

dear the opposite of cheap. ■ We begin letters: '*Dear* Mother', '*Dear* Jean', '*Dear* Sir', etc. ■ We all love Aunt Pat; she is a *dear*.

dearly John paid *dearly* for taking Joe's bicycle, for he fell off it and broke his leg. ■ We all love Aunt Pat *dearly*.

dearth shortage. The *dearth* of potatoes caused a famine in Ireland.

death On the *death* of King David, his son Solomon came to the throne.

deathly The injured man was so *deathly* pale that we knew that he hadn't long to live. The roar of the explosion was followed by a *deathly* silence.

debate an organized argument or discussion. ■ To *debate* is to argue.

debris (pron. dáy-bree) scattered pieces, e.g. The explosion in the factory flung *debris* all over the nearby houses.

debt (pron. det) I owe Dad a *debt* of £1, which I shall repay as soon as I have the money.

debtor (pron. det-or) Dad has two *debtors*; one *debtor* owes him £1, and the other owes more than he can pay.

decamp The gypsies who were living in the park had to *decamp* hurriedly when the police arrived.

decay to go bad or rot, e.g. Your teeth are more likely to *decay* if you don't clean them. Leaves which

fall to the ground *decay* and become part of the soil.

deceased The widow wept as she spoke of her *deceased* husband. ■ The *deceased* had died of old age.

deceit lying or dishonesty.

deceitful It was *deceitful* of the beggar to pretend to be blind when he wasn't.

deceive to mislead or cheat. Susan put a bolster down the bed to *deceive* us into thinking that she was still in it.

December the last month of the year.

decency modesty. ■ Jack had the *decency* to apologize for his rudeness.

decent respectable. ■ In slang, '*decent*' means 'kind' or 'satisfactory', e.g He's a *decent* chap. It's a *decent* book.

deception Carol was guilty of *deception* in telling her teacher that she had been ill, when she had spent the day at the zoo.

deceptive The wild cat's likeness to a household pet is very *deceptive*, for he is actually a very savage little creature.

decide You must *decide* which of the two things you wish to do, for you cannot do both.

decided definite, e.g. There is a *decided* flavour of salt in sea water. ■ Jack *decided* to play cricket rather than go to the dance.

decidedly definitely, e.g. When we went bathing during the winter, the water was *decidedly* cold.

deciduous A *deciduous* tree is one like the oak, chestnut and apple, whose leaves fall off each autumn.

decimal The *decimal* system is a method of reckoning based on tens. A *decimal* point is a dot which separates tenths from whole numbers, e.g. 4·6.

decipher To *decipher* a code, or a piece of bad handwriting, is to find its meaning.

decision After much thought, we have come to the *decision* not to have a party, but to go to the theatre instead.

decisive We won the match by one goal to nil, the *decisive* goal being scored by Jones.

deck The ship's passengers came up on *deck* to see the aircraft overhead. ■ At Christmas time we *deck* the house with holly and paper chains.

declaration something which is stated firmly, e.g. the *Declaration* of Independence of the American colonists.

declare To *declare* is to state or announce, e.g. I *declare* this ship well and truly launched. The cricket captain *declared* the innings closed.

decline to refuse, e.g. I *decline* to tell you. ■ a weakening, e.g. a *decline* in someone's health, or in the nation's prosperity.

decompose to decay or rot.

decorate At festival times we *decorate* our church with flowers.

decorations Our Christmas *decorations* usually consist of holly, balloons, paper chains and mistletoe.

decoy one who attracts others into a trap. ■ To *decoy* is to trap, usually in a net.

decrease If you *decrease* speed, you go slower. ■ If you now weigh less than you used to, there has been a *decrease* in your weight.

decree an official order, e.g. 'There went out a *decree* from Caesar Augustus that all the world should be taxed.'

decrepit A *decrepit* person is one who is feeble through age or illness.

dedicate To *dedicate* something is to devote it to a special purpose in a solemn ceremony, e.g. The bishop came to *dedicate* the new church.

deduce As the boys were at the coach station with their swimming things, I *deduced* that they were going to the seaside.

deduct I shall *deduct* the money you owe me from your pocket money, so you will receive less than usual.

deduction The *deduction* from your pocket money is to pay for the window you broke. ■ After considering the clues the detective made the *deduction* that the criminal was a lame Italian.

deed Boy scouts are expected to do a good *deed* each day.

deep If you cannot swim you had better not jump into *deep* water.

deer The *deer* in the park have large, branching antlers.

decorations   **deer**

deface To *deface* a building, monument, etc., is to spoil its appearance, e.g. by writing or drawing on it.

defeat to beat. ■ A *defeat* is the opposite of a victory.

defective My bicycle chain came apart because of a *defective* link in it.

defence A shield was a *defence* against arrows; it is no *defence* against bullets. If you have stolen something, it is no *defence* to say that you found it.

defenceless Without his sword and shield Sir Giles was *defenceless* and at the mercy of his enemies.

defend The soldiers were there to *defend* the city against attack.

defensive People on the *defensive* do not attack, but they resist any attacks made against them.

defiance open and deliberate disobedience.

defiant A person is being *defiant* when he is openly disobedient and rebellious.

deficient If there is not enough lime in soil, it is *deficient* in lime. A mentally *deficient* person cannot think or understand as well as other people.

define To *define* anything you explain it or make clear its exact meaning.

definite Dad's orders were quite *definite*; there can be no doubt about what he wants us to do.

definitely That is *definitely* the boy we want; I know him by the scar on his nose.

definition In this dictionary, the *definition* of 'defiance' is 'open and deliberate disobedience.'

deflect Horatius managed to *deflect* the blow so that the sword missed him.

deformed A person is said to be *deformed* if he is misshapen in any way, e.g. a hunchback.

deformity being deformed.

defraud The coalman used to *defraud* his customers by charging for ten bags of coal when he had delivered only nine.

defy To *defy* is to refuse to obey. ■ *Defy* used to mean 'to challenge to a fight', e.g. Goliath defied the armies of Israel.

degree The temperature rose one *degree* (1°) centigrade. ■ That angle is one *degree* (1°) too big. A right angle is ninety *degrees* (90°).

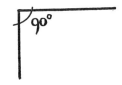

degree

deign To *deign* is to condescend. The boy shouted something at Diana, but she did not *deign* to answer.

dejected sad, depressed.

delay If we *delay* Jean, she will be late. ■ This *delay* has made me late.

delegate someone who represents a group of people at a conference, etc. ■ To *delegate* power or authority is to hand it over.

delegation a group of delegates, e.g. The British *delegation* has arrived for a meeting of the United Nations.

Delhi the capital city of India.

deliberate That was no accident, but a *deliberate* attempt to knock Jim off his bicycle.

deliberately on purpose, e.g. It was not an accident, for I saw the boy *deliberately* push Jim off his bicycle.

delicacy A *delicacy* is something especially tasty to eat, e.g. Strawberries and cream are a *delicacy*.

delicate A *delicate* child is one who easily or frequently becomes ill. ■ A *delicate* colour is one that is not too bright or strong.

delicious The ice cream was so *delicious* that we ate a lot of it.

delight We should have been pleased with a day's holiday, but, to our *delight*, we were given a week.

delightful charming, very pleasing, e.g. Aunt Beth is a *delightful* person. It was a *delightful* concert.

delinquent someone who has done wrong. Juvenile *delinquents* are boys or girls who have broken the law.

delirious A person is said to be *delirious* when illness causes him to become wildly excited or temporarily mad.

deliver The postman's job is to *deliver* letters.

deliverance rescue or saving, e.g. The sailors knelt and thanked God for their *deliverance* from the storm.

delivered The postman *delivered* the letters earlier than usual.

delivery Postmen are responsible for the *delivery* of letters to our houses.

delta *Delta* (Δ) is the Greek letter D. ■ A river mouth made up of many outlets is called a *delta* because it is shaped like Δ (delta).

delta

deluge very heavy rain. ■ By 'The *Deluge*' we mean Noah's flood.

delusion a false belief, especially a false belief caused by illness, e.g. The patient was under the *delusion* that the doctor was trying to poison her.

demand These apples are bad; I *demand* the return of the money I paid for them. ■ 'Where have you put your book?' *demanded* the teacher.

democracy a form of government in which people are governed by politicians whom they have freely elected.

democratic A *democratic* person or government is one that is in favour of democracy.

demolish The builders are going to *demolish* those old houses and build new ones in their place.

demon a devil or an evil spirit.

demon

demonstrate As Mother didn't know how to work the new washing machine, a man called to *demonstrate* it to her.

demonstration Mother didn't know how to use the new washing machine, so a man came to give her a *demonstration*.

demoralize To *demoralize* people is to destroy their courage. The killing of Goliath so *demoralized* the Philistine army that it turned and fled.

demure A *demure* girl is one who is quiet and shy.

den the place where a wild animal makes a habit of lying; ■ a place where thieves, etc., gather; ■ a small room.

denial In spite of the man's *denial*, we were sure that he had committed the crime.

Denmark a European country just north of Germany.

denote To *denote* the actual words said by someone, we use inverted commas, like this: " ".

dense The fog was so *dense* that we could see only a yard ahead.

dent The boy threw a stone which made a *dent* in the side of our car.

dental We go to the *dental* clinic when our teeth need attention.

dentist Our *dentist* does not hurt when he pulls out teeth.

deny It is useless for you to *deny* that you broke the window, for we saw you do it.

depart Our train is due to *depart* from London at 10 o'clock, and arrive in Dover about noon.

department If you require a table, you will have to go to the shop's furniture *department*.

departure We watched the *departure* of the train from the station.

depend You may *depend* on Jim; if he says he will do a thing, he does it.

dependable Jim is a *dependable* lad; if he says he will do a thing, he does it.

dependant a person kept by someone else, e.g. My dad has three *dependants*: my mother, my sister and me.

depict In her painting, Pat has tried to *depict* a sailing ship in a rough sea.

deport To *deport* someone is to send him out of the country. Many countries *deport* foreigners who break their laws.

deportment Jennifer's upright posture and dignified manner won for her the school *deportment* prize.

depose You *depose* a king, or any other official, by taking his job away from him.

deposit You may *deposit* your bags in the cloakroom. It is better to *deposit* your money in a bank than to keep it at home.

depot (pron. dép-oh) a storehouse.

depress to press down, e.g. When you *depress* a key of an organ, a note is sounded.

depressed Since her baby died, Auntie has been so *depressed* that she cries at the least thing.

depression a hollow (e.g. in the ground); ■ an area of low pressure, which causes rain.

deprive In order to punish the boys we will *deprive* them of their amusements for a week.

depth The *depth* of water at the deep end of the swimming bath is twice the *depth* at the shallow end.

deputation It was not possible for the whole school to go and see the headmaster, so we sent a *deputation* of four boys to tell him what we wanted.

deputize When the headmaster is away the senior master has to *deputize* for him.

deputy If the headmaster is absent, his duties are taken over by his *deputy*.

derelict A *derelict* car, ship, etc., is one (usually a wreck) that has been left somewhere because its owner no longer wants it.

derrick a crane for lifting things; ■ the framework constructed over an oil-well.

descant While we are singing a hymn, the choirboys sometimes sing a higher tune, called a *descant*.

descend Billy does not *descend* by the stairs; he slides down the handrail.

descendant Everyone is a *descendant* of his parents, grand-parents, great-grandparents, etc.

descent We watched the *descent* of the parachute all the way from the aircraft to the ground.

describe I would *describe* the man as young, tall and thin, very dark and remarkably good-looking.

description To give a *description* of a person is to say what he looks like

desert To *desert* (pron. de-zért) someone is to go away and leave him. ■ A *desert* (pron. déz-ert) is waste land, where nothing grows.

deserted The lamb had been *deserted* by its mother so we took it home and fed it from a bottle.

deserter a soldier who runs away from his companions.

desertion A man who goes away and leaves his wife is guilty of *desertion*.

deserts The bully got his *deserts* when the smaller boy punched him on the nose.

deserve In view of your bad behaviour, you do not *deserve* a birthday party.

design a plan, a scheme or a drawing.

designed The badge on our school blazer was *designed* by the art master.

desirable A *desirable* house, friend, etc., is one worth wishing for.

desire To *desire* something is to wish for it very much.

desirous 'She was *desirous* of meeting the duke' means that she wanted very much to meet the duke.

desist If you don't *desist* from teasing that cat, it will probably scratch you.

desk I keep my dictionary in my school *desk*.

oil derrick

desolate The South Pole is a *desolate* place, dreary and un-inhabited.

despair hopelessness. ■ To *despair* is to lose all hope.

despatch I will *despatch* the parcel to you by post (also spelt *dispatch*).

desperado a ruffian who will stop at nothing to get what he wants.

desperate without hope, e.g. As the tide rose in the cave the boys became *desperate*. A *desperate* man will stop at nothing to get what he wants.

desperately The boys worked *desperately*, bailing water from the rapidly sinking boat.

desperation In *desperation* the boys frantically bailed water from the sinking boat.

despicable To steal money from a blind beggar is a *despicable* act which would disgust any decent person.

despise to look down upon, e.g. You should never *despise* a person merely because he is poor or un-educated.

despite *Despite* his injured foot, David walked all the way home.

despondent After getting the sum wrong for the fifth time, Wendy became *despondent* and burst into tears.

dessert After dinner we had raw apples and oranges for *dessert*.

destination Your *destination* is the place you are going to.

destiny A man's *destiny* is what fate has in store for him, e.g. Hitler believed it was his *destiny* to rule all Europe.

destroy An atom bomb would *destroy* a city. ■ We would rather have a vet *destroy* our dog than let it live in pain.

destroyer a fast warship.

destruction The *destruction* of the city was so complete that not one house was left standing.

destructive Pamela was a *destructive* child; she broke or pulled to pieces almost everything she was given.

detach unfasten and remove. ■ A *detached* house is one not joined to another one.

detachable something that can be unfastened and removed, e.g. This mac. has a *detachable* hood.

detailed A *detailed* account is one that does not leave anything out.

details full particulars, e.g. I don't want to know the *details*; just tell me who won the game.

detain keep (waiting), e.g. As you are in a hurry I will not *detain* you for more than a few minutes.

detect It was not difficult to *detect* the guilty boy, for his pockets bulged with the stolen apples.

detection A fat boy cannot avoid *detection* by hiding behind a thin tree.

detective After studying the clues, the *detective* was able to say who had committed the crime.

detention Children who arrive late have to stay in school at 4 o'clock for an hour's *detention*.

deter (pron. de-tér) hinder, discourage, e.g. The barbed wire on top of the wall was to *deter* boys from climbing over it.

detergent a cleaning substance, such as soap.

deteriorate to become worse.

determination firmness. The boys showed such *determination* that there was no point in trying to make them change their minds.

determine to find out, e.g. Experts conducted an inquiry in order to *determine* the cause of the explosion.

determined I am *determined* to get home tonight, so if there are no trains or buses, I shall walk.

deterrent a means of discouraging people from doing something, e.g. The teacher's cane was a *deterrent* to naughty boys.

detest To *detest* something is to dislike it very much indeed.

detestable Dudley is a *detestable* boy; no one can bear him.

detour The journey was longer than usual because we had to make a *detour* to avoid road repairs.

detrimental harmful, e.g. Lime in the soil is *detrimental* to some plants.

devastate To *devastate* a country is to destroy all the buildings, crops, etc.

develop to grow or make progress. ■ To *develop* the film from a camera is to treat it so that the pictures can be seen.

development A person who asks 'What's the latest *development*?' wants to know what stage some event has now reached.

device an emblem on a shield; ■ a plan; ■ a scheme; ■ a tool, e.g. My pocket-knife has a *device* for removing stones from horses' hooves.

devil Satan, who tempts people to do wrong things; or any evil person or evil spirit.

devise to plan, e.g. We will *devise* a way of escaping from this prison.

devote to give, e.g. You *devote* too much of your time to games and neglect your work.

devoted very loving or loyal, e.g. Mrs. Jones had a *devoted* husband; he would do anything for her.

devotion The dog had such *devotion* to its master that it would not leave him, even when he was dead.

devour to eat greedily, e.g. Let's watch the lion *devour* that joint of meat. ■ We watched the flames *devour* the entire building.

devout very religious, e.g. My father is a *devout* man.

dew Often, early on a fine summer morning, the grass is wet with *dew*.

dexterity skill, cleverness with the hands, e.g. We all admired the *dexterity* of the conjurer in controlling six hoops at once.

diagonal the line joining opposite corners of a square, a rectangle, etc.

diagonal

diagonally A line was drawn *diagonally* across the room, from corner to corner.

diagram 86 **dignity**

diagram a drawing made to illustrate or explain something.

dial the face of an instrument such as a clock or a speedometer. ■ In order to talk to anyone on the phone, you have to *dial* his number.

dial

dice

dialect The Yorkshire *dialect* is the special way the people of Yorkshire speak. Similarly, the people of London, Somerset, etc. have their own distinctive *dialect*.

dialogue talk, conversation, e.g. Everyone was listening to the *dialogue* between Punch and Judy.

diameter The *diameter* of a circle is the distance from one side to the other, through the middle.

diamond The *diamond* sparkling in Mother's ring came from a mine in South Africa.

diary a record of the events of each day; ■ a book in which the events of each day are recorded.

dice A *dice* is a cube with its six surfaces numbered 1 to 6. We use *dice* in playing such games as Snakes and Ladders, Ludo, etc.

dictate To *dictate* is to say or read something aloud for someone else to write down. ■ To *dictate* to someone can also mean to give him orders.

dictation In *dictation* lessons we have to write down whatever the teacher reads out to us.

dictator a ruler who has power over all his countrymen, as Hitler had in Germany.

dictionary This *dictionary* tells you the meanings of 10,000 words.

die to stop living, e.g. The plant will *die* if you don't water it.

diesel The *diesel* engines used in buses, lorries and trains, burn oil, not petrol.

diet When I was ill, I was put on a *diet* of milk and fish, because all other foods made me sick.

differ The twins *differ* only in that one has a spot on his cheek and the other hasn't.

difference The *difference* between the twins is that one has a brown spot on his face and the other hasn't.

different not the same, e.g. My pen is *different* from yours.

difficult hard to do, e.g. That sum is too *difficult* for me.

difficulty My *difficulty* in arithmetic is that I cannot add up correctly.

digest Do not give the baby meat to eat, because he cannot *digest* it.

digestible food, such as milk, which the body can easily make use of, is said to be *digestible*.

digestion If you have a good *digestion* you can eat any food without ill effects, but if you have a weak *digestion* you may have pains after eating.

digit any one of the figures from 0 to 9; ■ a finger or toe.

dignified noble, stately, e.g. The duchess was a *dignified* old lady.

dignity It is beneath the *dignity*

of a senior boy to play infants' games.

dike (also spelt *dyke*) a bank built to keep back flood water; ■ a narrow water channel, or ditch.

dilapidated Buildings, furniture, clothing, etc., are said to be *dilapidated* when they are falling to pieces.

dilemma a difficulty in choosing between two things.

diligent hard-working, e.g. a *diligent* boy.

dilute made weak by the addition of water, e.g. *dilute* acid. ■ You *dilute* orange squash by putting a spoonful of it in a glass of water.

dimension A line has one *dimension*: length; a page has two *dimensions*: length and breadth; a box has three *dimensions*: length, breadth and height.

diminish To *diminish* is to become less, e.g. The amount of water in the pond will *diminish* as the dry season continues.

dimly In the half-light of dawn the boys could *dimly* see the outline of an animal.

dimple a little hollow in a person's chin or cheek.

dine to have dinner, e.g. We have our school dinner at midday, but when we are on holiday we *dine* in the evening.

dinghy (pron. ding-gy) a small boat, often carried on a bigger boat, or towed behind it.

dingy (pron. din-jee) unattractive and dirty-looking, e.g. Mother said the curtains looked *dingy*, so she bought new ones.

dining We always go into the *dining* room to have our dinner.

dinky (slang) attractive, neat and pretty.

dinner We eat our *dinner* at midday.

dint By *dint* of (by means of) courage and hard work the buried miners were rescued.

diphtheria a dangerous disease of the throat.

diploma Dad was so pleased with the *diploma* that I received for passing my exam that he had it framed.

diplomat a person who represents his country in a foreign country.

diplomatic taking care (like a diplomat) not to give offence, e.g. Ask your guests to go home now, but be *diplomatic* about it.

dire terrible and disastrous.

direct Can you please *direct* me to the post office? ■ Come by the *direct* route, not by a round-about way.

direction In which *direction* is north? ■ The *directions* which tell you how to assemble the model, are printed on the box.

directly 'I'll come *directly*' means 'I'll come at once.' ■ 'I'll come *directly* you call' means 'I'll come as soon as you call.'

director a manager, or the man responsible for the running of some organization or business.

dinghy

directory You can find our telephone number in the London telephone *directory*.

dirk A Scottish Highlander often carries a little dagger, called a *dirk*, in the top of his stocking.

dirk   disc

dirt Wash that *dirt* off your hands before you have your dinner.

dirty If your hands are *dirty*, you must wash them before you have a meal.

disable To *disable* a person or thing is to make him or it unable to work properly, e.g. One bomb can *disable* a ship.

disadvantage A *disadvantage* of being tall is that you frequently bump your head as you go through doorways.

disagree To *disagree* is to hold a different opinion or to quarrel.

disagreeable unpleasant, e.g. This medicine has a *disagreeable* taste, so I hate taking it. Wendy is a *disagreeable* girl; she quarrels with everyone.

disappear We saw the aircraft *disappear* behind a thick cloud.

disappoint I am sorry to *disappoint* you, but you will not receive a prize after all; your name was printed in the prize list by mistake.

disappointed Betty's name was on the prize list, so she was very *disappointed* when she didn't receive a prize after all.

disappointment It was a great *disappointment* to my parents when I failed the examination.

disapproval The crowd expressed their *disapproval* of the referee by booing.

disapprove Dad is sure to *disapprove* of Mum's new hat; he dislikes anything new.

disarm If you want to *disarm* a gunman, try to knock the gun out of his hand with a stick.

disarmament It was hoped that at the *disarmament* conference, nations would agree to get rid of all their weapons of war.

disaster The loss of 100 lives in the aircraft crash was a great *disaster*

disband We had to *disband* our Boys' Club because our clubroom was pulled down and we had no place in which to meet.

disbelieve not to believe.

disc A *disc* is anything circular and thin, such as a gramophone record or a coin.

discharge To *discharge* a gun, fire it. ■ To *discharge* a ship, unload

---

As the letters 'dis' before a word may merely give it the opposite meaning, many such words are not included here.

it. ■ To *discharge* a prisoner, free him. ■ The *discharge* from a sore is the matter that comes out of it.

disciple A *disciple* of Jesus was one of his followers.

discipline The *discipline* in our school is so good that the children carry out their orders even if there is no teacher present.

discoloured Sliced apples become *discoloured* and turn brown. The old newspaper was *discoloured* with age.

discomfort Jane suffered great *discomfort* because her shoes were too tight.

disconcert To *disconcert* someone is to upset him, e.g. Jim was *disconcerted* by the sudden bang.

disconnect An electric bell will not ring if you *disconnect* its wires.

disconsolate very unhappy.

discontented Freddy was *discontented* with his scooter because he wanted a bicycle.

discontinue to stop.

discord Stop quarrelling; we will not have *discord* in this house. ■ That horrible *discord* was caused by some members of the orchestra playing wrong notes.

discount money taken off a bill.

discourage You *discourage* Stella from playing the violin if you put your fingers in your ears.

discourteous rude, impolite.

discover When did Columbus *discover* America?

discovery Columbus is famous for his *discovery* of America.

discreet A *discreet* person does not say things that would cause annoyance or distress to anyone.

discretion judgement, e.g. Use your own *discretion* about the colour of your new frock.

discus a special, heavy disc which athletes throw.

discuss *Discuss* the matter with your friends; then you can tell me what would best suit you all.

discussion When we met to discuss the holidays, the *discussion* went on for hours.

disdain To *disdain* to do something is to think it beneath one's dignity to do it.

disease an illness.

disentangle The kitten got Mother's knitting wool into such a tangle that it took hours to *disentangle* it.

disfigure To *disfigure* anything is to spoil its appearance.

disgrace Brian made a rude remark and was sent out of the room in *disgrace*. ■ We will not take that rude boy to the party: he would *disgrace* us.

disgraceful Brian's behaviour was so *disgraceful* that he had to be sent out of the room.

disguise The detective wore a *disguise* so that no one would know him. ■ Sometimes a detective has to *disguise* himself so that no one will know him.

disgust Jane showed her *disgust* at Jim's dreadful behaviour by walking out of room.

disgusting Jim's behaviour was rude and vulgar, but Alan's was worse; it was *disgusting*.

dish Put the fruit in the *dish*. ■ My favourite *dish* is cauliflower cheese. ■ We're all ready, so you can *dish* up the pudding.

dishearten Don't tell the children that they still have many miles to walk; it would *dishearten* them.

dishevelled If you are *dishevelled*, your hair and clothes are in disorder, as if you had been pulled through a bush.

dishonest (pron. dis-ón-est) not honest.

disinclined 'Jack was *disinclined* to come' means that Jack did not feel like coming.

disinfect To *disinfect* anything is to kill the dangerous germs in it.

disinfectant The doctor washed his hands in *disinfectant* in order to kill any germs there might be on them.

disk A *disk* is anything circular and thin, such as a gramophone record or a coin (usually spelt *disc*, nowadays).

dislike To *dislike* something is not to like it, or to object to it.

dislocate You *dislocate* a limb when you cause a joint to go out of place, e.g. Bob fell on his wrist and *dislocated* it.

dislodge We tried to *dislodge* the bone that had stuck in Dad's throat, by slapping him on the back.

disloyal unfaithful to friend, school, country, etc., e.g. A person is *disloyal* to his country when he helps its enemies.

dismal miserable, dreary.

dismantle To *dismantle* a piece of machinery, etc., is to take it to pieces.

dismay Arriving late for school, we found to our *dismay* that the headmaster was waiting for us at the gate.

dismiss To *dismiss* is to send away, e.g. The headmaster will *dismiss* the school early today.

dismissal sending away, e.g. On the last day of the school term, *dismissal* is earlier than usual.

dismount To *dismount* is to get off a horse, bicycle, etc., e.g. You must *dismount* from your bicycle and walk.

disobedience doing what you have been told not to do, or refusing to do as you have been told.

disobedient Adam was *disobedient* and ate the fruit that he had been told not to eat.

disobey If you *disobey* the headmaster's instructions, you will be punished.

disorder There was complete *disorder* in the classroom, with boys in heaps on the floor, desks turned over, and books scattered everywhere.

disorganize to upset plans or arrangements; to cause confusion.

disown If my puppy behaves badly, I *disown* him, pretending that he belongs to someone else.

dispatch *Dispatch* that letter by

As the letters 'dis' before a word may merely give it the opposite meaning, many such words are not included here.

the next post. ■ To *dispatch* an animal is to kill it (also spelt *despatch*).

dispensary the part of a hospital or a shop where medicines are mixed.

disperse send or go in different directions, e.g. The police had to *disperse* the crowd. The children *disperse* for the holidays.

displace To *displace* a person or thing is to remove it from its place.

display an exhibition, e.g. We enjoyed the fireworks *display*. ■ To *display* is to exhibit.

displease to annoy.

disposal The car is at your *disposal* (you may use the car as you wish). ■ See to the *disposal* of that rubbish (get rid of the rubbish).

dispose I don't care where you put the rubbish, but please *dispose* of it (get rid of it) before the visitors arrive.

disposition No one likes Anne; she has such a sulky *disposition*.

disprove To *disprove* a statement is to prove that it is untrue.

dispute a quarrel; ■ to quarrel.

disqualified Pat came first in the race, but she was not the winner because she was *disqualified* for running in the wrong lane.

disregard to take no notice of, e.g. If you *disregard* the policeman's instructions he may arrest you.

disrepair The car was in such a condition of *disrepair* that bits of it dropped off as we rattled along the road.

disreputable Elias was a *disreputable* old man, shabby in appearance and quite untrustworthy.

disrespect rudeness, the opposite of respect, e.g. It is wrong for a child to show *disrespect* to an adult.

disrespectful It is *disrespectful* to talk of your headmaster as 'the old man'.

dissatisfaction the opposite of satisfaction, e.g. Mother showed her *dissatisfaction* with the stockings by taking them back to the shop and demanding the return of her money.

dissolve Sugar will *dissolve* in tea more quickly if you stir it. ■ Pat will *dissolve* into tears at the least thing, the cry-baby.

dissuade (pron. dis-swade) *Dissuade* Jim from buying the bicycle (advise him against buying it, or persuade him not to buy it).

distance The *distance* from London to Paris is about 320 km. ■ The castle appeared like a speck in the *distance*.

distant The lighthouse is 8 km *distant* from here. ■ Man is not very like the apes, but there is a *distant* connection between them.

distasteful The medicine was so *distasteful* that Sally spat it out.

distilled *Distilled* water is very pure water.

distinct clear, definite, e.g. The writing was not *distinct*, so we could not read it at all well. ■ There was a *distinct* smell of gas in the school; no one had any doubt about it.

distinction difference, or honour, e.g. There is a *distinction* between asking and begging. ■ I had the *distinction* of shaking hands with the Prime Minister.

distinctive You can tell a robin from a sparrow by its *distinctive* red breast.

distinguish You can *distinguish* between a robin and a sparrow by the fact that a robin has a red breast.

distort Some newspapers *distort* news to make it seem more exciting. ■ You *distort* an object when you put it out of shape.

distract The plan was that one thief should *distract* the shop-keeper's attention, while the other stole money from the till.

distraction anything that takes your mind off something.

distress A ship in *distress* is in danger of sinking. ■ To *distress* a person is to cause him anxiety or sorrow.

distribute to share out money, food, etc.

district In the *district* where I live there are no factories, though there are some in other parts of the town.

distrust I *distrust* that boy; whenever he is out of my sight, I wonder what he is doing wrong.

disturb Don't *disturb* the head-master; he is busy.

disturbance disorder, usually noisy, e.g. There was such a *disturbance* in the room that every-one knew the teacher had gone out.

ditch (or dyke) a narrow water channel. ■ 'To *ditch* an aircraft' is airmen's slang, meaning 'to bring an aircraft down into the sea'.

ditto *Ditto* is used instead of repeating words; it means 'the same'. In place of the word *ditto*, we sometimes use a pair of commas, like this: „ .

divan a long, soft seat without a back, which can be used as a bed.

divan   **diver**

dive to plunge downwards, usually into water and head first.

diver A *diver* went down to the sea bed to examine the sunken ship.

diverge Lines, roads, etc., are said to *diverge* if they go in different directions from one starting point.

diversion Because of road re-pairs, there was a traffic *diversion*, which meant that we had to go down lots of side-streets before getting back on to the road.

divert When a road is being repaired, it is necessary to *divert* traffic down side-streets out of the way.

As the letters 'dis' before a word may merely give it the opposite meaning, many such words are not included here.

divide When you *divide* eight by four, the answer is two.

dividend the number to be divided, e.g. in the sum: $8 \div 4 = 2$, 8 is the *dividend*.

dividers *Dividers* look like compasses with two metal points but no pencil; they are used for measuring.

divine sacred, or having to do with God.

divinity *Divinity* is being divine. ■ A *divinity* is a god. ■ In *divinity* lessons, we study the Bible and learn about God.

division A *division* sum is one in which we divide one number by another.

divisor the number you divide by, e.g. in the sum: $8 \div 4 = 2$, the *divisor* is 4.

divorce to separate; ■ a lawful way of ending a marriage.

divulge (pron. die-vulge) tell. You are not to *divulge* the secret to anyone.

dizziness After spinning round and round lots of times, Jean couldn't stand because of *dizziness*.

dizzy After spinning round and round lots of times, Jean was so *dizzy* that she couldn't stand.

docile gentle and obedient, e.g. The huge elephant was so *docile* that it did whatever the little boy told it.

dock a broad-leafed weed. ■ When the ship was in *dock*, ■ the *dock* gates were shut to keep the water in. ■ In court, the prisoner stands in the *dock*. ■ To *dock* a ship is to tie it up in a dock.

docked The ship *docked* (i.e. tied up in dock) this morning.

docker a workman whose job is loading and unloading ships.

dockyard a place specially fitted for the repairing of ships.

doctor someone especially trained to cure sick or injured people.

document writing, printing, etc. which is evidence of some fact, e.g. your Birth Certificate is a *document* which shows where and when you were born. ◀

dodge a plan or trick (slang). ■ To *dodge* is to move quickly to one side, or to avoid.

doe female rabbit, deer, etc.

does *Does* Bob play cricket? Bob plays cricket and Barry *does* too.

doesn't (short for) does not.

dogged obstinate and determined.

dogmatic A *dogmatic* person is one who states things in an over-confident way.

doings things done, e.g. Give an account of your *doings* since you got up this morning.

doldrums a belt of ocean around the equator, which is almost without winds.

dollar Americans reckon their money by the *dollar* ($).

dolly The little girl played at putting her *dolly* to bed. ■ When Grandmother did the washing, she stirred the clothes about in a *dolly* tub with a *dolly* stick.

dolphin (pron. dol-fin) a small, frisky kind of whale.

dome a rounded top, e.g. the *dome* on St. Paul's Cathedral.

Domesday Book a record of the land of England, made for William the Conqueror.

domestic having to do with the home, e.g. In *domestic* science lessons, girls learn how to run a home.

dominion The *Dominion* of Canada is a self-governing member of the British Commonwealth.

domino a piece of wood, marked with spots for use in the game of *dominoes.*

domino   dormouse

donation Here is a *donation* of fifty p to the Famine Relief Fund.

donkey an animal like a small, long-eared horse; an ass. We ride on *donkeys* at the seaside.

donor giver, but especially the *donor* of a prize, or a blood *donor*, who gives some of his blood for use in hospitals.

don't (short for) do not, e.g. I *don't* know.

doom A person's *doom* is what is in store for him in the end.

doomed condemned, e.g. The wretched man was *doomed* to spend the rest of his life in prison.

door Open the *door* and let me into the room.

dope a drink, etc., that makes people unconscious; ■ a varnish, used on aircraft.

dormant behaving as if asleep, like hibernating animals and buds in winter.

dormice more than one dormouse.

dormitory In the school *dormitory* where we sleep, there are many beds.

dormouse a pretty little field mouse, often found asleep.

dose the amount of medicine to be taken at one time, usually a teaspoonful, or a tablespoonful.

dote To *dote* on someone is to be so fond of him that you behave foolishly about him. Some people *dote* on animals.

double If you *double* three, you get six. ■ The punch in the stomach made Joe *double* up with pain. ■ A *double* bassoon plays an octave lower than a bassoon.

doubt 'I *doubt*' means 'I am not quite sure.'

doubtful not certain, e.g. We were *doubtful* whether our car could climb the hill.

doubtless certainly, e.g. The old car would *doubtless* go faster downhill.

dough (rhymes with 'low') When *dough* has been baked, it is bread.

dove a bird like a pigeon.

dovetail a wood-work joint shaped like a dove's tail. ■ Two things are said to *dovetail* when they fit exactly into each other.

dovetail

dowdy old-fashioned and shabby.

down soft hair or feathers; ■ treeless high land, especially the grassy hills of southern England (*downs*). ■ Come *down* from that tree.

downfall heavy rain, e.g. That *downfall* of rain has flooded the roads. ■ ruin, e.g. Delilah was the cause of Samson's *downfall*.

down-hearted sad.

downwards Point the gun *downwards* so that the shot goes into the ground.

doze I do not fall completely asleep; I just *doze*.

dozen twelve. A 'baker's *dozen*' means thirteen.

drab dull; ■ a dreary brown colour.

drag The boys had to exert all their strength to *drag* the heavy log along the ground to their camp.

dragon a story-book monster like a crocodile, but having wings and breathing fire.

dragonfly a large flying insect with a long body and beautiful wings.

dragonfly   draughts

drain Ditches are dug through swampy land to *drain* away the water. ■ The rain water runs down a *drain* in the street.

drainage system of drains, i.e. pipes, ditches, etc., e.g. To make flooded land fertile we must improve the *drainage*.

drake male duck.

drama a play in the theatre; ■ an exciting event in which death might occur, e.g. a difficult rescue of the crew of a sinking ship could be called a *drama* at sea.

dramatic to do with drama or the theatre. ■ A *dramatic* rescue is one that is exciting.

draper someone who sells cloth, linen, etc.

drapery materials made of wool, linen, cotton, etc.

drastic A *drastic* action is one that is violent, and perhaps desperate.

draught (pron. draft) There is a *draught* blowing on my neck from that open window. ■ Bob drank the whole glass of water in a single *draught*.

draughts (pron. drafts) a game played on a squared board with thick wooden discs.

draughtsman (pron. draftsman) a man skilled in making accurate drawings; ■ a thick wooden disc used in playing draughts.

draughty (pron. drafty) The wind blew through the gaps in the walls of the hut, making it very *draughty* inside.

draw to make a picture; ■ to make equal scores (in a game); ■ to attract (a crowd, attention, etc.).

drawback disadvantage.

drawer a box-like container that slides in and out of a desk or a cupboard, etc.

drawing a picture in pencil or in one colour; ■ making such a picture.

drawl to talk in a slow, lazy way.

drawn I have *drawn* a picture with my pencil. ■ The match was *drawn*, the score being 2–2. ■ Crowds were *drawn* to the spot by the roars of laughter.

dread to fear very much.

dreadful terrible, e.g. Being in a run away car is a *dreadful* experience. ■ troublesome, e.g. We were glad when that *dreadful* child went home.

dream scenes or events imagined during sleep; ■ to imagine scenes or events during sleep.

dreary dull and cheerless.

dredge To *dredge* a river, harbour, etc., is to remove mud from the bottom.

dredger a ship specially constructed for removing mud from the bottoms of rivers, harbours, etc.

dredger   dromedary

dregs the unwanted drops of tea, etc., left after drinking.

drench This heavy rain will *drench* us, for we have no coats.

drenched made soaking wet.

dress *Dress* yourself in your best clothes. ■ Jean is wearing a new *dress*. ■ To *dress* a wound is to put ointment, bandages, etc., on it.

dresser a piece of kitchen or dining-room furniture with shelves, drawers and cupboards to hold crockery, cutlery, etc.

dressing putting on clothes; ■ bandage, ointment, etc., for a wound. ■ Salad *dressing* is a spicy cream to put on salad.

dribble to keep a football moving with a series of light kicks. ■ A baby is said to *dribble* when it lets liquid run from its mouth.

dried After swimming I *dried* myself with a towel.

drier more dry; ■ a machine, etc., used for drying something.

drift snow piled up by the wind. ■ A boat without motor, oars or sail, will *drift* with the wind and tide.

drill physical exercises; ■ narrow furrow in which seeds are sown; ■ tool for boring holes; ■ to bore a hole.

drily in a voice that does not express any feeling (also spelt *dryly*).

drink I like to *drink* water when I am thirsty.

drip a small drop of liquid, e.g. A *drip* of water fell from the tap.

dripping the fat from roasted meat. ■ A tap is *dripping* when drips of water fall from it.

drive *Drive* the car carefully, or you may run over someone. ■ *Drive* away those noisy cats; I want to sleep. ■ We walked up the *drive* from the entrance gates to the doors of the house.

drizzle light rain, or rain in very tiny drops.

dromedary a kind of camel, bred for riding; it usually has one hump.

drone male honey bee, which doesn't collect honey; ■ a lazy person; ■ a low humming noise.

droop to flag or hang down limply, e.g. Plants *droop* if they are not watered.

drop Give me a *drop* (i.e. a little) of water. ■ to fall or to let fall.

drought a long period of dry weather.

drove a group of animals being driven. ■ The cowboys *drove* the cattle from the ranch to the railway. ■ Dad *drove* the car to London.

drown A cruel way of killing a cat is to *drown* it in a bucket of water.

drowned A man fell overboard into the sea and was *drowned*. ■ The noise of the passing aircraft *drowned* our voices so that no one could hear us.

drowsy sleepy.

drudgery hard, uninteresting work.

drug a substance used to make medicine and swallowed or injected by people who want to feel sleepy and dreamy. ■ To *drug* someone is to give him a drug which puts him to sleep.

drugged made unconscious by a drug.

drum musical instrument which the player beats; varieties include: bass *drum*, kettle *drum*, side *drum*.

drunk The man was *drunk* and unable to walk steadily ■ because he had *drunk* too much beer.

drunkard someone who is often drunk.

dry After washing I *dry* my hands on a towel. ■ A *dry* book is an uninteresting one.

dryness absence of moisture.

dual double, divided into two, e.g. Cars in which people learn to drive sometimes have *dual* controls so that both learner and instructor can control the car.

dubious doubtful, e.g. I am *dubious* of his chances of passing the examination because he has not worked hard enough.

Dublin the capital city of the Irish Republic.

duchess When a girl marries a duke, she becomes a *duchess*.

duck a water bird that makes the sound, 'Quack, quack!' ■ to dip your head under the water; ■ a score of 0 at cricket.

due Our train is *due* (is expected to arrive) in Paris at noon. ■ Your club subscription is *due* on Monday and you must pay it then. ■ The accident was *due* to (caused by) the motorist's carelessness.

duel a fight between two people armed, usually, with swords or pistols. ■ To *duel* is to fight a duel.

duet a musical composition for two voices or two players.

duke a nobleman of the highest rank, e.g. the Duke of Wellington.

dull A *dull* person is stupid. ■ A *dull* knife is blunt. ■ A *dull* day or colour is not bright. ■ A *dull* book is boring.

dullness stupidity; ■ bluntness; ■ cloudiness.

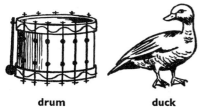

drum   **duck**

duly rightly, properly, e.g. Ellen won the race and was *duly* presented with the prize.

dumb unable to speak; ■ stupid (slang).

dummy an imitation, e.g. That is not a real person in the shop window, but a wooden *dummy*.

dump a heap of something, usually rubbish; ■ to unload or put down heavily.

dumps To be down in the *dumps* is to be miserable.

dunce old-fashioned name for a pupil at school who had difficulty in learning.

dune low mound of loose sand, often found on the sea shore.

dunes

dung animal droppings, especially when used to manure land.

dungeon an underground prison cell.

durable likely to last a long time, not easily worn out.

during You may not talk *during* the examination (while the examination is on).

dusk semi-darkness, nightfall.

dusky dark-coloured.

dust fine, dry particles of earth or other material. ■ To *dust* is to remove dust, e.g. with a duster, ■ or to sprinkle with dust.

duster a cloth for removing dust.

dusty covered with dust.

Dutch The *Dutch* are the people of Holland. ■ *Dutch* butter, bacon, etc., are made in Holland.

dutiful A *dutiful* person is one who does what he ought to do, e.g. Brian was a *dutiful* son (he did what a son ought to do for his parents).

duty something that you ought to do; ■ a tax on goods.

dwarf anything much smaller than normal size, e.g. *dwarf* beans. ■ A *dwarf* is a very small man.

dwell to reside or live, e.g. The pygmies *dwell* in the Congo forests. ■ To *dwell* on a subject is to talk or write about it at length.

dwindle to become smaller or grow less.

dwindling becoming smaller or growing less, e.g. The population of the village is *dwindling*.

dye substance used for colouring things. ■ To *dye* something is to colour it.

dyke

dyeing colouring.

dying coming to the end of life.

dyke a bank built to keep back flood water; ■ a narrow water channel or ditch (also spelt *dike*).

dynamite a powerful explosive. ■ To *dynamite* something is to blow it up with dynamite.

dynamo a machine for making electricity.

each   If you have four apples you can give four boys one *each*.

eager   keen and enthusiastic.

eagerly   The boys scrambled *eagerly* into the coach, impatient to get away on their holiday.

eagerness   We knew by the boys' *eagerness* to start that they were looking forward to an exciting holiday.

eagle   a large, powerful bird that kills and eats small animals and other birds.

eagle   ear of corn

ear   You hear with your *ear*. ■ An *ear* of corn is the bunch of seeds at the top of a corn-stalk.

earache   a continuous pain in the ear.

earl   a nobleman, e.g. The *Earl* of Leicester.

earlier   The train left *earlier* than usual, so when we arrived at the station it had gone.

early   The train arrived five minutes *early*, at 8.40 instead of 8.45.

earn   When I start work I hope to *earn* many pounds a week.

earned   My grandfather *earned* his living by selling newspapers.

earnest   serious, e.g. I am not joking; I am in *earnest*.

earnestly   The men were talking *earnestly* (i.e. the conversation was serious and important).

earnings   After a week's work my *earnings* were £10.

earth   That pile of *earth* came from the hole we dug in the ground. ■ The *earth* is one of several planets revolving round the sun.

earthen   made of earth, i.e. baked clay.

earthenware   pottery made of baked clay, e.g. jugs, basins, etc.

earthquake   During the *earthquake*, houses were shaken down and great cracks appeared in the ground.

earthworm   The bird tugged an *earthworm* from the ground and swallowed it.

earwig   a long dark insect with lots of legs.

ease   That's not difficult; I could do it with *ease*. ■ To stand at *ease* is to stand comfortably, i.e. not at attention.

easel   The blackboard stands on an *easel*; so does a picture while being painted.

easily   That's not difficult; I could do it *easily*. ■ In her race, Jill was *easily* first, several yards ahead of the second girl.

east   The sun rises in the *east* and sets in the west.

Easter   a Christian festival (holiday) to celebrate Christ's rising from the dead. ■ *Easter* holidays come in the spring.

eastern   If you wish to see the sun rise, watch the *eastern* sky at dawn.

easy   That was an *easy* sum; we all got it right.

eat We stop work at midday to *eat* our lunch.

eatable fit to be eaten, e.g. The apple was sour but *eatable*. ■ *Eatables* are things that can be eaten.

eaves the lower edges of the roof which overhang the walls of a building.

eccentric An *eccentric* person is one who is peculiar in habits, dress, etc.

echo the noise reflected (sent back) from a mountain, or, in an empty room, from the walls.

eclipse An *eclipse* of the sun is when the moon comes between the earth and the sun, and so casts a shadow on the earth. An *eclipse* of the moon is when the earth comes between it and the sun, and so the moon is put in shadow.

economical not wasteful.

economize to reduce expenses; to save.

economy cutting out all unnecessary expenditure of money.

eddy a spiral of water whirling round and round.

edge a border; ■ the cutting side of a knife.

edible fit to eat, not poisonous.

Edinburgh the capital city of Scotland.

edit To *edit* a book, newspaper, etc., is to prepare material for printing by making corrections, alterations, additions, etc.

edition the number of copies of a book or paper printed at one time, e.g. The first *edition* of the book was 20,000 copies.

editor someone who edits a book, newspaper, etc.

editorial to do with an editor. The *editorial* article in the paper is written by the editor himself.

educate Teachers are employed to *educate* children.

education My *education* began in the Infants' School and I hope to continue it in college.

eel a fish like a slippery snake.

eerie An *eerie* place, building, etc., is one that is strange and rather frightening.

effect The *effect* of the rattle was to make the baby laugh louder.

effective The medicine was *effective*, for the patient was better after taking it.

effeminate like a woman.

efficiency being efficient.

efficient An *efficient* person or machine is one that does its job well, without waste of time, effort or materials.

effigy an image. We made an *effigy* of Guy Fawkes, to burn on our bonfire.

effort the use of strength, e.g. It required an *effort* to lift the heavy rock. ■ an attempt, e.g. I'll make an *effort* to finish the job.

effortless easy, making no effort.

e.g. (short for) for example.

egg A hen laid the *egg* which I ate for breakfast. ■ To *egg* on is to encourage.

Egypt country in N.E. Africa, through which the River Nile flows.

Egyptian a citizen of Egypt.

eiderdown a bed cover stuffed with small soft feathers.

eight (8) I have *eight* fingers and two thumbs.

eighteen (18) *Eighteen* months are a year and a half.

eighteenth ($\frac{1}{18}$) one divided by eighteen. ■ (18th) Jim's birthday is on the *eighteenth* of June.

eighth ($\frac{1}{8}$) one divided by eight. ■ (8th) On your *eighth* birthday you had lived eight years.

eightieth ($\frac{1}{80}$) one divided by eighty. ■ (80th) The *eightieth* page is the one after the 79th.

eighty (80) eight tens.

either I will give you *either* a book or a pen, but not both.

ejaculate to cry out suddenly, e.g. to call 'What's that?'

eject to throw out, e.g. Police were at the meeting to *eject* trouble-makers.

elaborate complicated, not simple, e.g. Peter worked out an *elaborate* scheme for raising the money.

elapse to pass, e.g. We let an hour *elapse* before we returned home.

elastic Things that return of their own accord to their original length or shape after being stretched, etc., are *elastic*, e.g. rubber bands, balloons.

elated excited.

elbow the joint in the middle of the arm. ■ To *elbow* someone is to push him aside.

elder the person of greater age, e.g. Jim was the *elder* of the two brothers. ■ My *elder* brother is Jim.

elderly getting old, e.g. The mayor is an *elderly* man.

eldest the person of greatest age, e.g. Joe was the *eldest* of all the children ■ My parents' *eldest* child is Joe.

elect to choose, especially to choose a person by voting, e.g. We *elect* our school captain by a show of hands.

election At the *election* most people voted for Kay Smith and so she was elected.

elector someone who has a right to vote, e.g. Many of the *electors* voted for Kay Smith.

electric *Electric* lights and fires work by electricity.

electrical having to do with electricity, e.g. an *electrical* engineer, *electrical* apparatus.

electrician someone qualified to install and repair electrical equipment, such as fires, lights, etc.

electricity Electric lights, fires, etc., work by *electricity*, which is made by generators in power stations.

electrify to change from steam, etc., to electricity, e.g. to *electrify* the railways.

elegant graceful and refined, e.g. an *elegant* lady.

elementary simple.

elements the simplest forms of anything; ■ the forces that make up the weather – rain, hail, wind, etc.

elephant a large animal with tusks and a trunk.

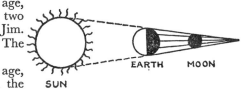

eclipse of the moon

elevate to lift up.

elevation being lifted up; ■ height, e.g. The cave was at an *elevation* of 300 metres above sea level.

elevator Farmers use an *elevator* to raise hay, straw, etc., to the top of a stack. ■ also American for a lift, used in tall buildings.

eleven (11) one more than ten.

eleventh (¹⁄₁₁) one divided by eleven. ■ (11th) The *eleventh* of May is the day following the tenth.

elf a mischievous little fairy.

elicit to draw out (information, etc. from a person), e.g. We could *elicit* no information from the guide.

eligible (pron. el-i-ji-b'l) suitable, e.g. All children who are between 10 and 11 years old are *eligible* for the examination.

eliminate to remove, e.g. We *eliminate* most of the runners in the heats; only the best run in the final.

Elizabethan having to do with either of the Queen Elizabeths or their times, but more especially with Elizabeth I, e.g. Drake was an *Elizabethan* seaman.

ellipse an oval shape.

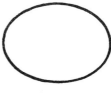

ellipse

elm The *elm* tree grows in woods in many parts of Europe.

elongate to make longer.

elope Girls *elope* when they run away from home with a lover.

eloquent An *eloquent* speaker is one skilled in the use of words.

else Who *else* was there besides Jane and Jill? If you have nothing *else* to do, you can always read.

elsewhere somewhere else, e.g. Very difficult words are not included in this dictionary; you must look for them *elsewhere*.

elude to dodge, get away from, e.g. Tom managed to *elude* his pursuers by hiding in a hay-stack.

elusive hard to catch.

elves mischievous little fairies.

embalm The Egyptians and other ancient peoples could *embalm* a dead body with spices, etc., so that it was preserved for centuries.

embankment To prevent flooding, a strong *embankment* of earth, stones, etc., was built along the river.

embark to board a ship or an aircraft.

embarrass to make someone feel awkward and uncomfortable.

embarrassing Most boys find it *embarrassing* when mothers kiss them in front of their school friends.

emblem The *emblem* of Scotland is a thistle, the *emblem* of Ireland a shamrock and the Welsh *emblem* a leek.

embrace to clasp a person in one's arms.

embrocation a liquid for rubbing on an injury.

embroider to decorate with needlework.

embroidered Jane *embroidered* the cloth with a pattern in yellow and green stitches.

embroidery decorative needlework.

emerald a bright green; the colour of ■ a precious stone called an *emerald*.

emerge We saw Jim *emerge*, dripping, from the pond. The rabbit will not *emerge* from its hole while you are there.

emergency You pull the communication cord in the train only in the event of some such *emergency* as fire or accident.

emigrate As Dad cannot find suitable work in England, we shall *emigrate* to Australia and make our home there.

eminent famous.

emit Why does the rocket *emit* those long streams of flame and smoke?

emotion feeling. We couldn't tell whether Dick was feeling angry, worried or excited, for he showed no *emotion* at all.

emperor the ruler of an empire.

emphasize To *emphasize* a word you say it with special force. ■ To *emphasize* a fact you draw special attention to it.

emphatically To speak *emphatically* is to give special force to your words.

empire a number of countries ruled over by one government, or by an emperor.

employ to give work to, e.g. The making of the road will *employ* many men.

employed busy, occupied; ■ given work, e.g. Fifty men were *employed* at the factory.

employee a person who works for someone.

employer someone for whom people work.

employment work, e.g. The new factory provided *employment* for many men.

empress an emperor's wife. ■ a woman who rules an empire.

empty There is nothing in an *empty* box, bag, etc.

emulsion a milky liquid consisting of particles of oil suspended in water and made by mixing water and oil vigorously together. ■ *Emulsion* paints are similarly made of resin in water.

enable to make able, e.g. This map will *enable* you to find the place.

enamel An *enamel* dish, saucepan, etc., is one covered with a hard, glossy material, ■ which is called *enamel*. ■ To *enamel* anything is to coat it with enamel.

enchant to charm or bewitch.

enchanting delightful, charming.

encircle to surround.

enclose to fence in, e.g. Farmers often *enclose* their land with hedges.

encore (pron. ong-kor). People at a concert shout '*Encore*' when they want to hear the music again.

encounter an unfriendly meeting, e.g. an *encounter* with cannibals; ■ a chance meeting.

encourage To *encourage* someone is to increase his will to do something.

encouragement Our team's victory was partly due to the *encouragement* given by its supporters among the spectators.

encyclopaedia, encyclopedia a book containing information on any or all subjects in alphabetical order.

end Put a full stop at the *end* of the sentence. ■ *End* the sentence with a full stop.

endanger to put in danger.

endeavour to try.

endless having no end.

endure Travellers in space have to *endure* many discomforts in their rockets.

enemy Our soldiers fought against the *enemy*. Disease is the *enemy* of all mankind.

energetic I don't feel *energetic* enough to rush about, so I'll sit down.

energy Dad was so tired that he hadn't the *energy* to get out of his chair.

enforce Some people do not keep the law unless a policeman is there to *enforce* it.

engage We *engage* a man to do the work for £25 a week. ■ You *engage* Bill's attention while I hide his book.

engagement I knew my sister was engaged to be married when I saw her *engagement* ring. ■ I can't meet you this evening for I have another *engagement*.

engine You don't often see a steam *engine* pulling a train. ■ The car wouldn't go because the *engine* had gone wrong.

engineer a person who makes or repairs machinery, bridges, etc.

enjoy To *enjoy* something is to like doing it. ■ To *enjoy* yourself is to have a good time.

enjoyable An *enjoyable* holiday, concert, etc., is one that gives pleasure.

enjoyment pleasure.

enlarge This photograph is too small; please *enlarge* it for me.

enlargement The *enlargement* of a photograph is bigger than the original photograph.

enlighten inform, e.g. If you do not know why we wash before eating, I will *enlighten* you.

enlist to join the army.

enmity the opposite of friendship; hatred.

enormous very large.

enough I have *enough*, so please do not give me any more.

enquire (also spelt *inquire*) Tell people who *enquire* after Dad's health that he is better.

enraged very angry indeed.

enrol, enroll to write someone's name on a list (of people who want to join something, etc.).

ensign (pron. én-s'n) The red *ensign* is the flag flown by British merchant ships; ships of the Royal Navy fly the white *ensign*.

ensure to make sure.

entail Going for a swim will *entail* all the bother of carrying a costume and towel and finding somewhere to undress.

entangle to mix up, to make tangled, to catch in a snare.

enter You *enter* by the door marked 'Way in'.

entertain We will *entertain* our guests with music and games.

entertainment There were music, games and dancing for our *entertainment*.

enthrone to place (a king, bishop etc.) on a throne.

enthusiasm keenness, great interest.

enthusiastic full of enthusiasm, e.g. John never missed an attendance at the local football match: he was an *enthusiastic* supporter of his club.

entice The keeper *enticed* the animal back into its cage by offering it bits of food.

entire whole, e.g. We searched the *entire* building to satisfy ourselves that Billy was nowhere in it.

entirely It is not *entirely* my own work, for Jane helped me with it.

entitled You are not *entitled* to wear our school tie if you do not attend the school. ■ The book is *entitled* 'Oliver Twist'.

entrance (pron. én-trance) a way in; ■ (pron. en-tránce) to charm.

entrant someone who enters (for a competition, into a profession, etc.).

entrust If I *entrust* something to you, I expect you to take care of it for me.

entry an entrance, e.g. The only *entry* was an iron gate set into the wall. ■ an item in a book, e.g. The last *entry* in my diary is 'I'm tired of keeping a diary.'

envelop (pron. en-vél-op) to wrap, e.g. The building was *enveloped* in flames.

envelope (pron. én-vel-ope) Address an *envelope* and put the letter in it.

envious 'Jane was *envious* of Mary's good looks' means that Jane was annoyed because Mary was better looking than she.

envy dislike for someone because he is more fortunate than you.

epic a poem, film, etc., about heroic deeds.

epidemic any disease which affects many people in a district at the same time.

episode part of a story.

epistle a letter, but especially one of the letters in the Bible, e.g. The *Epistle* of Paul to the Romans.

equal An hour is *equal* to sixty minutes (1 hr. = 60 min.).

equality being equal, e.g. *Equality* of opportunity means that all people have equal opportunities.

equalize to make equal. We are losing the match by three goals to two; so we can *equalize* by scoring another goal.

equally If you share the apples *equally* between Peter and Paul, they will have the same number each.

equator an imaginary line round the middle of the earth, half way between the North Pole and the South Pole.

envelope   equator

equatorial of or near the equator, e.g. *equatorial* forest.

equilateral An *equilateral* triangle has sides of equal length.

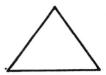

equilateral triangle   **escalator**

equinox March 20th or 21st, and Sept. 22nd or 23rd, when day and night are of equal length.

equip to provide (things necessary for a journey, etc.).

equipment the things that have to be taken for a journey, etc.

equivalent equal, having the same meaning.

era a period of the time dating from a particular event; e.g. the Christian *era*.

erase to rub out, e.g. You can *erase* pencil marks with a rubber.

erect upright, e.g. The soldier stood *erect*. ■ to build or set upright, e.g. The builder is going to *erect* a block of flats here.

erection something erected, a building.

erosion gradual destruction, wearing away, especially the wearing away of rocks by the weather, rivers, etc.

err to sin; to make mistakes. ■ To *err* on the safe side is to be inexact in the interests of safety, e.g. to under-load an aircraft rather than risk putting in too heavy a load.

errand An *errand* boy is employed to take messages, parcels, etc., short distances; ■ a short journey of this kind is an *errand*.

erratic uncertain, unreliable.

error a mistake.

erupt The volcano may *erupt* and shoot up smoke, ashes and molten rock.

eruption During the *eruption* of the volcano, smoke and hot ashes were shot high into the sky.

escalator a moving stairway.

escapade a foolish or mischievous adventure.

escape to get free.

escort The prisoner had an *escort* (pron. és-cort) of soldiers to guard him. ■ There were soldiers to *escort* (pron. es-córt) the prisoner.

Eskimo one of a race of people who live in the Arctic regions (also spelt *Esquimau*).

especial particular, chief, e.g. My *especial* friend is Jean.

especially I like all fruit, *especially* apples.

espy to catch sight of.

essay For homework, I have to write an *essay* entitled 'My Friends'.

essence a strong perfume, flavouring, etc., e.g. *essence* of almonds, a few drops of which can flavour a large cake.

essential very necessary.

establish to set up, e.g. The business was *established* in 1864.

estate The duke's *estate* included a house and gardens, woods and farms.

esteem to value highly.

estimate an opinion (about the size, weight, cost, etc., of anything). ■ to judge, to form an opinion.

estimation judgement, opinion.

estuary   a river mouth.

estuary

etc. (short for) *et cetera*, meaning 'and the rest', e.g. 'A newsagent sells books, papers, *etc.*' means that he also sells other things such as magazines, cards, pens and pencils.

eternal that always has and always will exist, e.g. *eternal* God.

eternally always; ■ (slang) too often, e.g. You children are *eternally* quarrelling.

eternity the future life, time which has no beginning or end.

Europe The continent of *Europe* includes Britain, France, Germany, Italy and many other countries.

European Britain, France and Germany are three *European* countries.

evacuate to empty, to remove, e.g. Because there was danger of the fire spreading, firemen had to *evacuate* people from the near-by houses.

evade to avoid.

evaporate to change from liquid to vapour, e.g. Wet pavements soon dry when there is wind or sunshine to *evaporate* the water.

evaporation a changing from liquid to vapour, e.g. *Evaporation* takes place more quickly when there is wind or sunshine.

evasive avoiding, e.g. *Evasive* action is action taken in an effort to avoid something. An *evasive* answer is one given in an attempt to avoid answering the question.

eve evening. ■ Christmas *eve* is the day before Christmas.

even An *even* surface is smooth and level. ■ An *even* number will divide by two. ■ A brave man is admired, *even* by his enemies. ■ (in poetry, short for) evening.

evening the end of the day, between sunset and bedtime.

evenly smoothly.

event A General Election is an important *event*, and so is your birthday.

eventful An *eventful* day is one on which something very important happens.

eventual final, resulting.

eventually in the end.

ever Do you *ever* wash your neck? (i.e. at any time). ■ Must I stand here for *ever*? (i.e. for all time).

evergreen An *evergreen* shrub or tree has leaves on it all the year round.

everlasting lasting for ever.

evermore for ever.

every each one, e.g. I wash *every* day.

evidence The policeman gave *evidence* at the trial. The policeman's *evidence* was that he saw the prisoner break the window.

evident It was *evident* from the puddles in the roads that there had just been a rainstorm.

evidently He was *evidently* an important person, for all the policemen saluted him.

E

evil bad, harmful. An *evil* deed is a sin or a crime.

ewe (pron. you) a female sheep.

ewe

exact There were about 10,000 people at the match; I don't know the *exact* number.

exactly There were *exactly* 9,997 people at the match (i.e. neither more nor less).

exaggerate to say something is greater than it is, e.g. to say someone is 'wet through' when only his top coat is wet.

exaggeration It is an *exaggeration* to say that it rains every day, if some days are dry.

examination an inspection, e.g. An *examination* showed a crack in the metal. ■ a test, e.g. In our school *examination* we answer questions on what we have learnt.

examine to inspect; ■ to test.

example a pattern or model, e.g. to set a good *example*. There have been great English writers, Shakespeare, for *example*.

exasperate to irritate (a person).

excavate to dig out, e.g. A group of men arrived with spades to *excavate* the buried Roman villa.

exceedingly extremely, very.

excel To *excel* in something is to be specially good at it.

excellence high quality, e.g. We were praised for the *excellence* of our singing.

excellent extremely good.

except All the boys were at school *except* Jim, who was ill in bed.

excepting leaving out (used only after 'not'), e.g. All the boys were late, not *excepting* Jim.

exception All the boys were at school with the *exception* of Jim, who was ill in bed.

exceptional unusual.

excess more than enough, extra.

excessive An *excessive* amount is far too much.

exchange I'd like to *exchange* my pen for your knife. ■ In the telephone *exchange*, callers are connected to the persons they wish to speak to.

excitable easily excited.

excite to cause someone to show strong feelings (of great happiness, amusement, anger, sorrow, etc.).

excited Pat was so *excited* at the good news that she yelled wildly and danced for joy.

excitement The crowd yelled with *excitement* as the queen's carriage came near.

exciting An *exciting* adventure or story, etc., is one that arouses strong feelings in a person.

exclaim to cry out.

exclamation something exclaimed, e.g. 'Good heavens!' or 'Oh!'

exclude to leave out.

exclusive reserved for certain persons only; ■ not including, e.g. The price of the outing is £1 *exclusive* of food.

excursion a pleasure trip, an outing.

excusable John's failure in the exam was *excusable* because he had been absent from school through illness.

excuse (pron. ex-kúze) to forgive, pardon; ■ to try to explain away misbehaviour. ■ (pron. ex-kéwss) an apology; ■ an attempt to show that you are not to blame.

execute to put to death; ■ to do; ■ to put into effect, e.g. to *execute* a will.

execution putting to death; ■ doing; carrying out, e.g. The soldier showed bravery in the *execution* of his duty.

exercise Do the first *exercise* in your English book. ■ We take physical *exercise* to keep ourselves fit. ■ *Exercise* more care or you'll cause an accident.

exert Jim had to *exert* all his strength to pull the man out of the river.

exertion The *exertion* of pulling the man out of the river made Jim pant for breath.

exhale breathe out.

exhaust The *exhaust* fumes from a car escape through the *exhaust* pipe. ■ The climb will *exhaust* (i.e. tire out) the boys.

exhausted tired out, e.g. The boys were *exhausted* after their long run. ■ used up, e.g. The diver had to surface because his air supply was *exhausted*.

exhaustion People suffering from *exhaustion* are seriously overtired.

exhibit to put on show; ■ something put on show.

exhibition At an *exhibition* things are put on show.

exhilarating making cheerful and lively, e.g. Tobogganing down the snow-covered hill is most *exhilarating*.

exile to send away from home or country; ■ someone who has been sent away from home or country.

exist to live, e.g. You cannot *exist* long without food and water. ■ to be, e.g. Slavery doesn't *exist* in our country.

existence life, being, e.g. To be without home or friends is a terrible *existence*.

exit way out.

exodus a going forth (out), especially the *exodus* of the Jews from Egypt, ■ described in the Bible book of *Exodus*.

exotic *Exotic* plants, creatures, etc., are those from abroad.

expand to get larger, e.g. When metals are heated, they *expand*.

expanse a large area, e.g. That *expanse* of water is Lake Windermere.

expansion increase, usually in length, e.g. The gaps between lengths of railway line are to allow for the *expansion* of the metal on hot days.

expect I *expect* a present from Uncle Tom and so I shall be disappointed if he doesn't send one.

expectant waiting hopefully.

expectation We came with the *expectation* of seeing Uncle Bob (i.e. We thought [with pleasure] that we should see Uncle Bob when we came.)

expedition I'd like to join the *expedition* which is going to explore the moon.

expel to turn out, e.g. The headmaster may *expel* the boy from the school.

expend to spend.

expenditure The Christmas party will involve an *expenditure* of £15.

expense cost.

expensive That watch is too *expensive* for me; have you a cheaper one?

experience I have no *experience* of camping (i.e. I have never been camping.) ■ Falling down a cliff is a terrifying *experience*.

experienced An *experienced* person is one who has had much experience.

experiment a test, e.g. The scientist carried out an *experiment* to see what would happen when the two chemicals were mixed.

expert a person who has great skill or knowledge of a particular subject.

expire to die, e.g. At the end of the play we see the hero *expire* in the girl's arms. ■ Our TV licence will *expire* next week, so we shall then need a new one.

expiry the end, e.g. At the *expiry* of the time allowed for the exam., everyone had to stop writing.

explain I do not understand long division; will you please *explain* it to me?

explanation a statement that explains something.

explicit definite and clearly explained, e.g. *explicit* instructions.

explode Don't hold that firework in your hand; it may *explode* and blow off your fingers.

exploit a brave or daring deed. ■ To *exploit* someone is to use him for your own advantage.

explore To *explore* a country is to travel through it to find out what it is like.

explorer someone who explores.

explosion The *explosion* of the bomb could be heard miles away.

explosive a substance that explodes – gunpowder, dynamite, T.N.T., etc.

export something sold to another country; ■ to sell something to another country.

expose to uncover or leave unprotected. ■ To *expose* a film in a camera is to let light fall on it to make pictures.

exposed uncovered or unprotected. ■ Camera film on which pictures have been taken is called *exposed* film (because it has been *exposed* to light).

exposure showing up; ■ the time during which film is exposed in taking a picture. ■ The man lost on the mountain died of *exposure* (i.e. because he had not been protected from the weather).

express An *express* train is a specially fast one. ■ These words *express* my feelings, 'Thank God you have come.'

expression the look on a person's face; ■ something said, e.g. a vulgar *expression*; ■ the feeling put into the voice when saying something, or into an instrument when playing music.

exquisite very beautiful indeed.

extend to reach; ■ to make larger.

extension an additional part, e.g. The school was not big enough so an *extension* was built on to it.

extensive far-reaching, spacious, e.g. a large house with *extensive* grounds.

extent size, amount, e.g. When the smoke blew away we could see the *extent* of the damage.

exterior the outside, e.g. The *exterior* of the building was dirty.

exterminate to destroy them all, e.g. We must *exterminate* the rats on our farm.

external outside.

extinct An *extinct* animal is one of a kind that no longer exists. ■ An *extinct* volcano is one which will not again erupt.

extinguish (pron. ex-ting-gwish) Firemen *extinguish* fires by spraying water on them.

extinguisher (pron. ex-ting-gwish-er) We can put out the flames with a fire *extinguisher*.

extra The shopkeeper weighed out the apples and gave me an *extra* one for myself.

extract to take out.

extraction Our dentist is very good at the *extraction* (pulling out) of teeth. ■ Betty is of African *extraction* (i.e. she has African ancestors).

extraordinary very unusual indeed.

extravagance being foolishly wasteful.

extravagant foolishly wasteful.

extreme very great, e.g. We were in *extreme* danger. ■ Farthest point, e.g. The cat was at the *extreme* end of the branch.

extremely very.

extricate The cat was so tangled up in the net that we had to cut it to *extricate* him.

eye I see with my *eye*. ■ You thread the cotton through the *eye* of the needle.

eyeball the whole eye, which is shaped like a ball.

eyebrow the line of hair just above the eye.

eyelash one of the hairs along the edge of the eyelid.

eyelet the lace-hole in a shoe, etc.

eyelid the skin covering of the eye.

eyesight You have good *eyesight* if you can see well without glasses.

eyesore something ugly or unpleasant to look at.

eyrie nest of a bird such as an eagle, built high on rocks, etc.

fire extinguisher

eyrie

fable a story with a moral (usually about animals).

fabric woven cloth; the walls and roof of a building, e.g. The floods ruined the furniture and fittings of the house, but the *fabric* was not damaged.

fabulous astonishing; ■ untrue.

face There is a smile on Pat's *face*. ■ To *face* a person is to have your front towards him. ■ There is a number on each *face* of a dice.

facetious amusing, e.g. Don't be *facetious*; this is a serious matter.

facilities opportunities (provided), e.g. At our club there are *facilities* for music, dancing, games, acting, etc.

facing When you are *facing* someone your face is towards him. ■ an outer covering, e.g. different material on the cuffs or collar of a dress.

facing   fairy

fact something known to be true.

factor As $2 \times 3 = 6$, two is a *factor* of six, and so is three.

factory That is the *factory* where cars are made.

faddy having odd ideas, usually about not eating certain things.

fade to lose colour, e.g. The curtains *fade* in the sun. ■ to dis-

appear gradually, e.g. The noise of the rocket will soon *fade*.

fading losing colour; ■ gradually disappearing.

Fahrenheit 32°F means 32° *Fahrenheit*, which is freezing point on a *Fahrenheit* thermometer.

fail You either *fail* an exam or pass it.

failure Tom's *failure* in the exam was to be expected, for he had done no work.

faint to lose consciousness, e.g. Some people *faint* at the sight of blood. ■ pale, indistinct, e.g. The writing was so *faint* that we could not read it.

faintly indistinctly.

faintness paleness, indistinctness, e.g. We couldn't read the message because of the *faintness* of the writing.

fair moderately good; ■ having light-coloured hair and complexion; ■ just (i.e. no cheating involved); ■ a market with stalls for the sale of goods, entertainments, roundabouts, etc.

fairly not very, e.g. Joe's a *fairly* good swimmer. ■ with no cheating, e.g. The game was played *fairly*.

fairness justice; showing no favouritism; ■ involving no cheating.

fairy a small, imaginary creature with magical powers.

faith trust; belief. Though lost in dangerous country, we were not worried because we had *faith* in our leader (i.e. we were certain that he could get us out of any difficulty). ■ belief in religious ideas that cannot be proved.

faithful loyal, e.g. A *faithful* friend can be relied upon never to let you down.

faithfully loyally. ■ The usual ending to business letters is: 'Yours *faithfully*,' followed by the writer's name.

faithfulness loyalty.

fake That is not the real diamond, but a *fake*, made of glass.

falcon a bird that eats other birds and is trained to catch them for men, as a sport.

falcon   **fang**

fall Billy saw an apple *fall* from the tree. ■ In the U.S.A., the *fall* is the name for autumn.

fallacy a mistaken idea.

fallen An apple has *fallen* from the tree on to the ground.

fallow *Fallow* land is ground that is ploughed, but no crops are grown in it for a year, so that there are more plant foods in the soil for the following year's crop. ■ *Fallow* deer are quite small and yellow-brown in colour.

false untrue; ■ not real.

falsehood a lie; an untruth.

falter to hesitate.

fame reputation, e.g. 'The *fame* of Napoleon spread to every country' means that people in every country knew about Napoleon.

familiar Being *familiar* with something (or someone) means knowing it (or him) well.

familiarity treating someone as if he were a person you know very well. ■ *Familiarity* with a subject is knowing it well.

family Your *family* consists of your parents, brothers and sisters.

famine There is *famine* in a place when the people there are seriously short of food.

famished very hungry.

famous well known.

famously excellently.

fanatic someone who is too enthusiastic – about religion, for example.

fancy to imagine, e.g. *Fancy* Geoffrey as a pop singer! ■ ornamental. ■ At a *fancy* dress party people dress up as characters in stories, etc.

fanfare a special short tune played on trumpets (usually) as a greeting, or to announce the arrival of someone important.

fang a long, pointed tooth, especially of dogs.

fantastic odd, unreal. Tony gave a *fantastic* account of his adventures in the woods (i.e. he described exciting things that he had only imagined).

farce a funny play, e.g. We went to the theatre and saw a *farce* so funny that my sides ached with laughter.

fare My bus *fare* to school is 5p.

farewell goodbye.

farm On his *farm* the farmer grows wheat and keeps cows.

farther at a greater distance, e.g. The sun is *farther* from us than the moon is.

farthest most distant, e.g. the *farthest* corner of the field.

fascinate to charm; to attract very strongly, e.g. Railway engines *fascinate* Robert.

fascination charm; ■ power of attraction, e.g. Robert could never resist the *fascination* of whirring machinery.

fashion The *fashion* (e.g. in ladies' shoes) is the style that is considered smart and up-to-date.

fashionable smart and up-to-date.

fast quick; ■ quickly; ■ to go without food. ■ A dye (colour) that is *fast* will not fade or wash out.

fasten to attach firmly; to fix.

fastener something with which to fasten things, e.g. a paper *fastener*.

fastening something which fastens things, e.g. a bolt.

fatal deadly. A *fatal* accident is one in which someone is killed.

fatally Anyone *fatally* injured will die of his injuries.

fate Your *fate* is the future which is in store for you.

fated doomed. 'Alim was *fated* to be drowned' means that Alim was sure to die by drowning.

father A boy is the son of his *father*.

fathom 1·8 m. The depth of the sea is often shown in *fathoms* on maps.

fatigue (pron. fa-teeg) tiredness (as a result of working or playing hard).

fatigued (pron. fa-teeg'd) tired out.

fatten to make fat.

fault The accident was my *fault*; I wasn't looking where I was going.

faulty A thing that is *faulty* has something wrong with it.

favour To do someone a *favour* is to do something for him out of kindness.

favourable A *favourable* reply is one that is friendly, or consents to what was asked.

favourite Your *favourite* uncle, book, etc., is the one you like best.

favouritism having favourites.

fawn a young deer, ■ or its colour (a light brown).

fawn feather

fear They run away because they *fear* the enemy. ■ We show *fear* by running away.

fearful afraid.

fearless not afraid.

feast a grand meal; ■ a religious festival, e.g. Easter.

feat a remarkable act, especially one requiring skill or daring.

feather The bird could not fly properly because it had lost a *feather* from its wing.

feature The *feature* film is the most important one in a cinema programme. ■ A *feature* in a newspaper is a specially important article. ■ *Features* are the most noticeable parts of the face: nose, mouth, eyes, etc.

February the second month of the year.

federation the union of several states or countries under one government.

fee a payment or charge. The admission *fee* is the money you pay before you are allowed in a cinema, swimming-bath, etc.

feeble weak.

feebly weakly, e.g. The sick man *feebly* raised his arm.

feed We *feed* our dog on bones and dog-biscuits.

feel It was so dark that we had to *feel* our way along the wall with our hands.

feelers long, thin growths, like those on the heads of some insects, with which they feel their way about.

feeling If you are *feeling* ill, send for the doctor.

feelings The unkind words hurt Jane's *feelings* so that she began to cry.

feet We stand and walk on our *feet.* ■ Three *feet* make one yard (3 ft. = 1 yd.).

feign (pron. fayn) to pretend.

feint (pron. faynt) a pretended attack, meant to deceive the opponent (in boxing, etc.).

fell Mary slipped on the edge of the river and *fell* into the water. ■ To *fell* is to knock down.

fellow a companion; ■ a man or boy, e.g. Poor *fellow*! ■ being alike in some way, e.g. a *fellow*-sufferer.

fellowship friendliness, companionship.

felt cloth made of wool pressed and stuck together. ■ The water *felt* warm as we dived in.

female A girl or a woman is a *female*; a boy or a man is a male.

feminine to do with women or girls.

fence railings, posts and wire or boards, round a garden, field, etc.; ■ to fight with special thin swords, as a sport; ■ someone who deals in stolen goods.

fern a plant with feathery leaves which uncurl as they grow.

ferns   ferret

ferocious very fierce, cruel.

ferret a thin, furry little animal, like a weasel; used for hunting rabbits, rats, etc., in their holes.

ferry A *ferry*-boat takes people backwards and forwards across a river or channel. ■ Such a crossing is called a *ferry*.

fertile fruitful, e.g. Plants grow well in *fertile* soil.

fertilize to make fertile, e.g. A farmer can *fertilize* his land with manure.

fertilizer manure; material to make ground, etc., more fertile.

fester A wound is said to *fester* when poisonous matter forms in it.

festival a joyful celebration; ■ a special kind of entertainment (e.g. a music *festival*) in which the performers are judged.

festive gay.

festivity gaiety, rejoicing.

festoon a chain of flowers, leaves, decorations, etc., hung in a curve between two supports.

festoon   fife

fetch to go and get.

fête a festival or entertainment, usually out of doors.

feud hatred between two people, families or tribes, that goes on and on, often from generation to generation.

feudal Under the *feudal* system (in the Middle Ages) a lord provided land for his men in return for their services as soldiers, etc.

fever an illness which causes the patient to have a high temperature, e.g. scarlet *fever*, typhoid *fever*, etc.

feverish having a fever or a high temperature.

few not many.

fibre a thin hair-like strand, e.g. of cotton, wool, etc.

fickle unreliable, changeable.

fiction imagined (made up) stories.

fictitious imaginary; not real or true.

fiddle a violin. ■ To *fiddle* with something is to fidget with it. ■ (slang) a piece of cheating; ■ to swindle or cheat.

fidelity faithfulness, accuracy, e.g. A high-*fidelity* radio (or gramophone) is one specially made to produce sounds almost exactly like those made by the original orchestra, singer, etc.

fidget to move about in a restless manner.

field an area for grazing animals, playing games, etc.; ■ an area where minerals are found (coal-*field*, oil-*field*, etc.); ■ place where a battle is fought (battle*field*).

fiend a devil.

fierce violent, wild, e.g. a *fierce* quarrel, a *fierce* storm.

fiery (pron. fire-ry) blazing; fire-like.

fife a small flute, used in military music.

fifteen (15) ten and five.

fifteenth ($\frac{1}{15}$) one divided by fifteen. ■ (15th) The *fifteenth* day, etc., is the one after the fourteenth.

fifth ($\frac{1}{5}$) one divided by five. ■ (5th) The *fifth* is the one after the fourth.

fiftieth ($\frac{1}{50}$) one divided by fifty. ■ (50th) The *fiftieth* is the one after the forty-ninth.

fifty (50) five tens.

fight Boys *fight* ■ (or have a *fight*) by hitting each other with their fists; soldiers fight with guns, etc.

figure a number, e.g. the *figure* seven (7); ■ a shape, e.g. A triangle is a three-sided *figure* (△).

file a steel tool with a rough surface, which you rub on things to wear them down or smooth them; ■ a folder, container, etc., for loose papers.

fill to make full.

fillet a piece of meat or fish from which the bone has been removed.

filling material used to fill (e.g. a tooth or a cushion); ■ making full.

film a thin layer or coating; ■ the material on which photographs are taken; ■ a picture shown at a cinema.

filter You strain the little solid pieces out of a liquid by pouring it through a *filter*. ■ To *filter* a liquid is to pass it through a filter.

filth disgusting dirt.

filthy disgustingly dirty.

fin A fish swims by movements of its *fins*.

final last.

finally lastly.

finance the management of money. ■ To *finance* an expedition, etc., is to find the money for it.

financial *Financial* difficulties are difficulties about money.

financier an expert in money matters.

finch a bird like a sparrow but prettier and a better singer.

find Look for the book until you *find* it. ■ the discovery of something important.

fine of good quality. ■ *Fine* weather is warm and sunny. ■ A *fine* powder is made up of very small particles. ■ money paid to a law court as a punishment.

finger We all have four *fingers* and a thumb on each hand.

finish to end; ■ the end.

finished ended.

Finland a country in northern Europe.

Finnish the language of the Finns; ■ anything from or of Finland.

Finns, Fins the people of Finland.

fir an evergreen tree which produces cones and is used as the Christmas Tree.

fir   fireplace

fire We cooked our food on a *fire* of logs. ■ To *fire* a gun you pull the trigger.

fire-alarm a device for giving warning that a fire has broken out, in a building usually.

fire-arms rifles, revolvers, pistols, etc.

fireplace A fire to warm a room burns in the *fireplace*.

fireproof able to resist fire, e.g. the *fireproof* curtain in a theatre.

fireworks showy, colourful, explosive devices such as rockets, crackers, squibs, etc.

firm not easily moved; ■ a business owned by more than one person.

first If something is happening for the *first* time, it has not happened before.

firth a narrow arm of the sea, e.g. the *Firth* of Forth in Scotland.

fish cold-blooded creatures which live in water and are covered with scales. ■ To *fish* is to try to catch fish.

fisherman a man who tries to catch fish.

fishermen men who try to catch fish.

fishmonger a man whose business is selling fish.

fission Nuclear *fission* is the splitting of atoms by which much power is released (in bombs or power stations).

fist tightly closed hand with which people thump or punch.

fit suitable, e.g. food *fit* for a king; ■ correct size and shape, e.g. The shoes are a perfect *fit*. ■ The shoes *fit* me. ■ in good health, e.g. Sam couldn't play in the match because he wasn't *fit*. ■ A sudden attack of illness, e.g. The man collapsed on the floor in a *fit*.

fitness suitability; ■ healthiness.

fitted The shoes *fitted* me perfectly (i.e. they were of the correct size and shape.)

fittings the fixtures (hooks, handles, shelves, etc.) and furniture in a house, shop, etc.

five (5) one more than four.

fix to fasten, e.g. You *fix* a bracket to the wall with screws. ■ To be in a *fix* is to be in difficulty.

fixed fastened; settled.

fixture something that is fixed, e.g. a date, or a shelf, e.g. Our

school team's next *fixture* is against your school team.

fizz a hissing sound, e.g. made by a mineral drink when poured out; ■ to make this hissing sound.

flabby soft and limp, e.g. I hate being offered a *flabby* hand to shake.

flag The British *flag*, the Union Jack, ■ was flying from the *flag*-pole. ■ to hang down loosely; to become weak; ■ a plant of the iris family, often seen growing beside streams.

flagon a large bottle, often with handle, spout and lid.

flagon   flange

flagrant easily noticed, e.g. a *flagrant* piece of bad driving (i.e. anyone could see that the car was being badly driven).

flake a small, flat piece, e.g. of paint off a wall; ■ a snow*flake*.

flaky *Flaky* things (pastry, for example) easily break into flakes.

flame A candle burns with a yellow *flame*.

flaming blazing.

flange Train wheels have a *flange* on the inside edge, which keeps them on the rails.

flank the side (of an animal, an army, a mountain, etc.).

flannel soft woollen material; 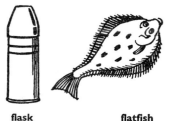 a piece of material with which people wash themselves.

flap a broad strip fastened along one edge; ■ to move up and down like wings.

flare a light used as a signal or a marker by aircraft, ships, etc. ■ To *flare* up is to burst suddenly into flame or temper.

flash A *flash* of light lasts only an instant.

flask a narrow-necked bottle, e.g. a vacuum *flask* for keeping liquids hot (or cold).

flask   flatfish

flat a set of living rooms on one floor of a building; ■ a *flat* surface is level. ■ Singing is *flat* when the notes are too low.

flatfish fish like plaice and sole, which are flat and have both their eyes on the top side.

flatten to make flat.

flatter To *flatter* someone is to give him more praise than he deserves.

flattery praise that is not really meant.

flaunt to show off.

flavour the special taste of a food, e.g. the *flavour* of meat, cheese, etc. ■ To *flavour* something is to add flavouring.

flavouring a substance which gives a special flavour to food (e.g. salt, vanilla, almond, etc.).

flaw A *flaw* in a piece of metal, etc., is a crack or a weak spot of any kind.

flax The *flax* plant produces linseed, and linen is made from its stem.

flaxen *Flaxen* hair is yellowish in colour.

flay to peel off the skin; ■ to whip or beat someone so that his skin is stripped off.

flea a small jumping insect which bites people or animals. ■ A *flea*-bite is a small, unimportant matter.

fled ran away.

fledgeling a young bird.

flee to run away.

fleece the mass of wool which covers a sheep. ■ To *fleece* someone is to strip him of his money.

fleecy like a fleece.

fleet a group of ships, aircraft, taxis, etc., under one person's control; ■ swift.

fleeting passing rapidly away, quick, e.g. a *fleeting* glance.

flesh Our arms and legs consist of bones covered with *flesh*.

flew The bird *flew* up into a tree. The aircraft *flew* from London to Paris.

flex flexible insulated wire connected to electric table lamps, etc.

flexible Wire, etc., is *flexible* if it will easily bend about without breaking.

flick a light, quick blow with a whip, duster, etc., or with the fingernail.

flicker A flame is said to *flicker* when it waves to and fro or burns unsteadily.

flickering A *flickering* light (or flame) is one that shines unsteadily.

flier a bird, airman, etc., that flies; ■ a fast train, coach, etc. (also spelt *flyer*).

flies flying insects that spread disease. ■ The bird walks slowly but *flies* very quickly.

flight a journey by aircraft; ■ the action of flying; ■ a set of stairs or hurdles; ■ running away.

flighty A *flighty* person is one whose likes and dislikes keep changing.

flimsy weak, e.g. a *flimsy* structure, a *flimsy* excuse.

flinch to draw back. The heavy blow caused the boxer to *flinch*.

fling to throw. ■ A Highland *fling* is a lively Scottish dance. ■ To have your *fling* is to have a spell of doing just what you like.

flint a hard, grey, shiny stone, often white on the surface.

flippant A *flippant* remark is one that makes light of a serious subject.

flirt to make love insincerely, just for the fun of it.

flit to move (to another house); ■ to fly about lightly.

float Wood will *float* on the surface of water, but stone sinks to the bottom. ■ A cork, etc., put on a fishing line to show when a fish is at the bait is called a *float*.

flock The shepherd had charge of a *flock* of sheep.

floe (pron. flo) a sheet of floating ice.

flog to beat with a stick, whip, etc.; ■ (slang) to sell.

flogging a beating, a whipping; ■ beating, whipping; ■ (slang) selling.

flood During the *flood*, farms and streets were covered with water. ■ Rice farmers *flood* their fields with water.

flooding The river overflowed, *flooding* the surrounding countryside.

floor We'll cover that *floor* with a carpet, or lino.

flop to sit or drop carelessly; ■ a failure, e.g. The concert was a *flop*.

floral *Floral* decorations, patterns, etc. are made up of flowers.

florin The former British silver coin worth two shillings, and now called a 10p piece; ■ a silver or gold coin.

florist someone whose work is with flowers.

flounce to jerk the body about in order to show displeasure, etc.

flounder to struggle; ■ a small flat-fish.

flour We make *flour* by grinding corn.

flourish to do well, to prosper. ■ To *flourish* a sword, etc., is to wave it about.

flourishing doing well, prospering, e.g. a *flourishing* business.

flow The rivers *flow* into the sea.

flower My favourite *flower* is the rose. ■ To *flower* is to bear flowers.

flowering A plant is *flowering* when the flowers growing on it are open.

flowing The river was *flowing* under the bridge.

flown The nest was empty, for the birds had *flown* away.

flu (short for) influenza, an illness causing pains in the limbs, running nose, etc.

flue a pipe, etc., which carries smoke or fumes from a fire.

fluent A *fluent* speaker is one whose words flow smoothly because he knows just what to say and how to say it.

fluff little bits of light, woolly stuff from blankets, etc.

fluid a liquid or gas, e.g. Water and air are *fluids*.

fluke a lucky, accidental stroke, e.g. when a ball you do not see hits your bat and goes away to the boundary.

flung thrown carelessly or violently.

flurried worried and confused, e.g. Grandma was so *flurried* when visitors arrived unexpectedly that she did not know what to do.

flurry to worry and confuse. ■ A *flurry* of snow is a very short snowfall.

flush To *flush* a drain, etc., is to clean it out with a flow of water. ■ to blush, i.e. to go red in the face.

fluster To *fluster* someone is to cause him to become nervous and confused.

flute a musical wind instrument, held across the face when being played.

flute

flutter to wave to and fro like a flag in a breeze; ■ (of birds, moths, etc.) to flap wings without flying anywhere.

fluttered The flag *fluttered* in the breeze. ■ The moths *fluttered* round the light (i.e. flapped their wings without flying).

fly a flying insect which spreads disease; ■ to travel through the air with wings or in an aircraft.

flyer a bird, airman, etc., that flies; ■ a fast train, coach, etc. (also spelt *flier*).

flying An aircraft is *flying* overhead. The birds are *flying* to their nests.

foal a young horse or donkey.

foam the mass of tiny bubbles that form on a liquid, e.g. on sea water when waves break.

focus to adjust a camera, binoculars, etc., so as to get a clear picture.

fodder dried food provided for cattle in sheds, e.g. hay.

foe an enemy.

fog thick mist, e.g. The *fog* was so thick that we could see only a few yards ahead.

fogey, fogy an old-fashioned old man.

foggy A *foggy* day is one when there is fog (i.e. thick mist).

foil to outwit, e.g. To *foil* the robbers we put a dummy package in the safe. ■ paper-thin metal used as wrapping for chocolate, etc.

foist To *foist* something on to someone is to get him to have it against his will.

fold To *fold* a piece of paper, etc., is to double it over. ■ an enclosure for sheep.

folder a cover of thin cardboard in which to keep loose papers.

foliage leaves (of plants).

folk people.

folksong a song by no known composer, which has been passed down through generations of people by word of mouth.

follow to understand an explanation. ■ To *follow* someone is to walk behind him, or to come after him.

followed The dog *followed* at the heels of his master.

follower a supporter or admirer.

folly foolishness.

fond To be *fond* of someone, or something, is to like him or it very much.

fondle to stroke lovingly.

fondness liking or affection. Jane has such a *fondness* for sweets; she spends all her pocket money on them.

font a structure at the west end of a church, which contains the basin in which the water for baptism is placed.

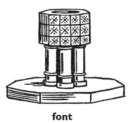

font

food The *food* we eat most often is bread.

fool a stupid person.

foolhardy A *foolhardy* person is one who foolishly takes unnecessary risks.

foolish silly, stupid.

foolproof so simple or so carefully worked out that even a fool could manage it.

foolscap paper which is about 13 in. wide by 17 in. long.

foot You have five toes on your *foot*. ■ 12 inches = 1 *foot*.

football a game in which a large ball is kicked (soccer); ■ a game in which a large oval ball is kicked and thrown (Rugby football); ■ the ball used in soccer or Rugby football.

foothold a place where the foot can get a firm support, e.g. when climbing.

footpath a path suitable only for people on foot.

footprint the mark left by a foot, e.g. in the snow.

footstep the sound of a foot on the ground.

footwear boots, shoes, slippers, etc.

forage to search about; ■ food for horses and cattle.

forbid 'I *forbid* you to do this' means that I order you not to do it.

forbidden If you have been *forbidden* to do something, you have been ordered not to do it.

force To *force* someone to do something is to make him do it, although he doesn't want to. ■ strength, power.

forced I did not want to be here, but Jim *forced* me to come.

forcible done by force.

ford At the *ford* the river is shallow enough for us to walk across.

fore at the front, e.g. the *fore* part of a ship.

forearm the part of the arm between the elbow and wrist.

forecast To *forecast* the weather is to say in advance what the weather is expected to be. ■ A weather *forecast* is a statement of what the weather is expected to be.

forefather grandfather, great-grandfather, etc.

forefinger the finger next to the thumb.

foregone A *foregone* conclusion is something about which you have made up your mind in advance.

forehead the part of the face which is above the eyebrows.

foreign having to do with countries other than your own, e.g. *foreign* language, *foreign* coin.

foreman a workman whose job is to tell other workmen what to do.

foremost first or most important.

forest a large area of trees and undergrowth.

forestall You *forestall* someone when you get in before him and do something that he had intended to do.

foretell The fortune-teller says he can *foretell* the future.

forfeit something paid as a penalty – especially in party games; ■ paid as a penalty, e.g. His life was *forfeit*.

forgave The boy said he was sorry, so we *forgave* him (i.e. let him off).

forge The blacksmith worked at his *forge*, heating the iron and hammering it into shape. ■ To *forge* someone's signature is to imitate it.

forger someone who copies papers, etc., dishonestly.

forgery the crime committed by forgers.

forget People who have bad memories *forget* things.

forgetful likely to forget things.

forgive If you are sorry for your mistake I will *forgive* you (i.e. let you off).

forgiveness pardon.

forgotten If something you used to know has gone from your mind, you have *forgotten* it.

fork We eat food with a knife and *fork*. ■ Dad digs the garden with a *fork*. ■ the place where two roads or branches (of a tree) meet.

table fork   garden fork

forlorn A *forlorn* hope is an idea that is pretty sure to fail. ■ sad and lonely.

form a long seat without a back; ■ a class in school; ■ a paper to be filled in. ■ To *form* something is to shape it or make it.

formal following the custom, e.g. Anything *formal* is done because it is necessary or proper, and not out of friendliness, e.g. a *formal* visit, a *formal* letter.

formality something that has to be done, even though it seems to be unnecessary.

formation forming, e.g. The heater prevents the *formation* of mist on the car windows.

former past, e.g. Mr. Greene is a *former* headmaster of the school. ■ first-mentioned, e.g. Jones and Smith are old boys; the *former* was school captain.

formidable difficult to overcome and rather frightening.

formula a set of symbols used in algebra, science, etc., e.g. πr^2 (the *formula* for the area of a circle), or H_2O (the *formula* for water).

forsake to give up, to desert, e.g. Never *forsake* a friend when he is in trouble.

forsaken given up, deserted, e.g. Why have you *forsaken* your old friend?

forsook gave up, deserted, e.g. 'They *forsook* him and fled' means they ran away and left him.

fort a strong building for defence against enemies.

forth To go *forth* is to go forward.

fortieth (40th) On your *fortieth* birthday you have lived 40 years. ■ ($\frac{1}{40}$) one divided by forty.

fortifications walls, banks of earth, towers, etc., which made a place strong (to resist attack).

fortify to make strong.

fortress a military stronghold; especially a town with fortifications and containing soldiers.

fortunate We were *fortunate* in having a fine day for our sports.

fortunately *Fortunately* it was a fine day for our garden party.

fortune My uncle died and left us a *fortune* of £500,000. ■ I had the good *fortune* to have a kind and happy mother.

forty (40) four tens.

forward, forwards Jean swung backwards and *forwards* on the swing. We walked *forward* to greet our friends.

fossil the hardened remains of an ancient plant or animal, found in the earth.

foster As Betty's parents were dead, she was brought up by a *foster*-mother.

fought The knights drew their swords and *fought* till one of them was killed.

foul unfair, e.g. a *foul*, ■ or *foul* throw, in football; ■ filthy, disgusting, e.g. *foul* language.

found I have *found* the book that I lost; here it is.

foundation the strong base on which a thing is built, e.g. the concrete *foundation* of a house.

founded That school was *founded* (i.e. started) many years ago.

foundry a factory where metal is melted and put into moulds to make such things as cast-iron pipes.

fountain The jets of water squirting up from the *fountain* look very pretty.

fountain

four (4) You have *four* fingers and a thumb on each hand.

fourteen (14) ten and four.

fourteenth (14th) On your *fourteenth* birthday you have lived 14 years. ■ ($\frac{1}{14}$) one divided by fourteen.

fourth (4th) On your *fourth* birthday you had lived four years. ■ ($\frac{1}{4}$) a quarter; one divided by four.

fowl a bird, especially a chicken (cock or hen).

foxglove a plant with lots of purple or white flowers on a tall stem.

foxglove

fraction a part; especially a vulgar *fraction*, e.g. $\frac{1}{4}$, $\frac{2}{5}$, etc., or a decimal *fraction*, e.g. ·6, ·75, etc.

fracture a break, especially a break in a bone. ■ To *fracture* a bone (or anything else) is to break it.

fragile easily broken.

fragment a piece that has been broken off something.

fragrance pleasantness of smell, e.g. the *fragrance* of a rose.

fragrant A *fragrant* flower is one that has a pleasant smell.

frail weak and feeble.

frame We put the picture in a wooden *frame* and hung it on the wall.

framework The building started with a steel *framework* which was later filled in with bricks and concrete.

franc the unit of French money; 1 *franc* = 100 centimes.

France a large country in the west of Europe.

frank To be *frank* is to say what you really think.

frankly To speak *frankly* is to be completely honest and hide nothing.

frantic mad with pain, anger, etc.; ■ wildly excited, e.g. Jim became *frantic* as the boat sailed away leaving him alone on the island.

fraud a dishonest trick.

fray That watch-strap will *fray* your shirt-cuff (i.e. rub it and make it ragged). ■ a noisy quarrel or fight.

frayed ragged at the edges.

freak A *freak* (of nature) is a creature that is wrongly formed in some way, e.g. a sheep with six legs.

freckles light brown spots on the skin.

free You do not have to pay for these books; they are *free*. ■ To *free* a prisoner is to let him go. ■ During the holiday we are *free* to do as we like.

freedom being free.

freely without hindrance, without payment.

freeze If you *freeze* water it becomes ice.

freight cargo carried by an aircraft, etc. (apart from passengers).

French The *French* are the people of France, ■ and *French* is the language they speak. ■ *French* things are things from or of France. ■ *French* leave is leave taken without permission.

frenzy To be in a *frenzy* is to be mad with fury or excitement.

frequency the number of times per second that something happens – or the number of times per minute, hour, etc.

frequent (pron. fré-quent) 'He pays *frequent* visits to our house' means that he comes often. ■ (pron. fre-quént) 'He *frequents* our house' means he is often there.

frequently often.

fresh *Fresh* eggs, fruit, etc., have been recently laid, gathered, etc. ■ *Fresh* air is clean, cool air.

freshen to make fresh or clean.

fret to worry; especially to worry about something you regret.

friar a kind of wandering monk who lived by begging.

'fridge, 'frig, 'frige (short for) refrigerator. We keep food cool and make ice cubes in the *'fridge*.

fried Fish and chips are *fried* in boiling fat.

friend someone you like and know well and who likes you.

friendly behaving like a friend.

friendship Our *friendship* has lasted for years (i.e. we have been friends for years).

frigate one of the larger warships.

fright a sudden feeling of fear.

frighten To *frighten* someone is to make him afraid.

frightened We *frightened* the birds away by waving and clapping our hands.

frightful A *frightful* noise, sight, etc., is one that makes you feel afraid.

frigid cold.

frill a decoration; ■ a strip of material gathered into folds at one edge.

friar   frigate

frill   fringe

friction Oil is put in machinery to reduce the *friction* (i.e. so that the parts move on each other more easily). ■ If there is *friction* between people they do not get on well together.

Friday the sixth day of the week.

fringe the edge; especially an edge consisting of threads of material left loose or short hair hanging straight down the forehead.

frisky An animal (or person) that is *frisky* jumps about in a lively manner.

fritter a slice of fruit, meat, etc., covered with batter, and fried. ■ To *fritter* away time, etc., is to waste it.

frivolous unimportant, silly, e.g. Don't waste my time by asking *frivolous* questions.

fro backwards. To and *fro* means forwards and backwards.

frock Jill has a new blue *frock* to wear at the party.

frog a small, jumping animal that lives in water and on land.

frog

frolic to play in a gay and lively way.

frolicsome playful.

from The aircraft flew *from* London to Paris.

front There are white lights on the *front* of a car and red lights on the back.

frontier the part of a country that is next to another country.

frost There is a *frost* when the temperature is below freezing point.

frostbite sore places caused by frost.

froth the mass of little bubbles formed on some liquids when they are shaken up or stirred.

frown to show displeasure by wrinkling the brows, etc.; ■ a look of displeasure.

froze turned into ice.

frozen Ice is *frozen* water.

fruit I like all *fruit*, especially apples and oranges. ■ To *fruit* is to bear fruit.

fruiterer We buy fruit from a *fruiterer*.

fruitful A *fruitful* tree, bush, etc., is one that bears lots of fruit.

frump a woman whose clothes are old-fashioned and shabby.

frustrated To feel *frustrated* is to feel that you are being prevented from achieving something.

fry to cook in boiling fat, usually in a frying-pan.

fuel a substance used for burning, e.g. coal or oil.

fugitive someone who is running away.

fulfil To *fulfil* a prophecy is to cause the events that were foretold to happen. ■ To *fulfil* conditions, etc., is to satisfy them. To *fulfil* duties is to carry them out (i.e. do them).

fulfilled Jane was the only one who *fulfilled* all the conditions; she was of the required age, height and colour.

full A container (jug, box, etc.) that is *full* will not hold any more.

full stop the dot (.) which must be put at the end of every sentence.

fully completely.

fumble to use your hands uncertainly as when they are frozen, or when you are feeling for something in the dark.

fumes The *fumes* from car engines come out of the exhaust pipe at the back of the car.

fumigate to use fumes (e.g. from burning chemicals) to kill the germs in a room, in clothes, etc.

fuming giving off fumes; ■ angry.

function The school prize-giving is an important *function*. ■ That machine does not *function* (i.e. it doesn't work).

fund money put aside for a special purpose, e.g. The swimming-pool *fund* is the money collected for a new swimming pool.

funeral The coffin was taken into church for the *funeral* service.

fungus a plant such as a mushroom, a toadstool, or mould.

funnel a tube, wide at one end, used when pouring liquids through narrow holes; ■ a ship's chimney.

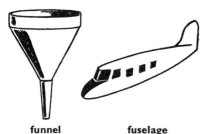

funnel   fuselage

funny A *funny* story makes you laugh.

fur Cats are covered with soft *fur*.

furious very angry indeed.

furl to roll up (a sail or an umbrella).

furlong an eighth ($\frac{1}{8}$) of a mile; 220 yards.

furnace a special enclosed fire-place (for melting metal, for heating water for the radiators in a building, etc.).

furnish To *furnish* a room is to provide it with furniture.

furnished provided with furniture.

furniture chairs, tables and other such things that are necessary in a house.

furrow the narrow trench made by a plough.

furry A *furry* coat, etc., is one that is made of fur, or has fur on it.

further 'Further away' means 'at a greater distance'.

furthest farthest. The boy *furthest* from you is the one who is the greatest distance away.

furtive sly, secret. A person has a *furtive* manner when he seems to be trying to escape notice.

fury violent anger.

fuse When too much electricity is used, a special little piece of wire, called a *fuse*, melts and so cuts off the supply. ■ the part of a bomb, mine, etc., which causes it to explode.

fuselage the body of an aircraft.

fuss To *fuss*, ■ or to make a *fuss*, is to make a great ado about something unimportant.

fussy A *fussy* person is one who makes a great ado about unimportant things.

futile A *futile* struggle, argument, etc., is one that is useless or has no effect.

future that which is yet to come, e.g. Do not worry about the *future*. ■ Christians look forward to a *future* life.

gabble to talk too quickly.

gaberdine a fine, tough cloth (also spelt *gabardine* – especially when it means a gabardine macintosh).

gable the triangular end of a roof.

gable   galleon

gadget a small mechanical device, e.g. Mother has a new *gadget* for opening tins.

gaiety being gay.

gaily merrily, happily.

gain If you buy something for £20 and sell it for £23, you *gain* £3, ■ or you make a *gain* of £3.

gait The sailor has a rolling *gait* (i.e. way of walking).

gala People come to our school swimming *gala* to watch the swimming and diving competitions.

galaxy one of many vast systems of stars, planets, etc., in space. Our *galaxy* includes our earth, the sun, the planets and the stars, etc., of the Milky Way.

gale a strong wind.

gall a bitter substance which animals make in their livers.

gallant A *gallant* soldier is one who is brave and splendid. ■ A

gentleman may be described as *gallant* if he makes a point of being very courteous to ladies.

galleon a large and grand old-time Spanish sailing ship.

gallery In a theatre, the *gallery* is the floor nearest to the roof. ■ An art *gallery* is a building or room where pictures are on show.

galley a ship's kitchen; ■ an old-time ship driven by oars and sails.

galling annoying and humiliating, e.g. It is *galling* to have to pay to get back something stolen from you.

gallon 1 *gallon* = 8 pints, or about 4½ litres.

gallop We saw the horse *gallop* away as fast as he could go.

gallows an Γ-shaped structure on which people were hanged.

galore In the pond there were fish *galore* (i.e. enormous numbers of fish).

gamble to play games for money; ■ to bet; ■ to take risks.

gambling We knew the card players were *gambling*, for we could see the piles of money on the table.

gambol to leap about in a lively manner, e.g. like a lamb.

gambolling leaping about in a lively manner, e.g. We love to watch the lambs *gambolling* in the field.

game birds and animals that are hunted for sport – pheasants, grouse, etc. ■ Football is the boys' favourite *game*.

gander a male goose.

gang A *gang* of workmen were digging a hole in the road. A *gang* of criminals raided the bank.

gangster one of a gang of criminals.

gangway The passengers walked down the *gangway* from the ship to the shore. ■ There is a narrow *gangway* between the rows of chairs in a theatre, etc.

gaol (pron., and also spelt, *jail*) prison.

gaoler (pron., and also spelt *jail-er*) a man who has charge of prisoners in a gaol.

gap The dog scrambled through a *gap* in the fence.

gape to stare open-mouthed at something.

garage a building in which a car is stored; ■ a place where cars are repaired.

garden We grow flowers in the *garden* in front of our house, and fruit and vegetables in the *garden* at the back.

gargle You *gargle* by holding a small amount of liquid in your throat and breathing out through it. ■ A *gargle* is the special liquid with which you gargle.

garland The girl hung a *garland* of flowers round the hero's neck.

garland

gauntlet

garlic an onion-like plant.

garment an article of clothing.

garnish to decorate (food, usually).

garrison the soldiers provided to defend a fortress, town, etc.

garter an elastic band for holding up a stocking.

gas Air is a *gas* consisting of a mixture of other *gases*, such as oxygen, nitrogen and carbon dioxide. The *gas* burnt in ■ *gas* cookers and *gas* fires is coal gas.

gash The knife slashed Brian's leg and made a long, deep *gash*.

gasp The runner was completely exhausted and had to *gasp* for breath.

gastric having to do with the stomach, e.g. *gastric* juices.

gate If you leave the *gate* open, the cows may stray out of the field.

gateway I couldn't shut the gate because a cow was standing in the *gateway*.

gather We will *gather* a basketful of fruit from the bushes.

gathering picking (flowers, etc.); ■ a collection of people; ■ a swelling on the body, containing poisonous matter.

gaudy (pron. gor-dy) unsuitably gay and showy, over-decorated.

gauge (pron. gage) an instrument for measuring, e.g. a rain *gauge*.

gaunt thin and grim-looking (man).

gauntlet a glove with a wide wrist; ■ a knight's armoured glove.

gauze (pron. gorz) a thin material used to cover wounds, etc. ■ Wire *gauze* is made by weaving wire into sheets.

gave Uncle *gave* me a present.

gay very cheerful.

gaze to look hard for some time; ■ a steady look.

gazelle a small, elegant, deer-like animal.

gazelle   gem

gazetteer a dictionary of names of countries, towns, rivers, mountains, etc.

gear equipment, e.g. We put our camping *gear* in the truck. ■ You change *gear* in a car when you want to climb a steep hill.

gelatin, gelatine a substance obtained by boiling animal skins, bones, etc., and used in making jellies.

gem a precious stone, such as a diamond or emerald.

gender Feminine *gender* is the *gender* of girls, women, hens, cows, etc. (all called 'she'). Masculine *gender* is the *gender* of boys, men, cocks, bulls, etc. (all called 'he'). Neuter *gender* is the *gender* of things, books, houses, etc. (all called 'it').

general including all, e.g. The *general* weather forecast includes all regions. ■ An army is commanded by a *general*.

generally usually.

generate to produce, e.g. A dynamo is used to *generate* electricity.

generation production, e.g. the *generation* of electricity. ■ My *generation* is all the people born

about the same year as myself. My father's *generation* is all the people born at about the same time as my father.

generator an apparatus that generates electricity (or steam).

generosity Uncle is well known for his *generosity* (i.e. his freeness in giving away money, or ■ his readiness to forgive people who offend him).

generous A *generous* person is one who freely gives away money, or ■ who is always ready to forgive people who have offended him.

genial kind and good-natured.

genius great cleverness; ■ an exceptionally clever person.

genteel outstandingly polite and good mannered; ■ belonging to the upper class (i.e. the nobility, the well-born.).

gentle light and soft, e.g. a *gentle* touch, *gentle* rain.

gentleman Mr. Smith is the *gentleman* who lives next door to us.

gentlemen The two *gentlemen* we met were Mr. Smith and Mr. Brown.

gentleness The nurse handled the baby with such *gentleness* that it didn't even wake.

gently Handle that vase *gently* for it will easily break.

genuine real, not imitation.

geographical having to do with geography.

geography In *geography* lessons we learn about countries and the people in them.

geology the study of rocks and other such materials that make up the earth's crust.

geometrical having to do with geometry, e.g. Compasses, set squares, etc., are *geometrical* instruments.

geometry the study of lines and the shapes and angles they make.

geranium a house or garden plant with showy red or white flowers and perfumed leaves.

geranium geyser

germ a very tiny living thing that causes diseases.

German the language spoken by Germans. ■ *German* things are things from Germany.

Germans the people of Germany.

Germany a big country in the centre of Europe.

germinate Put the seed in warm, moist soil and it will *germinate* (i.e. start to grow).

gesticulate to make movements with the hands and arms (or to make other such signs) which have a meaning.

gesture (pron. jést-ure) a movement of the hand, arm, etc., which has a meaning, e.g. shrugging the shoulders to mean, 'How do I know?'

get Please *get* me a book from the library. ■ I shall *get* into trouble.

getting Tom is *getting* me a book from the library. ■ I am *getting* tired of waiting.

geyser a device, usually worked by gas, for heating water in a kitchen or bathroom; ■ a spring from which hot water is sent up into the air.

ghastly horrible.

ghost It is said that the *ghost* of the dead queen is to be seen walking along the haunted gallery.

ghostly ghost-like.

giant an imaginary, man-like creature of enormous size; ■ a very big man, machine, etc., e.g. a *giant* rocket.

giddiness dizziness; the unsteady feeling you have after spinning round and round.

giddy dizzy. If you spin round and round many times, you feel *giddy* and unable to stand.

gift a present, something given.

gifted A *gifted* person is one who is unusually clever at something.

gigantic very big indeed.

giggle a silly little laugh; ■ to make a silly little laugh.

gild to cover with a very thin layer of gold.

gill (pron. jill) a quarter of a pint (4 *gills* = 1 pint); ■ (pron. gill) the opening behind a fish's head through which it breathes.

gilt covered thinly with gold, e.g. a *gilt*-edged book. To take the *gilt* off the gingerbread is to make something seem less attractive.

gimlet a small, T-shaped tool for boring holes.

gin a strong, colourless drink, made from grain. If people drink much *gin* they become drunk.

ginger a brown root with a hot and spicy taste, used to flavour cakes, etc.

gingerbread cake flavoured with ginger.

gingerly with extreme care, e.g. We must walk *gingerly* over this thin ice.

gipsy a member of a tribe who live in caravans and wander around in many European countries (also spelt *gypsy*).

giraffe an African animal with a very long neck.

giraffe   gimlet

girder A great steel *girder* goes across from one wall to the other to support the roof.

girdle a band, belt, cord, etc., which is worn round the waist.

girl Mary is the prettiest *girl* in the class.

give I will *give* you a birthday present.

giving Mother is *giving* the baby his breakfast.

glacier Thick layers of snow on a mountain become compressed into a mass of ice called a *glacier*, which moves slowly down the slope.

glad pleased.

glade an open space in a wood or forest.

gladiator a man whose job was to fight with weapons to entertain the people of ancient Rome.

gladly with pleasure.

gladness pleasure, joy.

glamorous charming and very beautiful.

glamour charm and beauty.

glance a quick look. ■ To *glance* is to take a quick look. ■ An arrow would *glance* off a knight's armour (i.e. without going into it).

gland There are *glands* in various parts of the body (e.g. the neck), which make special juices needed by the body. If you are ill, certain *glands* may swell up into lumps.

glare We could see nothing because of the *glare* of the car's lights. ■ To *glare* at someone is to stare at him angrily.

glaring staring with hate or anger. ■ A *glaring* mistake, etc., is one that anyone would notice.

glass There is *glass* in windows. ■ Please give me a *glass* of water to drink.

glasses I drank several *glasses* of water. ■ John wears *glasses* to improve his eyesight.

glassware things made of glass – dishes, glasses, vases, etc.

gleam a small, or brief light.

glee delight.

glen a narrow valley (in Scotland).

glib A *glib* story is one told confidently and without hesitation.

glide to go smoothly.

glider an aircraft without engines.

glimmer A *glimmer* of light is a faint light, seen only for a moment.

glimpse To have a *glimpse* of something is to see it only for an instant.

glint to flash or sparkle; ■ a flash or sparkle.

glisten, glitter to sparkle, e.g. The diamonds *glisten* (*glitter*) under the light.

glittering sparkling.

gloat A miser will *gloat* over his money (i.e. gaze at it greedily). ■ A man may *gloat* over his enemy's misfortunes (i.e. think about them with pleasure).

globe a ball-shaped map of the earth; ■ anything shaped like a ball.

    globe   glow-worm

gloom darkness, sadness.

gloomy Sylvia is feeling *gloomy*, so go and cheer her up. ■ It is so *gloomy* in the cave that you will need to take a light.

glorify to praise in a grand manner.

glorious magnificent, grand and splendid, e.g. a *glorious* sunset.

glory honour and praise, e.g. *Glory* to God. ■ To *glory* in something is to take a delight in it.

gloss To put a *gloss* on anything is to make it shiny.

glossy shiny.

gloves I wear *gloves* to keep my hands warm.

glow The flames of the fire have died down, but the ashes still *glow* (i.e. give out warmth and a dull light).

glower to look angrily, to scowl.

glowing The flames had died away, but warmth and a dull light still came from the *glowing* ashes.

glow-worm a beetle which shines at night with a pale, green light.

glucose a kind of sugar.

glue Stick the broken pieces together with *glue*. ■ *Glue* the broken pieces together.

glum gloomy, miserable.

glut Farmers had such a *glut* of apples last year that they didn't know how to get rid of them all.

glutton someone who eats too much.

gnarled (pron. narled) rough and twisted, like an old tree-trunk or an old man's crippled hands.

gnash (pron. nash) To *gnash* your teeth is to grind them together (in anger, etc.).

gnat (pron. nat) a small, flying insect, which sucks your blood, leaving an itchy spot.

gnaw (pron. naw) To *gnaw* an apple, etc., is to eat it with lots of small bites, as a dog *gnaws* a bone.

gnome (pron. nome) a fairy dwarf, especially one living in the ground.

gnu (pron. nu) an African deer-like animal.

goal the aim; the purpose for which you do something; the place you are trying to get to, e.g.

The *goal* of the space-men was Venus. ■ Johnny scored a *goal* in the football match.

goat a sheep-like animal, with horns, but covered with hair, not wool.

goat   goblet

gobble to eat quickly and noisily; ■ to make a noise like a turkey.

goblet a wine-glass shaped like a small bowl on a stem; ■ (in olden days) a metal or glass drinking-vessel.

goblin an impish fairy – usually ugly.

goddess The Greeks worshipped the *goddess* Diana.

goggles Racing drivers, etc., wear *goggles* over their eyes to protect them.

gold A *gold* ring is very valuable and never loses its bright, yellow-ish colour.

golden made of gold; ■ gold-coloured.

goldsmith a man who makes things from gold.

golf In the game of *golf*, a player hits a little white ball into a series of holes in the ground, with long-handled clubs.

gone Mother has *gone* to London.

gong a metal disc, hit with a drumstick, etc., to make a noise in music, or for calling people to dinner, etc.

good One apple is bad; the rest are *good*. ■ Susan does not mis-behave; she is a *good* girl.

goodbye I must go now. *Good-bye* (shortened from 'God be with you').

goodness Thank you for your *goodness* to me when I was ill. ■ My *goodness* ! (no special meaning, just an expression of surprise.)

goods Traders buy and sell *goods* of all kinds. ■ A *goods* train carries all kinds of things, but no passen-gers.

goose In appearance, a *goose* is halfway between a duck and a swan. ■ a good-humoured name for a silly person.

gooseberry a small, round, hairy fruit, which grows on a prickly bush.

gorge to eat greedily; ■ a narrow pass between hills.

gorgeous very beautiful, especi-ally beautifully coloured.

gorilla a large, fierce monkey, with some likeness to a man.

gong   gorilla

gorse a prickly bush with yellow flowers, which grows wild on commons and heaths.

gosling a young goose.

gospel St. John's *Gospel* is one of four *gospels* in the Bible, all of which are about the life of Christ.

gossip to chatter just for amusement; ■ a person who chatters idly.

gouge a tool for scooping out grooves in wood.

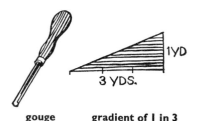

gouge　　　**gradient of I in 3**

govern To *govern* a country (or school, etc.) is to conduct its affairs, i.e. to be in command of it.

government The *Government* consists of the Prime Minister and the other ministers who together govern the country.

governor someone who governs.

gown a grand dress for a lady; ■ a special garment, like a thin, black cloak, worn by some teachers, lawyers, etc.

grab To *grab* something is to take hold of it suddenly.

grabbed The thief suddenly *grabbed* the bag and dashed off with it.

grace a prayer said at meals; ■ time allowed for paying a debt, etc., e.g. 3 days' *grace*; ■ charm in movement and manner.

graceful A *graceful* lady is one who is charming in her movements and manner. ■ A *graceful* spire (or other structure) is one that is slender and beautiful.

gracious kind and charming.

grade to sort out into groups according to size, quality, etc., e.g. to *grade* eggs; ■ The music exam. has eight grades; I've passed *Grade* 1, the easiest.

gradient The *gradient* of a hill is said to be 1 in 3 if you get 1 metre higher for every 3 horizontal metres.

gradual A *gradual* change, etc., is one that happens slowly, a little at a time.

gradually In summer-time the sea water becomes warmer *gradually*, not suddenly.

graft A gardener can *graft* a twig from one tree on to another tree so that it grows there.

grain The best-known *grains* are wheat, barley, oats, rye and maize. ■ The *grain* in wood is the pattern of markings which have grown in it.

grammar Sally hopes to go to a *Grammar* School when she is eleven. ■ In *grammar* lessons we learn about words and how to use them correctly.

gramme a very small weight. 1,000 gm = 1 kg.

gramophone record-player.

granary a place in which grain is stored.

grand splendid and important.

grandchild You are your grandfathers' (and grandmothers') *grandchild*.

grandchildren My grandad has many *grandchildren*, including my brothers and sisters and me.

grandad, grand-dad, grand-father the father of either of your parents.

grandma, grandmother the mother of either of your parents.

grandparent a parent's parent (i.e. a grandfather or a grandmother).

granite hard, speckled, grey stone, used for kerb-stones and for building.

granny grandmother; ■ a reef knot tied wrongly.

grant To *grant* a request is to agree to what is requested.

granulated *Granulated* sugar, etc., is in small particles, but it is not as fine as a powder.

grape the fruit of a vine, from which wine is made.

grapefruit A *grapefruit* is like a large, bitter orange.

graph a line drawn on squared paper to show how one thing varies in relation to another (e.g. how temperature varies from day to day).

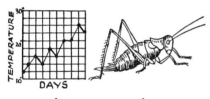

graph   grasshopper

grapple to grip.

grasp to hold firmly; ■ to understand.

grass Cows were feeding on the *grass* growing in the field.

grasshopper a long, jumping insect which makes a chirping noise with its legs.

grate an iron or brick container for a room fire. ■ You *grate* cheese into small pieces by rubbing it on a rough surface.

grateful People who are *grateful* can show it by saying, 'Thank you.'

gratefully thankfully.

gratify to please or to satisfy.

grating *Grating* anything (cheese, carrot, etc.) is rubbing it into small pieces on a rough surface; ■ a set of metal or wooden bars, parallel or crossed.

gratitude thankfulness.

grave serious, e.g. We knew by his *grave* face that he was not amused. ■ a hole dug for the burial of a dead body.

gravel large sand particles and small pebbles.

gravely seriously, e.g. Tom was *gravely* ill.

gravity seriousness; ■ the force that pulls things towards the earth.

gravy the juice that comes from cooking meat, or a similar liquid made to pour over meat and vegetables.

gray (usually spelt *grey* - except in U.S.A.) a colour between black and white.

graze to eat grass from a field, as cows, sheep, etc., do; ■ to touch in passing; ■ to scrape off skin with a glancing blow.

grease a thick, oily substance, especially that used to lubricate cars, etc., or animal fats such as lard and dripping. ■ (pron. greez) to put grease on the moving parts of a car, etc.

greasy smeared with grease, e.g. a *greasy* pole, etc.

great big, important.

greatness bigness, importance.

Grecian Greek (used chiefly to describe things connected with dress or art from Greece, e.g. *Grecian* vase).

Greece a country in the Mediterranean Sea between Italy and Turkey.

greed, greediness wanting more than is good for you.

greedy That *greedy* boy ate so many cakes that he was sick.

Greek the language spoken in Greece. ■ *Greek* things are things from or of Greece.

green the colour of grass, leaves, etc. ■ *Greens* are vegetables such as cabbages.

greengage a kind of plum which is greenish when ripe.

greengrocer We buy vegetables and fruit from a *greengrocer*.

greenhouse a glass-house in which plants are grown.

greet to welcome.

greetings words of welcome; ■ good wishes, e.g. Christmas greetings.

grew The little plant *grew* into a big tree.

grey a colour between black and white (sometimes spelt *gray* – especially in U.S.A.).

greyhound a big, fast, thin dog, bred for racing.

grief great sadness.

grievance To have a *grievance* is to feel that someone has given you cause for complaint.

grill To *grill* food is to cook it on a framework of bars, with heat from above. ■ A *grill* is an apparatus for grilling food. ■ food which has been grilled.

grim very serious or stern.

grime dirt which has gone deep into the skin.

grimly sternly.

grimy dirty.

grin showing the teeth in a rather forced smile; ■ to smile in a forced way.

grind to sharpen something, or to wear it down, by rubbing on rough stone. ■ To *grind* something to powder is to powder it by crushing. ■ an unpleasantly hard task.

grindstone a revolving stone wheel on which knives, etc., are sharpened.

grinning showing the teeth in a forced smile.

grip to hold firmly.

gripe to cause a sharp pain in the abdomen (i.e. a severe stomach-ache).

grisly terrifying.

gristle the tough, rubbery part of meat.

grit tiny particles of sand.

grizzly The *grizzly* bear is a very large and powerful North American animal.

groan the low sound made by a sick or injured person, or by someone who is irritated.

greyhound   grindstone

grocer From a *grocer* we buy the various things needed to run a house – tea, sugar, cheese, cleaning materials, etc.

groceries the goods sold by a grocer – tea, sugar, cheese, etc.

groin the part of the body between the abdomen and the thigh.

groom to brush and smarten up; ■ to care for a horse; ■ a man whose job is to attend to horses.

groove The glass front of a cupboard slides along in a *groove* cut into the wood.

grope to feel about with the hands like someone searching for something in the darkness.

gross 144; twelve dozens. ■ The *gross* weight of anything is the total weight, including wrappings, etc. ■ clear, glaring, e.g. *gross* carelessness.

grotto a pretty little cave.

ground Corn is *ground* into flour in a mill. ■ The apple fell to the *ground*. ■ *Grounds* are reasons, e.g. We had *grounds* for being angry.

groundless Our fears were *groundless* (i.e. there was no reason for them).

group a number of people or things together; ■ to arrange people or things in a group.

grouse a moorland bird, shot for sport; ■ (slang) to grumble.

grove a group of trees.

grovel to humble yourself before someone by lying face downwards; ■ to be very humble and apologetic.

grovelling being very humble and apologetic.

grow The boy will *grow* into a man. ■ The seed may *grow* if you plant it in soil.

growing The plant is *growing* (i.e. getting bigger) all the time. ■ If you water the seeds they may start *growing* (i.e. coming to life.)

growl The dog gave a low *growl* to show that he was displeased.

growling The dog was quietly *growling* to show his annoyance.

grown Billy has *grown* taller since we last saw him.

growth something that has grown; ■ an increase in size, e.g. These plants have made no *growth*.

grub larva, maggot. An insect's egg hatches into a *grub*, a caterpillar-like creature which later turns into the adult insect. ■ (slang) food.

grub

grubby dirty.

grudge To bear (or owe) someone a *grudge* is to wish him ill. ■ To *grudge* someone his success, etc., is to be envious of it.

grudgingly To give *grudgingly* is to give unwillingly.

gruel thin, watery soup.

gruelling very exhausting, e.g. a *gruelling* race.

gruesome terrible and horrifying, e.g. a *gruesome* sight.

gruff A *gruff* voice is one that is rough and unfriendly.

gruffly in a rough and unfriendly way, e.g. The man spoke *gruffly* to us.

F

grumble to complain, especially to complain quietly or at length.

grumbling complaining.

grumpy in a bad humour.

grunt the deep, gruff noise made by a pig; ■ to make a noise like a pig.

guarantee to promise, e.g. The makers *guarantee* that the watch is reliable. ■ a promise, e.g. With my new watch was a *guarantee* that it will keep good time.

guaranteed This garment is *guaranteed* fireproof (i.e. the makers promise that it is fireproof).

guard to protect, to keep from harm; ■ someone who protects; ■ the man in charge of a train.

guardian Derek has no parents; the man who looks after him is his *guardian*.

guess I do not know Mary's age, but I *guess* that she is 13.

guessed John didn't know Mary's age, but he *guessed* that she was 13.

guest In addition to the family, we have a *guest* staying at our house.

guffaw a loud burst of vulgar laughter.

guidance advice, help, e.g. We were glad of Father's *guidance*.

guide Without a *guide* to show them the way, the explorers would have been lost. ■ Stella is a Girl *Guide*.

guild a society which people (e.g. merchants) form in order to help each other.

guildhall a town hall; ■ a hall in which guilds met in the Middle Ages.

guillotine a machine for cutting off people's heads, made famous in the French Revolution; ■ a machine for cutting paper, cardboard, etc.

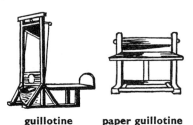

guillotine   paper guillotine

guilt The prisoner admitted his *guilt* (i.e. he admitted that he had committed the offence).

guilty Prisoners found *guilty* of a crime are punished; those who are innocent are set free.

guinea Old fashioned name for twenty-one shillings (originally a gold coin worth 21 shillings [£1·05]).

guitar a musical instrument with six strings, which the player plucks.

guitar   gull

gulf a partly enclosed sea, e.g. The *Gulf* of Mexico, The Persian *Gulf*.

gull a sea-bird, usually white and grey with long wings.

gullet the passage through which food passes from the mouth to the stomach.

gully a channel (e.g. gutter) for draining away water from a house; ■ a deep, narrow valley cut out by a stream.

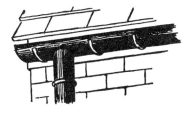

gutter

gulp With one *gulp*, the wolf swallowed the bird whole. ■ To *gulp* something down is to swallow it quickly or with difficulty.

gum glue; ■ a tough jelly-like sweet. ■ Your teeth grow out of your *gums*.

gumboil a painful swelling on the gums.

gurgle the bubbling sound made by water, e.g. when running from a bottle.

gurgling I love to hear the *gurgling* noise made by a brook flowing over stones.

gush A sudden *gush* of oil from the well swept everything before it. ■ When we strike oil it will *gush* from the well in great quantities.

gushing The oil *gushing* from the well swept everything before it. ■ A *gushing* person is one who talks a great deal, usually sentimentally.

gust A sudden *gust* of wind blew my hat off.

gusty A *gusty* day is one when there are lots of short, sudden, violent winds.

gut Some violin strings are made of *gut*. (Though called cat-*gut*, it is actually made from the insides of sheep, etc.) ■ To *gut* a fish is to remove its insides.

gutted The cook *gutted* the fish (i.e. removed its insides). ■ The fire *gutted* the house (i.e. the inside was burnt out of the building).

gutter a channel to drain water from the roof of a house, or from a street, etc.

guttural A *guttural* sound is one made in the throat, e.g. the letter 'g'.

guy a stuffed figure of Guy Fawkes, burnt on bonfires to celebrate the Gunpowder Plot; ■ a rope which holds a tent steady.

guy   guy-rope

gym, gymnasium At school we do our physical exercises in the *gymnasium* (*gym* for short).

gymnastic having to do with a gymnasium or with the work done in it, e.g. *gymnastic* exercises, *gymnastic* apparatus.

gypsy (usual spelling, *gipsy*) a member of a tribe who live in caravans and wander around in many European countries.

haberdashery In the *haberdash-ery* department of a shop they sell needles, cottons, buttons, ribbons, etc.

habit Mary has a *habit* of twisting her hair whenever she is thinking.

habitable fit to live in.

habitual done as a habit, e.g. There is a *habitual* grin on Jim's face.

habitually The child *habitually* sucks her thumb (i.e. she makes a habit of it).

hack to cut with rough, chopping strokes. ■ A *hack*-saw is for cutting metal.

had When I was a baby I *had* curly hair.

haddock a large salt-water fish.

hadn't had not, e.g. The shop-keeper *hadn't* any apples.

hag an ugly old woman; ■ in olden days, a witch.

haggard looking wild because of worry, tiredness, hardship, etc.

hail In a *hail*-storm, small balls of ice called *hail*-stones ■ or *hail* fall from the clouds. ■ to call out in greeting.

hair We have *hair* growing on our heads; but it grows all over such animals as dogs.

hake a large salt-water fish.

half *Half* six is three.

halfpenny (**ha'penny**) the least in value of all English coins.

halibut a very big flat fish.

hall The school *hall* is a large room in which the whole school can assemble.

hallo, halloo A good way of attracting someone's attention is to cry out, '*Hallo!*'

hallow to make holy.

hallowe'en October 31st, the evening before All Hallows' (Saints') Day.

halo a ring of light sometimes seen round the sun or moon; ■ (in pictures) a ring of light round saints' heads.

halt If a sentry shouts '*Halt!*' you must stop. ■ The travellers made a *halt* for an hour. ■ (as used in the Bible, etc.) crippled.

halter a strap or rope put round a horse's head, by which to hold or lead him.

halve If you *halve* anything you make it into two pieces of equal size.

halves If you cut something in *halves*, you make it into two pieces of equal size.

halving cutting into two equal parts.

hamlet a small village.

hammer To knock in a nail, you hit it with a *hammer*.

hammock

hammock I like to lie in a *hammock* hung between two trees.

hamper to hinder; ■ a large basket, usually with a lid.

hamster a pretty, furry, rat-like animal, popular as a pet.

hamster   **handcuffs**

hand You have four fingers and a thumb on each *hand*. ■ *Hand* me that book, please.

handcuffs a pair of metal rings joined by a short chain, and locked round a prisoner's wrists to fasten his hands together.

handful Billy put his hand in the bag and grabbed a *handful* of sweets.

handicap a disadvantage; ■ to put a handicap on someone (e.g. to make a race more fair).

handiwork If you say that something is your own *handiwork*, you mean that you have made it yourself.

handkerchief You wipe your nose on your *handkerchief*.

handkerchiefs The children are expected to wipe their noses on their *handkerchiefs*.

handle You carry a basket by the *handle*. Doors, drawers, etc., have *handles* by which you can hold them. ■ to touch or feel with the hands.

handlebar You steer a bicycle by turning the *handlebar*.

handsome good-looking, e.g. My uncle is a *handsome* man.

handwork In *handwork* lessons we make things.

handwriting I cannot read the letter you have written because the *handwriting* is so bad.

handy The rolling-pin was *handy* (i.e. near at hand), so Mother hit the burglar with that.

hang *Hang* the washing on the line to dry. We *hang* pictures on the walls of our house. ■ To *hang* a person is to kill him by suspending him by a rope round his neck.

hangar a large building in which aircraft are kept.

hanged The murderer was *hanged* (killed by being strung up by means of a rope round his neck).

hanger A paper-*hanger* is a man who sticks wallpaper in place. ■ A coat-*hanger* is a frame on which you put a coat in order to hang it up.

hanky (short for) handkerchief, e.g. Betty can't wipe her nose because she has lost her *hanky*.

ha'penny (short for) halfpenny, a coin valued at half a penny.

haphazard not following any scheme or plan; by chance, e.g. The flowers were pushed into the vase in a *haphazard* way.

happen We know about your accident, for we saw it *happen*.

happened The accident *happened* while Pat was cycling to school. ■ I *happened* to look out of the window (i.e. it was just by chance that I looked out).

happening We could not see what was *happening* because the light had gone out.

happily Tommy ran *happily* home, whistling gaily.

happiness joy.

happy Jean laughs and sings when she is *happy* and cries when she is sad.

harass to worry (someone).

harassed worried (by someone).

harbour a place where ships may shelter from rough seas. ■ To *harbour* a criminal is to give him shelter.

hard When set, concrete is as *hard* as stone. ■ I can't do *hard* sums.

harden The soft concrete will *harden* till it is like stone.

hardhearted A *hardhearted* person is one who does not care about the pains or sorrows suffered by others.

hardly I had *hardly* (i.e. not quite) reached the door when Jane called me back.

hardness Because of its *hardness*, a diamond can be used to cut glass, rock, etc.

hardship misfortune; ■ great suffering.

hardware things sold by an ironmonger – cooking pans, kettles, buckets, dustpans, etc.

hardy A *hardy* plant (or person) is one that can stand up to such severe conditions as cold, shortage of water, infection, etc.

hare an animal like a large rabbit.

hark listen.

harm damage, e.g. There was no *harm* done. ■ to hurt, e.g. The dog won't *harm* the baby.

harmful *Harmful* things are those which do harm.

harmless The grass-snake is a *harmless* creature (i.e. it cannot hurt you).

harmonious Notes that are *harmonious* make a pleasing sound when played together.

harmonize Notes that *harmonize* make a pleasing sound when played together.

harmony a combination of notes making a pleasing sound.

harness A horse wears a leather *harness*, to attach him to the cart which he pulls.

harp a roughly triangular musical instrument, with many strings, which are plucked.

harp   harrow

harpoon a special kind of spear with a rope attached, used for catching whales.

harrow a large tractor-drawn farm rake, like a big iron frame with spikes under it.

harsh rough, e.g. a *harsh* voice; ■ cruel, e.g. *harsh* treatment of someone.

hart a male deer.

harvest a season's crop. ■ To *harvest* a crop is to gather it in. ■ *Harvest*-time is when the various crops are harvested.

hash a stew made of chopped meat.

hasn't (short for) has not. It *hasn't* rained for weeks so there is a shortage of water.

haste hurry; ■ to hurry.

hasten to hurry; to make haste.

hastily quickly.

hasty quick – usually, too quick; ■ quick-tempered.

haversack

hatch Birds *hatch* their eggs by keeping them warm. ■ When eggs *hatch*, the baby creatures come out of them. ■ a hole built into a wall or door.

hatchet a short-handled axe.

hate to dislike very much; ■ hatred.

hateful A *hateful* person (or thing) is one that arouses feelings of hatred in you.

hatred intense dislike; enmity; hate.

haughty proud.

haul The boys had to fasten a rope round the man and *haul* him up the cliff.

haulage A *haulage* contractor is someone who undertakes to carry goods by lorry (or cart).

haunt A ghost is said to *haunt* a place if it is sometimes seen there.

haunted We dare not go along the *haunted* gallery for fear of seeing the ghost.

have I *have* a sweet in my pocket. ■ I *have* to do this job, though I don't want to.

haven a place of safety, e.g. A harbour is a *haven* for ships.

haven't (short for) have not. I cannot pay you because I *haven't* any money.

haversack When I go on a walking tour, I carry my belongings in a *haversack* hung on my back.

having We were *having* a swim when Bill arrived. ■ I don't like *having* to go to bed early.

havoc destruction, ruin, e.g. The storm made *havoc* of our flower garden.

haw The may blossom on hawthorn bushes produces little red berries, called *haws*.

hawk a bird that catches and eats other creatures; ■ to carry goods from door to door in an effort to sell them.

hawker someone who carries goods from door to door in order to sell them.

hawthorn a prickly bush on which may (blossom) grows.

hay grass which has been cut and dried (for cattle food).

haystack a great pile of hay – often shaped like a house.

hawk   haystack

haze thin fog.

hazel a tree that bears long yellow catkins (lambs' tails) in spring, and cob nuts in autumn.

hazy a little bit foggy.

head An animal has eyes in its *head*. ■ The *head* man of a tribe is called the chief.

headache a continuous pain in the head.

headlight The *headlight* of the car lit up the road far ahead.

headline Right across the top of one page of the newspaper, in big print, was the *headline*, 'Earthquake in Persia'.

headquarters The *headquarters* of an organization is the place from which it is run.

headstrong Billy is a *headstrong* boy; he will not take anyone's advice.

headway The boat made no *headway* against the tide (i.e. the tide prevented the boat from going forward).

heal A sore place will *heal* (i.e. become well) if you keep it clean. ■ No ointment can *heal* (i.e. make well) a broken arm.

health To be in good *health* is to have no kind of illness.

healthy A *healthy* person is one who has no kind of illness.

heap The things were piled on top of each other in a *heap*.

hear If you listen you can *hear* the music.

heard We *heard* the sound of music.

hearse a special car for carrying dead people to burial.

heart We knew the animal was alive, for we could feel its *heart* beating in its chest.

heartbroken Sally was *heartbroken* at the loss of her pet, and cried for hours.

heartfelt sincere; really meant, e.g. *heartfelt* thanks.

hearth the floor of a fireplace. ■ A *hearth*rug is a rug placed in front of the fire.

heartily very, e.g. I'm *heartily* tired of your silly jokes. ■ To eat *heartily* is to eat with a good appetite.

heartless cruel; showing no pity.

hearty To give *hearty* thanks is to express sincere gratitude. ■ A *hearty* appetite is a big appetite. ■ *Hearty* cheers are lusty and sincere ones.

heat If you stand in front of the fire you can feel the *heat* from it. ■ We use electric fires to *heat* our house.

heater The car soon gets warm if you switch the *heater* on.

heath flat waste land, often covered with heather and prickly bushes.

heathen people who do not worship the Christian or Jewish God.

heather a tough, heath-land plant, which produces little bell-like white or purple flowers.

heave To get the car out of the ditch the boys had to *heave* on the rope with all their strength.

heaven To Christians, *heaven* is where God and the angels are.

heavenly absolutely delightful. ■ A *heavenly* body is an object in the sky, such as a star. ■ Our *Heavenly* Father is God.

heavens   the sky.

heavily   Jim slipped backwards and sat down *heavily* (i.e. with great force) on the ice.

heaviness   great weight.

heavy   The bag was so *heavy* that I couldn't lift it.

Hebrew   a Jew; ■ Jewish; ■ the language of the Jews.

hectare   an area of 10,000 m² (100 ha = 1 km²).

hectic   wildly exciting.

hedge   a fence of growing bushes.

hedgehog   a little wild animal covered with prickles.

hedgehog

hedgerow   a row of bushes forming a hedge.

heed   to pay attention to.

heel   the back of the foot.

hefty   big and strong-looking, e.g. Jim is a *hefty* lad.

heifer   (pron. héff-er) a young cow.

height   The *height* of the building is 50 metres.

heir   (pron. air) Stephen is Uncle's *heir* (i.e. when Uncle dies, Stephen will receive his property).

heiress   (pron. air-ess) Jean is an *heiress* (i.e. she is to receive property on the death of its present owner).

heirloom   (pron. air-loom) something highly valued by a family because it has been passed on from generation to generation.

helicopter   an aircraft driven by air screws (propellers) revolving over it, which can move it straight up as well as forwards.

helicopter   **hemisphere**

hell   a terrible, wicked place; ■ (to Christians) where Satan is, and where wicked people go after death.

hello   a greeting, e.g. 'Hello! How are you?'

helm   the wheel or handle by which a ship's rudder is worked.

helmet   A motor-cyclist wears a crash *helmet* to protect his head.

help   I cannot do this by myself; I need *help*. ■ You cannot do this by yourself, so I will *help* you.

helpful   George was very *helpful*; we could not have done the job without him.

helpless   A *helpless* person is one who can do nothing for himself.

Helsinki   the capital city of Finland.

hem   To make a *hem* you double over the edge of a piece of material and sew it down. ■ To *hem* material is to put a hem on it.

hemisphere   half a sphere (i.e. the shape of half a ball) – especially half the earth.

hemp   an Indian plant from which fibre for rope is obtained.

hence   Baby found a pot of paint, *hence* all the marks on the wall.

herald In olden times a *herald* went ahead to announce the coming of the king.

herring a fish, common in the seas off Europe and eaten fresh, or as a bloater or kipper.

herald   heron

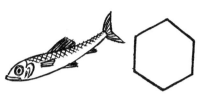

herring   hexagon

herb a plant, especially one whose leaves are used for flavouring.

herbaceous *Herbaceous* plants are those with soft stems which die down after flowering.

herd There were many cattle in the *herd* being driven to market. ■ To *herd* cattle is to drive them together.

here in, or to, this place, e.g. I am *here*. Come *here*.

hereditary passed on from parents to children, e.g. Certain diseases are *hereditary*.

heritage something you receive, or expect to receive, on the death of its owner.

hermit someone who chooses to live alone – usually in a cave or cell.

hero a brave man or boy.

heroes brave men or boys.

heroic brave.

heroine a brave woman or girl.

heroism The man who risked his life to save us was awarded a medal for his *heroism*.

heron a large bird with long legs, often seen standing in the edges of English streams and lakes.

hers Give this back to Jean if it is *hers*.

herself I know that Pat doesn't want to come because she told me so *herself*. ■ Mother gave us two each and kept one for *herself*.

hesitate to pause uncertainly before doing something.

hesitation Without a moment's *hesitation*, the fireman plunged straight into the blazing building.

hew If a tree is in the way, Jack will *hew* it down with his axe.

hexagon a shape consisting of six equal sides.

hibernate Animals are said to *hibernate* when they sleep through the winter.

hiccup the noise made by jerks of breath in the throat – usually caused by eating or drinking quickly.

hidden I have *hidden* the book so that Father cannot see it.

hide Let's *hide* the book so that Susan doesn't see it. ■ the skin of an animal.

hideous horrible; e.g. a *hideous* crime, a *hideous* sight.

hiding We could not see Jim because he was *hiding* behind the curtain. ■ To give someone a *hiding* is to thrash him.

high The shelf was so *high* that no-one could reach it without steps.

highlands The *highlands* (e.g. of Scotland) are where the mountains are.

highway road. ■ The *Highway Code* is a list of rules for road-users.

highwayman a man (e.g. Dick Turpin) who held up travellers on roads, and robbed them.

highwayman   **hippopotamus**

hilarious merry, an occasion for laughter, e.g. a *hilarious* party.

hill We hauled our sledges to the top of the *hill* in order to have the pleasure of sliding down again.

hilt You hold a sword or dagger by the *hilt* (handle).

himself I know that George was there because he told me so *himself*. ■ Dad gave us two each and kept one for *himself*.

hind a female deer. ■ The *hind* legs of an animal are the two at the back.

hinder We should have finished the job sooner if those boys had not been there to *hinder* us.

hindmost (those) at the rear.

hindrance something that hinders.

Hindu one of a race of people in India; ■ anyone who believes in the religion of the Hindus.

hinge a metal fastening which holds a door or lid at one edge, while allowing it to swing open.

hint to suggest something without actually saying it. ■ As a *hint* that it was time for us to go, Mr. Brown looked at his watch.

hippopotamus a large African river-animal.

hire to borrow something for money, e.g. You can *hire* a boat for 50p an hour. ■ If you buy goods by *hire*-purchase you have the use of them while they are being paid for in weekly or monthly instalments.

hiss the noise made by escaping steam, air, etc.; a similar noise made by a person, a snake or a goose.

historian a man who writes history.

historic A *historic* event is something of special importance in history.

historical having to do with history, e.g. a *historical* novel, a *historical* building.

history In *history* lessons we learn about people and events of the past.

hitch something that delays progress for a time. ■ To *hitch* up your trousers, skirt, etc., is to lift them with a jerk.

hither The ants rushed *hither* and thither (i.e. here and there).

hive a place in which bees are kept (for their honey).

hoard The squirrel had a *hoard* of nuts stored up for the winter. ■ A miser will *hoard* all the money he can get and never spend any of it.

hoarding a high fence put round a building during repairs, or a similar structure on which advertisements are pasted. ■ A miser loves *hoarding* (i.e. storing up) money.

hoarfrost white ice-crystals covering everything in frosty weather.

hoarse Tom's voice was *hoarse* after shouting so loud and long at the football match.

hoax to deceive someone by a trick, just for a joke; ■ a trick meant to deceive someone, just for a joke.

hobble People who have injured a leg cannot walk properly; they can only *hobble* along.

hobby something you enjoy doing in your spare time.

hockey a game like football, but played with a small, hard ball and curved sticks.

hoe a garden tool on a long handle, used for loosening the surface of the soil.

hoist to raise up (by pulling on a rope, usually), e.g. to *hoist* a flag.

hold Mother let Jean *hold* the baby in her arms. ■ To *hold* your breath is to stop breathing. ■ Cargo is carried in the *hold* of a ship.

holder A pen-nib is held in a pen-*holder*, and a cigarette in a cigarette-*holder*.

hole The money fell through a *hole* in my pocket. ■ The workmen dug a *hole* in the road in order to repair a water pipe.

holiday We shall have no work to do tomorrow because it is a *holiday*.

holiness great goodness; being holy. ■ The Pope is known as His *Holiness*.

Holland the Netherlands, a small west European country.

hollow having a space inside, like a drum; not solid.

holly an evergreen bush with prickly leaves and red berries, used chiefly for Christmas decorations.

holly   holster

hollyhock a garden plant with large flowers at intervals down a very tall stem.

holster The cowboy keeps his gun in a *holster* strapped to his waist.

holy belonging to God, or devoted to God, e.g. A saint is a *holy* man; a church is a *holy* place.

homage honour and respect, e.g. We pay *homage* to the queen. ■ (in the Middle Ages) a declaration of loyalty to an overlord.

home Your *home* is the place in which you live.

homeless A *homeless* person is one who has no home.

homely A *homely* person is one who is simple and open (i.e. he does not pretend to be what he isn't).

homesick unhappy (ill) as a result of being away from home.

honest (pron. ón-est) An *honest* person is one who does not cheat or steal.

honesty (pron. ón-est-y) There is no doubt about Fred's *honesty* (i.e. we're sure he would not cheat or steal).

honey a sweet, sticky liquid obtained from bees.

honeycomb a network of six-sided wax cells in which bees put their eggs and honey.

honeycomb   hook

honeymoon the holiday that couples take immediately after they are married.

honeysuckle woodbine, a sweet-smelling climbing plant.

honour (pron. ón-our) To (do) *honour* (to) someone is to show him great respect. ■ 'On my *honour*' means 'I promise'.

honourable (pron. ón-our-a-b'l) worthy of honour; ■ a title given to members of the government and the nobility.

hood a head covering that comes down over the neck.

hoof A horse-shoe is nailed to the horse's *hoof*.

hook a piece of bent metal for hanging things on, or (sharpened) for catching fish.

hooligan a young ruffian who misbehaves in the streets.

hoop a wooden or metal ring, especially one of the kind put round barrels.

hoot the noise of an owl or of a car-horn.

hooter a device, usually worked by steam or electricity, for making a loud noise.

hooves Horseshoes are nailed to horses' *hooves* (also spelt *hoofs*).

hope to expect and wish (for), e.g. I *hope* that I shall pass my examination.

hopeful To be *hopeful* is to have a feeling that things will go well.

hopeless A situation is *hopeless* when there is no chance that it will go well.

hoping We are *hoping* for fine weather when we go on holiday.

horde A *horde* of savages rushed upon the travellers.

horizon the line where the earth and sky appear to meet.

horizontal level with the horizon, or like this dash —.

horn Cattle have *horns* on their heads. ■ a metal musical wind-instrument, circular in shape.

hoof   horns

hornet a stinging insect like a big wasp.

hornpipe a lively dance for one person, especially the sailor's *hornpipe*.

horrible, horrid extremely unpleasant.

horrify The news will *horrify* your mother (i.e. give her a feeling of horror).

horrifying causing a feeling of horror, e.g. *horrifying* news.

horror great fear and dislike. ■ *Horror*-struck means made to stand still, tremble, etc., with horror.

horse The knight rode on a *horse*.

hovercraft

horsepower (usually, *h.p.* for short) Dad's first car had an 8 *horsepower* engine; his new 30 *h.p.* car can go faster and carry more weight.

hose stockings; ■ a plastic or rubber tube through which water passes to water the garden, wash the car, etc.

hosiery In the *hosiery* department of a shop you may buy stockings and various knitted garments.

hospitable A *hospitable* person is one who is pleased to see visitors and makes them welcome.

hospital a place where sick people are taken for treatment.

hospitality The natives are noted for their *hospitality* (i.e. for making visitors welcome and providing food, etc., for them).

host the landlord of an inn or hotel; ■ any man who is entertaining a guest.

hostage The bandits kept Tom as a *hostage* until we had done what they asked.

hostel (in olden times) an inn; ■ (nowadays) a place where students, etc., are boarded.

hostess a woman (girl) who is entertaining a guest.

hostile unfriendly.

hotel There were many holiday-makers staying at the Beach *Hotel* this summer.

hound a dog used for hunting, e.g. a fox-*hound*.

hour (pron. our) 60 minutes. From 1 o'clock to 2 o'clock is one *hour*.

house (pron. howss) We live in the *house* at the corner of the street. ■ (pron. howz) To *house* someone is to provide him with a house.

household all those who live in a house, e.g. The *household* consists of Mr. and Mrs. Smith, their son, two daughters and a lodger.

houses Most people in England live in *houses* made of bricks.

hovel The beggar lived in a filthy little *hovel*, too small and dingy to be called a house.

hover to stay in one place in mid-air (e.g. by fluttering the wings like a *hover*-fly).

hovercraft a vehicle which travels over water or land on a cushion of air.

how I do not know *how* to do this sum. ■ *How* are you? (i.e. Are you well or ill?)

however I'm sure the shop is shut; *however*, let's go and see.

howl the long, cheerless cry of an animal such as a dog; ■ a long cry of pain or mockery (by people); ■ to make a long, cheerless noise.

howler an easily-noticed (and usually amusing) mistake, e.g. 'A dead-heat is when the fire is out.'

hub the spokes of a wheel are all attached to the *hub* at the centre.

hub   **hull**

hubbub a loud and confused noise.

huddle Animals *huddle* together to keep each other warm. ■ (slang) To go into a *huddle* with someone is to have a private discussion with him.

hue colour. ■ A *hue* and cry is a noisy chase (e.g. after a thief with shouts of 'Stop thief!', etc.).

huff a fit of sulking. ■ To take *huff* is to take offence. ■ to remove an opponent's draughtsman from the board as a penalty.

huge The *huge* rocket towered high above the buildings around it.

hull the body of a ship.

hullabaloo The crowds of excited people made such a *hullabaloo* that we could not hear ourselves speak.

hum to sing with the lips closed.

human People are *human* beings; animals are not.

humane A *humane* person would not hurt any creature.

humanity the human race; ■ kindness and sympathy.

humble A *humble* person is one who does not consider himself to be important.

humbly in a humble way.

humbug a person who tricks or deceives you; ■ a big, hard sweet, usually peppermint flavoured.

humid damp, e.g. Washing does not dry very well on a *humid* day.

humiliate To *humiliate* anyone is to make him feel humble or ashamed.

humility humbleness, modesty.

hummed We *hummed* the tune (i.e. sang it with lips closed).

humming singing with lips closed. ■ A *humming*-bird is a tiny tropical bird whose wings make a *humming* noise.

humorist a funny (amusing) person.

humorous amusing, funny.

humour mood, e.g. Dad is in a good *humour* today. ■ A sense of *humour* is an ability to see the funny side of things.

hump The camel has a *hump* on his back.

humbug   **hump**

humus decayed vegetation (i.e. leaves, etc.), a valuable plant food.

hunchback a person with a hump on his back.

hundred (100) ten tens.

hundredth ($\frac{1}{100}$) one divided by 100. ■ Grandad has lived exactly 100 years, for today is his *hundredth* birthday.

hundredweight (usually written 1 cwt.) 112 lbs., a twentieth part of a ton.

hung The light *hung* from the ceiling on a piece of wire.

Hungarian the language of Hungary; ■ a citizen of Hungary. ■ *Hungarian* things are those from or of Hungary.

Hungary a European country between Austria and Roumania.

hunger If people have nothing to eat they die of *hunger*.

hungry We have had nothing to eat all day, so we are very *hungry*.

hunk Tom pulled a great *hunk* of bread off the loaf and crammed it into his mouth.

hunt The natives go off into the forest to *hunt* wild animals, which they kill for food.

hunter The *hunter* tracked the animal for hours before getting near enough to kill it.

hurdle a gate-like barrier, ■ especially one over which runners jump in a *hurdle* race.

hurl The tribesmen picked up great rocks to *hurl* at us.

hurrah, hurray a cheer or shout, e.g. Hip, hip, *hurray*!

hurricane The *hurricane* blew with such force that trees were uprooted.

hurried I *hurried* home as fast as I could.

hurriedly quickly or too quickly, e.g. The boys *hurriedly* washed their hands and ran in to dinner.

hurry to go faster than usual. ■ *Hurry* up, or we shall miss the train.

hurrying going faster than usual, e.g. The boys were *hurrying* to school.

hurt Billy's broken leg *hurt* him so much that he cried. ■ Anne fell off her cycle and *hurt* her knee.

hurtle The bridge collapsed and we saw the train *hurtle* into the river far below.

husband Mr. Smith is Mrs. Smith's *husband*.

hush A *hush* came over the crowd so that you could hear a pin drop. ■ *Hush!* or you'll wake the baby.

husk a tough outer skin, especially that on wheat, barley, etc.

husky Eskimo dog. ■ Joe has shouted so much that his voice is *husky* (i.e. hoarse).

hustle (pron. huss'l) to push roughly and in haste, e.g. I saw the police *hustle* the bandit into a car.

hut The poor old man lived in a little wooden *hut*.

hutch We keep our pet rabbit in a *hutch* made from a wooden box and wire netting.

hyacinth a scented spring flower

hurdle   **hyacinth**

like a large bluebell, though not always blue.

hydraulic worked by water (or some other liquid), e.g. Our car has *hydraulic* brakes.

hydrogen an invisible gas which burns easily and is used for filling balloons, etc., because it is lighter than air.

hydroplane a fast boat that skims over the surface of the water.

hydroplane

hyena a flesh-eating, dog-like animal. The howl of the laughing *hyena* sounds like laughter (also spelt *hyaena*).

hygiene In *hygiene* lessons we learn the rules for healthy living.

hymn We begin our religious service by singing a *hymn*.

hyphen There is a *hyphen* in the middle of the word 'ill-treat'.

hypnotism the art of putting a person into a deep sleep by talking to him.

hypnotize To *hypnotize* someone is to cause him to go into a deep sleep by talking to him.

hypocrite someone who pretends (to be good, or to be sorry, etc.).

hypotenuse the longest side of a right-angled triangle.

hysterical A *hysterical* person is one so wildly excited that he can't control himself.

hysterics an attack of wild excitement during which the sufferer cannot control himself.

ice If you make water very cold, it turns into solid *ice*.

iceberg a large lump of ice, like a rugged hill, floating in the sea.

iceberg   **icicle**

ice-cream cream, or more often custard, flavoured and frozen.

icicle Water trickling from a gutter or roof freezes into a V-shaped *icicle*.

icing *Icing* sugar is sugar in the form of a fine white powder. ■ This, when mixed with water and spread over cakes, sets to form a hard, sweet, white covering called *icing*. ■ Jane is *icing* the cake (i.e. she is covering it with icing).

icy very cold indeed, e.g. The skater fell into the *icy* water. ■ covered with ice, e.g. The car skidded on the *icy* road.

idea something thought up, e.g. Betty first thought of the *idea* of a fancy dress parade.

ideal Jack is the *ideal* boy to play the part; you couldn't imagine anyone more suitable.

idealist a person who is satisfied only with the very best.

identical exactly alike in every way, e.g. *identical* twins. The two new pennies are *identical*.

identify I can *identify* that watch as mine by the scratches on the back.

idiot a person whose mind is so weak that he constantly does silly things.

idiotic extremely silly, e.g. an *idiotic* motorist. It was an *idiotic* thing to do.

idle That *idle* boy hasn't done a stroke of work.

idleness We weren't surprised that Jack was punished for his *idleness*, for he had done no work at all.

idling Instead of working, Jack was *idling* away his time (i.e. he was doing nothing).

idly While we worked, Jack stood *idly* watching (i.e. doing nothing).

idol The *idol* that the people worshipped was a golden calf.

idolize to worship; ■ to love too much, e.g. My cousins *idolize* their dog.

i.e. (short for) that is.

igloo an Eskimo's snow house.

igloo

ignite to set fire to, e.g. George will *ignite* the fuse. ■ to catch fire, e.g. The wood will not *ignite* because it is wet.

ignoramus an ignorant person.

ignorance lack of knowledge, e.g. The reason for Jim's *ignorance* is that he has paid no attention to the lesson.

ignorant An *ignorant* person is one who has no knowledge.

ignore to take no notice of, e.g. The boys were so rude that we decided to *ignore* them.

ill If you are *ill* (unwell), you should call a doctor. ■ evil, e.g. an *ill*-natured person.

illegal not lawful, a crime, e.g. It is *illegal* to cycle without a light after dark.

illness The last *illness* I had was measles, which kept me in bed for several days.

ill-treat to treat badly, e.g. People who *ill-treat* children or animals deserve to be punished.

illuminate to light up, e.g. We need a lamp to *illuminate* this dark cupboard.

illuminations many lights, put up for some kind of festivity.

illusion It seemed to us that the magician cut the lady in halves, but this was an *illusion*, for the lady was not cut at all.

illustrate I *illustrate* a story by drawing pictures to show what is happening.

illustration One *illustration* in the book was a picture of the fight mentioned in the story.

image a likeness of someone; ■ a statue.

imaginary The events described in the book are *imaginary* (i.e. they didn't actually happen).

imagination Helen has a good *imagination*; she can make up marvellous stories (or pictures).

imaginative An *imaginative* person is one who can think up new and strange ideas.

imagine As I lie in bed I like to *imagine* that I am in a space-ship.

imitate to copy, e.g. *Imitate* Joyce and you will be able to dance as well as she does.

imitation a copy, e.g. That fur is not real fox, but an *imitation*.

immediately I didn't wait a moment, but came *immediately* you called.

immense very big indeed.

immensely very much, e.g. We were *immensely* relieved when Dad returned safely from the mine.

immerse To *immerse* something in a liquid is to put it right under the surface.

immigrate Many people from the Commonwealth *immigrate* to England (i.e. come to England to live).

immoral wicked.

immortal An *immortal* is supposed to live for ever, e.g. a god or a fairy. ■ *Immortal* God means God who lives for ever.

immune To be *immune* from an illness is to be safe from the danger of catching it.

immunize To *immunize* someone (e.g. by vaccination) is to make him safe from the danger of catching a disease.

imp a little devil; ■ a mischievous child.

impact The bull charged at the tree and the *impact* of his head on the trunk shook down all the apples.

impartial not favouring either side in a contest, argument, etc., e.g. A judge should be *impartial*.

impassable We could not go any farther along the road because a fallen tree had made it *impassable*.

impatience crossness, irritation, caused by inability to put up with delay, stupidity, etc., calmly, e.g. The accident was caused by the motorist's *impatience*.

impatient unable to put up with some delay or annoyance calmly, e.g. The *impatient* traveller kept getting up to look out of the window of the train to see if his station was in sight.

impede to hinder, e.g. You *impede* the workman if you get in his way.

imperfect not perfect, e.g. The aircraft made an *imperfect* landing which gave the passengers a nasty jolt, but did no damage.

imperfection a fault, e.g. The car's only *imperfection* was a scratch on the door.

imperil to put in danger, e.g. By wasting the water supply you *imperil* everyone in the expedition.

impertinence rudeness, insolence (usually by a child to an adult), e.g. The child had the *impertinence* to call his teacher a silly woman.

impertinent saucy, cheeky, e.g. That *impertinent* child called his teacher a silly woman.

impetigo contagious (catching) sores on the skin.

impetuous rash. An *impetuous* person is one who does things too violently or suddenly (e.g. without sufficient thought beforehand).

impish childishly mischievous.

implement a tool or instrument, e.g. The best *implement* for digging a garden is a spade.

implicate to involve, e.g. Several boys were *implicated* (i.e. mixed up) in the crime.

implore to beg, e.g. I *implore* you not to drown the kitten.

impolite rude, e.g. It is *impolite* to turn your back on someone who is speaking to you.

import We *import* into England many foods which have been grown abroad. ■ One *import* that comes into England (from abroad) is tea.

importance You realize the *importance* of taking care on the roads when you hear that thousands of road users are injured every year.

important We knew our visitor was an *important* person because the policemen saluted him.

imposing The mayor looked *imposing* in his scarlet robes and splendid gold chain.

imposition Bob has to do (write) 100 lines as an *imposition*, because he was talking in class.

impossible It is *impossible* to count the grains of sand on a beach (i.e. it cannot be done).

impracticable An *impracticable* idea (or plan, etc.) is one that may seem possible, but cannot in fact be done.

impress To *impress* something on someone is to fix it in his mind. ■ To *impress* someone is to have a strong effect on him, e.g. We hope our new car will *impress* the neighbours.

impressed The inspector was *impressed* by the smartness of the boys.

impression a mark made by pressing a hard thing into a softer

one, e.g. by pressing your thumb into clay; ■ an idea, e.g. I have the *impression* that Joan does not like me.

impressive The royal wedding was very *impressive* (i.e. it had a strong effect on my mind).

imprison to shut up, especially to shut up in a prison.

improbable not likely, e.g. It is *improbable* that you will have snowstorms during your summer holiday in England.

improper wrong, e.g. That was a most *improper* thing to say.

improve You could *improve* your bicycle by cleaning it and giving it a coat of paint.

improvement This composition is a great *improvement* on the one you wrote last week (i.e. it is a great deal better).

impudent insolent, cheeky. e.g. When caught out doing wrong, the *impudent* boy didn't stop, but looked the teacher straight in the eye and grinned.

impulsive An *impulsive* person is one who does things on the spur of the moment, without thought.

impure containing other substances that shouldn't be there, e.g. *impure* water or food; ■ indecent, disgusting.

inability Because of his *inability* to swim Henry is likely to drown if he falls out of the boat.

inaccessible The cave was *inaccessible*, high up the face of a cliff which no-one could climb.

inaccurate The speedometer was *inaccurate*, for it showed 60 m.p.h. when we were going at only 50 m.p.h.

inactive For a whole day the enemy remained *inactive* (i.e. they did nothing).

inadequate not enough, e.g. The child's clothing was *inadequate* for such a cold day.

inanimate not alive, e.g. A book is an *inanimate* object.

inattentive not attentive, e.g. Bob doesn't know what the lesson was about because he was *inattentive* (i.e. took no notice).

inaudible If anything is *inaudible* it cannot be heard.

incapable not capable, unable, e.g. The injured man was *incapable* of walking, so he had to be carried.

incense a spice burnt in religious ceremonies to give a sweet-smelling smoke.

incentive As an *incentive*, the teacher offered a bar of chocolate for the first boy to get all his sums right.

incessant The traffic thundered past our house all night and its *incessant* noise gave us not a moment's peace.

inch 1″: a twelfth part of a foot (about 2½ centimetres).

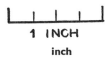

1 INCH

inch

incident anything that happens, e.g. Tell me everything that happened while I was away, every *incident*.

incivility rudeness, e.g. If you don't answer when people talk to you they may accuse you of *incivility*.

inclination liking, e.g. I have no *inclination* to go bathing in winter-time. ■ slope.

incline slope, e.g. The ball rolled down the *incline* into the river. ■ To *incline* the head (or body) is to bend it forwards and downwards.

inclined I am *inclined* to agree with you (i.e. I feel I ought to agree).

include You have four fingers on each hand, five if you *include* the thumb.

inclusion I do not agree to the *inclusion* of Sally in the party; leave her out.

inclusive including everything (or a great deal), e.g. *inclusive* charges at a hotel. ■ 'Read pages 6–9 *inclusive*,' means that you have to read both page 6 and page 9 as well as those in between.

income the money a person receives from his work, business, etc., e.g. Mr. Smith has an *income* of £2,000 a year.

incomplete not finished.

inconsiderate To do something without thinking of its effect on other people is *inconsiderate*.

inconsistent To change your mind often about your likes and dislikes is *inconsistent*.

inconspicuous not easily noticed.

inconvenience something that puts you to some trouble, e.g. It is an *inconvenience* to live a long way from the shops.

inconvenient A thing is *inconvenient* when it does not fit in with your plans or wishes.

incorrect wrong; not true.

increase Dad will *increase* your pocket money from 25p to 35p. ■ an *increase* of 10p.

incredible 'It is *incredible*,' means 'I cannot believe it.'

incriminate In answering questions, a person suspected of wrong-doing may *incriminate* other people (i.e. suggest that they too were mixed up in the trouble).

incubator a container in which eggs are kept warm in order to hatch chicks from them.

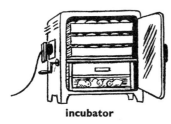

incubator

incur If you break a window you will *incur* the anger of the householder.

incurable An *incurable* disease (or person) is one that cannot be cured.

incurred All expenses *incurred* by our football team are paid by the school.

indebted We are *indebted* to Mr. Smith for these new books (i.e. we owe thanks to Mr. Smith because he gave them to us).

indecency behaviour that is disgusting (usually because it involves private parts of the body).

indecent An *indecent* person (or *indecent* behaviour) is disgusting (usually because of exposing some private part of the body, or talking improperly about it).

indeed very much so, e.g. I am very tired *indeed*.

indefinite not definite, e.g. We are staying for an *indefinite* time (i.e. no time has been fixed).

indelible An *indelible* mark is one that cannot be removed.

independence freedom from the control of other people.

independent not under the control of other people.

indescribable The scene was one of *indescribable* beauty (i.e. beauty that cannot be described).

indestructible An *indestructible* thing (e.g. a toy, etc.) is one that cannot be destroyed.

index In the *index* of a book, all the things mentioned in the book are listed in alphabetical order.

India a large country to the south of Asia. ■ *India* rubber is used to rub out pencil marks.

Indian a citizen of India. ■ *Indian* things are those from India (or from the American Indians). ■ one of the original natives of South America or North America (e.g. Red *Indians*). ■ *Indian* corn is maize.

indicate to show, e.g. You can *indicate* the direction by pointing with your finger.

indication a sign or hint, e.g. The motorist gave no *indication* of his intention to stop, so when he stopped we ran into the back of his car.

Indies the islands off south east Asia (the East *Indies*). ■ The West *Indies* are the islands between the U.S.A. and South America.

indifferent not interested, e.g. The savages quietly talked together, quite *indifferent* to our cries for help. ■ neither good nor bad, e.g. The actor gave an *indifferent* performance.

indigestible *Indigestible* foods are those which the stomach has difficulty in making use of, and may therefore cause pains or sickness.

indigestion discomfort or pain in the stomach, caused by its difficulty in absorbing something you have eaten.

indignant angry (at being unfairly treated, etc.), e.g. James was *indignant* at being blamed for something he hadn't done.

indignation anger (caused by unfair treatment, etc.), e.g. To James's *indignation*, he was blamed for damage that he hadn't caused.

indignity an insult, e.g. Bill suffered the *indignity* of having his face washed while the younger boys were looking on.

indigo a dark shade of blue.

indirect We came home by an *indirect* route (i.e. not by the shortest way).

indiscreet An *indiscreet* person is one who cannot keep a secret.

indiscriminately not in any special way, nor to any special persons, e.g. The knight slashed around him *indiscriminately* with his sword (i.e. at anyone and everyone.).

indispensable An *indispensable* thing is one you cannot do without.

indisputable A statement, etc., that is *indisputable* is one that is so certainly true that there cannot be argument about it.

indistinct blurred so as not to be clearly seen or heard, e.g. His voice was *indistinct*. The writing was *indistinct*.

indistinguishable If two (or more) things are *indistinguishable* you cannot tell one from another.

individual one person or thing. ■ The *individual* prize is given for an effort by one person (not a team).

individually one at a time, not all at once, e.g. The headmaster will see the boys *individually*.

indolent lazy.

indomitable An *indomitable* person is one who does not give in.

indoors Come *indoors* (i.e. into the house) out of the rain.

induce to persuade, e.g. Can you *induce* your baby to return Aunty's glasses?

inducement something which persuades, e.g. At this shop customers are offered a free sponge as an *inducement* to buy washing powder.

indulgent An *indulgent* parent is one who too easily agrees to let his children do what they like.

industrial having to do with industries, factories, etc., e.g. an *industrial* town.

industrious hard-working, busy, e.g. Brian is an *industrious* boy.

industry The building *industry* consists of all the firms and businesses occupied in building, the chemical *industry* with all those whose business is making chemicals.

inedible not fit to eat, e.g. Rotten apples are *inedible*.

ineffective having no result, useless, e.g. Our car has an *ineffective* silencer (i.e. the silencer does not reduce the noise).

inefficient not doing its job well (or at all), e.g. a machine may be described as *inefficient* because it is too slow, it does the work badly, or it uses too much fuel, etc.

inevitable sure to happen, e.g. Defeat was *inevitable* after two of our team had been injured.

inexhaustible The people living beside the river have an *inexhaustible* supply of water (i.e. more water than they can possibly use).

inexpensive cheap.

inexperienced The accident happened because the driver was *inexperienced* and not used to handling the car.

inexplicable The disappearance of the aircraft was *inexplicable* (i.e. no explanation of the disappearance could be found).

infallible A thing that is *infallible* cannot go wrong (or fail); e.g. an *infallible* cure.

infancy Children are in their *infancy* when they are babies.

infant a baby. ■ The *Infants'* School is for children under seven.

infatuated so very fond (or in love) as to behave foolishly, e.g. Jenny is *infatuated* by the latest pop singer.

infect People who have such diseases as colds *infect* the air around them and may thus pass on the disease to other people.

infection You can guard against *infection* (i.e. picking up a disease from the air) by wearing a mask over your face.

infectious An *infectious* illness is one that can be caught by breathing in germs that are in the air.

inferior less good, e.g. I won't pay top prices for goods of *inferior* quality. ■ less important, e.g. A captain is *inferior* in rank to a general.

infest to have large numbers of unpleasant creatures about, e.g. The house was *infested* with rats. The island was *infested* with pirates.

infinite endless, beyond measure.

infirm ill, weak because of old age.

infirmary hospital.

inflame to cause something to become hot or ablaze, but, more usually, to cause a person to become hot with anger.

inflamed red and swollen (part of the body), e.g. an *inflamed* eye.

inflammable Petrol is an *inflammable* substance (i.e. it catches fire very easily).

inflammation heat, swelling and redness (of a part of the body). You can see by the *inflammation* that there is something wrong with Jane's ankle.

inflate to blow up (a balloon, a cycle tyre, etc.).

inflated blown up (i.e. swollen with air or gas), e.g. an *inflated* balloon; ■ blew up, or pumped up, e.g. Fred *inflated* the football.

inflict You *inflict* pain on a creature when you beat it with a stick.

infliction I hate the *infliction* of suffering upon any creature.

influence the power of a person or thing to affect another person or thing, e.g. The moon has an *influence* upon the earth; it causes the tides. Pat has a good *influence* upon Paul (i.e. Pat causes Paul to be a better person).

influential An *influential* person is one who is able to affect the ideas or actions of others.

influenza an illness causing pains in the limbs, running nose, etc. (often called 'flu' for short).

inform to tell (by written or by spoken words), e.g. The letter was to *inform* me that I had passed the exam.

informal simple and without ceremony, e.g. the Queen paid an *informal* visit to our school.

informant someone who tells (you) something, e.g. I was told that we had won the match, but my *informant* couldn't tell me the score.

information news, knowledge, e.g. I have no *information* about the holidays.

informer someone who tells tales (i.e. gives information that is likely to get someone into trouble).

infuriate to make terribly angry, e.g. The man is already angry; any further annoyance will *infuriate* him.

ingenious An *ingenious* person is one clever at thinking up new ideas. ■ An *ingenious* idea is one that has been cleverly thought out.

ingenuity cleverness (at thinking up new ideas).

ingot an oblong lump of metal, usually gold.

ingratitude failure to show pro-

per appreciation for something given to or done for you.

ingredient One *ingredient* needed when making a cake is flour; another is sugar.

inhabit To *inhabit* a place is to live there.

inhabitant An *inhabitant* of a place is someone who lives there.

inhale to breathe in.

inherit Jim will *inherit* his father's farm. (i.e. The farm will be Jim's when his father dies.)

inhospitable An *inhospitable* person is one who does not make visitors welcome, or who shows that he is not pleased to see them.

inhuman cruel, beastly, e.g. The guards were punished for their *inhuman* treatment of the prisoners.

iniquity wickedness, e.g. The house was a den of *iniquity*.

initial The *initial* letter of the word 'London' is L. ■ George Paul Smith's *initials* are G.P.S.

initiative Peter took the *initiative* in clearing up the mess, and the other boys followed his example.

inject The doctor uses a syringe to *inject* (squirt) drugs, etc., into people's flesh.

injection When a doctor gives you an *injection*, he squirts liquid into your flesh with a syringe.

injure When a man shoots an animal, the bullet may *injure* it, not kill it.

injury When Susan fell off her cycle, her only *injury* was a twisted ankle.

injustice unfairness, e.g. You do Brenda an *injustice* if you say she is lazy; she is tired because she is unwell.

ingot   injection

ink Dip the pen in the *ink* and write your name.

inkling a hint, e.g. The boys had no *inkling* of what was to happen at the party, so they were very surprised at the games we played.

inland not near the sea.

inlet a branch of sea reaching into the land; a creek.

inlet   insects

inmate someone who is in a prison, etc., for a time.

inn a place where people may buy drink, food or lodgings; a public house (the slang abbreviation is 'pub').

innings It is your *innings* at cricket, rounders, etc., when it's your turn to bat.

innocence The prisoner proved his *innocence* so the judge did not punish him.

innocent An *innocent* person is one who has not done wrong.

innocuous harmless, e.g. The drink looked horrible, but it was quite *innocuous*.

innumerable too many to be counted, e.g. *Innumerable* wild animals live in the woods.

inoculation the injection into a person's flesh of a liquid containing germs of a disease. (This gives him a mild form of the disease and so protects him from the serious form.)

inoffensive not likely to give offence, e.g. Joe is an *inoffensive* person, who wouldn't be unpleasant to anyone.

inquest an official inquiry (held by a coroner) into the cause of someone's death.

inquire As we didn't know the way to the station we had to *inquire* of a passer-by, who gladly told us (also spelt *enquire*).

inquiry I made an *inquiry* and was told all I wanted to know (also spelt *enquiry*).

inquisitive An *inquisitive* person is one who is ever trying to find out about things – by asking questions, looking into places, etc.

insane mad. When people are *insane*, they are put away in mental hospitals to be cured.

inscription Come and read the *inscription* on this gravestone.

insect a small, six-legged creature, such as a beetle, ant, or bee.

inseparable Anne and Pam were *inseparable* friends (i.e. they could not be separated).

insert to put in, e.g. To get chocolate from the machine, you *insert* a coin in the slot and pull out the drawer.

inside *Inside* the wolf was the duck he had swallowed.

insight a thorough understanding, e.g. I worked on a farm for a long time and so got an *insight* into the life of a farmer.

insignificant of no importance, e.g. It was such an *insignificant* item of news that none of the papers printed it.

insincere An *insincere* person will

offer sympathy or compliments which he does not really mean.

insinuate to hint; to suggest something without actually saying it, e.g. Do you *insinuate* that we cheated?

insipid having no flavour, e.g. I cannot enjoy *insipid* food (or drink).

insist I *insist* on quietness (i.e. there really must be quietness).

insistent I didn't want the medicine, but the nurse was so *insistent* that I finally agreed to drink it.

insolence impertinence, cheek, e.g. The boy had the *insolence* to accuse the headmaster of cheating.

insolent impertinent, insulting, cheeky, e.g. An *insolent* boy accused the headmaster of cheating.

insoluble An *insoluble* problem is one to which no answer can be found. ■ An *insoluble* substance is one that will not dissolve, e.g. Sand is *insoluble* in water.

inspect to examine carefully, e.g. Before the match the captains *inspect* the pitch to satisfy themselves that it is fit for play.

inspection a careful examination, e.g. An *inspection* of the pitch showed that it was not fit for play.

inspiration a splendid idea, e.g. Jim had an *inspiration*; 'Let's go by canoe,' he said. ■ power from God, like that which guided the writers of the Bible.

inspired To explain how an artist (writer, painter, musician, etc.) is able to produce some exceptionally great work, people say that he was *inspired*.

install to put in, to fit, e.g. A man came to *install* a telephone in our house.

instalment a part payment, e.g. I paid for my bicycle in 20 weekly *instalments*. ■ one of the parts of a serial story or play.

instance example, e.g. I wish we grew fruit in our garden – apples, for *instance*.

instant moment, e.g. You must come the *instant* I call. ■ immediate, e.g. When I give an order, I expect *instant* obedience.

instantly If you press the switch the light comes on *instantly* (i.e. at once).

instead I pressed the wrong button, so *instead* of the bell ringing, the light came on.

instep the top of the foot between toes and ankle, e.g. Shoe laces fasten over the *instep*.

instep

instinct the urge that causes people and animals to do things without thought, e.g. A bird knows by *instinct* how to build a nest. A man's *instinct* is to run away when he is frightened.

instinctive The *instinctive* act of a frightened person is to run away (i.e. he will do it without thinking).

institute a society or organization, e.g. The Women's *Institute*. ■ To *institute* an inquiry, search, etc., is to start one.

instruct to order, e.g. *Instruct those boys to wait there.* ■ to teach, e.g. *My job is to instruct you in arithmetic.*

instructions explanations, e.g. *If you want to know how to use this stuff, read the instructions on the packet.*

instructor *I was taught to swim by the swimming instructor at the baths.*

instrument any kind of tool, e.g. a drawing *instrument* (compasses), a writing *instrument* (pen), a musical *instrument* (violin).

insufficient *If you have insufficient money for your journey, tell me how much more you need.*

insulate We *insulate* wire by putting round it rubber, etc., through which electricity will not pass. ■ We *insulate* water pipes by wrapping round them material which prevents them from getting cold (or hot).

insulation *Insulation* (made of rubber, etc.) is put round wire to prevent the electricity from getting out (into people or things that the wire may touch).

insulator a substance through which electricity (or heat) will not easily pass, e.g. rubber or porcelain.

insult an offensive (rude) remark or action. ■ To *insult* someone is to be rude or offensive to him.

insulting An *insulting* remark (or piece of behaviour) is one that makes someone feel hurt or offended.

insurance Each year we pay a few pounds *insurance* on our car; then if it is damaged, ■ the *insurance* company pays for the repairs.

intact The parcel arrived *intact* (i.e. all in one piece, undamaged).

intellect, intelligence power of understanding, or quickness at understanding, e.g. *I wish I had an intellect like the professor's.* ■ An *intelligence* test is used to pick out those quickest and best at understanding things.

intelligent An *intelligent* person is one who is good (or quick) at understanding things.

intelligible An *intelligible* answer (or explanation, etc.) is one that can be understood.

intend *I intend to get up early tomorrow morning* (i.e. I plan to get up early).

intensely very, very, e.g. *The water was intensely cold.*

intent *Bob was so intent on lighting the camp fire that he didn't notice the bull charging across the field.*

intention *It is my intention to catch fish, so I shall not go away till I have done so.*

intentional done on purpose, not by accident, e.g. *That blow on the head was intentional; it was no accident.*

intentionally *Letting that animal escape was no accident; you did it intentionally.*

intercept to stop, especially to stop someone (or something) on his way from one place to another, e.g. *The enemy may intercept our messenger.*

interest *I can see that you have no interest in the lesson by the way you look around and yawn.* ■ money paid to you for the use of money you have lent to someone (or put in the bank, etc.).

interested No-one is *interested* in your story, so please do not bore us by telling it.

interesting It was such an *interesting* book that I could think of nothing else while I was reading it.

interfere to get in the way; ■ to give unwanted help with something that someone else is doing.

interference We could do this job better without your *interference* (i.e. unwanted help). ■ The picture on our TV is spoilt by *interference* from your vacuum cleaner.

interior inside, e.g. We paper the *interior* walls of our house.

interloper someone who forces his way into other people's business, e.g. None of us wants Barry at this meeting; he's just an *interloper*.

interminable endless, or too long, e.g. The day's outing was spoilt by the *interminable* wait for the bus home.

intermingle to mix (together), e.g. If the escaped prisoners *intermingle* with the crowd we shall never find them.

intermittent An *intermittent* sound (or light, etc.) is one that keeps on stopping and starting.

internal inside, e.g. A stomach-ache is an *internal* pain.

international An *international* conference (or exhibition, competition, etc.) is one in which a number of nations take part.

interpret to explain the meaning; ■ to translate from another language, e.g. Please, someone, *interpret* this Chinese boy's remarks so that I can understand them.

interpreter An *interpreter's* job is to change foreign speech into language that the listener understands.

interrogate to question, e.g. The police *interrogate* a prisoner in an attempt to learn the truth about a crime.

interrupt You *interrupt* someone talking (or doing something) when you stop him before he has finished.

interruption There was an *interruption* during the lesson, when a man came into the classroom to remove a cupboard.

interval a space, e.g. The trees were planted beside the road at 50-ft. *intervals*. ■ a pause, e.g. Between the two parts of the concert is an *interval*, when we can buy ice-cream.

intervene The argument between the two boys became so fierce that Dad had to *intervene* and tell them to behave.

intervention The two men would have continued fighting but for the *intervention* of a policeman, who ordered them to stop.

interview a meeting, arranged for a special purpose, e.g. My father had an *interview* with the headmaster to discuss my work.

intestine yards of tubing in the abdomen into which food passes after leaving the stomach.

intimidate The bully would so *intimidate* (frighten) smaller boys that they would do whatever he told them.

intolerable An *intolerable* noise (or insult, situation, etc.) is one which you cannot put up with.

intolerant An *intolerant* person is one who cannot bear ideas different from his own.

intoxicated drunk, e.g. The man had drunk so much beer that he was *intoxicated* and couldn't walk steadily.

intrepid very brave, e.g. The *intrepid* explorer seized the lion by the tail and pulled.

intricate very complicated, e.g. Inside the machine is an *intricate* arrangement of wires.

intriguing arousing great curiosity, e.g. An *intriguing* notice said, 'All boys are to take an old toothbrush to the gym at 4.30.'

introduce Mary does not know John, so will you *introduce* him to her? ■ to bring something into use, e.g. Raleigh is said to have *introduced* tobacco smoking into England.

introduction The *introduction*, printed at the beginning of a book, usually tells the reader something about the book or its author. ■ Raleigh was responsible for the *introduction* of tobacco smoking into England.

intruder someone who comes in without being asked, e.g. an uninvited guest, or a burglar.

invade To *invade* a country, an enemy enters it with an army.

invader an enemy who enters a country with an army.

invalid a person who is weak because of illness or injury, e.g. We went to visit the *invalid* in hospital.

invaluable beyond price, very valuable, e.g. The thieves stole an *invaluable* painting.

invariably always, e.g. When I ask Mother anything she *invariably* replies, 'Ask your father.'

invasion In 1066 William the Conqueror brought his army across the sea for the *invasion* of England.

invent to make something that (so far as you know) has never been made before, e.g. Marconi *invented* radio. ■ to make up an untrue story.

invention discovery by experiment, e.g. Before the *invention* of gunpowder, men fought with bows and arrows. ■ something invented, e.g. Radio is a useful *invention*.

inventor a person who makes something that has not been made before.

invert to turn upside down.

invest To *invest* money you buy shares in a business and so receive each year your share of the profits of the business.

investigate to inquire into, e.g. The detective was sent to *investigate* the crime.

investigation an inquiry or examination, e.g. At the end of his *investigation* the detective knew who had committed the crime.

invigorating making (a person) lively and energetic, e.g. A swim in cold water is very *invigorating*.

invisible It is not possible to see anything that is *invisible* – e.g. a voice, air, etc.

invitation If you want Betty to come to your party, send her an *invitation*.

invite to ask someone to come (e.g. to your house); ■ to ask someone to do something that you believe he will like to do (e.g. to have a piece of cake).

inviting I am not *inviting* (asking) parents to my party. ■ On a hot day the swimming pool looks very *inviting* (attractive).

invoice a list of goods sent and their cost, e.g. We send an *invoice* with every parcel of our goods.

involved Joan was *involved* (i.e. mixed up in) the trouble. ■ Painting the room *involved* (i.e. included) moving out the piano.

irate angry, e.g. The *irate* farmer ordered the campers off his land.

Ireland the island between Britain and the Atlantic Ocean.

iris a tall blue or yellow flower with leaves like big blades of grass; ■ the coloured part of the eye.

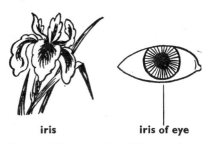

iris   iris of eye

Irish The people of Ireland. ■ *Irish* things are those from Ireland, e.g. *Irish* bacon.

irksome An *irksome* job is one that you find dull and irritating.

iron a grey metal used for making nails, tools, etc. ■ To *iron* clothes is to make them smooth ■ by sliding a hot *iron* over them.

ironmonger We buy such iron goods as buckets, saucepans, dustpans, etc., from an *ironmonger*.

irregular not evenly spaced, e.g. *irregular* school attendance, *irregular* teeth; ■ not according to rule (or custom), e.g. You cannot bring your cat to school; that would be very *irregular*.

irresistible I cannot refuse this offer; it is *irresistible*.

irresponsible An *irresponsible* person is one who does not care whether what he does is right or wrong (or kind or unkind, wise or foolish).

irreverent lacking in respect (for religious things usually), e.g. That *irreverent* boy was making fun of our prayers.

irrigate If there isn't enough rain, farmers *irrigate* their land by flooding it from streams or wells.

irrigation In rainless countries farmers depend on *irrigation* (the use of water from streams, etc.) to water their crops.

irritable easily made angry, e.g. Grandad is *irritable* when he wakes up.

irritate Spoilt children *irritate* me (i.e. cause me to become angry). ■ If you get bits of hair down the back of your shirt they will *irritate* you (i.e. make you feel uncomfortable).

irritation annoyance, e.g. My *irritation* is caused by being called to the door for nothing. ■ itchy discomfort, e.g. The *irritation* is caused by the bits of hair the barber let slip down my back.

island As Cyprus has water all round it, it is an *island*.

isle   The *Isle* of Wight has water all round it.

isn't   (short for) is not, e.g. *Isn't* it time you were in bed?

isobar   a line on a map joining places where the air is at the same pressure. (*Isobars* are the lines which make the patterns on weather maps.)

isobars

isolate   To *isolate* anything (or anybody) is to put it on its own, apart.

isolated   Brenda had to be *isolated* (kept away from everyone) because she had an infectious disease. ■ Mac lived in an *isolated* village on the moor (a village cut off from others).

Israel   The country of the Jews, called *Israel*, is at the eastern end of the Mediterranean Sea. ■ the Jewish people.

Israelites   the Jews.

issue   to send out, e.g. to *issue* instructions; ■ to come out, e.g. water *issued* from the crack. ■ the result, e.g. The *issue* of the contest is very uncertain.

isthmus   a narrow strip of land joining two larger pieces, like the *Isthmus* of Panama.

Italian   a citizen of Italy, or his language. ■ *Italian* things are those from (or of) Italy.

italics   *sloping printing, like this.*

Italy   a country shaped like a Wellington-boot, in the middle of the Mediterranean Sea.

itch   an irritation of the skin, often caused by an insect bite, which makes you want to scratch.

itching   This spot on my arm is *itching* so much that I simply must scratch it. ■ The boys were *itching* (longing) to let off their fireworks.

item   The last *item* in our concert is a song by Betty.

its   belonging to it, e.g. The animal was feeding *its* babies.

it's   (short for) it is, e.g. *It's* time you were in bed.

itself   The bird made *itself* a nest.

I've   (short for) I have, e.g. *I've* lost my money.

ivory   The tusks of elephants, walruses, etc., consist chiefly of a valuable hard, white material called *ivory*.

ivy   a climbing evergreen plant, often found covering the walls of old buildings.

isthmus   **ivy**

jab to poke; ■ a poke, e.g. Joe woke me with a *jab* in the ribs. ■ a stab; ■ to stab, e.g. Inoculation is easy; the doctor will *jab* a needle into your arm.

jabbed Jane *jabbed* a finger into Bob's ribs to wake him up. ■ The doctor *jabbed* a needle into the patient's arm.

jabber to talk quickly and indistinctly, e.g. If you *jabber* like a monkey we cannot understand what you say.

jack a device for lifting a car, etc., e.g. when changing a wheel.

jack   jackal

jackal a small, dog-like wild animal.

jackdaw a small kind of crow which can be taught to talk, and likes collecting shiny objects.

jacket A suit of clothes consists of *jacket* and trousers.

jaded tired (or worn) out, e.g. Mother looked *jaded* after being up all night with her sick baby.

jagged The *jagged* edges of broken glass are very dangerous.

o

jaguar a large spotted wild animal of the cat family. ■ A *Jaguar* is a fast car.

jail A prisoner is locked up in *jail* as a punishment (also spelt *gaol*).

jailer, jailor A *jailer* has charge of prisoners (also spelt *gaoler*).

jam Mother makes *jam* by boiling fruit and sugar together. ■ A traffic *jam* is formed when there are so many vehicles using a road that little or no movement is possible.

jamboree a large meeting, in camp, of Boy Scouts.

jammed squeezed, e.g. I hurt my finger badly when I *jammed* it in the door. ■ Your clothes are full of creases because of the way you *jammed* them in your case.

jangle an unpleasant noise made by people squabbling or by untuneful bells; ■ to make such an untuneful noise.

January the first month of the year.

Japan a country consisting of islands off the east coast of Asia.

Japanese the people of Japan, or their language. ■ *Japanese* things are those from (or of) Japan.

jar We buy jam in a glass *jar*. ■ to jolt.

jargon a kind of talk that is difficult to understand because it includes too many long or unusual words or phrases.

jarred The tuneless noise so *jarred* upon our nerves that we told the boys to stop it.

jaunt a pleasure trip or outing.

jauntiness Billy swaggered along with such *jauntiness* that anyone could see he was very pleased with himself.

jaunty Billy swaggered along in a *jaunty* manner which showed he was very pleased with himself.

javelin a throwing spear, used nowadays in athletics.

javelin   **jellyfish**

jaw one of the two bones that your teeth are fixed in (the upper *jaw* and the lower *jaw*).

jay a brilliantly coloured European bird which chatters noisily. ■ A *jay*-walker is someone who steps carelessly into the traffic (on a road).

jazz a type of music invented by negroes in the southern states of America, which has a special kind of rhythm.

jealous Paul was *jealous* of his mother's new baby (i.e. he was annoyed because he would have liked the attention the baby was getting).

jealousy worry and annoyance because parents (or lover, etc.) give to someone else attention or love that you would like.

jeans tight, rather short trousers, made of tough cotton cloth (worn by both boys and girls).

jeer It is unkind to *jeer* (mock) at the boy who comes last in a race.

jelly When warm, a *jelly* is watery like fruit juice, but it sets solid when cool.

jellyfish The *jellyfish* looks like a lump of jelly floating in the sea, but it can sting you.

jerk a short sudden pull, e.g. The fish gives a *jerk* on the line when it takes the bait.

jersey a close-fitting woolly with sleeves. ■ *Jersey* is one of the Channel Islands.

jest a joke, e.g. The *jest* was that Harry joined in the laughter without knowing that we were laughing at him.

jester In olden times kings and other rich people employed *jesters* at their courts to amuse or cheer them.

Jesus (to Christians) the son of God, born on the first Christmas Day.

jet A *jet* of water spurted into the air from the hole in the pipe. ■ *Jet*-black is a deep, shiny black.

jet-propelled *Jet-propelled* aircraft (called jets for short) are driven by hot gases forced out of the backs of their engines.

jettison If a ship is in danger of sinking, the crew may *jettison* (throw overboard) the cargo.

jetty a landing-stage (like a seaside pier) at which ships can tie up and unload.

Jew one of the people of Palestine (now called Israel) whose history is told in the Bible.

jewel a precious stone, such as a diamond, ruby, emerald, etc.; ■ an ornament that has jewels in it.

jeweller You buy jewels, and other expensive ornaments, from a *jeweller.*

jewellery The *jewellery* consisted of rings, bracelets, necklaces, etc., set with precious stones.

jig-saw A *jig-saw* puzzle is made up of lots of odd-shaped pieces which can be fitted together to make a picture.

jig-saw   ankle joint

jilt Tom had expected to marry Mary until she *jilted* him and went off with Clive.

jingle We heard Dad's keys *jingle* as he fitted one into the lock. ■ Has anyone heard the *jingle* of Father Christmas's sleigh bells?

jive a form of jazz that became popular in the 1950's, and the dance performed to this music.

jockey a man (or boy) who rides race-horses.

jockey

join You can *join* two pieces of string by tying them together. ■ Do *join* our club; we would love to have you as a member.

joiner a woodworker, like a carpenter, but who sees to the lighter jobs, such as the fittings in a house.

joint a place where things join, e.g. the ankle (where the foot joins the leg) ; ■ a piece of meat, cut off for cooking, e.g. a *joint* of beef.

joke something said or done to make people laugh.

jolly It was a *jolly* party (i.e. there was laughter and gaiety).

jolt The bus suddenly stopped with a *jolt* that shook us all out of our seats.

jostle to push against, e.g. When you are in a big crowd you must expect that people will *jostle* you.

journalist a person, such as a reporter or editor, who writes for a newspaper or magazine.

journey You can make the *journey* from London to New York by sea or by air.

jovial A *jovial* person is one who is good natured and full of fun.

joy happiness, gladness.

joyful Christmas is a *joyful* day (i.e. a day of happiness).

jubilee a period of rejoicing; ■ the 50th anniversary of something (a Silver *Jubilee* is the 25th anniversary).

judge the person who is in charge during a trial in a court of law. ■ Will you *judge* the pictures in our art competition? (i.e. decide which picture is the best.)

judgement, judgment In my *judgment* (opinion), smoking is silly. ■ The *judgment* of the court is that the prisoner will go to prison for a year.

jug You hold the *jug* by the handle and pour out the milk from the lip.

Chinese junk

juggle to do conjuring tricks, e.g. The juggler could *juggle* with several plates, all spinning in the air at the same time.

juice the liquid that may be squeezed out of fruit or vegetables.

juicy When you bite a *juicy* pear, the juice from it runs down your chin.

July the seventh month of the year.

jumble to mix (muddle) up, e.g. If you *jumble* (up) our clothes, no-one will be able to find his own. ■ A *jumble* sale is a sale of mixed up cheap articles (for charity, usually).

jump That gate will not keep the horse in the field for he will *jump* over it.

jumper Jones is the school champion high-*jumper*. ■ Mother is knitting Mary a woollen *jumper* (a garment reaching from neck to hips).

junction A road (or railway) *junction* is a place where several roads (or railways) join.

June the sixth month of the year.

jungle land thickly covered with trees, bushes, etc., as in the Indian *jungle*.

junior Billy is the *junior* (younger) brother. ■ A *Junior* School is for the younger children (between 7 and 11 years old). ■ A *junior* partner in a business is the partner of least importance.

junk These things are only *junk* (rubbish), so throw them away. ■ a large Chinese sailing ship.

junket curds and whey; milk which has been made to set into a jelly-like state, by putting in it a special liquid called rennet.

Jupiter the largest of the planets which revolve round our sun; ■ (in olden times) the chief of the gods.

jury In English law courts a *jury* of twelve people listen to the evidence and decide whether or not the prisoner is guilty.

just A judge must be a *just* (fair) man. ■ I have *just* (a moment ago) arrived. ■ The pain is *just* (exactly) there.

justice fairness, e.g. A prisoner can be sure of *justice* in this court. ■ A *Justice* of the Peace (*J.P.* for short) is a judge in a Magistrates' Court.

justify To *justify* (show to be right) his theft of the bread, the man said that his children were starving.

jut A mass of rock that *juts* out into the sea is a danger to shipping.

jute fibre (threads) from an Indian plant, used to make sacks, etc. ■ The *Jutes* were a German tribe who invaded England long ago.

juvenile a young person. ■ Young people who want work apply to the *Juvenile* Employment Office.

kangaroo   an Australian animal which moves along in great leaps. The female carries her babies in a pouch on the front of her body.

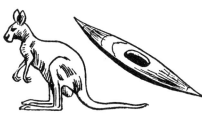

kangaroo   kayak

kayak   an Eskimo canoe, made by stretching seal-skins over a wooden frame.

keel   the length of heavy wood or metal which runs under the bottom of a boat or ship from end to end.

keen   Joan is so *keen* on horses that she spends all her spare time at the stables. ■ That knife has a *keen* (sharp) edge. ■ The wind is *keen* (sharp).

keenness   enthusiasm, eagerness.

keep   I *keep* rabbits in this hutch. ■ I shall not eat the apple now; I shall *keep* it till break.

keeper   At the zoo, the *keeper*'s job is to care for the animals. ■ A game-*keeper* protects the animals and birds on his employer's estate.

keepsake   a gift that you value because it reminds you of the person who gave it to you.

kennel   Our dog lives in a wooden *kennel*.

kept   Robert *kept* white mice as pets until his mother found out. ■ Sheila *kept* the apple so long that it went bad.

kerb   the edging of a path or pavement, e.g. It is dangerous to step off the *kerb* into the road without looking (also spelt *curb*, chiefly in the U.S.A.).

kernel   You crack the nut, throw away the shell and eat the *kernel* from inside it.

kestrel   a kind of small hawk.

ketchup   a sauce (to eat with meat, etc.) made of tomatoes, vinegar, salt, spices, sugar, etc.

kettle   Fill the *kettle* with water and put it on the stove to boil.

key   I cannot unlock the door without a *key*. ■ The *key* on the map explains the meanings of the different colours, lines, etc. ■ If you press a *key* of a piano (or organ, etc.) a note is sounded. ■ The men sang in a low *key*; the boys sang the same tune in a high *key*.

kick   To *kick* something (e.g. a ball) is to hit it with your foot.

kid   a young goat. ■ *Kid* gloves, etc., are made from the skins of kids.

kidnap   to seize someone and take him away. To *kidnap* a child is to steal him from his parents.

kennel   kernel

kidnapped The criminals who had *kidnapped* the boy would not set him free until his father had paid them money.

kidney All animals (including ourselves) have a pair of *kidneys* inside their bodies (small rounded things, low down in the back, which cleanse the blood). We buy ox-*kidneys* from the butcher, to eat.

kill I know the mouse is dead for I saw the cat *kill* it.

kiln We make our clay models hard by baking them in a hot oven called a *kiln*.

kilogram 1,000 grammes (about 2¼ lbs.) weight.

kilometre 1,000 metres (about 3,280 ft.). The distance from London to Paris is more than 300 *kilometres*.

kilowatt 1,000 watts (about the amount of power used by one bar of an electric fire).

kilt The *kilt* worn by Scottish Highlanders is a long length of cloth fastened round the waist like a skirt.

kilt   kingfisher

kin relatives. A person's next of *kin* is the relative most closely related to him.

kind Which *kind* of chocolate do you prefer, milk or plain? ■ Betty didn't have to walk home because a *kind* lady paid for her to ride in the bus.

kindergarten a school for very young children.

kindle On getting up in the morning, the first job is to *kindle* (light) the fire.

kindly *Kindly* stop that horrible noise! ■ When Billy was lost, a policeman *kindly* brought him home in his car.

kindness Mother thanked the neighbours for their *kindness* in helping to look after Billy when she was taken ill.

kindred relatives, e.g. Ian is lonely away from all his *kindred*. ■ similar (like), e.g. Mr. Smith teaches arithmetic, geometry and *kindred* subjects.

kingdom a land ruled by a king or a queen, e.g. The United *Kingdom*.

kingfisher a small, brightly-coloured bird which lives beside rivers and eats fish.

kink a loop which comes un-wanted into a wire (or chain, rope, etc.) when it is wrongly twisted.

kiosk A telephone *kiosk* is a small glass structure in the street, from which anyone may telephone. An ice-cream (or newspaper) *kiosk* is a small covered stall from which you may buy ice-cream (or news-papers).

kipper a herring split open along the backbone, and salted and smoked.

kiss Mother puts her lips to my cheek (or lips) to *kiss* me goodbye.

kitchen the room in a house (or restaurant, school, etc.) where food is prepared and cooked.

kitchenette a small kitchen.

kite a bird, like a hawk, that eats other birds or small animals; ■ a light wooden frame covered with material which, let up on a string, will fly high in the air on windy days.

kite   knave

kitten Your pretty little *kitten* will grow into a cat.

* **knack** The trick is easy when you have the *knack* (i.e. when you have learnt the special skill required).

* **knapsack** When I go on a walking holiday I pack all my luggage in a *knapsack*, which I carry on my back.

* **knave** (in playing-cards) the Jack (i.e. the picture card lowest in value); ■ a rather bad, but not very bad man.

* **knead** You *knead* dough or clay (to get it properly mixed) by squeezing it about with your hands and knuckles.

* **knee** the joint in the middle of your leg.

* **kneel** to go down on to your knees (e.g. when saying prayers).

* **knelt** The people in church last Sunday *knelt* down (on their knees) to pray for the hungry.

* **knew** Jack is not a stranger; I *knew* him when we were in the Infants' School.

* **knickers** The children made their *knickers* dirty by sitting in the mud.

* **knick-* knack** some unimportant, small, and usually decorative, article of furniture, dress or food.

* **knife** Jim cut the apple into pieces with his *knife*.

* **knight** When Mr. John Smith is made a *knight*, he is called Sir John Smith. ■ Story-book *knights* of old used to wear armour, ride horses and rescue ladies in distress.

* **knit** If I had knitting needles, I could *knit* a scarf with this wool. ■ Mother *knit* (or knitted) that woolly last year.

* **knives** Put the *knives* and forks on the table ready for dinner.

* **knob** a rounded end (as a handle or a decoration, etc.), e.g. You must turn the *knob* to open the door. There is a *knob* on the top of the stair post.

* **knock** You *knock* on a door, by banging it hard with your knuckles or with the door-knocker. To *knock* out a boxer is to hit him so hard that he cannot get up before he is counted out. ■ A *knock*-out (blow), k.o. for short, is a blow that knocks out anyone and prevents him from fighting any more.

---

* The 'k' is not sounded in any of these words.

* **knocked** The old man was *knocked* down in the street by a bus, and injured. I *knocked* on the door and the householder opened it.
* **knocker** The door-*knocker* is hinged to the letter box so that you can bang on the door with it.

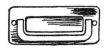

knocker

* **knot** There is a *knot* where the pieces of string have been tied together. ■ a hard place in wood (where a branch joined the tree trunk); ■ the unit by which speeds at sea are measured (a *knot* is one sea mile [6,080 ft.] per hour).
* **knotted** The string is so *knotted* (tightly tangled) that we cannot untie it.
* **know** I *know* Jane is there because I can see her.
* **knowing** *Knowing* that we were safe at home, Dad did not worry about us. ■ A *knowing* person is one who is artful.
* **knowledge** Dad has no *knowledge* of cooking; he can't even cook an egg.
* **known** John is no stranger; we have *known* him for years.
* **knuckle** any one of the bones at your finger-joints, but especially one of those where the fingers join the hands.

 Kremlin the headquarters of the government of the U.S.S.R. (Soviet Union) in Moscow.

label a piece of paper or card attached to luggage, a parcel or a bottle, etc., to show who owns it, what is in it, etc.

laboratory a room specially equipped for the conduct of scientific experiments, e.g. the school science *laboratory* (*lab* for short).

laborious A *laborious* task is one requiring hard work.

labour work; ■ to work, e.g. The workers *labour* all day for 50p. ■ The *Labour* Party is a political party originally formed by working people.

labourer a man who does hard work requiring no special skill, e.g. A bricklayer has a *labourer* to bring him the bricks and mortar he uses.

laburnum In spring, long clusters of yellow flowers hang from the *laburnum* trees, followed later by seed pods.

lace a cord used to fasten shoes; ■ to fasten (shoes, etc.) with a lace; ■ a network of thread, making patterns, and used for decoration, e.g. a *lace* collar on a dress.

lack Our defeat was due to a *lack* (need) of ammunition. ■ The only thing the campers *lack* (need) is a tin-opener.

laconic A *laconic* remark is one that uses only a few words.

* The 'k' is not sounded in any of these words.

lacquer (pron. lák-er) varnish, a special hard, glossy, Japanese varnish for painting wooden, etc., articles, or a gold-coloured coating for brass. ■ To *lacquer* anything is to coat it with lacquer.

ladder The workman rested the *ladder* against the house and climbed up it to the roof.

laden The poor donkey was *laden* with so many packages that he could hardly carry them.

ladies These *ladies* are our mothers.

ladle a special spoon with a long handle and big bowl, for serving gravy, soup, etc.

ladle   ladybird

lady This *lady* is my mother. ■ Lord Dory's wife is called *Lady* Dory.

ladybird a little flying beetle with spots on its back, liked by gardeners because it destroys greenfly.

ladylike Mary is a *ladylike* girl (i.e. she has the perfect manners of a lady).

lag If we walk slower than the others we shall *lag* behind them. ■ To *lag* pipes, boilers, etc., is to cover them with materials which will prevent heat escaping.

lagging Some of the party are *lagging* behind so we will wait for them to catch up with us. ■ covering pipes, etc., with materials that will prevent them from freezing; ■ the material used for lagging pipes, etc.

lagoon an area of sea water completely (or almost) cut off from the sea by a strip of land such as a sand-bank, coral reef, etc.

laid Our hen *laid* an egg yesterday. ■ Jane *laid* her book on the desk. ■ Mother *laid* the table (i.e. put on it the things needed for a meal).

lain Joan has *lain* on her bed asleep all the afternoon.

lair den; the place where a wild beast goes to lie down.

lake a large area of water surrounded by land, e.g. *Lake* Victoria (in Africa).

lamb A mother sheep is not as pretty as her little woolly *lamb*.

lame Jim is so *lame* after injuring his leg that he has great difficulty in walking.

lament to mourn, e.g. The woman continued to *lament* the death of her child. ■ a mournful song, e.g. The tribesmen are singing a *lament* for the death of their chief.

lamentable We made a *lamentable* mistake (i.e. a mistake for which we were afterwards very sorry).

lamp Move the *lamp* so that its light shines on your book.

lance a long spear used by horse-soldiers. ■ To *lance* a boil, etc., is to cut it open or pierce it.

land About a third of the earth's surface is *land*; the rest is water. ■ The ship's passengers will *land* in England today. ■ We hope the space rocket will *land* safely on 'Mars.

landing the piece of floor at the top of a flight of stairs. ■ The ship's passengers are *landing* in England now. ■ The space travellers made a successful *landing* on the moon.

landlady a woman who keeps an inn (public house) ■ or takes in lodgers, ■ or owns houses, etc., for which people pay her rent.

landlord a man who keeps an inn (public house); ■ a man who owns land or houses which he lets to others for rent.

landmark an object such as a church spire, factory chimney, etc., which is easily seen from a distance.

landscape a painting of a country scene; ■ a view of the countryside. ■ A *landscape* gardener is one who lays out grounds to look like natural scenery.

landslide Returning after the *landslide*, we found that masses of earth had slipped down the hillside and buried our camp.

lane a narrow road, usually between hedges.

language The *language* of England is English; French people speak the French *language*. ■ Bad *language* is speech which includes swearing or curses.

lanky A *lanky* person is one who is very tall and thin.

lantern a transparent case in which a light (especially a candle or oil lamp) is protected from the weather.

lantern   lapel

lap Mother was sitting with the baby on her *lap*. ■ Each *lap* (round) of our running track is 200 m. ■ Cats *lap* milk (drink by scooping it up on their tongues).

lapel the folded-back front part of the collar of a jacket or coat.

lapped Before the end of the race Bob had *lapped* Jimmy (i.e. was more than a lap ahead of him). ■ The cat *lapped* up the spilt milk (i.e. scooped it up with its tongue).

lapse a slight mistake or piece of misbehaviour, e.g. Tom's misbehaviour was just a *lapse*, nothing serious. ■ John speaks properly in school, but in the company of friends he will *lapse* into slang.

larch a cone-bearing tree which provides tough timber, and bark for tanning leather.

lard the soft, white fat obtained by roasting pork, and used in cooking and for making ointments, etc.

larder a cupboard or small room in which food is kept.

large The duke lived in a *large* (big) country house. ■ The soldier reported that a prisoner was at *large* (free).

largely chiefly, e.g. This illness is *largely* caused by smoking.

lark The *lark* flew off its nest in the grass and fluttered high in the sky, singing gaily.

larva a caterpillar-like grub which hatches out of an insect's egg and later changes into an adult insect.

lash It is cruel to *lash* that horse with your whip. ■ The prisoner was given ten *lashes* with the whip as a punishment.

lass (used chiefly in northern Britain and by poets) a girl.

lasso To *lasso* an animal a cowboy throws a loop of rope called a lasso over its head. ■ The loops of *lassos* are made with slip-knots so that they can be pulled tight round the animal's neck.

lasso   lines of latitude

last I hope this sunny weather will *last* to the end of the holiday. ■ There is no-one to come after Dick; he is the *last* boy. ■ You put shoes on an iron foot called a *last*, when repairing them.

lasting This shower is *lasting* a long time. ■ The punishment had a *lasting* effect on Tom (i.e. the effect did not soon wear off).

lastly in the last place, e.g. at the end of a speech: '*Lastly*, I would like to thank you all for listening so patiently.'

latch You must lift the *latch* before you can open the gate.

late Joan came to school *late* and missed the first lesson. ■ This prize was given by the *late* Mr. Smith (i.e. the Mr. Smith who is now dead).

lately We have not seen Betty *lately* (i.e. it is a long time since we saw Betty).

lateness Please excuse my *lateness*, but my bicycle broke and I had to walk.

lath a thin, narrow strip of wood, e.g. of the kind used to support tiles on a roof.

lathe a machine on which wood or metal is turned round and round so that it can be shaped by a cutting tool held against it.

lather a mass of air bubbles made by shaking or stirring soapy water; ■ the frothy sweat on a horse.

Latin the language spoken by the ancient Romans and still used in the Roman Catholic Church.

latitude Lines of *latitude* are east–west rings round the globe, the ring round the equator being 0°. (The United Kingdom lies between latitudes 50° and 60°.)

latter Here are Daphne and David; the *latter* (second one mentioned) is my brother.

laugh The joke was so funny that it made us *laugh* loudly.

laughed We *laughed* so long and loudly at the funny man that our sides ached.

laughing We were *laughing* at the funny man's jokes. ■ This is no *laughing* matter (i.e. it is serious).

laughter You know by the boys' loud *laughter* that they are enjoying the joke.

launch To *launch* a rocket is to send it up from its launching pad. ■ To *launch* a ship is to cause it to slide into the water. ■ We travelled down the river in a motor-*launch* (boat).

launder to wash and iron (clothes), e.g. Mother will *launder* your shirts.

laundry We send our clothes, bed-linen, etc., to the *laundry* to be washed and ironed.

laurel an evergreen bush with big, glossy leaves.

lava During the eruption of the volcano, red-hot *lava* came up from the crater, poured slowly down the slope and cooled to form rock.

lava

lavatory a water-closet or toilet (i.e. where you go to be 'excused'); ■ a room containing wash-basins but not necessarily a toilet.

lavender a plant with tough, grey-green leaves and very sweet-smelling mauve flowers.

lavish To *lavish* money (or love, etc.) on anyone is to give him all the money (or love, etc.) that you possibly can.

law When a *law* (rule) has been made by Parliament, those who do not keep it are punished. ■ Policemen arrest *law*-breakers.

law-abiding A *law-abiding* person is one who does not break any laws.

lawful A *lawful* act is an act which the law allows.

lawless A *lawless* person is one who breaks laws (i.e. a criminal).

lawn You must keep the grass on a *lawn* closely cut. ■ very fine linen cloth – almost like silk.

lawyer a person who makes his living by helping or advising people who are in difficulty about the law (e.g. he may defend a prisoner in court or help to draw up a will).

lay a song or poem. ■ A *lay*man is anyone who is not a clergyman. ■ *Lay* the patient on the bed. ■ A hen's job is to *lay* eggs. ■ *Lay* the table for tea (i.e. put on it the things needed). ■ Last night as I *lay* asleep, the bed broke.

layer I can see a *layer* of dust on this polished table. ■ That hen is a good *layer* (i.e. she lays many eggs).

lazily Bob, who had no intention of working, leaned *lazily* on his spade.

laziness No-one can accuse us of *laziness*, for we have worked hard all day.

lazy That *lazy* boy hasn't done a stroke of work.

lea grass-land, a meadow.

lead (pron. leed) The blind man had a dog to *lead* him (show him the way). ■ (pron. led) a very heavy, rather soft, grey metal. ■ *Lead* pencils contain ■ black-*lead* (a form of carbon, also called graphite).

leader someone who goes in front, shows the way or sets an example; ■ a person who leads or commands.

leadership The team's success was due to Dick's *leadership* (i.e. Dick's ability to show them what to do).

leading most important, e.g. our *leading* scientist; a *leading* article in a newspaper. ■ The dog is *leading* a blind man along the street.

leaf This *leaf* of the book has page 183 on the front and page 184 on the back. ■ The *leaf* of a plant is usually thin, flat and green.

leaf　　　**leapfrog**

leafless A *leafless* plant is one that has no leaves on it.

leaflet a small leaf or part of a big leaf; ■ a single sheet (sometimes folded) of printed paper, usually handed out free or put through your door.

leafy full of leaves, e.g. Most English trees are *leafy* in summer, but leafless in winter.

league a distance of about 3 miles; ■ an organization of people (or groups), formed to help each other, e.g. The members of our Chess *League* arrange games with each other.

leak I know there is a *leak* in the kettle because water is dripping on to the stove. ■ If secrets *leak* out, people gradually get to know about them.

leakage a leaking out of information that should have been kept secret.

leaky If you put water in that *leaky* kettle, it will drip out on to the stove.

lean *Lean* meat has no fat in it. ■ If you *lean* on (rest against) those wet railings you'll dirty your sleeve. ■ *Lean* the pole against the wall (i.e. put it in a sloping position).

leaning Joe stood at the street corner, *leaning* on a lamp-post for support. ■ Anything in a *leaning* position is not upright (e.g. The *Leaning* Tower of Pisa).

leap to jump; ■ a jump. ■ *Leap*-frog is a game in which some players jump over others who are bending down.

leap-year every fourth year, when there are 29 days in February instead of the usual 28.

learn You come to school to *learn* how to read and write, do arithmetic, etc.

learned (pron. learn-ed) A *learned* person is one who knows a great deal.

learner An L on a car means that the driver is a *learner* who is being taught how to drive.

learning We are *learning* how to spell these words. ■ knowledge gained by reading, attending lessons, etc.

learnt Dad will not let me go out in the boat till I have *learnt* to swim.

leash When I take my dog for a walk I keep him on a *leash* so that he cannot run into the road.

least smallest (amount), e.g. John had done less work than Jim, but Jane had done *least* of all. ■ Pat is not the *least* bit afraid.

leather a tough material made from the skins of animals (chiefly cattle) and used to make shoes, etc.

leave *Leave* it here (do not take it away). ■ *Leave* the room (go out of it). ■ Mother would not run away and *leave* (forsake) us. ■ I have *leave* (permission) to be away from school tomorrow. ■ Uncle says he will *leave* me his gold watch (i.e. in his will).

leaves When he *leaves* the room we will follow him. ■ In autumn the *leaves* fall off such trees as the oak and apple.

leavings The *leavings* from our dinner plates are sent to the farmer's pigs.

lectern a church reading-desk. The *lectern* on which the Bible rests is usually in the form of an eagle with outstretched wings.

lecture The police officer gave us a *lecture* (talk) on road safety.

led Jane took the blind man by the hand and *led* him across the road.

ledge John was half-way up the cliff on a *ledge* hardly wide enough for him to stand on.

ledger a payments book, e.g. The amount of every sum of money paid out or received by the business is written down in the *ledger*.

lee If you stand on the *lee* (side) of a building, etc., you are sheltered from the wind.

leek an onion-like vegetable, the national emblem of Wales.

leer a glance which has a sly, naughty expression (and sometimes called in slang, 'a dirty look').

left Most people cannot write with their *left* hands. ■ I *left* my bicycle out in the rain and it rusted. ■ Jim *left* (went out of) the room. ■ Uncle *left* me all his money (i.e. in his will).

legal having to do with the law, e.g. a *legal* document; ■ allowed by law, e.g. Is it *legal* to take birds' eggs?

legend an old story thought by many people to be true, e.g. The *legends* of ancient Greece and Rome, or of King Arthur.

legendary A *legendary* person is one known only in legends, not in history.

lectern   lens

legible Be sure that your handwriting is *legible* (easy to read).

legion a very large number (originally, a group of 3,000–6,000 Roman soldiers). ■ The British *Legion* is an organization of old soldiers.

legitimate lawful, e.g. If your actions are *legitimate* you need not hide them from the police.

leisure spare time, when you can do what pleases you.

leisurely We had a *leisurely* meal (i.e. we didn't hurry over it).

lemon a fruit like an orange, but pale yellow in colour and more sour; ■ the colour of a lemon.

lemonade a drink made from lemons; or a similar-looking drink having the taste of lemons.

lend If I *lend* you something, you keep it for a time, then give it back to me.

length The *length* of this rope is ten metres. ■ The *length* of this lesson is one hour.

lengthen Mother has to *lengthen* my coat because it is too short for me. ■ The days *lengthen* (become longer) as summer approaches.

lengthways, lengthwise When elastic stretches *lengthways* (or *lengthwise*) it becomes longer.

lengthy The visitor gave us a *lengthy* talk (i.e. the talk was longer than we expected or wanted).

lenient A judge who is *lenient* will not punish people severely.

lens a disc of glass with curved surfaces (i.e. it is not the same thickness in the middle as round the edge). *Lenses* are used in cameras, spectacles (glasses), telescopes, etc.

lent I *lent* John my bicycle and he hasn't yet returned it to me. ■ *Lent*, to church people, is a period of fasting (the six weeks before Easter).

leopard a large, spotted, wild animal of the cat family.

leopard

leper someone who has leprosy, a disease which causes the body to waste away.

leprosy a horrible disease which causes scales to form on the skin and which slowly eats the body away.

less A bicycle costs *less* than a car.

lessen I'm taking these apples out of my bag to *lessen* the load I have to carry.

lesser the smaller one of two things, e.g. the *lesser* celandine (a flower, the smaller one of two kinds); the *lesser* of two evils.

lesson At school, our first *lesson* today is arithmetic.

lest We dare not play jokes on Mr. Kane *lest* he should become angry.

let Please *let* me see your book. ■ If I *let* a house to someone, he pays me rent for the use of it, but the house remains mine.

lethal A *lethal* weapon (or dose, etc.) is one that can kill.

letter   Z is the last *letter* of the alphabet. ■ Write a *letter* to Uncle to thank him for the birthday present.

lettuce   a green, cabbage-like vegetable, eaten raw in salads.

level   A *level* surface is one that is horizontal with no hollows or bumps on its surface. ■ To *level* ground is to make it level. ■ A (spirit) *level* is an instrument that shows, by a bubble in a tube of liquid, whether or not a surface is horizontal.

levelled   We *levelled* our cricket pitch last season (i.e. we made it level). ■ He *levelled* the gun at me (i.e. he took aim).

lever   a strong bar used to lift heavy things, or to force open doors, boxes, etc. ■ To *lever* something up is to lift it with a lever.

lever

liable   Careless motorists are *liable* to meet with accidents. ■ A husband is *liable* for his wife's debts (he is forced, by law, to pay them).

liar   someone who says things that are not true.

libel   something printed (or written) that causes people to have a bad opinion of someone. ■ To *libel* someone is to cause people to think ill of him by printing or writing something (even though it is true).

liberal   A *liberal* person is one who gives away things in large quantity (often all he can afford, or more). ■ A *Liberal* is a member of ■ the *Liberal* (political) Party.

liberate   to set free, e.g. *Liberate* all the prisoners.

liberty   All prisoners want their *liberty* (freedom). ■ The prisoners were set at *liberty* (freed). ■ To take a *liberty* is to do something that is not allowed. ■ You are at *liberty* (free) to say what you like.

librarian   the person in charge of a library.

library   a collection of books, e.g. The professor has a *library* of thousands of books. ■ a room in which books are set out on shelves. e.g. This room is the *library*.

lice   insects which live in people's (and animals') hair and suck their blood, causing itching.

licence   You have to buy a *licence* (a paper giving permission) before you are allowed to run a car, work a TV set, own a dog, etc.

license   to grant a licence to, e.g. We want the council to *license* our hall for dancing. That shop is *licensed* to sell tobacco.

lick   To *lick* (your lip, etc.) is to wet it with your tongue. A cat will *lick* its fur to clean it.

licorice   a black substance from a plant-root, used to make sweets, etc. (usually spelt *liquorice*).

lie   something that you say or write, knowing that it is not true. ■ To *lie* is to say something that is not true. ■ On Sundays I *lie* in bed till 9 o'clock.

lieutenant   an officer of low rank in the army, navy, etc.

life I have lived here all my *life* (i.e. ever since I was born). ■ Your *life* begins when you are born and ends when you die.

lifeless The explorers found their comrade's *lifeless* body and buried it. ■ The orchestra gave a *lifeless* (dull) performance of the music.

lifelike The statue was so *lifelike* that people actually spoke to it.

lift Please *lift* this case from the floor on to the table for me. ■ We can travel up in the *lift* instead of climbing the stairs.

light When it is day*light* we can see things by the *light* of the sun. ■ Switch on that *light* so that I can see. ■ If you *light* the lamp they will see it in the darkness. ■ *Light* red is pink. ■ The parcel is so *light* that a baby could lift it.

lighten I took some of the parcels from Tom to *lighten* his load. ■ You can *lighten* the room by drawing the curtains or by switching on the light.

light-hearted You feel *light-hearted* when you are not worried about anything.

lightly If you tread *lightly* your footsteps will not be heard.

lightning During the storm flashes of *lightning* appeared in the sky.

lightning   **lilac**

likable Simon is a *likable* boy (i.e. people soon or easily like him).

like I *like* sweets (i.e. I enjoy eating them). I *like* Joan (i.e. I enjoy being with her). ■ Margaret looks very *like* her sister Jane.

likelihood There is no *likelihood* that I shall win the race (i.e. it is not to be expected.)

likely It is *likely* to rain today (i.e. rain is to be expected). ■ A *likely* candidate is one whom we expect to be successful.

liken You can *liken* your eye to a camera (i.e. show ways in which the eye is like a camera).

likeness I see no *likeness* between chalk and cheese (i.e. they are different in every way). ■ Betty painted a *likeness* (picture) of Pat.

likewise Harry fell over the rope and Jim did *likewise* (i.e. Jim also fell over it).

liking Is the drink to your *liking*? (i.e. Is it so made that you will enjoy it?) ■ John has a *liking* for adventure stories (i.e. he enjoys reading them).

lilac a bush that has cone-shaped clusters of sweet-smelling tiny flowers, mauve or white in colour; ■ the mauve colour of lilac flowers.

lily a plant that grows from a bulb and bears showy flowers – usually white and strongly perfumed. ■ The *lily* of the valley is small, sweetly perfumed and has many bell-like flowers hanging from each stem.

limb an arm, leg, or wing of a creature; ■ the branch of a tree.

lime a white substance, made by burning limestone, which becomes hot if you wet it; ■ a fruit like a lemon; ■ a European tree with heart-shaped leaves and sweet-smelling yellow blossom.

limelight Sheila likes being in the *limelight* (i.e. she likes to be the centre of attention and admiration). ■ (years ago) a bright stage light made by heating lime.

limerick a silly, amusing rhyme of five lines (usually beginning: 'There was a young —— of ——').

limestone a hard rock formed long ago under the sea, now used for making cement, etc.

limit There is a speed *limit* of 30 m.p.h. in towns.

limited Only a *limited* number of people can travel in the coach (i.e. not more than a certain number). ■ A *limited* company, such as J. Smith & Co. *Ltd.*, can be made to pay debts only up to a certain fixed amount.

limousine a large saloon car.

limp not stiff; ■ to walk with difficulty owing to injury to foot, leg, etc.

limpet a small shell-fish which clings to rocks, etc., very tightly.

line This is a line ——; ■ a thin rope or wire, e.g. a washing *line*. ■ To *line* a garment is to sew a thinner material inside it.

linen cloth made of fibres from the stalk of the flax plant.

liner a passenger ship or aircraft which regularly travels to and from certain places.

linger Though Joe has said goodbye, he still *lingers* about the place, unwilling to go.

lingering a *lingering* death, etc., is one that lasts a particularly long time.

liniment an oily liquid for rubbing into the body where there are pains caused by rheumatism, etc.,

lining a layer of (usually thinner) material sewn inside a garment. ■ The bird is *lining* its nest with a lining of moss.

link Each *link* that makes up a chain is equally important. ■ *Link* (join) hands to make a circle.

links Dad goes to the *links* to play golf. ■ A ferry *links* England with the Isle of Wight. ■ Cuff-*links* are little ornamental chains for fastening cuffs.

linnet a small, brown song-bird.

linoleum a floor covering made of canvas coated with hardened linseed oil, etc., and usually ornamented with coloured designs (*lino* for short).

linseed the seed of the flax plant. ■ (*Linseed* oil is squeezed out of it.)

lint linen cloth made fluffy on one side by scraping, and used for covering sore places and cuts.

lion The *lion* is so brave and handsome that he is called the king of beasts.

limpet

lion

lioness a female lion.

liquefy to make liquid, e.g. You can *liquefy* ice by warming it. You can *liquefy* air by compressing it.

liquid If you melt butter it becomes *liquid*. ■ Other *liquids* are oil, milk and water.

liquidate To *liquidate* an organization is to bring its activities to an end. To *liquidate* people is to get rid of them (often by violent means).

liquor a drink such as beer, whisky, etc., which can make people drunk.

liquorice a black substance, made from a plant root, and used to make sweets, etc. (also spelt *licorice*).

Lisbon the chief city of Portugal.

lisp People who *lisp* use the sound 'th' instead of 's' when they speak, e.g. 'thing uth a thong', for 'sing us a song'.

list In the register is a *list* of the names of all the children in the class. ■ The ship has a *list* (i.e. it is leaning over to one side).

listen If you *listen* you can hear the music.

listened If you had *listened* you would have heard what I said.

listener After the programme had been broadcast over the radio, one *listener* wrote to complain about it.

listening That nasty child was standing behind the door *listening* to what we were saying.

listless too tired to be interested in anything – especially anything requiring an effort.

lit When darkness came we *lit* the lamp.

literally 'We are wet through' usually means simply, 'We are very wet'; but 'We are *literally* wet through' means that the rain has actually come right through to our skins.

literature books, poems, etc., by the best writers. ■ In our *literature* lessons we study Shakespeare's plays and stories by Dickens.

litre the unit for measuring liquids, equal to 1,000 cubic centimetres (about 1¾ pints).

litter The beauty spot was spoilt by the *litter* (i.e. waste paper, tins, bottles, etc.) left by sight-seers. ■ The sow had a *litter* of ten piglets (i.e. ten baby pigs were born on the one occasion).

litter   litter of piglets

little We need a *little* (not much) water. ■ Mike is a *little* (small) boy. ■ Stay a *little* (short time) longer.

live (pron. liv) I *live* in that house. ■ The doctor says the patient will *live* (i.e. stay alive). ■ (pron. live) That is a *live* fish (i.e. not dead). ■ That is a *live* wire (i.e. electricity is running through it). ■ *Live*-stock are farm animals.

livelihood A person's *livelihood* is what he does for a living – his work.

lively full of life and energy, e.g. The baby is a *lively* little thing.

liven To *liven* anything (e.g. a party) is to put life and gaiety into it.

liver a part of your body, inside you, which makes juices to aid digestion, etc. We had (sheep's) *liver* and bacon for dinner.

liverish Uncle is *liverish* (bad-tempered) today. (Strictly, it means that there is something wrong with his liver.)

lives (pron. livs) Betty *lives* in that house. ■ (pron. lives) We have been in England all our *lives* (i.e. ever since we were born).

livid the colour of a bruise (black and blue). ■ (In slang, 'He was *livid*' means that he was very angry.)

living We are *living* in this house now. ■ What does your dad do for a *living*? ■ Most of the people *living* now will be dead in 100 years.

lizard a four-footed animal like a tiny crocodile, which likes hot, dry places.

lizard   llama

llama a South American animal like a small, hairy camel without a hump.

load To *load* a gun is to put the shell or cartridge into it. ■ The lorry was carrying a *load* of sand.

■ The men had to *load* the lorry with sand.

loaded A *loaded* gun is one containing a bullet, etc., ready for firing. ■ The men *loaded* the lorry with the goods it was to carry.

loaf Buy a *loaf* of bread for our tea. ■ To *loaf* (about) is to loiter around, doing nothing.

loaf   lobe

loafer someone who loiters about lazily.

loam a good soil, in which plants grow well.

loan This money is a *loan* from James, which I must pay back.

loath unwilling, e.g. I am *loath* to get out of bed on cold mornings (also spelt *loth*).

loathe I *loathe* (hate) big, hairy spiders.

loathing extreme dislike, e.g. Jean couldn't hide her *loathing* for the horrible creature.

loathsome That huge, hairy spider is a *loathsome* creature (i.e. it is so very unpleasant that you want to get away from it).

loaves We must buy several *loaves* of bread to feed all those boys.

lobby an entrance-hall or porch; ■ the big hall in the House of Commons where people may go to meet their Members of Parliament.

lobe The *lobe* of your ear is the flat, soft piece at the bottom.

lobster a shell-fish with a long tail and big claws. ■ Lobsters are caught in basket-work *lobster*-pots.

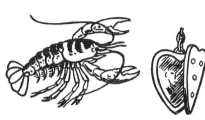

lobster   locket

local Your *local* cinema (or church, shop, public house, etc.) is the one in the district in which you live.

locality Betty does not live in our *locality* (the area where we live).

locally The fruit we buy is grown *locally* (i.e. in our own district).

locate To *locate* something is to find out exactly where it is, e.g. Before the doctor can remove the coin Baby has swallowed, he must *locate* it.

location Film actors are on *location* when they are making a film away from the studio. ■ First, we must decide on the *location* of our new swimming pool (i.e. where it is to be built).

loch a Scottish lake, e.g. There is said to be a monster in *Loch* Ness.

lock a length of canal in which the water level can be raised or lowered, ■ and which has *lock* gates at each end. ■ You *lock* a door ■ by turning the key in the *lock*.

locker Each boy has a *locker* (small private cupboard) in which to keep his belongings.

locket There is a picture of Dad in the *locket* that Mother wears on the gold chain round her neck.

locomotive Our train was pulled by a steam *locomotive*.

locust a flying insect, like a grass-hopper. (They invade hot countries in swarms and do enormous damage by eating every green leaf.) ■ a tree whose fruit is the *locust*-bean.

locust   loganberry

lodge I *lodge* with Mrs Smith (i.e. I pay to live in her house). ■ Bill managed to *lodge* the parcel on the top of the wall (i.e. he placed it so that it wouldn't fall). ■ a beaver's lair.

lodger someone who pays to live in another person's house.

lodgings room(s) which you pay to live in (not in a hotel).

loft a room in the roof of a building.

lofty The town's buildings were overshadowed by the *lofty* mountain peaks high above them.

loganberry a fruit like a large raspberry.

loin the part of the body between the hips and the bottom ribs.

loiter We must not *loiter* (wait about) or we shall be late for school.

loll You look lazy when you *loll* in your chair in that careless way.

London the capital city of England.

lone In that cloudy sky only one *lone* star could be seen.

loneliness I couldn't bear the *loneliness* of a desert island; I must have someone with me.

lonely Grandma lives on her own, so she is *lonely* if no-one goes to keep her company.

long This ruler is a foot *long*. ■ How *long* will it take you to dress? ■ Fifty years is a *long* time. ■ To *long* for something is to wish for it very much. ■ A *long*-winded person is one who goes on talking too long.

longing I am *longing* for the holidays (i.e. I am looking forward to the holidays very much indeed).

longitude Lines of *longitude* go from north to south round the globe like hoops, passing through both North and South Poles. The line of 0° *longitude* passes through Greenwich (London).

lines of longitude

look *Look* there and tell us what you see. ■ Help me to *look* for my lost ring. ■ I know you are pleased by the *look* on your face.

looking Jane is *looking* at the television. ■ We are *looking* for a lost ring. ■ Jennifer is a good-*looking* (beautiful) girl.

loom a machine on which thread is woven into cloth; ■ to appear indistinctly, e.g. I don't like the strange shapes that *loom* out of the fog.

loop the shape made when a curved line crosses itself.

loop   **loophole**

loophole a narrow slit in a castle wall through which arrows could be shot; ■ a way of getting round a rule or law.

loose The dog's collar was so *loose* that it came off over his head. ■ To *loose* an animal is to untie him.

loosen If your belt is too tight, *loosen* it.

loot things taken by soldiers from an enemy (or any goods wrongly taken). ■ To *loot* a city is to take away valuables.

lop To *lop* a tree is to cut branches off it. ■ hanging down loosely, e.g. a *lop*-eared rabbit.

lop-sided Your drawing of the vase is *lop-sided* (i.e. one side is bigger than the other).

lord The *Lord* is God or Christ. ■ *Lord* Nelson was a famous sailor. ■ a master or ruler, e.g. The *lord* sent his servant to buy food.

lorry   A *lorry* came along the road carrying a load of sand.

lorry   louse

lose   If you *lose* your ring through carelessness, don't expect us to help you to find it. ■ If we *lose* the battle, the enemy will win.

loss   If you lose anything valuable you should report your *loss* to the police.

lost   Give us a description of the *lost* dog, and we will try to find it. ■ I have *lost* my way; please tell me how to get home. ■ I do not know where my dog is; I have *lost* him.

loth   unwilling, e.g. I am *loth* to part with my dog (also spelt *loath*).

lotion   a liquid put on the skin to heal sore places, etc.

lottery   In a *lottery*, many people buy tickets, but only those whose tickets have the same numbers as those drawn out of a hat win a prize.

loud   The radio is so *loud* that people in the street can hear it. ■ The colours in your tie are too *loud* (bright).

loudspeaker   The sound of a radio or television set comes from the *loudspeaker*.

lounge   a room in which to sit at ease; ■ to stand or sit in a lazy way.

louse   an insect that lives in the hair or skin of animals or people, and causes itching by biting, sucking, etc.

lout   a rough, ill-mannered young man or boy.

lovable   A *lovable* baby is one whom people can't help loving.

love   If you *love* someone you will want to please him and make him happy. ■ Bob is in *love* with Anne and hopes to marry her one day.

loveliness   great beauty.

lovely   The bride looked *lovely* (i.e. very beautiful). ■ (slang) pleasing, e.g. It was a *lovely* party.

lover   someone who is in love. *Lovers* are a boy and girl in love. ■ A music-*lover* is someone who enjoys music very much.

loving   To show that I am fond of Mother, I end my letters to her with the words, 'Your *loving* son, John.'

low   You can step over a *low* wall. ■ Women sing the high notes and men the *low* ones. ■ Names beginning with W come *low* down an alphabetical list.

lower   We went down steps to a *lower* room. ■ *Lower* the bucket into the well to get some water. ■ Good-mannered people would not *lower* themselves to be so rude.

lowland(s)   low-lying country.

lowly   A *lowly* person is one who has not a high opinion of himself – is not at all proud.

loyal   A *loyal* person is one who does not say or do anything that could cause harm to his queen, country, government, school, etc.

loyalty   loyal behaviour.

lozenge a small sweet, especially one sucked as a medicine, e.g. a throat *lozenge*. ■ *Lozenge*-shaped is diamond-shaped (◇).

lubricant Any substance (e.g. grease) used to make parts of a machine move more easily on or in each other is a *lubricant*.

lubricate To *lubricate* a machine is to put oil or grease in it so that the parts move more easily.

lubrication To ensure the *lubrication* of a car, you pour oil into the engine and squeeze grease into the joints.

luck There is no way of knowing how to pick a winning ticket out of the hat; it is just *luck* (chance).

luckily by chance, e.g. The rain was unexpected, but *luckily* we had our coats with us.

lucky A *lucky* person is one to whom something pleasant happens by good fortune.

ludicrous It is *ludicrous* for a big, fat boy like John to act the part of a fairy.

lug It was only by a great effort that the boys were able to *lug* (drag) the heavy log to their camp. ■ Fishermen find *lug*-worms for bait by digging in sandy beaches.

luggage The travellers' *luggage* consisted of a variety of cases, bags and trunks.

lukewarm neither hot nor cold, e.g. I don't like *lukewarm* soup. ■ neither keen on something nor against it.

lull A *lull* in a storm is a period of calm. ■ To *lull* a baby to sleep, you could try rocking it, or singing to it.

lullaby a special kind of quiet song intended to lull a baby to sleep.

lumber roughly cut wood (still in logs). ■ In the *lumber* room we keep the various household things, such as pieces of furniture, for which we have no use at the moment.

lumbering the cutting down and trimming of trees, e.g. *Lumbering* is an important industry in Canada.

lumberjack a man who cuts down and trims trees.

lumberjack

luminous Things that are *luminous* can be seen in the dark because they give off light (e.g. the hands of a *luminous* clock).

lump a swelling, e.g. Mike has a *lump* on his head through hitting it on the door. ■ a piece of no particular shape, e.g. a *lump* of rock.

lumpy This custard is *lumpy* (i.e. it contains lumps).

lunacy madness (i.e. being a lunatic).

lunar having to do with the moon, e.g. A *lunar* eclipse is an eclipse of the moon. A *lunar* month is from one new moon to the next (usually taken as four weeks; actually, it is $29\frac{1}{2}$ days).

lunatic a madman whose madness was once thought to be connected with changes in the moon. ■ any very foolish person, e.g. Who was the *lunatic* who gave the baby matches to play with?

lunch, luncheon the midday meal.

lung You have two *lungs* in your chest and when you breathe in, you fill them with air.

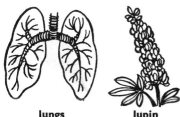

lungs   **lupin**

lunge We saw the man *lunge* forward with his sword and run it through his opponent's body.

lupin a tall blue, white or yellow garden flower. (On each stem are many small flowers, which together make a big spike of blossom.)

lurch The rough road caused the bus to *lurch* from side to side. ■ To leave anyone in the *lurch* is to leave him when he is in difficulties.

lure You can *lure* the animal out of its hole by putting down a tasty piece of food nearby.

lurid A *lurid* description is one that gives special details of all that is most exciting or frightful. ■ *Lurid* clouds, complexion, etc., have an unnatural, fiery colour.

lurk Robbers may *lurk* (be waiting) in those dark caves.

luscious delicious and sweet, e.g. This is a *luscious* peach.

lusty very fit and strong, e.g. a *lusty* young man.

lute an old-time musical instrument, like a guitar with a rounded back.

Luxembourg a small country with a capital city of the same name, which lies between France, Belgium and Germany.

luxurious *Luxurious* things are those bought at great expense to make life easy and comfortable, e.g. expensive cars, houses, etc.

luxury something which is intended to give pleasure or comfort, but which you can easily do without.

lying Bob was *lying* in bed, asleep. ■ The man is *lying* (not speaking the truth).

lynch A mob of people *lynch* a man when they hang him unlawfully after a mock trial.

lyre an ancient harp-like instrument, but having its strings arranged like those on a guitar – of about equal length and passing over a bridge.

lute   **lyre**

lyric the words of a song, i.e. a kind of poem.

M. (short for) Monsieur, the French for 'Mister', e.g. *M.* Fauré is a Frenchman.

ma'am (short for) madam, a polite way of addressing a lady, e.g. Can I help you, *ma'am*?

macaroni long, brittle tubes of dried flour paste, which become soft when cooked (used to make milk puddings, etc.).

macaroon a small cake or biscuit, made of ground almonds, egg, sugar, etc.

mac, mack (short for) macintosh, a thin overcoat specially coated with rubber, etc., to keep out the rain.

mace a heavy club with spikes on it, once used for fighting; ■ an ornamental club like that carried before mayors, or placed in the House of Commons when Parliament is sitting.

machine This motorcycle is a powerful *machine*. Mother uses a sewing *machine*. ■ It will take less time to *machine* the curtains than to sew them by hand.

machinery In the factory we saw the *machinery* which makes lumps of metal into car engines.

mackerel a sea-fish, caught for food.

macintosh a thin overcoat specially treated with rubber, etc., to keep out the rain.

mad A *mad* person is one whose mind is diseased, causing him to do and say wild and foolish things. ■ (slang) very angry, e.g.

I was *mad* with the puppy for tearing my coat.

madam a polite way of addressing a lady, e.g. Can I help you, *madam*?

madame French for 'Mistress' (Mrs), e.g. *Madame* Fauré is M. Fauré's wife.

madden to make mad, or, more usually, to make very angry, e.g. It would *madden* you to see those lovely animals being shot.

maddening It is *maddening* (i.e. it makes you very angry) to walk all the way to school and then remember that it is closed for a holiday.

madman a man who is mad, e.g. The *madman* had to be held to prevent him from injuring himself.

madness The man's *madness* caused him to do very foolish and wild things. ■ It would be *madness* (extreme foolishness) to swim in that rough sea.

Madrid the capital city of Spain.

magazine a weekly or monthly paper or book, often on glossy paper and with many coloured pictures.

maggot When a fly's egg hatches, a *maggot* (little caterpillar) comes out of it. A *maggot* in an apple has hatched out of a moth's egg.

mace   mackerel

magic a power, which magicians pretend they have, to make things happen as they wish, e.g. to make a rabbit appear from an empty top hat.

magician The *magician* pulled a rabbit from his empty top hat. ■ The *magician* in the fairy story turned the woman into a toad.

magistrate The police take law-breakers to the local court (a *Magistrates'* Court), ■ where a *magistrate* is the judge.

magnet If a piece of iron is a *magnet*, it will pull other pieces of iron to it. The ends of a *magnet* suspended by a thread, or balanced on a point, will point north and south.

magnetic A *magnetic* needle points to the north and pulls iron objects. ■ A *magnetic* person is one who attracts others.

magnetism If a magnet loses its *magnetism* it will no longer attract things.

magnificent The palace is *magnificent* (large and expensive), worthy of a great man.

magnified The glass *magnified* the object so that we saw it bigger than its proper size.

magnify If you *magnify* anything (e.g. with a magnifying glass) it appears to be bigger than it really is.

magpie a handsome black and white European bird which chatters noisily.

mahogany a reddish-brown wood used for making furniture, etc.

maid female servant, e.g. Mrs Browne's *maid* brought in a tray of tea. ■ a girl, e.g. The *maid* called her father.

maiden a girl. ■ A *maiden* lady is an unmarried lady. ■ an over (6 balls) in cricket in which no runs are scored.

mail metal armour, e.g. chain-*mail*. ■ A *mail* van carries letters, etc. ■ To *mail* a letter is to send it by post.

maim to cripple or cause other severe injuries to the body, e.g. That dangerous old car may one day *maim* someone.

main chief, most important, e.g. a *main* line train. ■ A water *main* is an important, big water pipe. ■ To do something with might and *main* is to do it with all your strength.

mainland The *mainland* of Britain is the biggest part (England, Wales and Scotland), but Britain also includes other smaller islands, such as the Isle of Wight, the Hebrides, etc.

mainly Many eastern people live *mainly* on rice (i.e. most of their food is rice).

maintain To *maintain* a road, etc., is to keep it in repair. ■ I *maintain* that anyone can learn to spell (i.e. I insist that this is true).

maize Indian corn. (Many large, yellow maize seeds grow tightly packed together on each corn cob.)

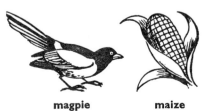

magpie   maize

majestic grand, stately and impressive, e.g. The lion is a *majestic* animal. The king, wearing his crown and robes of state, was a *majestic* figure.

majesty We hope to see Her *Majesty* (the Queen).

major an army officer next in rank above a captain. ■ The *major* part of anything is the greater or larger part.

majority The *majority* of the children here speak English (i.e. more children speak English than do not).

make Let us *make* a model aircraft. ■ *Make* me a cup of tea. ■ If Ben does not wish to come we must *make* (force) him. ■ What *make* of television is yours? (i.e. Which firm made it?)

maker A dress-*maker* is someone who makes ladies' clothes. ■ By 'Our *Maker*', we mean God.

makeshift As there was no proper stage in the hall, we had to use a *makeshift* one made of tables tied together.

making Mother is *making* the bed (i.e. getting it ready). ■ Betty is *making* mud pies. ■ James has the *makings* of a good school captain (i.e. he has the necessary abilities).

malaria a serious illness passed to people by the bite of a mosquito.

male Men, boys, bulls and cocks, etc., are *male*; women, girls, cows and hens, etc., are female.

malice a desire to be unkind or hurtful. ■ To bear *malice* is to hope for revenge on someone.

mallet a hammer with a big, wooden head.

malt To make *malt* you cause barley (or other grain) to sprout and then heat it. *Malt* is used in brewing beer and other drinks.

mammal any animal that feeds its young on its own milk, e.g. a cow, dog, etc.

mammoth a huge, hairy elephant with long curved tusks, that used to live in Europe thousands of years ago.

manage to control or run (a business, etc.). ■ I don't think I can be there by six, but I will try to *manage* (arrange) it.

management Mother hasn't much money and it is only by good *management* (i.e. using it cleverly) that she is able to buy all we need.

manager the person in charge of the running of a shop, football team, etc.

mane the long hair on the neck of a horse or lion.

manfully bravely, e.g. Billy bore the pain *manfully*.

mange a skin disease which affects the hair or wool of animals.

mangel (mangel-wurzel) a large, pale kind of beetroot, grown for cattle food (also spelt *mangold*).

mallet   mammoth

manger a container for animals' food (hay, etc.), like a long box, open at the top. Jesus, who was born in a stable, was put in a *manger* to sleep.

manger   mangle

mangle a wringer, a machine in which washing is squeezed between rollers to remove water from it. ■ To *mangle* washing is to put it through a mangle. ■ To *mangle* other things is to hack them about.

mangled Yesterday, I *mangled* the washing (i.e. put it through the mangle). ■ The cat was badly *mangled* (hacked about) by the car that hit it.

manhood When a boy reaches *manhood*, he should behave like a man.

mania Helen has a *mania* (craze) for ponies. ■ Strictly, *mania* is a kind of madness which makes people violent.

maniac a noisy, screaming madman.

manicure To *manicure* your hands is to make them more beautiful, e.g. by cutting and polishing finger-nails.

mankind *Mankind* (i.e. the people of the earth) must learn how to grow more food or millions will starve.

manly A *manly* fellow (boy or man) is one who behaves as you would expect the best of men to behave – e.g. bravely, gallantly, etc.

manner The Chinese eat their food in a strange *manner* (way) with chopsticks.

manners People who have good *manners* are polite and considerate to others.

manœuvre a movement of soldiers, ships, etc., e.g. The general won the battle by a clever *manœuvre*. ■ a crafty, sly plan, e.g. By some *manœuvre* the boys managed to arrive too late to do the work.

manor a lord's lands – ■ usually including his *manor*-house.

mansion a big house. ■ The *Mansion* House is the official home of the Lord Mayor of London.

manslaughter the unplanned killing of someone. (Planned killing is murder.)

mantel, mantelpiece Round a fireplace there is usually a *mantelpiece* of tiles or bricks, on top of which you can stand a clock or ornaments.

mantle a woman's garment, like a loose overcoat without sleeves. ■ A gas *mantle* is a tube of special material placed over a gas flame so that it gives out a bright light.

manual *Manual* work is work done with the hands. A carpenter is a *manual* worker.

manufacture That factory was built for the *manufacture* of furniture. ■ The workers in that factory *manufacture* furniture.

manufacturer If goods are not well made you should complain to the *manufacturer* (i.e. the person or firm who made them).

manure animal droppings, spread over land so that crops grow better. ■ Artificial *manures* are chemicals, put into the soil to improve crops. ■ To *manure* land is to spread manure on it.

many There are *many* children in a school.

maple a broad-leafed tree; some kinds produce sugar, others are grown because they are decorative. ■ The *maple*-leaf is the emblem of Canada.

maple-leaf   **marigold**

mar To *mar* anything is to spoil it completely, e.g. A thunderstorm would *mar* the picnic.

Marathon The *Marathon* is the longest race in the sports; the runners have to go a good many miles.

marble a hard stone which can be polished and is much used for making gravestones, memorials, statues and for building. *Marble* is found in Italy, Greece, etc., in many colours, but the commonest is white. ■ A *marble* is a small ball of glass or clay, ■ with which a boy plays the game of *marbles*.

March the third month of the year.

march The soldiers *march*, 'Left, right, left, right,' ■ while the band plays a *march*.

mare a female horse.

margarine Though *margarine* looks like butter, it is not made from milk, but from such things as beef fat, nut oil, etc.

margin Draw a *margin* 1 in. wide down the edge of your paper.

marigold a garden plant with golden or yellow, daisy-like flowers.

marine a soldier who serves on a warship. ■ *Marine* creatures are those which live in the sea.

mariner a sailor or seaman.

mark If I *mark* your sums you will know how many are right. ■ The *mark* I was given for arithmetic was 9 out of 10. ■ The dog's dirty paw made a *mark* on my coat. ■ If you don't *mark* your linen before sending it to the laundry, they will not know whose it is.

marked I have *marked* your work and given you 8 out of 10 for it. ■ A *marked* man is one who is being carefully watched (to see whether he does anything wrong, etc.).

market Farmers go to (the) *market* to buy and sell animals. ■ To *market* goods is to put them on sale. ■ You can buy almost anything in a street *market*.

marmalade jam made from oranges and sugar and usually eaten on toast at breakfast.

maroon a crimson-brown colour. ■ To *maroon* a person is to leave him alone on a desert island.

marquee a tent as big as a school hall.

marquess, marquis a nobleman who ranks between a duke and an earl, e.g. The *Marquis* of Queensberry.

marred completely spoilt, e.g. Our firework display was *marred* by a thunderstorm.

marriage On her *marriage* to Mr. Smith, Miss Jones became Mrs. Smith.

married When Miss Jones *married* Mr. Smith, she became his wife, Mrs. Smith.

marrow a large fleshy vegetable with seeds in the middle; ■ a soft substance found in the middle of bones. (It boils out, leaving the bones hollow.)

vegetable marrow   **martin**

marry A girl must *marry* Mr. Smith in order to become his wife, Mrs. Smith.

Mars the ancient Roman god of war. ■ That red star in the sky is the planet *Mars*.

marsh low, muddy ground.

marshal The officer of highest rank in the army is the Field *Marshal*. ■ To *marshal* people or things is to arrange them in order.

mart a market or fair.

Martian a person or creature supposed to live on the planet Mars.

martin a bird like a swallow, which often builds its mud nest on the wall of a house where the roof overhangs.

martyr someone who is killed, or severely punished, for something he believes in, e.g. Christian *martyrs*, killed because they believed in Christ.

marvel This new rocket is a *marvel* (i.e. something very wonderful). ■ People will *marvel* (be very surprised) at the new rocket.

marvellous surprising and wonderful, e.g. a *marvellous* idea, a *marvellous* invention.

marzipan a paste made of almonds, sugar and egg, and used to make cakes, or to cover (ice) a cake.

mascot some thing or person supposed to bring luck, e.g. a toy black cat.

masculine Male things (e.g. boy, man, bull) are of *masculine* gender. ■ A *masculine* fellow is one who is particularly manly.

mash To *mash* potatoes you crush them and mix them up. ■ We feed our chickens on a *mash* made of bran and potatoes, etc.

mask We could not recognize our friends at the party, for everyone wore a *mask* over his face.

mask

mason a man who works in stone – cuts it, builds with it, etc.

masonry A great lump of *masonry* (stonework) fell from the ruins.

masquerade a ball (party) at which the guests wear masks. ■ To *masquerade* is to appear in a character that is not your true one.

mass a church service (Holy Communion). ■ A *mass* meeting is one attended by many people. ■ His body was a *mass* of sores (i.e. his body was covered with sores).

massacre the killing of a large number of people.

massage to rub a muscle or a joint as a cure for an ache or pain, e.g. I will *massage* your sprained ankle.

massive big and heavy, e.g. Several strong men were needed to open and close the *massive* gates to the castle.

mast a big pole which supports a ship's sails, etc.

master The *master* of a ship is the man in charge of it. ■ A school *master* is a male teacher. ■ To *master* something is to get to know all about it. ■ A dog's *master* is his owner. ■ an expert.

masterful A *masterful* person is one who will not take anyone's advice.

masterly The actor (or pianist, etc.) gave a *masterly* performance (i.e. he showed that he was an expert).

masterpiece This painting is a *masterpiece* by Holbein (i.e. one of that great painter's best works).

match To light a *match*, you strike it on its box. ■ Bob is playing in a football *match*. ■ Mother needs a hat to *match* her new coat.

matches Mother's new hat *matches* her coat. ■ Here is a box of *matches* for lighting the fire. ■ Our football team has won several *matches*.

matchless If a thing is *matchless*, you cannot equal it.

mate a workman's helper or fellow worker; ■ a bird, etc., which is one of a pair; ■ the officer on a ship responsible for seeing that the captain's orders are carried out. ■ To *mate* birds, etc., is to pair them off, male with female.

material My coat is made of a woollen *material*.

materialize to appear (out of nowhere, like a ghost), e.g. While you are searching for the cat, he will suddenly *materialize* on the grass beside you.

mathematics In *mathematics* lessons such as arithmetic, algebra, geometry, etc., we learn about numbers.

matinée The *matinée* performance at a theatre, etc., is in the afternoon.

matrimony Bill and Anne have had a year's experience of *matrimony* (i.e. they have been married a year).

matron the woman in charge of the nurses in a hospital; ■ the woman in charge of the health, clothes, etc., of boarding-school children; ■ a married woman.

matted tangled, e.g. My hair is so *matted* that I cannot pull a comb through it.

matter What is the *matter*? (i.e. What is troubling you?) ■ Don't worry about the broken cups; they don't *matter* (are of no importance). ■ pus, the yellowish substance produced by festering sores.

mattress To make a bed soft and comfortable, you must put on it a *mattress* (a big box-shaped bag, made of material and stuffed with springs, horse-hair, etc.).

mature fully developed, grown up, or ripe, e.g. a *mature* animal; a *mature* person; a *mature* plant.

maul to treat or handle anyone, or anything, so roughly as to cause injury or damage.

mauve pale purple (colour).

maximum Today's *maximum* temperature is the highest temperature reached today.

May the fifth month of the year.

may the sweet-smelling blossom of the hawthorn. ■ It *may* (perhaps) rain tomorrow.

maybe Let's call on Auntie and *maybe* (possibly) she will ask us to stay for tea.

mayor the head of the corporation or council of a city, borough or town. His Worship the *Mayor* presides over council meetings.

mayoress the mayor's wife, or some other lady who carries out the official duties of a mayor's wife.

maze a puzzle provided in pleasure gardens (e.g. Hampton Court), and consisting of paths with many turnings, between high hedges. (The object is to find a way to the centre of the *maze* and out again, which is difficult because many of the turnings are false.)

meadow The grass growing in the *meadow* is eaten by the farm animals, or cut and dried to make hay.

meal At supper-time all the boys sat down to a *meal* of sausages and bacon.

mean I did not *mean* to hurt you; it was an accident. ■ Bob is so *mean* that he puts only a penny in the collection. ■ It is a *mean* trick to hide a boy's book so that he gets into trouble for losing it. ■ 6 is the *mean* (i.e. halfway) quantity between 3 and 9.

meaning The *meaning* of 'Shut up !' (slang) is 'Be quiet !' ■ A *meaning* glance is one that has in it a special message.

meaningless The letter is *meaningless* to me (i.e. I do not understand anything in it).

meanness Scrooge was famous for his *meanness* (he would not give anything away if he could avoid it).

means 'Hurry up !' *means* 'Be quick !' ■ We would like to come to your party, but we have no *means* of getting there (i.e. there are no buses, etc., and we have no cycles, cars, etc.).

meant I *meant* (intended) to return your book, but I forgot. ■ I didn't know what the word *meant*, so I looked it up in a dictionary.

meantime, meanwhile Put the kettle on to boil and in the *meantime* we'll cut the bread and butter. Jack ran for a doctor; *meanwhile* we stayed with the patient.

measles When you are suffering from *measles* you have red spots on your skin and you feel as if you have a cold.

measure To *measure* the length of the curtain, ■ I used a tape-*measure* marked in feet and inches.

H

measurement My waist *measurement* is 32 inches (i.e. it is 32 inches round my waist).

meat The *meat* we ate for dinner was mutton, which is the flesh of sheep. (We also eat the *meat* of cattle, pigs, birds, etc.).

mechanic a man whose work is looking after machinery, e.g. The *mechanic* was busy repairing the machine.

mechanical *Mechanical* things are those which have working parts, e.g. machines.

mechanically In this factory the bottles are filled *mechanically*; no hand touches them. ■ The tall man was so used to hitting his head in doorways that he ducked *mechanically* (i.e. from habit) every time he went through one.

mechanism Roy took the back off his clock in order to see the *mechanism* that worked the alarm.

mechanize When you *mechanize* an activity like farming, you put in machinery to do work which has previously been done by men.

medal a metal disc like a coin, pinned to a person's chest as a reward for bravery, a reminder of an important event, etc.

medal

meddle Do not *meddle* (take part) in things that do not concern you.

mediaeval of the Middle Ages (roughly between the times of William the Conqueror and Christopher Columbus – 11th to 15th centuries), e.g. a *mediaeval* castle, *mediaeval* music, etc. (also spelt *medieval*).

medical A doctor gives a patient a *medical* examination to find out whether there is anything wrong with him. ■ *Medical* treatment consists of cures (medicines, etc.) which do not include an operation.

medicine To cure my illness, the doctor gave me a bottle of *medicine* to drink, a spoonful at a time.

medieval of the Middle Ages (also spelt *mediaeval* – see above).

meditate to think long and seriously.

Mediterranean The *Mediterranean* Sea stretches along the south of Europe and the north of Africa.

medium The *medium*-sized packet is bigger than the small one and smaller than the big one. ■ We can send messages anywhere through the *medium* of wireless. ■ A spiritualist's *medium* is the person through whom he claims to contact the spirits of dead people.

meek A *meek* person is one who offers no resistance to those who hurt or annoy him, e.g. Jane is as *meek* as a lamb.

meekness Because of the *meekness* of the thief, we had no difficulty in tying his hands and leading him to the police-station.

meet When Auntie comes by train we go to the station to *meet* her. ■ To tunnel through a hill you can drill holes from each side which *meet* in the middle.

meeting All parents are invited to a *meeting* in the school hall, to discuss the new plan for education.

megaphone a big, cone-shaped tube through which you shout when you want your voice to be heard a long way off.

megaphone   melon

melancholy sad, e.g. the *melancholy* sound of an owl.

melodious A *melodious* sound is one that you find sweet and tuneful.

melody Peter played a delightful *melody* on his flute.

melon a large, juicy fruit usually sliced and eaten with sugar.

melt If you warm ice it will *melt* into water.

melting Water dripped from the *melting* icicles. ■ The butter is *melting* in the heat (i.e. it is changing into a liquid).

member Tim is a *member* of our football team (i.e. he is one of the team.)

membership being a member, e.g. *Membership* of the club is a great honour.

memento something which you keep to remind you of a person or an event.

memorable The visit of the queen was a *memorable* occasion (i.e. one to be remembered).

memorial That building (or monument, etc.) is a *memorial* to those who were killed in the war (i.e. something to remind us of them).

memorize If you *memorize* a poem (or a part in a play, etc.), you can say it without looking at a book.

memory John has a good *memory* (i.e. he does not forget things).

menace a threat, e.g. A careless driver is a *menace* to all road users. ■ to threaten, e.g. The tiger continued to *menace* us by walking round and round our tent.

menagerie In a *menagerie* you can see various wild animals on view in cages.

mend You *mend* a puncture in your bicycle tyre by sticking a piece of rubber over the hole. You *mend* a broken ornament by sticking the pieces together.

mensuration In the arithmetic lesson we did *mensuration* (i.e. sums to do with the lengths, areas, etc. of things).

mental A *mental* (hospital) patient is one whose mind is diseased. ■ You do *mental* arithmetic in your head (i.e. without using paper).

mentality A person of low *mentality* is one who is not clever. ■ Tim has not the *mentality* of Brian (i.e. Brian is the cleverer one.)

mentally A person who is *mentally* ill is one whose mind is unwell. ■ Do these sums *mentally* (i.e. in your head, without using paper).

mention   Jim did not *mention* (say anything about) the matter to us.

menu   a card on which are printed the names and prices of the foods provided in a hotel, restaurant or café.

merchant   We buy coal from a coal *merchant*. A timber *merchant* sells timber.

merciful   A *merciful* judge is one who gives a prisoner a light sentence because he takes pity on him.

merciless   heartless, showing no mercy, e.g. In spite of the victim's screams, his *merciless* enemy continued to thrash him.

mercury   a heavy, silvery liquid metal, used in thermometers, barometers, etc. ■ That bright star is *Mercury*, the planet nearest to our sun. ■ Pictures of the ancient Roman god *Mercury* usually show him with winged helmet and shoes.

mercy   You can show *mercy* to an enemy by not punishing him even though you have the chance to do so.

mere   It is a *mere* 100 metres from my house to the school (i.e. only 100 m).

merely   The boys are doing no harm; they are *merely* playing (i.e. they are doing nothing more than playing).

merge   The council are going to *merge* our school in the big new County School (i.e. our school is to become part of this new one).

merit   An order of *merit* is a list of people arranged in order of goodness, or cleverness, etc. (i.e. the best at the top, then the

next best and so on, and ending with the worst at the bottom).

merited   deserved, e.g. That brave deed *merited* a better reward.

mermaid   an imaginary sea creature whose top half is girl and bottom half fish.

mermaid   meteor

merrily   happily and gaily, e.g. The children ran *merrily* after the Pied Piper.

merriment   Hearing the sounds of gay laughter, we asked the cause of the *merriment*.

merry   A *merry* person is one who is full of fun and laughter.

mesh   This net has a fine *mesh* (i.e. the spaces between the threads are small).

mesmerize   to hypnotize; to cause someone to go into a deep sleep by talking to him.

mess   The room is in a *mess* (dirty and untidy). ■ To make a *mess* of a job is to do it very badly.

message   information sent on paper or by word of mouth, e.g. Please give your mother this *message* from me.

messenger   someone who carries a message.

Messiah   In the Bible the Jews were promised that the *Messiah* would come and save them from their enemies. Christians say that Christ is the *Messiah*.

metal any such substance as iron, brass, gold, silver, aluminium, etc.

metallic A *metallic* substance is one made from some kind of metal. ■ A *metallic* noise is the kind of noise made when you hit a piece of metal.

meteor a shooting star; a small piece of material from space which glows brightly as it passes through the earth's air.

meteorologist a person who studies the air and its movements, etc., and so is able to forecast the weather, etc.

meter A gas *meter* measures the amount of gas you use; an electricity *meter* measures the amount of electricity.

method What is your *method* of keeping warm on cold days?

methodical A *methodical* person is one who does things in a careful, orderly way; he doesn't muddle through a job.

Methodist *Methodists* are supporters of ■ the *Methodist* Churches, which were founded by Wesley and others in the 18th century.

methylated spirit a liquid like alcohol, but unsuitable for drinking; used in picnic stoves, etc.

metre We now measure length in *metres*.

metric In the *metric* system, measurements are made in metres (length), grammes (weight), and litres (capacity).

metropolitan of (connected with) a country's capital city, e.g. The *Metropolitan* Police is the police force of England's chief city, London.

mettle courage, pluck. To be on your *mettle* is to be under pressure to do your best.

mew When you hear the cat *mew*, open the door and let him in.

Mexican a citizen of Mexico.

Mexico the country on the southern borders of the United States.

mice Our cat has caught a mouse each day this week; that is seven *mice* altogether.

Michaelmas the festival of Saint Michael, 29th September. ■ *Michaelmas* daisies grow in clumps on tall, stiff stems.

microbe a very tiny creature or plant (it cannot be seen without a microscope), which causes disease, etc.

microphone When people broadcast over the radio, they speak into a *microphone*.

microphone   microscope

microscope magnifying glasses so arranged in a stand that when you look at a tiny object through them, it looks very much bigger.

microscopic A *microscopic* object is one so small that you cannot see it without a microscope.

midday We have our *midday* meal about 12 o'clock, noon.

middle From the *middle* the distance to each end is the same. ■ The *Middle* Ages lasted from about the 11th century to the 15th century.

midge a tiny fly which bites people, causing itchy spots.

midget a very small person.

midnight At *midnight* you hear the clock strike twelve.

midst We have an enemy in our *midst* (among us).

midsummer the time of the year when the midday sun is at its highest in the sky – about June 21st in the northern half of the earth.

might great strength, e.g. Jack pulled with all his *might*. ■ We *might* (perhaps will) see Dick at the party. ■ You *might* help me (i.e. you ought to help, but you don't).

mighty very strong, powerful, e.g. The blacksmith is a *mighty* man.

migrate In winter many of our birds *migrate* to warmer countries. ■ People often *migrate* to another town (or country) to find work.

migration The birds assemble in groups ready for their winter *migration* (i.e. their journey to another country). ■ There has been a *migration* of people from the country to the towns (i.e. country people have moved into towns).

milage The *milage* (miles travelled) shown on the car's speedometer is 5,000 (sometimes spelt *mileage*).

mild *Mild* weather is warm and pleasant. A *mild* punishment is one that is light (not severe).

mildew a growth on plants, or on things kept in damp places, which looks like a powder.

mile about 1·6 km. A good runner can run a *mile* in about four minutes.

militant A *militant* supporter of a cause is one who fights for it in some way (e.g. by speeches, demonstrations, strikes, etc.).

military A *military* camp is one for soldiers. A *military* band is an army band, ■ or any band consisting only of brass, wood-wind and percussion instruments.

milk a white liquid made by animals such as cows, for feeding their young. ■ To *milk* a cow is to get milk from it.

milky A *milky* liquid is one that is white and cloudy, like milk. ■ The *Milky* Way is a bright band of stars very close together across the night sky, and it forms part of our galaxy.

mill a factory or machine, especially one in which things are ground into powder or pulp, e.g. a flour *mill*, a paper *mill*; but also, a cotton *mill*.

miller The *miller* works in his mill, grinding corn into flour.

millet a grass-like plant producing small seeds which are an important food crop in India, etc.

milliner a woman (usually) who makes ladies' hats.

million a thousand thousands, 1,000,000.

millionaire a very rich person (strictly, someone who owns a million pounds, or a million dollars, etc.).

millionth The *millionth* person to visit the exhibition was given a prize (including this person, a million people had visited the exhibition). ■ a *millionth* of a metre (a million of these make one metre).

millstone The corn is ground into flour between a pair of circular *millstones*.

mime something acted without words (i.e. by actions only); ■ to act by actions only (especially actions of the hands) and without words.

mimic someone who can imitate the sounds or movements of other creatures. Some birds are good *mimics* (i.e. they can imitate the sounds of other birds, or of people talking).

mince To *mince* meat is to chop it up small, usually in a mincer. ■ *Mince* pies contain a fruity filling called mincemeat. ■ Dad didn't *mince* his words (i.e. he said exactly what he meant).

mincemeat The *mincemeat* put into Christmas mince pies is made of currants, raisins, apples, candied peel, etc.

mind Do you *mind*? (Do you object?) ■ Will you *mind* (look after) the baby? ■ I'll bear it in *mind* (I'll take it into account). ■ My *mind* is made up (i.e. I have decided).

mine a container filled with explosive and buried in the ground, or put into the sea, to blow up an enemy. ■ This pen is *mine* i.e. it belongs to me. ■ To *mine* for coal, etc., is to dig ■ a *mine* into the ground in order to dig out coal, etc., below the earth's surface.

miner A *miner* works underground, digging out minerals such as coal, copper, diamonds, etc.

mineral a rock, metal, etc., obtained from the ground (i.e. something that is not animal nor vegetable). ■ *Mineral* waters are fizzy drinks.

mingle If we *mingle* (mix) with the crowd we shall not be noticed.

miniature We built a *miniature* village in our back garden.

minim a musical note that looks like a hollow oval on a stem, and is worth two crotchets.

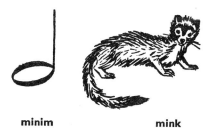

minim   mink

minimum least (amount), e.g. Today's *minimum* (lowest) temperature was 5°.

minister a clergyman (neither Anglican, nor Roman Catholic). ■ To *minister* to someone is to give him help or attention, e.g. a nurse *ministers* to the sick.

ministry The government department in charge of schools is the *Ministry* of Education. ■ A clergyman's *ministry* is his work of preaching, teaching, etc.

mink A *mink* coat is made of many furs ■ from *minks* (small, stoat-like animals).

minor less important, e.g. a *minor* road. ■ Smith *minor* is the younger of the two Smith boys. ■ In music, the major scale starts on doh, but the *minor* scale starts on lah. ■ a person under 21.

minority Only a *minority* of the children speak French (i.e. most of them don't speak French).

minster a cathedral or a very important church, e.g. York *Minster*.

minster   minstrel

minstrel a wandering musician and singer of medieval times and later. ■ *Minstrels* are present-day black-faced entertainers.

mint a plant with a strong smell whose leaves are chopped ■ to make *mint* sauce. ■ The *Mint* is the factory in South Wales where coins are made. ■ to make coins.

minuet a slow, dignified dance to three-time music; ■ or just the music, without the dance.

minus Five *minus* two is three (5 — 2 = 3).

minute (pron. mín-it) 60 seconds make one *minute*; 60 *minutes*, one hour. ■ The *minutes* of a meeting are the notes of what happened. ■ (pron. my-núte) very small indeed.

minutely carefully, e.g. After the accident we examined the car *minutely* for signs of damage.

minx a saucy, teasing girl.

miracle The car ran over the child, but by a *miracle*, he was unhurt (i.e. it was not possible to explain why he was unhurt). The Bible tells of *miracles* performed by Jesus, e.g. turning water into wine.

miraculous A *miraculous* happening is one which is very surprising, or for which you cannot give an explanation.

mirage the reflection from a layer of hot air, etc., which causes people in a desert or on a hot, dry road to think that they see water in the distance.

mirror If you look in a *mirror* you see yourself.

mirror

mirth Unable to control their *mirth* any longer, the boys burst into roars of laughter.

misbehave to be naughty.

misbehaviour naughtiness, e.g. John was punished for his *misbehaviour*.

miscalculate to work out something incorrectly, e.g. Dad *miscalculated* the load his boat would carry, so when we all got in, it sank.

miscellaneous of various kinds, e.g. a page of *miscellaneous* sums.

mischief To get into *mischief* is to do something naughty. ■ To make *mischief* is to cause disagreement or quarrelling between people.

mischievous A *mischievous* child is one who often gets into mischief. (pron. miss-chee-vus).

misconduct wrong behaviour or bad management, e.g. The Prime Minister's *misconduct* of the war caused our defeat.

misdeed For a serious *misdeed* (crime) a man may be sent to prison.

miser someone who stores up money and lives miserably rather than spend any of it.

miserable very unhappy.

miserly Mrs. Flint put a *miserly* penny in our collecting box (i.e. the amount you would expect from a miser).

misery great unhappiness.

misfit Joan's coat was a *misfit* (i.e. it didn't fit her).

misfortune bad luck, e.g. Tom had the *misfortune* to be ill on the day of the party.

misgivings After walking for hours without finding the village, we began to have *misgivings* about our map (i.e. we began to fear that the map might be incorrect).

mishap a slight, unfortunate accident.

misinformed 'You were *misinformed*' means that you were given incorrect information.

misjudge To *misjudge* anything is to form a wrong opinion about it.

mislay To *mislay* something is to put it where you cannot, for the moment, find it.

mislead To mislead anyone is to take him the wrong way ■ or to cause him to believe something that isn't quite true.

misleading A *misleading* remark, sign, etc., is one that gives people incorrect ideas about something.

misled Our guide *misled* us (took us the wrong way). ■ The salesman *misled* mother (caused her to believe something not quite true).

misplace to put in a wrong place. ■ *Misplaced* confidence is confidence put in a person or thing that later lets you down.

misprint a mistake in printing.

mispronounce to say a word wrongly, e.g. Some foreigners *mispronounce* our word 'which' and say 'vitch'

miss To *miss* a train, bus, etc. is to arrive too late to get on it. ■ When shooting, etc. at something if you do not hit it, you *miss* it. ■ A *miss* is a failure to hit. ■ *Miss* Smith is an unmarried lady.

missile something thrown or fired at an enemy by means of a gun or a rocket.

missing We must find the *missing* book. ■ There is a page *missing* (not there) from my book. ■ The shots are *missing* (not hitting) the target.

mission the life's work that a person feels he must do, e.g. The doctor's *mission* in life is to heal the sick.

missionary a religious person who tries to persuade others to believe in his religion, e.g. Dr. David Livingstone.

mis-spelling a wrong spelling.

mist tiny drops of water (or fine rain) in the air, through which you cannot see things clearly.

mistake If you make a *mistake* in your book, cross it through and write the correct word above it. ■ You may *mistake* an aircraft light for a star (i.e. think that it is a star).

mistaken Bob has the *mistaken* (wrong) idea that tomorrow is a holiday. ■ Joan has *mistaken* our visitor for the milkman and asked him for two bottles.

mistletoe a plant with narrow leaves and cream berries, which grows on apple and other trees, and is used as a Christmas decoration.

mistook The bird *mistook* the pebble for an egg and tried to hatch it.

mistress The *mistress* of a house is the woman in charge of it. ■ A school *mistress* is a woman teacher.

mistrust To *mistrust* someone is to feel that you cannot depend on him.

misty covered with mist (e.g. glass when you breathe on it). ■ On a *misty* day, tiny drops of water in the air make it impossible to see things clearly.

misunderstand To *misunderstand* someone is to have a wrong idea of what he means.

misunderstanding Owing to a *misunderstanding* (having a wrong idea of what we meant) Jim arrived when we were out. ■ Jean and John had a *misunderstanding* (quarrel), but they have made it up now.

misunderstood Told to do 50 lines, the new boy *misunderstood* and ruled 50 straight lines on his paper instead of doing 50 lines of writing.

misuse To *misuse* something is to use it for the wrong purpose, e.g. to use a handkerchief as a duster, a bath as a coal bin, etc.

mite a small child, e.g. The little *mite* could not reach the door knob. ■ a coin, mentioned in the Bible as being worth half a farthing ($\frac{1}{8}$d.).

mitten a glove which covers the hand and thumb, but not the fingers.

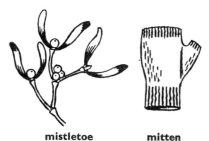

mistletoe   mitten

mix If you *mix* blue and yellow you make green.

mixed A *mixed* school has both boys and girls in it. *Mixed* bathing is bathing by boys and girls (men and women) together. ■ We *mixed* yellow and blue together to make that green paint.

mixture anything that is made up of things mixed together, e.g. a medicine containing more than one ingredient.

moan The injured man, too ill to talk, made a low *moan* as we lifted him.

moat To make attack by enemies more difficult, mediaeval castles and cities were often surrounded by a *moat* (ditch) filled with water.

moat

mob a disorderly crowd.

mobile A *mobile* crane is one that is easily moved from place to place; similarly, a *mobile* library (in a motor-van), etc.

mock imitation, not real, e.g. *mock* turtle soup. ■ To *mock* (at) someone is to make fun of him.

mockery I cannot stand *mockery* (being made fun of). ■ The trial was a *mockery* (not a real one, but a bad imitation).

mocking Poor Jim came last in the race, to the *mocking* cheers of some rude spectators.

mode fashion. To be in the *mode*, ladies must wear clothes that are smart and up to date.

model a person whom artists draw or paint; ■ a person employed in a shop to wear new clothes so that customers can see them being worn. ■ A *model* railway is a small-sized copy of a railway.

moderate (pron. mód-er-at) not extreme, e.g. A *moderate* price is one that is neither cheap nor dear. ■ (pron. mod-er-áte) The gale-force winds will *moderate* (become less strong).

moderation Sun-bathing in *moderation* (i.e. not too much of it) will do you no harm.

modern *Modern* fashions, ideas, times, etc. are those of the present time, or very recent time.

modernize To *modernize* anything is to bring it up to date.

modest A *modest* person is one who has not a high opinion of himself. ■ A *modest* charge, price, etc. is one that is not too high. ■ rather shy, especially about being seen incompletely dressed, etc.

modestly After bravely rescuing the boy, Jack *modestly* said that he had done nothing to make a fuss about.

modesty What we like most about the great man is his *modesty* (i.e. that he hasn't a high opinion of himself).

modification a slight change, e.g. a *modification* of a plan, or *modifications* to a machine.

modify To *modify* anything is to change it a little.

modulate To *modulate* your voice you speak lower or more quietly.

Mohammedan a follower of Mohammed, the Arab prophet who founded the Moslem (*Mohammedan*) religion.

moist slightly wet, e.g. A fruit cake should be *moist*, not completely dry.

moisten To *moisten* anything is to make it slightly wet, e.g. to *moisten* your lips with your tongue.

moisture The little drops of *moisture* which can be seen on plants on summer mornings are called dew.

molasses a sweet, dark, sticky liquid, obtained during the manufacture of sugar.

mole a little velvet-coated animal that burrows underground, eating worms. ■ a brown spot (sometimes quite large) on a person's skin.

mole   mongoose

molecule the smallest possible quantity of a substance, a particle too small to be seen.

molest Betty is busy doing her homework and you are not to *molest* her (i.e. do not annoy or interfere with her).

mollify Father is very angry; do try to *mollify* him (calm him down).

molten The hot, *molten* metal is poured into the sand to harden.

moment It took Jim only a *moment* to grab his coat and rush from the house.

momentary Anything that is *momentary* lasts for only a short time, e.g. a *momentary* pain.

momentous very important, e.g. Jack took a *momentous* decision – to run away from home.

monarch a king or queen (or other such ruler of a country), e.g. The *monarch* wears a crown.

monarchy Britain is a *monarchy* (i.e. the head of the state is a king or a queen).

monastery the home of monks, where they spend their time praying and working.

Monday the second day of the week.

money Have you enough *money* to pay for the things you are buying?

mongoose a little, furry Indian animal, able to kill poisonous snakes.

mongrel A *mongrel* (dog) is one whose mother was not of the same breed as its father, e.g. mother a spaniel and father a terrier.

monitor The form (or class) *monitor* has to give out books, and take charge of the class when the teacher is out, etc.

monk A *monk* lives in a monastery with other *monks* and spends his time praying and working.

monk   monkey

monkey The *monkey*, swinging through the trees, is a very human-looking animal. ■ A *monkey* nut (also called pea nut and ground nut) has a thin, pale shell and grows in the ground.

monkeys animals that live in trees and look remarkably like human beings.

monologue a long speech, all by one person (in a play or in conversation with friends).

monopoly As for the sale of coal in the town, Bloggs and Son have the *monopoly* (i.e. this firm is the only seller of coal in the town).

monotonous A *monotonous* noise is one that continues on the same note without changing, e.g. We soon became tired of listening to that *monotonous* voice.

monotony What Uncle hates about factory work is the *monotony* (i.e. doing exactly the same thing all day and every day).

monsoon a wind system like that in India, where there are dry north-east winds for part of the year and very wet south-west winds for the other part. The latter are known as the S.W. *monsoon*.

monster a creature that is frightening because it is very big, ugly, queer in shape, wicked, etc.

monstrosity something that is frightfully ugly, or very badly made, etc.

monstrous A *monstrous* creature is one like a monster. ■ A *monstrous* suggestion, accusation, etc., is one that is very insulting to someone, or completely ridiculous.

month There are twelve *months* in a year. The first *month* is January.

monthly It is called a *monthly* magazine because new copies appear each month.

monument something, usually a building, to remind people of an event or a person, e.g. The *Monument* (in London) is to remind

people of the Great Fire of London.

monumental A *monumental* mason is a stoneworker who makes monuments, gravestones, etc.

mood People in a good *mood* feel friendly and good-tempered.

moody miserable and bad-tempered.

moon The *moon* is the brightest object in the night sky. ■ To *moon* about is to wander around in a tired, uninterested way.

moonlight Come at night and see the lake by *moonlight*.

moor a large piece of waste ground with pools, streams, heather, etc. ■ To *moor* a boat is to fasten it with ropes to a buoy or to the shore.

moorings the place, or fixture, to which a ship is moored (tied up).

moose a Canadian animal, like a big deer.

moose   mop

mop a pole with (usually) a bunch of strands of thick cotton thread on the end, and used to dry, clean or polish floors. ■ To *mop* a floor is to rub it with a mop.

mope To *mope* is to show yourself unwilling to take an interest in anything.

moped (pron. móped) Joan *moped* all day because her dog was lost (i.e. she showed she wasn't interested in anything). ■ (pron. mó·ped) a bicycle fitted with a motor.

moping Joan sat at home *moping* all day because her dog was lost (i.e. she was showing that she had no interest in anything).

mopping Sam is busy *mopping* the floor (i.e. rubbing the floor with a mop).

moral having to do with right and wrong, e.g. You should receive *moral* training at home. ■ The *moral* of a story is the lesson to be learnt from it.

morale People's *morale* is their courage, discipline, and confidence that what they are working or fighting for is right, e.g. Although our men had lost the battle, their *morale* was high (good).

morals A person who has no *morals* (or has loose *morals*) does not mind doing wrong.

morass a marsh, an area of deep mud.

more Six is two *more* than four.

moreover You cannot go out because it is a stormy night; *moreover*, your homework hasn't been done.

morn, morning I usually get out of bed at 7 o'clock in the *morning*. (Poets sometimes use the shorter word *morn*.)

Morse The *Morse* code is a method of signalling letters of the alphabet by dots and dashes, e.g. three short taps (or flashes) followed by a long one (. . . —) is V.

morsel A *morsel* of food is a very small quantity.

mortal All living creatures are *mortals* (i.e. they do not live for ever). ■ A *mortal* blow is one that kills.

mortality The infant *mortality* is the number of infants who die (in a year, or a month, etc.).

mortally The soldier is *mortally* wounded (i.e. he has wounds from which he will die).

mortar You make *mortar* (for bricklaying) by mixing sand, lime and water.

mortuary a place in which dead bodies can be kept while awaiting burial.

mosaic pictures or designs (usually on floor or wall) made up of many tiny pieces of coloured stone or glass.

mosaic

Moscow the capital city of Russia and the centre of the government of the U.S.S.R.

Moslem a Mohammedan. ■ The *Moslem* religion was founded by its prophet, Mohammed, and is practised chiefly by Arabs (also spelt *Muslim*).

mosque a building in which Mohammedans worship.

mosque   mosquito

mosquito a flying insect whose bite may cause itchy spots. The bite of the malaria *mosquito* gives people malaria.

moss a small, green, flowerless plant which spreads over damp surfaces in woods (and on stones, etc.), like a thick, green carpet.

most *Most* (but not all) birds can fly. ■ Tom has 10p and Jim has 20p, but Ben has the *most*; he has 50p.

mostly The trees in this orchard are *mostly* apple trees (i.e. there are more apple trees than any other kind).

moth an insect like a butterfly, but which comes out at night. Clothes *moths* lay their eggs in clothes, etc. and when the maggots hatch out, they feed on the clothes.

mother When a woman has a baby she becomes a *mother*. ■ Auntie will *mother* the poor lost child (i.e. treat it as a mother would).

motion Anything that is in *motion* is moving. ■ The *motion* of a ship on a rough sea makes some people sick.

motionless We stood *motionless* as if turned to stone.

motive What was the *motive* (reason) for the boy's attack on you?

motor You do not turn this sewing machine by hand; it is driven by an electric *motor*.

motor-car Before you can drive a *motor-car* along the road you need a licence.

motorist The *motorist* stopped his car at the traffic lights.

mottled Some birds' eggs are *mottled* (i.e. they have spots or patches of colour on them).

motto words of good advice, etc. on a coat of arms or in a Christmas cracker.

mottoes The *mottoes* on coats of arms and in Christmas crackers usually give good advice.

moth   jelly mould

mould a woolly or furry growth that appears on cheese, jam, etc., when kept for a time in warm, damp place; ■ earth, soil; ■ a specially shaped container into which molten substances, etc. are poured so that they harden into the shape required, e.g. a jelly *mould*.

moulding   a pattern made along lengths of wood, plaster, etc., to decorate walls or ceilings.

mouse   Our cat caught the *mouse* as it ran out of its hole in the kitchen.

moulding   mouse

moustache

mouldy   *Mouldy* cheese has a furry stuff growing on it.

moult   When a bird *moults*, its feathers fall out (so that new ones may grow).

mound   a heap of earth.

mount   a mountain or hill, e.g. the *Mount* of Olives (in the Bible); ■ the space round a picture, or the card on which it is stuck. ■ To *mount* a horse or a bicycle is to get on it.

mountain   As you climb higher up the *mountain* it becomes so cold that the rocks are covered with snow.

mountaineer   someone who is good at climbing mountains.

mountainous   A *mountainous* country is one in which there are many mountains.

mourn   To *mourn* for a person is to feel very sorry and sad because he has died.

mournful   sad, e.g. the *mournful* sound of weeping.

mourning   Mrs. Smith wore *mourning* (black clothes) at her husband's funeral. ■ The tribesmen are *mourning* (showing sorrow for) the death of their chief.

moustache   the hair on a man's upper lip.

mouth   Put the sweet in your *mouth* and eat it. ■ The *mouth* of a cave is the hole through which you enter it.

movable   A thing that is *movable* can be moved.

move   We are going to *move* to London (i.e. we are leaving this town to go and live in London). ■ Please *move* your bag (i.e. put it in some other place). ■ In the game of chess, white has the first *move*.

movement   You can see by the *movement* of the leaves that there is a wind blowing.

moving   The Smiths are *moving* to their new house today. ■ A *moving* story or experience is one that makes you feel very sympathetic, sad, etc.

mow   I cannot *mow* (cut) grass with a scythe, so I use a lawn mower.

mower   We cut the grass on our lawn with a (lawn) *mower*.

mown   When you have *mown* the grass, put the grass-cuttings here.

Mr.   (short for) Mister. *Mr.* Smith is the man I mean.

Mrs. (short for) Mistress. *Mrs. Jones* is a married lady.

much If there is *much* rain the ground will be flooded.

muddle The papers are in such a *muddle* (not tidy) that it is difficult to find the one you want. ■ If you *muddle* the papers, you will have to put them back into order again.

muddy When you walk on *muddy* ground you get mud on your shoes.

muff a covering for keeping something warm, e.g. a car radiator *muff*. Ladies used to keep their hands warm in a tube-shaped fur *muff*.

muff   **mule**

muffin a kind of tea cake, eaten toasted and buttered.

muffle You can *muffle* the sound of a bell by wrapping the clapper in cloth. ■ If you *muffle* me up in that scarf I shall be too warm.

muffled Brenda was so *muffled* up in her scarf that she could hardly breathe. ■ The bells were *muffled* (wrapped in material, to quieten them).

muffler a scarf, worn to keep you warm.

mulberry A *mulberry* tree has fruit like big, dark raspberries and its leaves provide food for silk-worms.

mule a stubborn, horse-like animal whose father was a donkey and mother a horse (mare).

multiple Twelve is a *multiple* of four (i.e. 12 contains an exact number of fours, with no re-mainder).

multiplication '3 × 4 = 12' is a *multiplication* sum.

multiply If you *multiply* four by three the answer is twelve. ■ Rabbits *multiply* quickly (i.e. they have many young ones at frequent intervals).

multitude a crowd, e.g. The *multitude* filled the huge stadium. A large number, e.g. A *multitude* of people assembled in the stadium.

mumble Do not *mumble*; speak clearly.

mummy Many young children call their mother '*Mummy*'. ■ a dead body treated with spices, etc., and wrapped in cloth, to preserve it (prevent it from going bad).

mumps a disease which causes your neck and face to swell up.

munch to chew (e.g. an apple) steadily and noisily.

municipal The *municipal* build-ings are those in which a town's officials work. The *municipal* buses, dust-carts, etc., are those belonging to the town.

murder If you kill someone in-tentionally, that is *murder*.

murky dark, e.g. We wished for a moon to light up the *murky* lane that night.

murmur There was a *murmur* of many quiet voices, though we could not hear what anyone was saying.

I

muscle The big *muscle* on the back of your leg is your calf.

muscular A *muscular* person is one who has big and powerful muscles.

museum a building in which you can see a collection of things, e.g. things of scientific interest in the Science *Museum*.

mushroom a kind of fungus, an umbrella-shaped growth which grows in fields and is tasty to eat.

mushroom   **mussel**

musket

music *Music* may be made by an orchestra playing, by someone playing an instrument, or by someone singing.

musical *Musical* instruments include such things as trumpets, violins and pianos. ■ A *musical* person is one who enjoys making or listening to music.

musician someone who earns his living by playing or writing music. ■ any great or famous writer or player of music, e.g. Handel.

musket an old-fashioned kind of gun carried by soldiers years ago.

muslin thin cotton cloth, like very fine net.

mussel a dark, oval shell-fish which is good to eat.

must You *must* go to bed (i.e. whether you wish to or not). ■ We *must* see this new TV. show (i.e. let us be sure to see it).

mustard a field plant with bright yellow flowers, whose seeds are ground to powder to make ■ the hot yellow paste eaten with meat, etc.

muster You will need to *muster* all your courage for this dangerous job. ■ Tell the sergeant to *muster* (call together) his soldiers.

mustn't (short for) must not, e.g. You *mustn't* run into the road.

musty Hay, etc., which is stale and damp, or mouldy, gives off a *musty* smell.

mute a person who cannot speak; ■ a thing fitted to a musical instrument to deaden the sound.

mutilate To *mutilate* a creature or a plant is to injure it by pulling or cutting parts off it.

mutineer a soldier or sailor who deliberately refuses to carry out orders given him.

mutinous The ship's crew became *mutinous* and refused to carry out the lawful orders given by their officers.

mutiny a revolt of soldiers or sailors, etc., against their officers.

mutter to grumble in a low and indistinct voice, e.g. We heard the man *mutter* (something) as he walked away.

mutton meat from a sheep, e.g. We had *mutton* for dinner today.

mutual By our *mutual* love, we mean the love that each of us has for the other. Something that is to our *mutual* advantage will benefit each of us.

muzzle An animal's *muzzle* is his mouth and nose. ■ To *muzzle* an animal is to put a special little cage over its face to prevent it biting. ■ The *muzzle* of a gun is the end from which the bullet, or shell, etc. comes out.

muzzled The dog is *muzzled* so that he cannot bite anyone (i.e. there is a special little cage over his face).

myriad A *myriad* lights twinkled like stars in the distance (i.e. an enormous number of lights, more than could be counted).

myrrh a strongly scented gum, used to make incense and perfumes (one of the presents brought to Jesus by the Wise Men).

myself If no one else will act the part, I must do it *myself*.

mysterious No one could tell us anything about the *mysterious* stranger.

mystery The disappearance of the picture was a *mystery* (i.e. no one could explain how, why or where the picture had gone.)

mystified We were *mystified* by the disappearance of the picture (i.e. we could think of no explanation).

mystify My new conjuring trick will *mystify* the audience (i.e. they will not be able to explain how it is done).

mythical A *mythical* creature (e.g. a dragon) is one that exists only in stories, not in history nor in real life.

nag a horse; ■ to go on and on complaining, finding fault, e.g. Some children complain that their parents *nag* (at) them.

nagging A *nagging* person is one who goes on and on complaining, etc. ■ A *nagging* pain is one that goes on and on hurting.

nail Our finger *nails* need cutting now and again. ■ To *nail* things together is to fasten them ■ by hammering a *nail* (or *nails*) through them.

naked Anyone wearing no clothes is *naked*.

name That boy's *name* is Robert. ■ To *name* anything (or anyone), e.g. a house, is to give it a name.

nameless Some *nameless* person (i.e. a person whose name is not being mentioned) has spilt ink on the floor.

namely There are three colours in the British flag, *namely* red, white and blue.

namesake Your *namesake* is another person who has the same name(s) as you.

nanny a woman paid to look after young children (in their own house, usually). ■ A *nanny* goat is a she-goat.

nap a short sleep; ■ the fluffy surface on cloth; ■ a game played with cards.

napkin The *napkin* pinned round a baby's bottom has to be changed when he wets it. ■ A (table) *napkin*, or serviette, is a square of material to protect your clothes while you eat.

narcissus a trumpet-shaped spring flower which grows from a bulb. A daffodil is one kind of *narcissus*.

narcissus   nasturtium

narrative a story.

narrator someone who tells a story.

narrow The stream is so *narrow* that you can step across it.

nasal Your *nasal* organ is your nose. *Nasal* drops are drops to put into the nose (as treatment for colds, etc.).

nasturtium a garden plant with trailing stems and bright orange flowers.

nasty unpleasant or dirty, e.g. *nasty* medicines; a *nasty* man; *nasty* weather; a *nasty* mess.

nation all the people ruled by one government, e.g. The British *nation*, the French *nation*.

national belonging to, or to do with, the whole nation, e.g. The British *National* Anthem is 'God Save the Queen'. The nation's coal mines are run by The *National* Coal Board.

nationality I am of British *nationality*; Pierre's *nationality* is French.

nationalize To *nationalize* anything (e.g. an industry, the railways, land, etc.) is to make it the property of the whole nation.

native A *native* of a country is anyone born in it.

Nativity The *Nativity* is the birth of Christ.

natural left as nature made it, i.e. not artificial, e.g. A *natural* wave in someone's hair is one that has grown there and not one made by a hairdresser. ■ In *natural* history lessons we study animal life.

naturalist someone who studies natural history (animal life).

naturally Hearing loud screams, I *naturally* thought that someone had been hurt or frightened.

nature Susan has a kind *nature* (she is a kind girl). ■ In *nature* study lessons we learn about animals. ■ What is the *nature* of Jim's complaint (i.e. what is he complaining about)?

naught nothing [o], e.g. Five *naught* two (502) is five hundred, no tens and two (also spelt *nought*).

naughtiness bad behaviour.

naughty A *naughty* child is one who behaves rather badly.

naval of the navy, e.g. a *naval* officer, a *naval* battle, etc. *Naval* stores consist of the various things used in ships.

navigate To *navigate* a ship, aircraft, etc. is to see that it goes in the right direction.

navvy a workman who does such heavy jobs as digging holes and trenches.

navy Our *navy* is made up of all our warships.

near I was so *near* Tom that I could have touched him.

nearly Grandad is *nearly* 80 (he will be 80 soon). We are *nearly* there (we have not far to go).

neat tidy, carefully done, e.g. Your last exercise is a *neat* piece of work.

neatly Dora does her sums *neatly* (i.e. carefully and tidily). ■ Harry stepped *neatly* (cleverly) aside and the bull charged into the tree.

neatness To get marks for *neatness*, your work must be very carefully and tidily done.

necessarily Rich people are not *necessarily* happy (i.e. it does not follow that because they are rich they are happy).

necessary It is *necessary* for me to see the headmaster (i.e. I must see him).

necessitate Moving the piano will *necessitate* (make necessary) taking the door off its hinges.

necessity Food is a *necessity* (i.e. we cannot do without it). ■ As the weather is dry there is no *necessity* for a mac.

neck As the giraffe has a long *neck*, his head and shoulders are a long way apart.

neck

necklace

necklace To add to her beauty the lady wears a diamond *necklace* round her neck.

nectar any particularly nice drink, but especially the sweet juices in flowers, which bees drink.

need If I am to write I *need* a pen. ■ You will *need* to wash your hands before dinner. ■ People in *need* are those who haven't such essential things as food, clothes, homes, etc.

needed Our team *needed* two more points to win the game.

needle We sew with a *needle* and cotton. A knitting *needle* is bigger than a sewing *needle* and has no hole through the end.

needles

needless *Needless* to say, the hungry boys soon ate all the cakes.

needlework In *needlework* lessons the girls sew (or knit). ■ That embroidered cloth is the most beautiful piece of *needlework* that I have seen.

needy poor, and in need of such things as food and clothes.

ne'er (short for) never (used chiefly by poets).

negative A *negative* answer is one that refuses, or says 'No'. ■ On a photographic *negative*, the parts which will be black in the finished picture are transparent, while the parts that will be white are black.

neglect To *neglect* something (or someone) is to fail to look after it (or him).

negligence People who do not look after things properly are guilty of *negligence*. The fire was caused by *negligence* (carelessness).

negligible A *negligible* quantity is one so small that you need not take it into account.

negotiate It is not easy to *negotiate* the obstacles in an obstacle race. ■ They met to *negotiate* (arrange by talking) a settlement of the quarrel between their peoples.

negress a coloured (black) woman.

negro a coloured (black) man.

negroes black men. American *negroes* invented jazz.

neigh the noise made by a horse. ■ To *neigh* is to make the sound of a horse.

neighbour someone who lives next door, or near by.

neighbourhood Billy doesn't live in this *neighbourhood* (district). ■ The cost is in the *neighbourhood* of (i.e. near) £50.

neighbouring When Mr. Smith's house blew up, the *neighbouring* houses were damaged too.

neither A cat is *neither* a bird nor a fish.

neon *Neon* lights are the variously shaped tubes of coloured light used in many advertisements.

nephew A boy is his uncle's *nephew*.

Neptune the god of the sea. ■ The planet *Neptune* goes round the sun as the earth does, but at a greater distance.

nerve If you have a *nerve* exposed in a bad tooth and anything touches it, a severe pain shoots through your jaw. ■ People are said to suffer from *nerves* if they are easily frightened or upset. ■ To lose your *nerve* is to become frightened. ■ (slang) You've got a *nerve* (cheek).

nervous To be *nervous* is to fear that something unpleasant may happen. ■ The *nervous* system is the network of nerves in the body.

nervously Robert stepped *nervously* forward to make his speech (i.e. he was very excited and rather frightened).

nest A bird lays eggs in the *nest* it has built. ■ Blackbirds often *nest* in that bush.

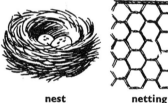

nest   netting

nestle In cold weather I like to *nestle* down under the bedclothes.

nestled The frightened child *nestled* into her mother's skirts for protection.

netting Wire *netting* is a net made of wire.

nettle a weed which stings if you touch it.

network The country is covered with a *network* of roads (i.e. the roads make a net-like pattern).

neuter neither male nor female, e.g. Man is masculine (male sex), woman is feminine (female sex), but a book is *neuter* (no sex).

neutral During the war, Switzerland remained *neutral* (i.e. she did not help either side).

never I *never* go to school without my clothes on.

nevertheless all the same, e.g. I know you can swim; *nevertheless* you are to wear a life jacket when you go out in your canoe.

new Today I am wearing my *new* coat for the first time.

Newfoundland an island off the east coast of Canada.

newly Joe leaned on the *newly* painted wall and stuck to the wet paint.

news For all the latest happenings, listen to the *news* broadcast over the radio or television.

newspaper You will find printed in a *newspaper* information about recent events, together with pictures, advertisements, etc.

newt a pond creature like a tiny crocodile.

newt   **nightingale**

New Zealand a country which consists of two islands south east of Australia.

New Zealander a citizen of New Zealand.

next If tomorrow is Monday, the *next* day will be Tuesday.

nibble to eat carefully, in little bites, e.g. a mouse may *nibble* cheese, or a fish *nibble* bait.

nice pleasant, pleasing, e.g. a *nice* house, a *nice* dinner (slang). ■ precise, subtle, e.g. A *nice* point (in an argument) is one difficult to grasp.

nicely Joan plays the piano very *nicely* (i.e. in a pleasing way).

nickel a hard metal that looks like silver; ■ an American coin worth 5 cents.

nickname a name by which people call you instead of your proper name. (My *nickname* is Ginger – because I have ginger-coloured hair.)

niece A girl is her uncle's *niece*.

nigh (used chiefly by poets) near.

night The sun shines by day and the moon by *night*.

nightingale a bird that sings beautifully by night as well as by day.

nightmare a very frightening dream.

nil nothing, e.g. We won the football match by two goals to *nil*.

nimble *Nimble* people are those who move quickly and lightly.

nimbly The boy *nimbly* dodged aside and his pursuer, unable to stop, rushed into the river.

nine (9) one more than eight.

nineteen (19) one more than eighteen.

nineteenth (19th) The *nineteenth* of May is the day after the eighteenth. ■ ($\frac{1}{19}$) If you divide one into 19 parts, each part is a *nineteenth*.

ninetieth (90th) When Grandad reaches his *ninetieth* birthday, he will have lived 90 years.

ninety (90) nine tens.

ninth (9th) The *ninth* of May is the day after the eighth. ■ ($\frac{1}{9}$) If you divide one into nine equal parts, each part is a *ninth*.

nippers pincers or pliers (used to pull out nails or to grip things).

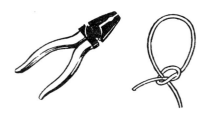

nippers   **noose**

nitrogen The air we breathe consists mostly of the gas *nitrogen*.

nobility The *nobility* are the people who have titles: the dukes, earls, lords, etc.

noble a nobleman. ■ A *noble* creature (e.g. a person, lion or horse, etc.) is one whose manner is dignified and admirable.

nobleman a lord, earl, or duke, etc.

nobly John *nobly* (i.e. in a dignified and admirable way) took the blame to protect his young brother.

nobody We don't know what it is like to live on Mars because *nobody* has been there yet.

nod If you *nod* your head it means 'yes'.

nodded Paul couldn't speak so he *nodded* his head, meaning 'yes'.

noise The *noise* from the engines is so loud that we cannot hear ourselves speak.

noiseless Because of their *noiseless* approach, the enemy were on us before we heard anything.

noisily The children rushed *noisily* to their seats (i.e. they made a great deal of noise).

noisy You can hear that *noisy* motor-cycle when it is in the next street.

nomad one of a tribe who wander from place to place (seeking grass for their animals, etc.).

nominate If you wish to *nominate* Joan for election as House Captain, you must hand in her name before the election.

none The last of our rabbits has died, so now we have *none*.

nonsense It is *nonsense* to say that the moon is made of cream cheese.

noon twelve o'clock, midday.

noose the kind of loop in a rope that tightens when the rope is pulled (used, e.g., in a lasso).

normal ordinary, e.g. Jim is quite a *normal* boy. ■ usual, e.g. We got up at our *normal* time.

north If you are facing the sun rising in the east, *north* is on your left. ■ Iceland is *north* of England ■ (i.e. nearer to the *North* Pole).

northerly A *northerly* wind is one that blows from the north.

northern *Northern* Ireland is that part of Ireland which is farthest north.

Norway a country on the north Atlantic coast of Europe.

Norwegian a citizen of Norway; ■ the language of the people of Norway.

Norwegians (the) people of Norway.

nose You smell things with your *nose*, and breathe through it.

nostril Each of the two holes in your nose is a *nostril*.

notably London contains many interesting buildings, *notably* St. Paul's Cathedral and the Tower.

notation the use of written shapes to represent numbers, or musical notes, e.g. The usual way of writing music, on five lines, is called staff *notation*.

notch a V-shaped cut which a person makes on a stick to help him to keep count, etc.

notch

note Mother wrote a *note* to the headmaster to explain my absence. ■ Jean spoilt her song by singing a wrong *note*. ■ That black *note* in the music is a crotchet. ■ You will *note* (notice) that the floor has been cleaned.

noted Holland is *noted* for bulbs and windmills. ■ The class *noted* (wrote down) the facts in their books.

nothing I am silent because I have *nothing* to say.

notice The *notice* on ■ the school *notice*-board was to tell us about sports day.

noticeable A *noticeable* bulge in Peter's pocket showed clearly where the apples were.

noticeably There was no doubt that the snake had swallowed the animal for it was *noticeably* fatter.

noticed As the policeman walked along he *noticed* an open door.

notification The mayor had received no *notification* of the queen's visit so he was very surprised when she arrived.

notified Before organizing that procession along the street we ought to have *notified* (told) the police.

notify Before organizing a procession along the street you should *notify* (tell) the police.

notion I have no *notion* (idea) of what Charles wants to do.

notorious A *notorious* person is one who is well known because of some piece of bad behaviour.

nought nothing. Five *nought* two is 502 (also spelt *naught*).

noun a word such as paper, ball, ship, etc., which is the name of something.

nourish to feed.

nourishment food that contains the things the body needs, e.g. There is not much *nourishment* in gravy.

novel a book, or a story, about imaginary happenings. ■ A *novel* idea (etc.) is one that no one has thought of before.

novelist a writer of novels, e.g. Charles Dickens.

novelty something new or un-usual, e.g. One *novelty* at Joan's party was a dance for dogs.

November the eleventh month.

novice a beginner, e.g. It was clear from the number of mistakes he made that our driver was a *novice*. ■ a person preparing to become a monk, or a nun.

now Do it *now* (i.e. at this time).

nowadays Years ago the crossing of the Atlantic took weeks; *nowadays* we can do it in a few hours.

nowhere We could find *nowhere* to park the car, so Dad had to drive it home again.

nozzle the end-piece fitted to a hose, etc., from which the water squirts.

nozzle

nuclear *Nuclear* fission is the splitting of atoms to release atomic energy (power). A *nuclear* reactor is the apparatus in which atoms are split. *Nuclear* weapons are atomic bombs or shells, etc. (i.e. A-bombs, H-bombs, etc.).

nudge to poke someone with your elbow in order to attract his attention, but without attracting the notice of other people.

nudging I had to keep *nudging* Rip (i.e. poking him with my elbow) to keep him from falling asleep during the lesson.

nuisance anything (or anybody) that annoys people, e.g. the smell from a factory, the barking of a dog, a troublesome child, etc.

numb My hands are *numb* with cold (i.e. they have no feeling in them).

number Mary lives at *number* 4 Wood St. ■ The *number* of toes on your foot is five. ■ *Number* your answers (i.e. put numbers beside them).

numerical To take things in *numerical* order is to take them in the order in which they are numbered, i.e. number 1 first, then number 2, and so on.

numerous many, e.g. On my birthday I receive *numerous* presents.

nun a woman who leads a relig-ious life in a convent or nunnery, with other such women.

nurse a woman (usually) who looks after people who are ill, especially in a hospital. ■ To *nurse* a baby is to feed it as a mother does, or just to hold it lovingly in your arms.

nun   **nurse**

nursery a young children's room; ■ a place where young plants are grown for sale or for later planting somewhere else. ■ A *nursery* school is for children under five.

nursing Julia is going in for *nursing* when she grows up (i.e. she intends to be a nurse). ■ Mother is *nursing* the baby (i.e. feeding it, or just holding it). ■ A *nursing* home is a kind of hospital, usually one for people who are recovering from an illness.

nutcrackers You crack nuts in the (or, a pair of) *nutcrackers*.

nutmeg a hard, round, sweet-smelling nut, bits of which are grated on to puddings, etc., as flavouring.

nutritious Herrings are very *nutritious* (i.e. they are a food which is very good for you).

nylon a plastic material which looks like silk.

nymph an imaginary, almost god-like young lady, supposed to live in the countryside – in rivers, hills, woods, etc.

nutcrackers   **nutmeg**

oak Acorns grow on *oak* trees.

oar The two boys each took an *oar* and rowed the boat to the bank.

oasis a place in the desert where there is water enough for trees, etc., to grow.

oast An *oast* house is a curiously shaped building in which hops are dried.

oath a swear-word, or a curse; ■ a solemn promise, especially one made to God.

oatmeal powdered oats, used to make porridge, cakes, etc.

oats a grain, like wheat and barley, and used for feeding people or horses.

oast houses   **oats**

obedience I admire your *obedience* (i.e. the fact that you do as you are told).

obedient An *obedient* person (or animal) does as he is told.

obeisance a bow made to some superior person as a sign of respect and humility.

obey To *obey* someone is to do what he tells you.

object (pron. ób-ject) What is that strange *object* (thing)? ■ What is the *object* (aim, purpose, point) of this expedition? ■ (pron. ob-ject) I *object* to (dislike) slugs in my salad.

objection What is your *objection* to (i.e. reason for not wanting or liking) cats?

objectionable An *objectionable* person, or action, is one you dislike strongly.

objective a thing aimed at, e.g. The climbers' *objective* is the top of that mountain.

obligation We are under an *obligation* to help our neighbours (i.e. we feel we ought to help; it is our duty).

oblige I'm looking after the baby to *oblige* Mrs. Smith (i.e. as a kindness to Mrs. Smith). Will you *oblige* me with a stamp? (i.e. let me have one, as a kindness.) ■ This fog may *oblige* (compel) me to walk home.

obliging John is an *obliging* boy (i.e. he is always ready to do things for people).

oblong a shape which, like this page, has four square corners and is longer than it is wide.

obnoxious very unpleasant, e.g. an *obnoxious* smell.

oboe a wood-wind (musical) instrument, whose beautiful, sad notes are produced by the vibrations of the double reed in its mouth-piece.

oboe

obscene indecent, e.g. An *obscene* book is one that contains objectionable stories or pictures (usually about sex).

obscure If you stand there you *obscure* our view of the race (i.e. you make it difficult for us to see). ■ The meaning of the message is *obscure* (not at all clear).

observant Harry is very *observant* (i.e. his eyes miss nothing).

observation a comment, e.g. Tom's *observation* as we watched the rocket was, 'I wish we were in it.' ■ An *observation* post is a place from which you can watch people (or animals, etc.).

observatory At the *observatory* is a big telescope through which scientists study the stars.

observe *Observe* that boy (i.e. watch him). ■ To *observe* a custom or a law is to keep it, e.g. We still *observe* the custom of giving money to carol singers.

obsolete out of date, e.g. Bows and arrows are now *obsolete*.

obstacle something that is in the way.

obstinate stubborn, e.g. This *obstinate* donkey won't move an inch.

obstruct To *obstruct* a road (or passage, etc.) is to block it or to prevent movement along it.

obstruction The water would not flow away because of an *obstruction* in the pipe.

obtain Will you *obtain* (get) a ticket for me?

obtuse blunt. An *obtuse* angle is one greater than a right angle, i.e. over 90°, e.g.. ⌐‾. ■ slow of understanding, e.g. You will not easily make Pat understand; he's very *obtuse*.

obvious It is *obvious* that this is Jane's pencil, for it has her name on it.

obviously The pencil is *obviously* Jane's, for it has her name on it.

occasion To mark a special *occasion* we sometimes have a day's holiday.

occasional We pay an *occasional* visit to the theatre (i.e. we don't go often).

occasionally *Occasionally* (not often) we go to a theatre.

occupant The *occupant* of a house is the person living in it.

occupation Mr. Brown's *occupation* (job) is brick-laying. ■ If you can think of no better *occupation* (thing to do), you had better weed the garden.

occupy How do you *occupy* your time all day (i.e. what do you find to do?). ■ Mr. and Mrs. Smith *occupy* the house next door.

occur It didn't *occur* to me (i.e. I didn't think of it). ■ Don't let it *occur* (happen) again.

occurred It *occurred* (came) to me that Mary might help us.

occurrence a happening, e.g. Any strange *occurrence* is reported in the newspapers.

ocean a big area of sea, e.g. the Atlantic *Ocean.*

o'clock The time is 3 *o'clock.*

octagon a shape which has eight sides.

octagon

octave the interval between a (musical) note and the one eight notes above or below it.

October the tenth month of the year.

octopus a sea creature with a small body and eight big arms with suckers on them.

octopus

odd An *odd* number is one that will not divide by two (e.g. 1, 3, 5, etc.). ■ An *odd* job is an occasional job. ■ How *odd* (queer) to see snow in summer!

oddity a strange object or event, e.g. I bought this *oddity* at the fair.

oddments A box of *oddments* will usually contain a variety of small articles for which there is no use at the moment.

odds *Odds* and ends consist of various small stray articles. ■ 'What's the *odds*?' means 'What does it matter?'

odious hateful, e.g. Who is that *odious* person?

odour a smell, e.g. an *odour* of bad eggs, an *odour* of expensive perfume.

o'er poets' word for 'over'.

off Billy fell *off* his horse. ■ We set *off* for school.

offence To commit an *offence* is to do something wrong. ■ Don't take *offence* (i.e. don't be annoyed).

offend If Billy takes Jane out he may *offend* (annoy) Janet.

offender someone who does wrong, e.g. The *offender* will be punished.

offensive insulting, e.g. The boy was *offensive* to Janet. ■ *Offensive* weapons are those intended for attack on someone.

offer Perhaps Mother will *offer* (show herself willing) to help. ■ Priests, especially in the Bible, *offer* sacrifices to their gods.

offered Jim *offered* to help us (i.e. he asked if we would like him to help). ■ The dog *offered* me his paw to shake.

offering Mother is *offering* you an orange; do take it. ■ a gift made to a god by a worshipper.

office a place of business, especially one where clerks, typists, etc., work. ■ Ted holds an important *office* in the club; he is the secretary.

officer a person in authority, especially in the army, navy or air force.

official a person holding some public office or ■ who has *official* duties, e.g. the school attendance officer, the income tax inspector. ■ The *official* opening of the new school was performed by the duke some time after we had begun to use the building.

officially Although the new road is being used, it has not yet been *officially* opened (i.e. declared open by some important person).

officious An *officious* person is one who causes needless disturbance in doing a job – by doing more than is necessary, or by doing

things that you do not require to be done, etc.

offset To *offset* the loss on his apples, the shopkeeper charged more for the cabbages.

offspring children, e.g. Mrs. Smith's *offspring* are all in bed by now.

oft old-time form of 'often', used nowadays only in such senses as *oft*-repeated.

often Brian *often* sleeps out of doors, so he is used to it.

ogre an imaginary giant, supposed to eat people.

oil (1) a greasy liquid obtained from the earth by drilling deep holes, ■ called *oil*-wells. ■ To *oil* a machine is to put oil in it (so that the parts slide over each other more easily). ■ (2) other oils, used chiefly for food, are obtained by squeezing linseed, olives, etc. (i.e. linseed *oil*, olive *oil*, etc.).

oily like oil, or covered with oil, e.g. an *oily* liquid, an *oily* rag.

ointment a greasy substance put on sore places to heal them.

old That *old* man has lived a very long time.

olden In *olden* times the quickest way of travelling was on a horse.

older Father is thirty years *older* than I am.

oldest Ben Smith is the *oldest* man in the village (i.e. the others are younger than Ben).

old-fashioned not up to date, e.g. Grandma is, of course, *old-fashioned*. ■ out of date, e.g. Grandma wears *old-fashioned* hats.

olive an evergreen tree, with fruits which are eaten green (pickled) or from which olive oil is squeezed. ■ The *olive* leaf (or branch) is a symbol of peace.

omelet, omelette To make an *omelette*, you beat an egg lightly and then fry it.

ominous *Ominous* sounds, signs, etc., are those that indicate that something terrible is about to happen.

omission Owing to the *omission* of the letter f, the notice said, 'In ants' instead of 'Infants'.

omit If you *omit* the letter f, 'infants' becomes 'in ants'.

omitted You have *omitted* my name from your list (i.e. you have not put my name in the list).

omnibus An *omnibus* (book) is one that contains a number of stories, etc. ■ (usually shortened to 'bus') a vehicle that carries people along roads, for short distances.

omnibus   onion

once You can only die *once*. ■ Don't all talk at *once* (i.e. together). ■ *Once* upon a time there lived a lovely princess.

one [1] *One* and *one* make two. ■ When *one* (any person) is angry, *one* does not stop to think.

oneself It is better to do a job *oneself* than to ask an unwilling person to do it for you.

onion a strong-smelling vegetable that makes your eyes water. It is eaten cooked, as a flavouring, or raw (pickled).

onlooker An *onlooker* sees a happening, but takes no part in it.

only I cannot pay £5 because I have *only* £4.

onslaught a fierce attack, e.g. The enemy *onslaught* drove our men back.

onward, onwards forward, e.g. 'Onward, Christian soldiers.' The explorers struggled *onwards*.

ooze wet mud, especially that on the bed of a river or the sea. ■ To *ooze* is to flow very slowly as mud would.

opaque You cannot see through a substance that is *opaque* (e.g. wood).

open You cannot walk into the room unless the door is *open*. ■ You have to *open* your mouth to sing 'Ah'.

opened Joan *opened* the door and let us in. ■ The meeting *opened* (began) with a speech by Jones.

opening He is *opening* the door to let us in. ■ The animal escaped through an *opening* (hole) in the fence.

openly To do something *openly* is to make no attempt to hide what you do.

opera An *opera* is a play set to music (the words are sung).

operate to perform an operation, e.g. The doctor had to *operate* on the patient. ■ Do you know how to *operate* (work) this machine?

operation cutting of the body as a way of dealing with an illness, e.g. Janet has gone into hospital for an *operation*.

opinion In my *opinion* (i.e. it is what I think), Jack is a good captain.

opium a drug made from the juice of poppies, which makes people sleepy if it is injected into them, or if they smoke it.

opponent the person against whom you play or fight.

opportunity The guard turned his back, and this gave the prisoner an *opportunity* to throw a message from the window.

oppose I shall *oppose* (work against) the idea of having shorter holidays.

opposite The butcher's shop is *opposite* the chemist's (i.e. facing it, on the other side of the road). ■ Jane says Billy is naughty; I think the *opposite* (i.e. that he is good).

optician a person who tests your eyes and supplies you with glasses.

optimist someone who sees the cheerful side of things, e.g. the person who misses his bus home and says, 'Well, the walk will do me good.'

optional Church attendance is *optional*; you don't have to come.

oral spoken, e.g. In an *oral* exam, you don't write the answers; you say them.

orange a soft, juicy fruit with a thick skin; ■ the reddish-yellow colour of oranges.

orangeade a drink, fizzy or still, made from oranges (or flavoured and coloured to resemble an orange drink).

orator someone who is good at making speeches.

oratorio a musical composition, usually on a religious subject, and like an opera except that the performers do not act and there are no costumes or scenery.

orb a sphere (a ball-shaped object). ■ The *orb* held by kings or queens at their coronation is a jewelled metal ball with a cross on the top.

orb   orbit

orbit the path followed by a planet in going round the sun, or by a space-craft going round the earth. ■ To *orbit* a star, etc., is to go round it.

orchard There are many fruit trees in the *orchard*, including apples, pears and plums.

orchestra a group of musicians playing various kinds of instruments together (most, or all, of the instruments will be stringed ones).

orchestral An *orchestral* concert is one given by an orchestra.

ordeal a very unpleasant experience, one which is a severe test of your courage and toughness.

order Arrange the boys in *order* of size. ■ When a master gives an *order*, he expects you to obey it. ■ *Order* (tell) those boys to go away.

■ Call at the butcher's and *order* a chicken for dinner (i.e. tell the butcher we shall require a chicken).

orderly Leave the room in an *orderly* (tidy) state. Leave the room in an *orderly* way (i.e. don't rush out in disorder).

ordinarily usually, e.g. *Ordinarily*, I do not talk to strange people.

ordinary If anything is *ordinary*, there is nothing unusual about it.

ore rock from which metals are obtained, e.g. iron *ore*.

organ No music came from the church *organ* when the organist pressed the keys, because the pump which blew air into the pipes had broken. ■ any special part of an animal or plant, e.g. your digestive *organs* (stomach, etc.), your hearing *organ* (ear).

organism a living plant or animal.

organist someone who plays an organ.

organization An *organization* is made up of people working together for some special purpose, e.g. the United Nations *Organization*.

organize To *organize* anything (e.g. a concert, a party) is to make all the arrangements for it.

oriental a person from the east, especially from China or Japan; ■ eastern, e.g. an *oriental* rug.

origin the beginning, or starting point, e.g. the *origin* of a rumour.

original the thing from which something has been copied, e.g. Where is the *original* of the picture you have painted? ■ An *original* idea is one that has not been copied from anyone.

originality What I specially like about the idea is its *originality* (i.e. the fact that it hasn't been copied from anyone else).

originally This is not what we *originally* (at first) set out to do.

ornament an article (or the carving, painting, etc., on an article), which is for decoration rather than use. ■ To *ornament* anything is to put some kind of decoration on it.

ornamental Dad has bought some *ornamental* iron gates (i.e. gates specially made to be decorative).

orphan a child whose father or mother (or both father and mother) has (have) died.

orphanage a home specially for orphans.

Oslo the capital city of Norway.

ostrich a large African bird with long legs and neck, which runs fast, but cannot fly.

ostrich   otter

other This book is better than the *other* one.

otherwise Joe is rather noisy; *otherwise* he is a pleasant boy. ■ Play the gramophone quietly; *otherwise* you will not be allowed to play it at all.

otter a furry, web-footed animal that lives in water and eats fish.

ought You *ought* to have a light on your bicycle when you ride at night (i.e. it is right, proper and wise to have a light).

ounce (usually shortened to oz.) a weight of 28 gms, a sixteenth ($\frac{1}{16}$) part of a pound.

our belonging to us, e.g. *our* parents, *our* books.

ours These books are *ours* (i.e. they belong to us).

ourselves We don't need help; we can do it *ourselves*.

oust To *oust* people (or animals) from a place is to force them out.

out Mother is *out* (not at home). ■ When a batsman is *out*, another man goes in to bat in place of him.

outbreak The school had to be closed because of the *outbreak* of a disease. In 1939 there was an *outbreak* of war.

outburst a sudden rush of angry or excitable words, e.g. There was an *outburst* from Peter as he heard the result of the match.

outcast a person rejected by friends, relatives or country.

outfit all the things needed for some purpose, especially the things to wear, e.g. Billy has a skin-diving *outfit*.

outing a journey (usually a short one) made for pleasure.

outlandish very strange, e.g. Jenny was dressed in an *outlandish* costume.

outlaw (long ago) a person not protected by the law, e.g. Robin Hood was a famous *outlaw*. ■ To *outlaw* someone is to order that he is not to be protected by the law.

outlay money paid for something, e.g. Our total *outlay* for the party was £5.

outlet The water could not get away from the tank because the *outlet* was blocked.

outline a drawing showing only the outer edge of something. ■ To give an *outline* (e.g. of an idea) is to explain without going into details. ■ To *outline* any object is to draw only the outer edge of it. ■ To *outline* an idea, etc., is to explain it without going into details.

outlook The (weather) *outlook* for today is wet and windy (i.e. wind and rain are to be expected).

output The whole of the *output* of the factory (i.e. all the goods produced) goes overseas.

outrage a piece of very serious misbehaviour.

outrageous The boy's behaviour was *outrageous* (very bad indeed).

outright all at once, not a little at a time, e.g. Dad bought the car *outright*. I would rather kill the animal *outright* than leave it to suffer.

outside Don't leave Pat *outside*; invite her into the house. ■ My new gloves have fur on the *outside*, and wool inside.

outspoken Uncle Frank is an *outspoken* man (i.e. he says plainly what he means, even at the risk of annoying people).

outstanding particularly good, e.g. Ivan is an *outstanding* chess player.

outward Jim showed no *outward* signs of the nervousness he was feeling. ■ A ship that is *outward* bound is going away from port.

outwardly *Outwardly* Jim looked calm, but inside he was feeling very frightened.

outwit To *outwit* someone is to prove yourself too clever for him.

oval the shape of a flattened circle.

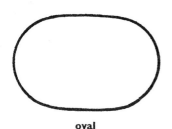

oval

ovation enthusiastic applause, e.g. The hero received a great *ovation* from the crowd.

oven You bake cakes, bread, etc. by putting them in an *oven*.

over The parcel weighs *over* (more than) 2 kg. ■ Hold an umbrella *over* your head to keep off the rain. ■ The cow jumped *over* the moon. ■ After paying my fare, I had 5p *over* (left).

overalls People who do rough or dirty work often protect their clothes by wearing *overalls*.

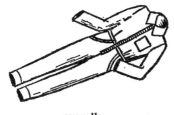

overalls

overboard The ship stopped because someone had fallen *overboard* (into the sea).

overcast The sky is *overcast* when it is covered with clouds.

overcoat When the weather is cold I put on an *overcoat* before going out of doors.

overdo To *overdo* anything is to do it too much and so spoil the result, e.g. Make-up improves a lady, provided she doesn't *overdo* it.

overdue The aircraft is *overdue* by several hours (i.e. it should have arrived several hours ago).

overflow If you get into a bath full of water some of the water will *overflow* on to the floor. ■ The *overflow* from the bath ran on to the floor.

overhaul Before going for a long ride I *overhaul* my bicycle (i.e. make sure that all the parts are in proper working order). ■ The police car began to *overhaul* (overtake) us.

overhead The aircraft circling *overhead* is waiting to land.

overjoyed very pleased indeed.

overlap Where the two carpets *overlap*, you have one on top of the other.

overlook Please *overlook* the mistakes in my letter (i.e. take no notice of the mistakes). ■ The neighbours in the upstairs flat *overlook* (see from above) our garden.

overseas Visitors from *overseas* have crossed the seas to get here.

oversight a mistake, e.g. Owing to an *oversight*, Betty's name was included in the list of boys.

overtake The police car is having to *overtake* (pass) the lorry.

overtime If a worker who should finish at 5 works till 7 o'clock, he has worked two hours *overtime*, for which he receives extra pay.

overture a short piece of music written to be played at the beginning of an opera, or concert, etc.

overturn We saw the canoe *overturn*, throwing its passengers into the water.

overwhelm Don't just win the match; *overwhelm* your opponents by about 20 goals to nil.

owe Please repay the 10p you *owe* me.

owing The aircraft cannot take off *owing* to the foggy weather.

owl a flesh-eating bird that flies at night.

own Do you *own* this dog (i.e. does it belong to you?). ■ Use your *own* pen (i.e. the one belonging to you). ■ I am on my *own* (i.e. there is no one with me). ■ I hope the boy who broke the window will *own* up (admit it).

owner Who is the *owner* of that dog? (i.e. To whom does he belong?)

oxen (more than one ox) cattle, especially cattle of the kind used to pull ploughs, etc.

oxygen one of the gases in the air we breathe, the gas without which neither animals nor plants can live.

oyster a shell-fish which is usually eaten alive. (Pearls are sometimes found in the shells of *oysters*.)

owl   **oyster**

pace I cannot walk at that *pace* (speed). ■ Take one *pace* (step) forward. ■ I measure the distance by *pacing* it out (i.e. by counting the number of steps).

pacific peaceful, peace-loving. ■ The *Pacific* Ocean lies between America and Asia.

pacifist someone who believes that there ought not to be wars.

pacify To *pacify* an angry person, or a war-like tribe, is to cause him (or them) to become calm and peaceful.

pack *Pack* your case (i.e. put things in it). ■ The tramp carried a *pack* (bundle) on his back. ■ A *pack* of hounds chased the fox. ■ Take the *pack* (set) of cards and deal some to each player.

package Among the parcels was a *package* for me.

packet I have a *packet* of sweets. Bring me a *packet* of tea. ■ A person's wage-*packet* is the envelope containing his week's wages. ■ A *packet* (boat) is one that carries letters and parcels.

pact an important agreement, e.g. The white men made a peace *pact* with the Indians.

pad a cushion-like piece of soft material, e.g. a *corn*-pad, a writing *pad*, a shoulder *pad*; or the soft cushion under an animal's foot. ■ To *pad* anything is to stuff it out with material to make it bigger or to make it soft.

padded We *padded* the seat of the chair with horse-hair to make it soft. ■ A *padded* cell is a room with *padded* walls in which violent lunatics may be safely kept.

padding material put in chair seats to make them soft, or into the shoulders of coats to shape them, etc.

paddle We took off our shoes and socks so that we could *paddle* in the sea. ■ We *paddle* our canoe along ■ with a *paddle*.

paddle padlock

padlock a lock which hangs by a loop of metal.

page a small boy who works as a servant, especially in hotels. ■ Each *page* of a book has a number on it.

pageant a spectacular historical play performed out of doors.

paid I *paid* you the money for those tickets yesterday.

pail A *pail* of water is too heavy for a small boy to carry.

page palette

pailful A *pailful* of water is about ten litres.

pailfuls We shall need many *pailfuls* of water to fill the fish-pond.

pain Betty is crying because she has a *pain* in her stomach. ■ To take *pains* over a thing is to go to a lot of trouble over it.

painful A broken leg is *painful* (i.e. it hurts).

painstaking Mr Carpenter is a *painstaking* workman (i.e. he takes great care with his work).

paint a thick, oily liquid put on things, with a brush or spray, to colour or preserve them. ■ You *paint* (put paint on) ■ with a *paint* brush. ■ I wish I could *paint* a picture.

painter a workman who paints houses, etc.; ■ an artist who paints pictures, etc.; ■ a rope in the bow (front) of a boat, used to tie it to a ship or a post, etc.

painting This *painting* is valuable because it was painted by a great artist. ■ The artist is *painting* a picture. ■ Father is *painting* the kitchen door.

pair I need a *pair* of shoes, one shoe for each foot.

Pakistan In 1947 the country that had been called India became two countries : *Pakistan* and India.

palace the home of a king or bishop, etc., e.g., The Queen of England lives in Buckingham *Palace*.

palatable pleasant to the taste, or to the mind, e.g. a *palatable* stew, a *palatable* idea.

pale Derek looked *pale* (whitish) after his frightening experience. ■ *Pale* red is pink, a lighter shade of red.

palette a flat, thin board on which an artist mixes his colours.

paling a strip of wood which, with other strips, is nailed upright across horizontal timbers to make a fence.

palings **palm**

palm a tree having a tall stem and no branches, and with a fan-like arrangement of leaves at the top, e.g. date-palm, coco-nut palm, etc. ■ He held out a coin in the *palm* of his hand.

palsy A person suffering from *palsy* is unable to move some part (or any part) of his body.

paltry not worth much, e.g. a *paltry* gift, a *paltry* contribution.

pampas the great treeless plains of South America. ■ The giant *pampas* grass, taller than a man, is grown in Europe as a garden plant.

pamper To *pamper* someone is to do everything (or far too much) that he wants – i.e. to spoil him.

pamphlet a thin paper-covered book.

pancake You make a *pancake* by frying a thin layer of batter in a frying-pan.

pandemonium disorder, noise and violence, e.g. There was *pandemonium* in the hall when the speaker insulted the audience.

pane There are usually several separate *panes* of glass in a window.

panel a separate, oblong part of the surface of a wall, or a door, etc., e.g. A door usually has four *panels*. ■ the team in a radio or television quiz game.

panelling Years ago, the inside walls of houses were often covered with oak *panelling* (i.e. panels made of oak).

panic sudden terror which causes people (or animals) to rush madly in an effort to escape. ■ To *panic* is to take fright and act too hastily in an effort to avoid danger or trouble.

pansy a big, colourful flower which grows from a small plant and is often to be seen in garden borders.

pansy

pant You *pant* (for breath) after running hard for a time.

panther a leopard, an animal like a big, wild, spotted cat.

pantomime a theatrical entertainment including comedy, music and dancing, and based on such children's stories as Cinderella, Puss in Boots, etc., but with the Principal Boy played by a girl and the chief female part, the Dame, played by a man (usually).

pantry   At home, we keep our food in the *pantry*.

pants   underclothing worn under trousers; ■ trousers.

paper   Books are printed on *paper*. Parcels are wrapped in brown *paper*. We decorate walls by sticking wall-*paper* on them. The newspaper is printed on large sheets of *paper*, made from wood-pulp. ■ To *paper* (a room) is to decorate it by sticking wall-paper on the walls.

parable   a story made up to explain some religious idea, e.g. the *Parable* of the Good Samaritan, in the Bible.

parachute   The man jumped from the aircraft and floated slowly to earth, hanging from his *parachute*.

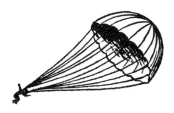

parachute

parade   a show, especially of soldiers lined up for inspection. ■ A *parade* (of shops) is a row of shops along a street. ■ To *parade* is to show off something, or to line up soldiers for inspection, etc.

paradise   a place of great happiness; ■ heaven.

paraffin   a thin oil (usually coloured pink, blue, or green) used in lamps, oil heaters, etc.

paragraph   When you write or print, each new *paragraph* must begin on a fresh line, and start farther in from the edge of the page than the other lines.

parallel   *Parallel* lines, like a pair of railway lines, never get closer or farther apart, no matter how long you make them.

parallel lines

paralysed   A person who is *paralysed* is unable to move some (or any) parts of his body.

parapet   the low wall on the edge of a bridge, or of a flat roof, etc.

parasite   a creature that lives on some other creature, e.g. by sucking blood out of it as a flea does, or like mistletoe, which gets its food from the branches of the apple tree on which it lives.

paratroops   soldiers who are dropped into battle by parachute.

parcel   You can make a number of articles into a *parcel* by wrapping them up together.

parched   hot and dry, e.g. All the crops in that *parched* soil had died.

parchment   specially prepared skin, usually of sheep or goats, on which people used to write or paint.

pardon   To show you are sorry for annoying someone you say, 'I beg your *pardon*.' ■ To *pardon* anyone is to forgive him.

pare   to cut (away), e.g. you *pare* your nails, or *pare* fruit (i.e. cut off the skin).

parent   To begin with, we all have two *parents*, a father and a mother.

Paris   the capital city of France.

parish Your *parish* church is the one specially provided, together with its clergyman, ■ for the *parish* (district) in which you live.

parishioner someone who lives in a parish, and who is therefore in the care of the clergyman of the parish church.

park an open space with trees, grass, flower gardens, etc., where people may walk or sit. ■ A car *park* is a place ■ where you may *park* (leave) your car.

Parliament the group of elected people who rule Britain. Members of *Parliament* are elected by the people of the country. *Parliament* meets in the Houses of *Parliament*, in London.

parlour the sitting room in a house or in a public house.

parrot a colourful bird with a hooked beak, which is able to repeat words or other sounds that it hears.

parrot   parsnip

parsley a garden plant with spicy-smelling, crinkly leaves, used for decorating food or for making sauces.

parsnip a root vegetable like a pale yellow beetroot.

parson a clergyman.

part I saw *part* (but not all) of the concert. ■ In the play, John plays the *part* of a knight. ■ To *part* your hair is to divide it with a comb. ■ To *part* people who are fighting is to separate them.

partial not complete, e.g. *partial* blindness, a *partial* eclipse. ■ I am *partial* to fried sausages (i.e. I like them).

partially The house was *partially* hidden behind the trees so we could not see all of it.

participate Everyone can *participate* (take part) in this game.

particle a tiny portion of anything, e.g. The boys ate and ate until not a *particle* of food remained.

particular On this *particular* (special) day we had to be at school early. ■ Any old thing will not do for Mary; she's very *particular*. ■ I only know there is to be a party; I don't know any *particulars* (i.e. details of time, place, etc.).

particularly very, e.g. It was a *particularly* pleasant day. ■ especially, e.g. John likes all the girls, *particularly* Joan.

parting a line on the top of the head from back to front, made by combing the hair away from it to right and left. ■ The girls cried at *parting* from (leaving) their mother.

partition There is a wooden *partition* across the room to divide it into two parts.

partly The floor is only *partly* scrubbed because the girls went home before they had finished the job.

partner the person with whom you take part in something, e.g. a dancing *partner*, a business *partner*.

partridge a land bird, about the size of a duck, which is shot for sport, and eaten.

partridge

party You invite your friends to a *party* so that you can have fun and eat together. ■ Political *parties* are made up of people who have similar political ideas, e.g. the Conservative *Party*, the Labour *Party*, the Liberal *Party*.

pass Please *pass* me the butter. ■ I hope that I *pass* my exam. ■ A bus or train *pass* is a ticket that shows that you haven't to pay. ■ A mountain *pass* is a narrow gap between mountains.

passable fairly good, e.g. The actor gave a *passable* performance.

passage a corridor joining rooms in a building; ■ a voyage, e.g. I hadn't enough money for my *passage* home. ■ Ruth read us a *passage* from the Bible.

passed I *passed* Jean as I cycled home. ■ I'm glad that I *passed* my exam. ■ Dad *passed* me the butter (i.e. handed it to me).

passenger someone (apart from the crew) who travels on a plane, bus, ship, etc.

passion strong feelings, e.g. of anger or love. ■ The *Passion* is the suffering of Christ on the cross.

passionate A *passionate* person is one who is easily roused to strong feelings – especially of anger or love.

passionately with strong feeling, e.g. John *passionately* denied that he had stolen the money.

passive You are *passive* when you allow things to happen, but do nothing, e.g. when you take no notice of things said or done to you.

passport A person who travels abroad has to carry a *passport*, a thin booklet which contains a photograph and description, etc., of him.

password a secret word which you have to say in order to get into a place (used chiefly in wartime).

past Jim rushed *past* me before I could speak. ■ The time is half *past* two. ■ The *past* week was an exciting one. ■ Grandad is always thinking of the *past*.

paste You can stick paper with *paste* made of flour and water. ■ Fish-*paste* is fish so treated that it can easily be spread on bread.

pastel a coloured chalk or crayon for making pictures on paper. ■ *Pastel* shades are light, delicate colours.

pastime an amusement, e.g. Colin's favourite *pastime* is playing chess.

pastry the crust over pies, tarts, etc., made by baking a mixture of flour, fat, water, etc.

pasture The farmer's sheep and cattle needed fresh *pasture*, so we had to move them to other fields.

patch a piece of material, rubber or metal, put on something to mend a hole. ■ A cabbage *patch* is a piece of ground on which cabbages grow. ■ To *patch* anything is to put a patch on it.

patchy If you paint a wall badly it may look *patchy* (i.e. patches of different colours may be seen). Billy's work is *patchy* (i.e. some parts are good, others are bad).

patent If you invent something, you can apply to the government for a *patent*, which will ensure that no one but you may sell your invention.

path a way or track for people travelling on foot.

pathetic The homeless children were in a *pathetic* state (i.e. a state that made people feel sad and sympathetic).

patience A person who has *patience* is not easily irritated, e.g. by worry or by having to do a job which requires much time and care.

patient a person being treated for an illness, especially in hospital. ■ A *patient* person is one who has patience.

patiently To do something *patiently* is to do it without getting cross.

patriotic A *patriotic* person is one who loves his country and stands up for it.

patriotism love for your country.

patrol To *patrol* a place, you go about in it to see that all is well, e.g. policemen *patrol* the streets.

patron a regular customer of a shop. ■ St George is the *patron* saint of England (i.e. the saint supposed to be England's special guardian).

patter You hear the *patter* of children's feet as they run across the floor. ■ A comedian's *patter* is his flow of quick, amusing talk.

pattern something to be copied, e.g. a paper *pattern* that dressmakers use when cutting out material. ■ a design used to decorate wallpaper, lino., etc.

pause to stop for a short time; ■ a short stop.

pavement People should walk on the *pavement*, not in the road.

pavilion an ornamental building, usually of wood, to be seen on a cricket ground or at the seaside etc.

pavilion   pawn

paving The pavement is made of large, oblong *paving*-stones. ■ We are *paving* our garden path with slabs of stone.

paw Our dog walked on a thorn and pricked his *paw*.

pawn the chess piece which is of least value in the game.

pay How much did you *pay* for the book you bought? ■ If you do not *pay* attention, you will not understand what I say. ■ The *pay* I receive for a week's work is £10.

payable The money is *payable* (due to be paid) on the first day of the term. ■ A sub of 25p is *payable* (has to be paid) by all members.

payment We receive a *payment* of 25p for each basket of fruit we pick.

pea *Pea* soup, *pea*-shooters and pease pudding ■ all require *peas*, which are the seeds of the pea plant and grow in neat rows in pods. ■ Sweet *peas* are beautiful, sweet-smelling garden flowers.

peak The *peak* of a cap is the stiff, flat piece that sticks out in front. ■ A mountain *peak* is the point at the top.

peal A *peal* of bells is a set of bells. ■ When the bellringers pull on the ropes, the bells *peal* out so that everyone in the town can hear.

peanut a small, pea-like nut which grows in a pod under the ground (also called monkey nut, or ground nut).

pea   peacock   peanut   pear

peace In 1945 the war ended and we had *peace*. ■ Grandma loves the *peace* (quiet and calm) of the countryside.

peaceable *Peaceable* people (or nations) dislike wars and quarrels.

peaceful We hope for a *peaceful* settlement of the quarrel between the countries (i.e. without war). ■ It is *peaceful* (quiet) in the countryside.

peach a fruit like a plum, but larger and with a yellowish velvet-like skin.

peacock a large bird with a tail composed of long, beautifully coloured feathers, which can be opened out like a fan. (The female bird is a peahen.)

pear a fruit like an apple, but different in flavour and shape.

pearl a precious stone, like a small, hard, whitish ball, found inside the shells of some oysters.

peasant someone who lives and works in the countryside.

peat a mass of partly decayed vegetation, which is cut out of the ground and dried for use as fuel, e.g. in Ireland.

pebble a small stone which has become rounded through being rolled about by the sea.

peck a measure of corn, etc.; 2 gallons = 1 *peck*. ■ The birds come and *peck* at the nuts hung up in the garden.

peckish (slang) hungry, e.g. I feel rather *peckish*.

peculiar This drink has a *peculiar* (strange) flavour. ■ I have my own *peculiar* (special) way of doing things.

peculiarity some special odd thing about someone, e.g. Jim pokes his tongue into his cheek, Jack's ears stick out and Mary has one grey eye and one blue one.

pedal The *pedals* on a bicycle or an organ, etc., enable you to work it with your feet. ■ To *pedal* a bicycle, etc., is to work the pedals (with your feet).

peddle To *peddle* (goods) is to sell small quantities by going from door to door.

pedestal the base on which something, especially a statue, stands.

pedestal   pelican

pedestrian anyone who is walking. ■ A *pedestrian* task, etc., is one which is neither interesting nor exciting.

pedigree a list of ancestors, made to show that some person (or animal) has descended from desirable people (or animals). ■ A *pedigree* animal is one whose ancestors have been so listed.

pedlar someone who goes from door to door selling small quantities of such goods as buttons, ribbons, laces, cotton, etc.

peel When you *peel* an orange, or a potato, etc. ■ you take off the *peel* (thick skin). ■ The skin will *peel* off your back if you expose it to too much sun.

peep *Peep* through the letter-box and see if anyone is at home. ■ I know what's in the secret letter, for I took a *peep* while no one was looking.

peeping Tom was *peeping* through a shutter at Lady Godiva.

peer a nobleman, such as an earl or duke, etc. ■ To *peer* at something is to look at it closely and carefully.

peeved (slang) annoyed, e.g. Jack was *peeved* because we would not wait for him.

peevish irritable, quietly bad-tempered.

peg You fasten washing to a line with a *peg*. ■ You hang clothes on a *peg* fixed to a wall or door. ■ Tent ropes are held down with tent-*pegs*. ■ The strings of violins, guitars, etc., are fastened to *pegs*. ■ To *peg* washing on a line is to fix it there with a peg. ■ To *peg* away at a task is to work at it steadily.

pegged Janet *pegged* the washing on the line (i.e. fixed it with pegs). ■ John *pegged* away at his work (i.e. he worked steadily at it).

Peiping, Peking the capital city of the Chinese Republic (China).

pelican a bird that catches fish and stores them in a big skin bag under its beak.

pellet a small ball, especially of paper, bread, lead, etc.

pelt the furry skin of an animal such as the fox. ■ Why did the boys *pelt* Joe with rotten apples? (i.e. throw them at him).

pelting The angry tribesmen are *pelting* the travellers with stones. ■ The rain is *pelting* down (coming down heavily).

penalty punishment, e.g. Years ago the *penalty* for stealing was death. ■ In football, a *penalty* kick is given against the team which breaks a rule.

pence A hundred *pence* make a pound.

pencil If you draw or write with a *pencil* the lines can be rubbed out.

pendulum Some clocks have a *pendulum*, which swings from side to side to keep the works moving at the right speed.

penknife The blades of a *penknife* can be closed so that you may safely keep it in your pocket.

pennies The shopkeeper gave me my 7p change all in *pennies*.

penniless A *penniless* person is one who has no money.

penny (1p) a British coin worth one-hundredth of a pound.

pension a regular payment made to people who are not able to continue working, e.g. the old age *pension*.

pensioner someone who is receiving a pension, e.g. an old age *pensioner*.

pentagon a five-sided flat shape.

pendulum   **penguin**   **penknife**   **pentagon**

penetrate to go through, e.g. No bullet can *penetrate* this tough steel. Rain will soon *penetrate* a thin coat.

penguin a sea bird that cannot fly and is usually seen standing upright.

peninsula a piece of land almost surrounded by water. The Peninsular War was fought in the Spain–Portugal *peninsula*.

peony a plant with big cabbage-like red or white flowers.

people All the *people* at the party were talking at once.

pepper a hot, spicy, powder which makes you sneeze. It is shaken on food to flavour it.

peppermint a kind of mint (plant) grown for its oil, which is used for flavouring, ■ e.g. in *peppermint* sweets.

per £5 *per* year means £5 each year. ■ 25 *per* cent (25%) means 25 out of every hundred.

perambulator (usually shortened to *pram*) Put the baby in its *perambulator* and I will wheel it home.

perambulator   perimeter

perch a stick, etc., that a bird sits or stands on. ■ Birds often *perch* (settle) on branches of trees. ■ a fresh-water fish.

percussion You make a *percussion* instrument sound by hitting it (e.g. a drum).

perfect If a thing is *perfect*, you cannot improve on it.

perfection The poet admires the *perfection* of a rose (i.e. the fact that there is nothing wrong with it).

perfectly I am *perfectly* (completely) happy. ■ This is *perfectly* (quite) ridiculous.

perforated A sheet of paper, or metal, etc., that is *perforated* has holes in it – usually in rows, e.g. a page of stamps.

perform The actors will *perform* their play this evening. ■ The mayor will *perform* the opening ceremony.

performance In the school play Dora gave a good *performance* (i.e. she acted well).

performer The best *performer* in the concert was the boy who played the piano.

performing I love to watch a conjurer *performing* tricks. ■ At the circus we saw some *performing* seals (i.e. seals which had been taught to do tricks).

perfume You can smell the *perfume* of the roses. ■ Mother puts *perfume* on her handkerchief to make it smell pleasant.

perhaps If we are good, *perhaps* the teacher will let us go home early (i.e. he may or he may not).

peril danger, e.g. those in *peril* on stormy seas.

perilous dangerous, e.g. a *perilous* voyage into space.

perimeter The *perimeter* of anything (e.g. a circle, a square, a field, etc.) is the distance, or the line, round it.

period Our school day is divided into eight *periods* of forty minutes each. ■ The Tudor *period* in history was the time during which the Tudor Kings and Queens reigned.

periodical a magazine, etc. that comes out at regular intervals, e.g. monthly or weekly.

perish to die, e.g. Many people *perish* in the floods each year.

perishable *Perishable* goods are those likely to go bad, e.g. fruit or fish.

perished To be *perished* with cold is to be so cold that you are miserable. ■ Many people *perished* (died) in the flood.

permanent intended to last a long time, or for ever, e.g. the *permanent* wave in a lady's hair.

permissible It is not *permissible* for children to bring their pets to school (i.e. it cannot be allowed).

permission May I have *permission* to go home early? (i.e. Will you allow it?)

permit Will you *permit* (allow) me to use your camera? ■ You may not collect money in the streets without a *permit* (written permission).

perpendicular upright, like a telegraph pole, or a string on which a weight is hung.

perpendicular

perpetrate to do (something that you ought not to have done), e.g. to *perpetrate* a silly practical joke, to *perpetrate* a crime.

perpetual everlasting. A *perpetual* motion machine was one which, its inventor hoped, would keep going for ever.

perplex to puzzle, e.g. If the problems *perplex* you, ask someone to explain them.

persecute To *persecute* someone is to keep on annoying or injuring him (usually because of an opinion he holds that you do not agree with), e.g. Saul set out to *persecute* the Christians.

persecution the annoying or injuring of people by others who dislike their opinions, e.g. the *persecution* of the Jews by Hitler.

persevere To *persevere* with a job, etc., is to keep at it, even when there is difficulty or discouragement.

Persia a country between Arabia and India, now called Iran.

Persian a citizen of Persia; ■ the language of Persia. ■ *Persian* things are those from (or connected with) Persia, e.g. *Persian* cats, *Persian* carpets.

persist To *persist* in something is to keep on doing it, especially against the wishes of others, e.g. Pat will *persist* in singing that horrible song.

persistent The salesman at the door was so *persistent* (he wouldn't take 'No', for an answer) that Mother finally bought something from him.

person Ask Dick, Joan, or any other *person*. ■ The Queen presented the prizes in *person* (i.e. herself).

personal That is my *personal* (own) opinion. ■ Don't make *personal* remarks (i.e. remarks about a person). ■ Your *personal* property consists of the movable things that you own.

personality character, e.g. A man's *personality* may be changed by illness. ■ A television *personality* is someone well known on television.

personally The queen *personally* (herself) presented the prizes. ■ *Personally*, I see nothing wrong with it (i.e. this is my own opinion).

perspective the art of drawing objects on a flat surface so that they seem to be solid, e.g. parallel railway lines are made to meet at the horizon.

perspire When you *perspire* drops of sweat form on your skin.

persuade I will *persuade* Derek to come (i.e. I'll talk him into it).

persuasion No amount of *persuasion* will make Derek come (i.e. you cannot talk him into coming).

pert saucy, cheeky, e.g. People dislike Angela because she is *pert*.

perturb to upset (someone), to make (someone) worried.

pessimist a cheerless person who thinks only of the worst side of things, e.g. someone who is miserable during a party because he is thinking of all the clearing up that will have to be done.

pest something (e.g. flies, factory smoke, a mischievous boy, etc.) that is a nuisance or does harm.

pester to annoy and trouble, e.g. Swarms of flies *pester* picnic parties. Little boys *pester* footballers for their autographs.

petal A flower such as the daisy has a yellow centre with many white *petals* round it.

pew   pheasant

petrified turned to stone. ■ To be *petrified* with fear is to be frightened stiff.

petrol, petroleum The fuel that drives motor-car engines is *petroleum*, *petrol* for short.

petticoat a thin under-skirt (worn under a skirt) for females.

petting cuddling and kissing, etc.

petty not important, e.g. You must not bother the headmaster with such a *petty* matter. ■ At the *Petty* Sessions, the courts deal with crimes which are not very serious.

pew a seat in a church ■ 'Take a *pew*' (slang) means 'Sit down.'

pewter a grey metal which consists, usually, of tin and lead.

phantom a ghost.

phase a stage through which something passes as it grows or develops, e.g. The *phases* of the moon include the new moon and the full moon.

pheasant a large, handsome bird which is (in Britain) shot for sport, and eaten.

philatelist a stamp collector, e.g. One *philatelist* I know has collected thousands of stamps.

philosopher a lover of the truth, a thinker, especially someone who likes to think deeply about life and its problems.

phone (short for) telephone.

phosphorus a yellowish substance that glows with a faint light in darkness.

photo (short for) photograph.

photograph The *photograph* that I took of Sandra with my new camera is very like her.

photography If you want to know how to take good pictures with your camera, you should ask someone who understands *photography*.

phrase a group of words which do not make a sentence e.g. 'at break of day'.

physical *Physical* exercises are activities such as running and jumping, which keep the body fit. ■ *Physical* things are those that you can see, touch, etc.

physics the branch of science in which you study heat, light, sound, magnetism, electricity, splitting atoms, etc.

pianist someone who plays a piano.

piano (short for) pianoforte The black and white keys of a *piano* work little hammers, which hit strings.

grand piano

pianoforte a large musical instrument, now usually called a piano.

Piccadilly a famous London street, noted for its smart shops, hotels, etc.

piccalilli a pickle made of vegetables, spices, mustard, etc.

piccolo When playing the small flute called a *piccolo*, you hold it sideways across your face and blow across a hole.

x

pick May I *pick* some flowers out of your garden? ■ *Pick* whichever sweet you like best. ■ You must *pick* up your litter and take it away with you. ■ This lovely flower is the *pick* (best) of the bunch.

pickaxe a big, heavy tool for breaking up hard surfaces. (It is often called, simply, a pick.)

piccolo   **pickaxe**

pickle To *pickle* onions you put them in vinegar with spices, etc. ■ A jar of *pickle* will contain pickled onions, or pickled cabbage, etc.

pickup the part of a record-player that holds the needle.

picnic We usually enjoy a *picnic* on the beach, even though sand does get into the food. ■ To *picnic* is to eat a meal out of doors.

picnicking having a picnic (i.e. having a meal out of doors).

pictorial This *pictorial* record of our holidays is made up of photographs of all kinds.

picture Joan has painted a *picture* of children playing in the snow. ■ Can you *picture* (imagine) Bill dressed as a fairy?

pictures We all went to the *pictures* to see an old film about cowboys and Indians.

picturesque Auntie lives in a *picturesque* village (i.e. one that would make a good picture).

pie a crust of pastry baked over meat or fruit ■ in a *pie*-dish.

piebald   pike

piebald A *piebald* horse is one with black and white patches.

piece Give Jack a *piece* of your chocolate. ■ When I dropped the cup it smashed to *pieces*. ■ Jane played a *piece* of music to us.

pied in two colours, e.g. the *Pied* Piper, whose coat was 'half of yellow and half of red'.

pier People at the seaside can walk out over the sea on the *pier*.

pier   pigeon

pierce To *pierce* anything is to make a hole through it.

piercing The tortured man let out a *piercing* scream (i.e. it was loud and shrill).

pigeon a bird, common in many cities, whose sound is, 'Coo-coo-coo.' There are also racing *pigeons*, homing *pigeons*, carrier *pigeons*, etc.

pigmy one of the little people who live in the hot forests of Africa (also spelt *pygmy*).

pigtail a plait of hair hanging from the back of the head (worn nowadays by girls, but once worn by Chinamen, sailors, etc.).

pike an axe on a very long handle, with which soldiers used to fight; ■ a large freshwater fish which eats other fish.

pilchard a small sea-fish which is caught and canned in south-west England and elsewhere.

pile A *pile* of things is made by heaping them on top of each other. ■ To *pile* things (up) is to heap them on top of each other. ■ a big post driven into the ground as foundation for a building, etc. ■ The *pile* on a carpet is made up of the strands of wool, etc., which stand up from the surface. ■ An atomic *pile* is an apparatus in which atoms are split for peaceful purposes.

pilfer to steal things which have little value, e.g. to *pilfer* from a shop.

pilgrim someone who travels to a holy place.

pilgrimage a pilgrim's journey, e.g. Those people are going on a *pilgrimage* to Lourdes, a holy place in France.

pill medicine in the form of a little ball, which is swallowed whole.

pillar The arch over the church doorway is supported on each side by a stone *pillar*.

pillion A motor-cyclist can carry a passenger sitting on the *pillion* (seat) behind him.

pillory In olden times a thief might be fastened in a *pillory* by his neck and wrists.

pillory   pincers

pillow In bed, I rest my head on a soft *pillow* filled with feathers.

pilot the person who drives an aircraft. ■ The job of a ship's *pilot* is to take charge while the ship is entering or leaving harbour.

pimple a small spot or sore place, especially on the face.

pinafore A girl, or a woman, wears a *pinafore* over the front of her clothes to protect them while she is washing up, cooking, etc.

pincers a carpenter's tool for pulling out nails, etc.; ■ the nippers with which a crab or lobster grips things.

pinch to squeeze something (especially a piece of someone's flesh) between your finger and thumb; ■ (slang) to steal.

pine A *pine* tree is an evergreen tree with needle-like leaves. ■ To *pine* for something is to long for it.

pineapple a large fruit which looks a little like a pine cone.

pining Helen is *pining* for her mother (i.e. longing very much).

pink a pale red colour; ■ a flower with crinkled petals and a strong, sweet perfume.

pinnacle a small, slender, ornamental tower or spire.

pinned Dad took a pin and *pinned* the flower to his coat.

pinning Pins are for *pinning* things together.

pint just over half a litre. A *pint* of liquid is about four cupfuls.

pioneer an explorer of unknown lands; ■ a person who first starts something new, e.g. The Russians were the *pioneers* of space travel.

pious religious. Auntie is a *pious* lady (i.e. she says prayers, attends church, etc., regularly).

pipe Water comes to the tap through a *pipe*. ■ Father smokes a *pipe*. ■ The piper is playing a tune on his *pipe*. ■ The piper will *pipe* a tune.

piping The children danced to the music that the pipers were *piping*. ■ lines of cord, covered with material, used to ornament furniture, etc.; ■ lines of icing on a cake.

pirate a sea robber. ■ In stories, *pirate* ships usually fly a black flag with a skull and crossbones on it.

pistol a small gun that can be fired with one hand.

pineapple   pistol

piston a metal cylinder which is forced down a circular hole in a car (or other) engine when petrol vapour is exploded in the space above it, thus working the engine.

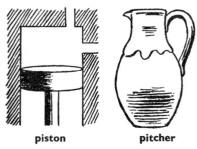

piston   pitcher

pitch a black solid substance obtained from tar, which becomes a thick, sticky liquid when hot. ■ To *pitch* a tent is to put it up. ■ The *pitch* of a note is the highness or lowness of it.

pitcher a big jar, usually with a handle, and a lip for pouring.

piteous A *piteous* cry is one that makes you feel sorry for the creature making it.

pitfall a trap, danger, or difficulty for which you are not prepared.

pith a whitish, rubbery substance which is found under the skin of an orange or in the stems of such plants as elder.

pitiable The injured animal was a *pitiable* sight (i.e. you couldn't help feeling sorry for it).

pitied Anyone having that terrible disease is to be *pitied* (i.e. you should feel sorry for him).

pitiful disgracefully bad, e.g. The actor gave a *pitiful* performance. ■ *Pitiful* people are those who show pity.

pitiless showing no pity, e.g. the *pitiless* sun (in a very hot country), a *pitiless* slave trader.

pitted The apples had been *pitted* by hailstones (i.e. the hail had made little holes in the surface).

pity the feeling of sadness that kind people have when unpleasant things happen to other people or creatures.

pivot a rod or bolt, etc. on which something turns, e.g. the screw in the top of a pair of compasses.

pivot   plaice

place London is the *place* where Janet lives. ■ I'll put some ointment on your sore *place*. ■ Sit in your usual *place* in the class-room. ■ *Place* a stone over the hole. ■ I cannot *place* (remember) you.

placid A *placid* person is one who does not easily become excited.

plague a serious nuisance. ■ The *plague* was an illness that used suddenly to appear in a country and kill many people. ■ To *plague* someone is to be a serious nuisance to him.

plaice a flat fish which lives on the sea bottom and is good to eat.

plain easy to understand, e.g. Dad made it *plain* that he was cross. ■ a level piece of country (i.e. with no hills); ■ not decorated, e.g. a *plain* wallpaper.

plainly If you speak *plainly* people can understand what you say. ■ You cannot see *plainly* through dirty windows.

plaintive A *plaintive* cry is one that is very sad.

plait (pron. plat) a rope of hair, straw, etc., made by weaving strands together, e.g. Mary wears her hair in a *plait*. ■ Mary has to *plait* her hair before coming to school.

plait   plane (wood)

plan a map which shows objects, or a single building, very big; ■ an idea or proposal. ■ To *plan* is to make arrangements before doing something.

plane (short for) aeroplane; ■ a sharp tool for smoothing wood; ■ a big broad-leafed tree. ■ To *plane* a piece of wood is to make it smooth with a plane.

planed The carpenter *planed* the piece of wood (with a plane) to make it smooth.

planet a world which, like our earth, goes round the sun, e.g. Mercury, Venus, Mars, Jupiter, Saturn, Uranus, Neptune, or Pluto.

plank A *plank* of wood is a long flat piece.

planned Last year we *planned* to go to Spain (i.e. we made arrangements).

plant If I want a *plant* to grow, ■ I *plant* it in the garden (or in a pot).

plantation a large group of plants, e.g. a tobacco *plantation*, a rubber *plantation*, etc.

planter a man who has a plantation, e.g. a tobacco *planter*.

plaster the substance spread over walls and ceilings to make them smooth; ■ some such substance as wet clay, bread, etc., put on sore places as a cure. ■ To *plaster* walls, etc., is to spread plaster on them.

plastic A *plastic* substance is one that can easily be given any required shape, e.g. by being pressed into a mould. ■ (Such substances are called *plastics*.)

plate We eat our food from a *plate*. ■ A (car) number *plate* is a flat piece of metal with a number on it. ■ To *plate* metal is to cover it with a thin layer of gold, or silver, etc.

plateau an (usually large) area of high ground.

platform The speakers stand on a wooden *platform* so that everyone in the hall can see them. ■ At a railway station, you can get out of the train on to the *platform*.

platinum a heavy metal that looks like silver, but is harder and more expensive.

plausible A *plausible* excuse, argument, etc., is one that you are likely to believe because it sounds reasonable. ■ A *plausible* person is one who is rather mistrusted because he can always talk so reasonably.

play Jack is going to *play* a game. ■ Jean will *play* the piano. ■ The *play* was acted in the theatre.

player someone who plays a game, ■ who plays an instrument, or ■ who acts in a play.

playful We have a *playful* kitten (i.e. it likes having fun).

plead Janet had to *plead* with (beg) her father to keep the stray dog.

pleasant Things that are *pleasant* are those that please you, e.g. a *pleasant* breeze, a *pleasant* person.

please *Please*, may I borrow your book? ■ Do it to *please* me (i.e. because I would like it). ■ You may have as many as you *please* (wish).

pleasure enjoyment, e.g. Some people get *pleasure* by listening to the radio. ■ A *pleasure* trip is one taken for amusement only.

pleat a fold in cloth made by doubling the material back on itself, e.g. There is a *pleat* in Jane's skirt. ■ To *pleat* cloth is to make a pleat in it.

pleat   pliers

pledge a solemn promise, e.g. I cannot tell you because I am under a *pledge* of secrecy. ■ To *pledge* your word is to promise solemnly.

plentiful There is a *plentiful* supply of fish in the river (i.e. as many fish as you could possibly want).

plenty We have *plenty* of cakes so you can all eat as many as you like.

pliable A *pliable* substance is one which you can easily bend without it breaking, e.g. copper wire.

pliers a tool for holding or bending wire, etc.

plight We were in a sorry *plight*, tired, lost and hungry.

Plimsoll The *Plimsoll* mark is a line painted on the side of a ship to show the depth to which it may safely be sunk into the water when being loaded.

plimsolls cheap shoes made of rubber and cloth. We wear *plimsolls* when doing physical exercises at school.

plod to walk, or work, hard, slowly and with determination.

plot a small piece of ground; ■ a plan for doing something wrong, e.g. the Gunpowder *Plot*. ■ To *plot* a graph is to draw it. ■ The *plot* of a play, story, opera, etc., is the outline of the main events.

plough The farmer's tractor pulls a *plough* through the soil to turn it over. ■ To *plough* a field is to turn over the soil in it with a plough.

plough   plover

plover a quite small long-legged wading bird.

pluck bravery, e.g. Few people have the *pluck* to face a bull. ■ To *pluck* a bird is to pull out its feathers.

plucky brave, e.g. Pat made a *plucky* attempt to rescue the drowning boy.

plug You put the *plug* in the bath to prevent the water running out. ■ To *plug* a hole is to put a plug in it.

plug   plum

plum a round, fleshy fruit with a stone in the middle, ■ which grows on a *plum* tree.

plumage A bird's *plumage* is its feathers.

plumber A *plumber's* job is to mend, or fit, water pipes, taps, etc.

plump A *plump* person is one who is rather fat.

plunder To *plunder* a place is to steal goods from it by force. ■ Goods so stolen are called *plunder*.

plunge I saw Jack *plunge* into the swimming baths with a great splash. ■ You *plunge* the red-hot iron into a bucket of water to cool it.

plural The *plural* of 'boy' is 'boys'.

plus Four *plus* three is seven $(4 + 3 = 7)$.

plush a material like velvet, but with longer and softer threads standing out from its surface.

Pluto the planet farthest from the sun; ■ the old-time god of the underworld.

plywood *Plywood* is made by sticking together a number of thin sheets of wood.

pneumatic A *pneumatic* tyre is one filled with air.

pneumonia a disease of the lungs.

poach To *poach* an egg, you break it open and drop the yolk and white into boiling water. ■ To *poach* game (i.e. animals or birds which people shoot for sport) is to trespass on private land to trap or shoot them.

poacher An egg *poacher* is a special pan in which to poach eggs. ■ A *poacher* will wander on private land in order to catch rabbits or pheasants, etc.

pocket I keep a handkerchief in the *pocket* of my coat. ■ To *pocket* anything is to put it in your pocket.

podgy A *podgy* person is one who is short and fat.

poem One *poem* in my first poetry book began: 'Twinkle, twinkle, little star.'

poet someone who writes poetry, e.g. Tennyson, Browning, Shakespeare, etc.

poetry a piece of writing in which thoughts or feelings are specially well expressed, with rhythm in the words and often with the end words of certain lines rhyming.

point I pricked myself on the *point* of the needle. ■ What is the *point* of (reason for) doing this? ■ *Point* with your finger to the next word. ■ You have scored a *point* (mark) for your team. ■ The ship sailed round the *point* (headland) and out of sight. ■ Is there any *point* (matter) that is not clear? ■ North-East (N.E.) is one *point* of the compass and South-West (S.W.) is another.

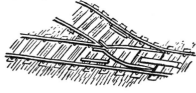

points

pointed Joe *pointed* to Jean with his finger. 'That's the girl,' he said. ■ A *pointed* stick is one that has a point on its end.

pointer a stick used to point out things on a map, blackboard, etc.

points special sections of railway lines which can be moved so as to make a train go from one set of rails to another.

poised The soldier held the sword *poised* in the air, ready to strike. The dancer remained for a time *poised* on one toe.

poison a substance that will kill you, or at least make you ill, if it gets into your body. ■ To *poison* anyone is to kill him, or make him ill, with poison.

poisoned His enemies *poisoned* him by putting poison in his food. ■ The *poisoned* arrow has only to scratch a man to kill him.

poisonous *Poisonous* snakes, berries, etc., are those which can poison you.

poke to push an object into something, e.g. to *poke* your finger into someone's ribs, to *poke* the fire (with a stick).

poker a metal rod with which to poke a (house) fire; ■ a card game.

poky small and shabby, e.g. The poor man lived in a *poky* room in a back street.

Poland a European country between East Germany and the U.S.S.R. (Soviet Union).

polar The *polar* regions are those near the North or South Poles. A *polar* bear is a big white bear that lives near the North Pole.

Pole A *Pole* is a citizen of Poland.

pole The great flag *pole* was the long slender trunk of a tall tree. ■ $5\frac{1}{2}$ yards = 1 rod, *pole*, or perch. ■ The North and South *Poles* are the two points at opposite ends of the earth, about which it revolves.

police The job of the *police* is to keep law and order in the streets. ■ A *police* car is for the use of policemen.

policeman A *policeman*'s job is to keep law and order in the streets.

policy I agree with the government's *policy* (i.e. the plan they are following.) ■ An insurance *policy* is the form on which is set out the agreement between a customer and an insurance company.

Polish (pron. Pole-ish) from or of Poland, e.g. the *Polish* language, *Polish* butter.

polish (pron. poll-ish) I *polish* my shoes until they shine. ■ If you get a good *polish* on your shoes they reflect the light.

polite If you are *polite* you say, 'Please,' and 'Thank you,' and you stand aside to let others go through doorways first, etc.

politely Bob *politely* stood aside and let the lady go through the doorway first.

politeness What people like about Bob is his *politeness* (good manners).

political Each *political* party (Conservative, Labour, Liberal, etc.) has its own ideas on how the country should be run. ■ *Political* geography has to do with the boundaries of countries.

politician a person, such as a Member of Parliament, who is interested in politics.

politics People who are interested in *politics* are concerned with the government of a country, or methods of government.

polka a cheerful dance that goes, '1, 2, 3, hop; 1, 2, 3, hop', etc.

poll (pron. pole) the number of votes (in an election), e.g. There was a heavy *poll* (many votes).

pollen the fine, yellowish powder on the stamens of flowers.

polling (pron. pole-ing) A *polling* station is a place where people go to vote in an election.

pollute to make dirty, e.g. If you burn coal on your fire the smoke will *pollute* the air we breathe.

pollution the dirtying of our surroundings, e.g. smoke in the air, oil on beaches, sewage in rivers and seas, etc.

polo a ball-game played on ponies; water polo is like handball played in water.

pomegranate a fruit with a tough skin, containing a mass of seeds, each covered with pink pulp.

pomp the show, splendour, ceremony, etc., suited to a very important person on a great occasion, e.g. at a coronation.

pompous A *pompous* person is one who gives the impression that he thinks he is important.

pond Ducks swim in the village *pond*.

ponder To *ponder* a matter is to think it over very carefully.

ponderous heavy and clumsy, e.g. The hippopotamus is a *ponderous* animal.

ponies My pony likes being with other *ponies*.

pontoon a card game; ■ a flat-bottomed boat used to support a section of a temporary bridge.

pony a small kind of horse.

pony-tail This girl likes to wear her hair in a *pony-tail*.

poodle a pet dog whose curly hair is usually left long on some parts of his body and cut short on other parts.

pool Jimmy can sail his toy boat in this *pool* of water left by the rain. ■ People pay small sums of money each week into football *pools* in the hope of winning a big prize.

pony-tail   **poodle**

poor The old lady is too *poor* to buy the things she needs. ■ *Poor* (unfortunate) Fred fell through a hole in the ice.

poorly ill, e.g. Sandra is feeling *poorly* today.

Pope The *Pope*, Bishop of Rome, is the head of the Roman Catholic Church throughout the world.

poplar a tall, slender tree that grows quickly.

poplar   poppy

poppy a showy flower with thin, papery petals, usually scarlet.

popular A *popular* girl like Janet always has lots of friends.

popularity Jack's *popularity* is shown by the fact that he always has lots of friends around him.

population The *population* of the United Kingdom is about 53 millions, and most of these people live in England.

porcelain a fine kind of earthenware used to make ornaments, electrical insulators, etc.

porch The *porch* over the door shelters callers from the rain.

porcupine an animal covered with long upstanding spikes, like a giant hedgehog.

pore Perspiration comes out of the body through countless tiny *pores* (holes) in the skin. ■ To *pore* over a book is to concentrate on it hard for a long time.

pork You would have to kill several pigs to provide all those people with roast *pork* for dinner.

porous The human skin is *porous* (full of pores). ■ Unglazed clay pots, etc., are *porous* (i.e. they are full of tiny holes through which gases or liquids can pass.)

porpoise a small kind of whale.

porridge To make *porridge* for your breakfast you boil oatmeal in water.

port Ships sail from one *port* to another. ■ *Port* wine is made from grapes. ■ The *port* (side) of a ship, aircraft, etc., is the one on your left as you look forward.

portable A *portable* radio, record-player, etc., is one that you can carry about with you.

porter A *porter*'s job is to carry luggage, especially on a railway station.

portion We were all given a *portion* of pudding to eat.

portrait a painting, drawing, or photograph, etc., of someone.

Portugal a country on the south-west coast of Europe.

porch   porcupine

Portuguese The *Portuguese* are the people of Portugal. ■ The language of Portugal is *Portuguese*. ■ *Portuguese* things are those from Portugal.

pose When you *pose* for a photographer or an artist, you hold yourself in some agreed position while he takes your photograph or paints your picture.

position place, e.g. I cannot see the blackboard from this *position*. ■ You must *position* yourself where you can see the blackboard. ■ state of affairs, e.g. The *position* is that we have ten miles to go and our car has broken down.

positive I am *positive* (sure) that the boy I saw was Jim.

possess I do not *possess* a bicycle; the one I use belongs to Peter.

possession The boys were already in *possession* of the tent (i.e. in it) when the girls arrived. ■ The native's only *possession* (thing he owns) is a knife.

possibility There is a *possibility* of his coming for Christmas (i.e. it could happen).

possible It is *possible* for a man to run a mile in less than four minutes (i.e. it can be done). ■ It is *possible* that Uncle James will come for Christmas (i.e. he may do so).

possibly You cannot *possibly* run a mile in two minutes (i.e. it is out of the question). ■ You may *possibly* (perhaps) have seen this before.

post The gate is hung from a *post* fixed upright into the ground. ■ You can *post* a letter ■ at the *post* office. ■ The *post* (delivery of letters) hasn't come yet. ■ Dad's first *post* (job) was in an office.

postage You pay the 3p *postage* on a letter ■ by buying a *postage* stamp.

postal When you send a letter to anyone you must write his correct *postal* address on the envelope. If you want to send money by post you buy a *postal* order.

poster To advertise our concert we will paint (or print) a *poster* to be put somewhere where lots of people will see it.

posterity the people who are not yet born, e.g. What will *posterity* think of the buildings we are erecting nowadays?

postman The *postman* brings our letters.

postpone To *postpone* a game (or any other engagement) is to have it later on.

postscript (usually shortened to *P.S.*) a note added to a letter after you have signed it.

posture Your *posture* is good if you stand and walk with your body in an upright, smart position.

posy a small bunch of flowers.

posy   bad posture

potato You can eat a *potato* baked, boiled, mashed, fried, or chipped.

potatoes Many new *potatoes* will grow from one potato planted in the ground.

potter a person who makes pots, vases, etc., of clay. ■ To *potter* (about) is to go slowly and without any special idea in mind.

pottery things made of clay. The Potteries is the part of the Midlands where most English *pottery* is made.

pouch a small bag, e.g. a tobacco *pouch*; the *pouch* in which a kangaroo carries its babies.

poultice a mass of some soft, hot material (e.g. wet bread), put on a sore place as a cure.

poultry The *poultry* kept on the farm includes chickens, ducks, geese and turkeys.

pounce The lion crouched on the rock, ready to *pounce* on any animal that passed below.

pound (1 lb.) 16 ounces = one *pound* (weight). ■ (£1) 100p = one *pound* (money). ■ To *pound* anything is to beat it to pieces or to pulp.

pour Please *pour* some milk from the jug into my cup. ■ To *pour* with rain is to rain very heavily.

pout to poke out your lips as a sign of thoughtfulness, sulkiness, annoyance, etc.

poverty poorness, e.g. You can relieve people's *poverty* by gifts of money or food.

powder a mass of dry, small, dust-like particles, e.g. Flour is a *powder*. ■ To *powder* a substance is to grind it to powder. ■ Ladies *powder* (put powder on) their faces.

power A judge has the *power* to send a person to prison. ■ This car has a 30 horse-*power* engine. ■ Electric *power* to light and heat our homes ■ is made in a *power* station.

powerful very strong, e.g. a *powerful* engine, a *powerful* smell.

practical In *practical* science lessons we do our own experiments ■ A *practical* joke is something that is done (not said) to cause amusement.

practically The jug is *practically* (nearly) empty.

practice You will never learn to play the instrument if you don't do your *practice*. ■ I do not make a *practice* of getting up at dawn (i.e. I do it only sometimes).

practise If you are learning to play an instrument you must *practise* every day.

Prague the capital city of Czechoslovakia, in the middle of Europe.

prairie a large expanse of grassland without trees, such as that in Canada.

praise To *praise* anything, or anyone, is to say how good it (he) is or how pleased you are with it (him).

praiseworthy A *praiseworthy* effort, or deed, etc., is one worth praising.

pram (short for) perambulator. Jane wheeled the baby along the street in his *pram*.

prance The noise made the horse *prance* (about) so that the rider had difficulty in staying on its back.

prank Just for a *prank* (something amusing to do) the boys brought a cow into the classroom.

prawn a fish like a big shrimp, which is boiled, skinned and eaten.

pray When people *pray* they say prayers to God.

prayer The *prayer* that many people say when they pray to God begins, 'Our Father, which art in heaven'.

preach Part of a clergyman's job is to *preach* sermons to people in church, or elsewhere.

preacher someone who preaches a sermon in a church, or elsewhere.

prearranged arranged beforehand, e.g. At a *prearranged* signal the boys sprang from their hiding place.

precarious uncertain, e.g. Farmers make a *precarious* living on that poor soil.

precaution The buckets of water are hung on the wall as a *precaution* against fire.

precious *Precious* metals or stones are those such as gold, diamonds, etc., which are worth a great deal of money.

precipice a very steep, or upright, face of a cliff or mountain.

precipice

precise The time is about four o'clock, or, to be *precise*, it is one and a quarter minutes past four.

predecessor Your *predecessor* in a job, etc., is the person who had the job before you.

predicament an awkward or dangerous situation, e.g. I was in a train going the wrong way, and my *predicament* was made worse by the knowledge that the next stop was 200 miles away.

predict Some fortune tellers say that they can *predict* future events.

preface the short introduction or explanation printed at the beginning of a book.

prefect The job of a school *prefect* is to see that the boys and girls behave properly in the absence of teachers.

prefer I *prefer* red to blue (i.e. I like red better than blue).

preferable A carpet is *preferable* to lino as a floor covering (i.e. people like a carpet better than lino).

preferably I would like some fruit please, *preferably* apples (i.e. apples are what I would like most).

preference Adam likes all fruit, but he has a *preference* for (likes best) apples.

prefix a title such as Mr., Mrs., Sir, etc., put before someone's name; ■ a group of letters put before a word to give it a different meaning, e.g. the prefix 'dis' put before 'please' makes the word 'displease'.

prehistoric *Prehistoric* events, animals, etc., are those that came before history (i.e. before the time when records of events were made).

prejudice Mary has a *prejudice* against ginger-haired boys (i.e. she has decided, even before meeting them, that she doesn't like them). But Joan has a *prejudice* in favour of ginger-haired boys (she, for no reason, likes them).

preliminary A *preliminary* exam (or talk, etc.) is one which is in preparation for something.

prelude some event or, more usually, a piece of music, which is an introduction to what is to follow.

premature The applause is *premature*, for Janet hasn't finished the song yet.

premeditated thought out beforehand, e.g. a *premeditated* crime.

premises Visitors may not remain on the school *premises* (buildings or grounds) without permission.

premonition a feeling that something terrible is about to happen, e.g. Auntie has a *premonition* that the ship is going to sink.

preoccupation Because of his *preoccupation* with his book, Dick didn't know we had come into the room (the book had all his attention).

preoccupied When Tom is *preoccupied* with his hobby he has no idea of what is going on around him.

preparation Joe is training in *preparation* for the next football match. ■ The *preparations* (getting ready) for the party took hours. ■ homework (usually shortened to *prep.*)

preparatory A *preparatory* (or prep) school is a private junior school, where parents pay for their children's education.

prepare You can help to *prepare* the dinner by peeling the potatoes.

prepared Ian has come in his macintosh and gum boots, *prepared* for rain. ■ Let's eat the meal that Mother has *prepared* for us.

preposition a word, such as 'at', 'in', 'on', 'by', which relates a noun to another word in a sentence, e.g. Tom is **in** bed. Put your feet **under** the table.

preposterous Betty has the *preposterous* idea that the moon is made of cheese.

prescribe What medicine did the doctor *prescribe* (tell you to take) for your illness?

prescription a list of drugs for making a medicine, and directions for its use. A doctor writes the *prescription* and a chemist makes it up for you.

presence Jill received her medal in the *presence* of the whole school (i.e. the whole school was there). ■ *Presence* of mind is quickness of thought or action (at a time of danger, etc.).

present (pron. préz-ent) a gift, e.g. a birthday *present*; ■ here, e.g. Pat is *present*; ■ for the moment, e.g. I require no help at *present*. ■ (pron. pre-zént) to give, e.g. The mayor will *present* the prizes.

presentable When you go to a party you must look *presentable* (fit to be seen by the people there).

presentation One of the mayor's jobs is the *presentation* (giving) of prizes at schools.

presently I will come *presently* (in a little while).

preserve You paint woodwork to *preserve* it (prevent it from rotting).

president the person who is head of a group of people and in charge at their meetings, etc. ■ The *President* of the United States (or France, etc.) is its chief citizen.

press You *press* clothes (with an iron) to make them smooth. ■ You *press* a bell-push to ring the bell. ■ Do not *press* (persuade) Pat to come if she doesn't want to. ■ A *press* report is a report in a newspaper.

pressure The air *pressure* in the car tyre is 24 lbs. per square inch.

prestige A person's *prestige* is the high opinion that people have formed of him.

presumably Jim was walking towards the baths with his costume and towel, so *presumably* he was going for a swim.

presume I *presume* (take it for granted) that you are hungry, so I'm making you some sandwiches.

pretence The boys made a *pretence* of looking for the book, but they weren't really looking at all.

pretend In this play Brian has to *pretend* to be dead.

prettily beautifully and daintily, e.g. The little girls danced *prettily*. The girls were *prettily* dressed for their party.

prettiness beauty, but usually of a small or childish kind, e.g. the *prettiness* of a little girl, or of a doll, etc.

pretty beautiful in a small or childish way, e.g. What a *pretty* doll!

prevailing The *prevailing* wind is the one that blows most often. In Britain the *prevailing* wind is from the south-west.

prevent John held Tom's hands to *prevent* him (from) hitting Billy.

prevention The Society for the *Prevention* of Cruelty to Children tries to stop people from being cruel to children.

previous If yesterday was Monday, the *previous* day was Sunday.

prey an animal hunted for food by other animals. ■ A bird of *prey* is one that hunts other creatures for food. ■ It is an eagle's nature to *prey* on small animals (hunt them for food).

price The *price* I paid for that book was 75p.

priceless A *priceless* picture is one worth more than any sum of money. ■ (slang) very amusing or strange, e.g. Fred is a *priceless* fool.

prick If you *prick* your finger with a needle, it bleeds.

prickle a sharp point on such a plant as holly or thistle, or on an animal such as the hedgehog.

prickles

prickly If you grab that *prickly* plant, you will prick your fingers.

pride a too high opinion of your own good points or cleverness. ■ To *pride* yourself on something is to be proud of it.

priest The *priest* who takes the services at that church is the Rev. P. Brown.

prig a person who considers that he is better than those around him.

prim fussy about details of behaviour, e.g. Aunt Agatha is a *prim* old lady.

primary A *Primary* School is one in which children up to the age of eleven may be educated free of charge.

prime The *Prime* Minister is the chief minister of the government. ■ A *prime* number is one such as 2, 3, 5, 7, etc., which you cannot divide by any other number. ■ *Prime* cuts of meat are the best ones.

primitive People who are *primitive* lead simple lives, and haven't houses, furniture, tools, etc., as civilized people have.

primrose a pale yellow spring flower.

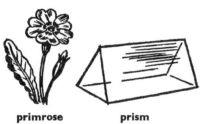

primrose   **prism**

prince *Prince* Charles is the son of Queen Elizabeth.

princess *Princess* Anne is the daughter of Queen Elizabeth.

principal The *principal* (chief) food of the Chinese is rice. ■ The *principal* of a college, etc., is the man or woman in charge of it.

principle a truth that is important to the person who holds it, e.g. Auntie won't let men give up their seats for her in buses on the *principle* that women are the equals of men.

print They *print* newspapers on very big sheets of paper. ■ Newspaper headlines are printed in big *print*.

printer The *printer* who printed that book put one word upside down.

printing A *printing* press is a machine that prints books, papers, etc. ■ Men work late at night *printing* tomorrow's newspapers.

prior the head of a priory. ■ *Prior* to (before) her marriage, my mother was a nurse.

priority Police directing traffic give *priority* to fire engines (i.e. they hold up other traffic to let them through).

priory a kind of monastery (or nunnery) whose head is a prior (or a prioress).

prism a solid whose ends are the same shape and whose edges are parallel; especially a triangular *prism* of glass, used to split light into colours.

prison As a punishment, the criminal was locked up in *prison* for six months.

prisoner There is more than one *prisoner* locked up in that prison.

privacy If you want to discuss secrets, you need *privacy* (i.e. not to have other people with you).

private for the use of certain people only, not for everyone, e.g. *private* roads, *private* hotels, *private* schools, rooms marked 'Private', etc.; ■ a soldier who is not an officer. ■ The *private* parts of the body ■ (the *privates*) are the parts always kept covered in public.

privately May I talk to you *privately* (i.e. in secret)?

privet a shrub grown chiefly to make hedges.

privilege a special right, e.g. As a *privilege*, prefects are allowed to use the front entrance to the school.

privileged Only *privileged* people such as prefects and visitors are allowed to use the front entrance to the school.

prize Anne's *prize* for being top of the form was a book.

probable It is *probable* (likely) that it will rain today.

probably We shall *probably* go to France for our holiday next year (i.e. it is likely that we shall go).

probation A criminal put on *probation* is given a period, perhaps a year, in which to prove that he can behave well. ■ During this time a *probation* officer tries to help him.

problem The *problem* is how to get this big piano through that little doorway. ■ A *problem* in arithmetic is an example about which you have to think carefully before you know what has to be done with the numbers given in it.

proceed After that pause we will now *proceed* (go on) with what we were doing.

proceedings happenings, especially official events, e.g. the *proceedings* in a court of law, or at the official opening of school, etc.

proceeds We sent the *proceeds* of our concert, amounting to £5, to the orphanage.

process Can you describe the *process* by which sugar is obtained from sugar beet?

procession a moving column of people, carriages, or boats, etc.,

e.g. the Lord Mayor's *procession*, a funeral *procession*.

proclaim to tell (something) officially, to everyone, e.g. A herald will *proclaim* the new king immediately the old one dies.

proclamation a public announcement ordered by a king or a government, e.g. The *proclamation* told people that the king's daughter was to be married.

prod to poke, e.g. The driver had to *prod* his donkey with a stick before it would move.

prodigal wasteful, e.g. the *prodigal* son in the Bible story.

produce (pron. pród-uce) Garden *produce* consists of the various things grown in a garden. ■ (pron. pr'dúce) to present something for people to see or hear, e.g. to *produce* a play, to *produce* evidence of something.

producer The *producer* of anything is the person who makes or grows it. ■ The *producer* of a play is the person in charge of its rehearsal and performance.

product the answer to a multiplication sum, e.g. The *product* of 2 and 3 is 6. ■ a thing made, e.g. Our car is a *product* of that factory.

production The factory was built for the *production* of cars.

profess I do not *profess* to be clever (I do not say that I am).

profession a job such as that of a lawyer, doctor, or teacher, which requires skill and knowledge.

professor a teacher at a university.

profile an outline of something, especially of a person's face, as seen from one side.

profile **projector**

profit If you buy a thing for £5 and sell it for £6, you make a *profit* of £1. ■ You do not *profit* by selling things at the price you pay for them.

profitable If a business is *profitable* it makes money for the owner.

programme In the *programme* you can read all about the items in the concert.

progress (pron. pró-gress) forward movement, e.g. We made slow *progress* over that rough country. ■ John is making good *progress* in arithmetic. ■ (pron. pro-gréss) to go forward, e.g. You will not be able to *progress* far along that road.

prohibit Many firms *prohibit* (do not allow) smoking in their shops.

project (pron. pró-ject) a plan, e.g. The new *project* is to build our own swimming baths. ■ (pron. pro- jéct) to stick out, e.g. Nails that *project* from the wall may tear your clothes. ■ to throw a picture, etc. (on to a screen).

projectile a bullet or shell, etc., that can be thrown by means of a gun or rocket, etc.

projecting I caught my coat on a nail *projecting* from that wall. ■ We are *projecting* our holiday pictures on to a screen so that lots of people can see them at the same time.

projector You use a (film) *projector* to show moving pictures on a screen.

prolific producing lots of fruit or young ones, etc., e.g. This is the most *prolific* of our apple trees. Rabbits are *prolific* animals.

prolong If the headmaster makes his usual speech, it will *prolong* the ceremony by ten minutes.

prolonged All those stops have *prolonged* the journey by hours. ■ The coach made a *prolonged* stop at a village while the engine was repaired.

promenade a place provided for people to walk along, especially at the seaside.

prominence The singer came into *prominence* (became well known) through appearing on television.

prominent easily noticed, e.g. Jean has a *prominent* part in the play. The church spire is a *prominent* landmark.

promise If you *promise* something, you must be sure to do it. ■ If you give your *promise* that you will do something, you must be sure to do it.

promised I *promised* Mary that I would wait for her, so I must do so.

promising A *promising* pupil (or actor, player, etc.) is one who is likely to do very well later on. ■ Paul is always *promising* things, but he doesn't keep his promises.

promote to move (someone) to a higher position, e.g. to *promote* a soldier from captain to major. ■ To *promote* a boxing contest is to arrange and organize it.

promoter A boxing *promoter* is someone who arranges boxing matches.

promotion To get a *promotion* is to be moved to a higher position (in the army, navy, or other employment, etc.).

prompt The drowning child was saved by Dick's *prompt* action (i.e. Dick acted without waste of time). ■ To *prompt* an actor is to tell him his words when he has forgotten them.

promptly without delay, e.g. Dick *promptly* dived to the rescue.

pron. used in this dictionary as an abbreviation of *pronounced*, meaning 'said' (sounded), e.g. knot (*pron.* not).

prone Mother is *prone* to headaches (i.e. she easily gets them). ■ Dick is lying *prone* (face downwards).

prong A dinner fork usually has four *prongs* on it.

prongs   propeller

pronoun a word, such as 'I', 'he', 'she', 'it' which is used instead of the name of a thing or a person, e.g. She has it (instead of 'Mary has the ball').

pronounce How do you *pronounce* (say) this word? ■ The judge will now *pronounce* the sentence (i.e. say what punishment the prisoner is to receive).

pronounced The word 'knot' is *pronounced* 'not'. ■ The judge *pronounced* the sentence on the prisoner. ■ Jean has a *pronounced* (easily noticed) French accent.

pronunciation Sam asked about the *pronunciation* of a word (i.e. how it should be sounded).

proof evidence that makes you sure of something, e.g. We have *proof* that this man committed the crime. ■ A rain-*proof* coat will keep out the rain.

prop to support, e.g. We had to *prop* up the shed roof with a post. ■ a support, e.g. We put a *prop* under the shed roof to hold it up.

propaganda information spread around in order to make people believe some particular idea (usually political).

propel Jet engines are used to *propel* the aircraft; propellers are used to *propel* the ship.

propeller It is the revolving of a *propeller* that drives ships along; some aircraft have *propellers* too.

proper That is not the *proper* (right) way of doing it. ■ respectable, decent, e.g. That is not a *proper* remark. ■ A *proper* noun is the name of a particular person, place, etc. (e.g. 'Smith', 'London').

properly You are not *properly* dressed if you appear at a wedding in your oldest clothes. ■ Paul misbehaved at the party and was very *properly* (rightly) sent home.

property That coat is my *property* (it belongs to me). ■ land with perhaps buildings, etc., on it.

prophecy (pron. próf-e-see) a forecast of future events. To have the gift of *prophecy* is to be able to foretell future events.

prophesy (pron. próf-ess-eye) To *prophesy* events is to tell beforehand that they are going to happen.

prophet someone who foretells future events; ■ an ancient Jewish teacher such as Isaiah or Jeremiah, mentioned in the Bible.

proportion a part, e.g. A large *proportion* of the country is desert. ■ A drawing, etc., is out of *proportion* if one part is too big or small in comparison with another part.

proposal a suggestion, e.g. Jane's *proposal* was that we should go for a swim. ■ especially a request to someone to marry you, e.g. Mary turned down John's *proposal* (that she should marry him).

propose I *propose* that we all go for a swim. ■ To *propose* to a girl is to ask her to marry you.

proprietor owner, e.g. The *proprietor* of that café is a Frenchman.

prose written or spoken words that are not poetry.

prosecute To *prosecute* someone is to bring him into court and charge him with having broken the law.

prosecuted brought into court and charged with breaking the law, e.g. Trespassers will be *prosecuted*.

prospect an outlook, e.g. The *prospect* of a holiday abroad pleases us all.

prospective Your *prospective* employer is the person who will, later on, be your employer (likewise, a *prospective* headmaster, wife, etc.).

prospectus a little book or pamphlet describing a school, college, or business, etc., for the benefit of people new to it.

prosper to succeed, do well, e.g. Cheats never *prosper*.

prosperity During periods of *prosperity* things go right for people and they become rich.

prosperous Margaret's father is a *prosperous* shopkeeper (i.e. he is doing well).

prostrate (pron. prós-trate) The man was *prostrate* (lying at full length) on the sand. ■ After so much hard work Mother was *prostrate* (exhausted). ■ (pron. pros-tráte) The natives *prostrate* themselves before their gods (i.e. they bow down to the ground.)

protect The king had a bodyguard to *protect* him from the attacks of his enemies.

protection We have this big dog as a *protection* against burglars.

protest (pron. pro-tést) They went to the Prime Minister to *protest* against the war (i.e. to say they didn't like it). ■ (pron. prótest) a formal complaint or objection, written or spoken.

Protestant The *Protestant* Churches were formed at the Reformation (16th century) by separation from the Roman Catholic Church. ■ A *Protestant* is a person who is a member of a Protestant Church.

protractor an instrument for measuring angles.

protractor

protrude The tramp's toes *protrude* from the front of his old shoes.

proud Anyone would be *proud* to have a father who is brave and famous. ■ The lady, though poor, is too *proud* to accept money.

proudly George *proudly* showed everyone the medal he had won (i.e. he was very pleased with himself for winning it).

prove To *prove* something is to show that it is really true, e.g. to *prove* the earth is round.

proverb a well-known, short, wise saying, such as, 'Too many cooks spoil the broth.'

provide Mother will *provide* all the food for the picnic.

provided Mother *provided* the food for last week's picnic. ■ You may go to the beach *provided* (on condition) that you don't bathe.

province one of the parts, like an English county, into which countries such as France are divided. ■ People who do not live in the capital city of a country are said to live in the *provinces*.

provision A man makes *provision* for his old age by putting aside enough money to live on when he is old.

provisions The *provisions* we took with us to camp included meat, bread, milk, sugar, etc.

provocation Jack would not have hit the boy without *provocation* (i.e. unless the boy had made Jack cross).

provocative A *provocative* remark (or person) is one which makes you feel cross.

provoke If you *provoke* the animal by teasing, he may bite you.

provoking irritating, e.g. Sally is a *provoking* child. ■ By *provoking* people you make them cross.

prowess courage and daring; skill.

prowl The lion was on the *prowl* (going about looking for some creature to eat).

proximity To be in the *proximity* of a place is to be near it.

prudent A *prudent* person is one who is careful and wise, especially about making provision for the future.

prune a dried plum, e.g. We had stewed *prunes* for dinner. ■ To *prune* a tree is to cut out unwanted branches and twigs.

pry To *pry* into a person's affairs is to try to find out things that are none of your business.

prying A person *prying* into someone's affairs is trying to find out things that don't concern him. ■ I cannot show you the secret note till we are away from *prying* eyes. (i.e. eyes that try to see things that don't concern them).

psalm (pron. sarm) any one of the 150 *psalms* (songs) in the Bible. The 23rd *Psalm* begins: 'The Lord is my Shepherd.'

public The *public* (everyone) ■ may walk in a *public* park. ■ A *public* house, or inn, is a place where people can buy drinks.

publicity The singer became well known through the *publicity* he received in the newspapers, and on television, etc.

publish To *publish* a book or magazine, etc., is to produce it and send out the copies.

pudding Among the *puddings* we have for dinner are: rice *pudding*, Yorkshire *pudding*, meat *pudding* and plum *pudding*.

puddle When rain falls, *puddles* form in all the little holes in the path.

puff A *puff* of wind (air) will blow out a candle. ■ There was a *puff* of smoke and a bang as the gun fired. ■ Girls put powder on their faces with a powder *puff*.

pukka real, e.g. Jim has a *pukka* space helmet (also spelt *pucka*).

pull If we *pull* on the rope we can bring the boat nearer to us.

pullet a young hen (female chicken).

pulley a special wheel having a groove into which a rope or belt fits, e.g. You haul up the washing line by a rope which passes over a *pulley*.

pulley   pullover

pullover a woolly outer garment that you pull on over your head.

pulp a soft, wet substance, like the flesh of plums, or paper that has been soaked in water.

pulpit A clergyman usually stands in a *pulpit* to preach his sermon.

pulse If you put your fingers on a person's *pulse* you can feel the blood passing along a blood vessel in time with his heartbeats. (The usual place to feel someone's *pulse* is on his wrist.)

pulverize To *pulverize* anything is to grind or smash it into dust.

puma a big American wild animal of the cat family.

pumice The *pumice* stone that you rub on your fingers to remove stains is lava from a volcano.

pummel To *pummel* anyone is to keep on punching him.

pump We use a *pump* to blow air into our tyres. ■ To *pump* up tyres is to blow air into them. ■ The fire-brigade came to *pump* water out of the flooded house.

pumpkin a big, round fruit which has soft, eatable flesh under its tough outer skin.

pulpit   pumpkin

pun a joke based on the fact that a word in it has two meanings, e.g. There were soldiers outside Buckingham Palace in their bear (bare) skins.

punch to hit with your clenched fist; ■ a tool for making holes in things; ■ a drink made of wine, spices, sugar, hot water, etc.

punctual If you are *punctual* you are not late.

punctuality Joan received a prize for *punctuality* (i.e. for not being late).

punctually Joan was not late; she arrived *punctually*.

punctuate To *punctuate* a piece of writing is to put in the full stops, commas, etc.

punctuation *Punctuation* marks are full stops, commas, etc.

puncture The *puncture* in the tyre was made by a nail going into it.

punish You can *punish* people who have misbehaved by beating them, making them pay fines, or sending them to prison, etc.

punishment As a *punishment* for being late, George had extra work to do after school.

punt a wide, flat-bottomed boat that you push along with a pole.

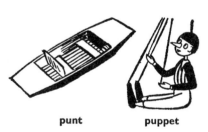

punt   puppet

pupil A teacher likes each *pupil* in his class to have work to do. ■ the little hole in the centre of your eye, through which you see (it looks black to other people).

puppet a little figure worked by strings or by someone's fingers fitted into it.

puppy a young dog. This *puppy* has the same mother as those *puppies*.

purchase I shall use this money to *purchase* a new coat.

pure not mixed with other things, e.g. *pure* milk, *pure* butter, *pure* water, etc.

purely I do this *purely* (only) for pleasure.

purify You *purify* drinking water by getting rid of the dirt and germs in it.

puritan The *Puritans* were strict, religious people who disliked ornaments, robes, ceremonies, etc., in churches, and who disapproved generally of gaiety and pleasure-seeking.

purity cleanness.

purloin to steal.

purple a colour made by mixing red and blue.

purpose The *purpose* of this meeting is to elect a new captain (i.e. that is why we are here). ■ That was no accident; you pushed him over on *purpose*.

purposely I did not bang the door *purposely*; it was just an accident.

purr the low, continuous noise made by a happy cat.

purse I keep my money in a leather *purse*. ■ To *purse* your lips is to draw them together to make them small.

purse

pursue If the enemy run away, we will *pursue* them until we catch them.

pursuit After a *pursuit* lasting all day we finally caught up with them.

push John reached out his hands and gave Peter a *push* that sent him into the water ■ Now Peter will *push* John into the water.

puss, pussy the name often used by people when calling a cat.

put I *put* the book on the table. ■ I have *put* sugar in your tea. ■ When I am writing, though I know what I mean, I don't know how to *put* it. ■ To *put* the shot (weight) in athletics, you heave a heavy iron ball as far as you can.

putrid rotten, going bad, e.g. like a diseased potato. ■ (slang) very poor, e.g. Jim's performance in the game was *putrid*.

putty a soft substance made of whiting and linseed oil, and used for fixing glass in windows, filling holes in woodwork, etc.

puzzle something that is very difficult to do, e.g. a jig-saw *puzzle*. ■ To *puzzle* someone is to set him to do something that is very difficult, or that requires very hard thinking.

puzzling I find this affair very *puzzling* (i.e. I cannot understand it, even after long and hard thinking).

pygmy one of the little people who live in the hot forests of Africa (also spelt *pigmy*).

pygmy

pyjamas Many people, both male and female, wear *pyjamas* when they are in bed.

pyjamas   pylon

pylon a metal framework in the form of a high tower, which holds up overhead electric cables.

pyramid a solid which has a (usually) square base, and triangular sides whose points meet at the top; but especially the ancient stone *pyramids* of Egypt.

pyramid

python a big snake which kills creatures by crushing them.

python

quack   the noise made by a duck. ■ A *quack* doctor is an ignorant person who pretends to be a doctor, or to have a doctor's knowledge.

quadrangle   a four-sided figure, usually a square or a rectangle; ■ a square or rectangular area between parts of a big building, such as a school.

quadrilateral   a figure that has four sides (whatever its shape).

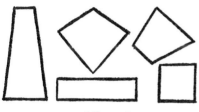

quadrilaterals

quadruped   a four-footed animal, such as a dog or a horse.

quail   a brown bird like a fat little partridge. ■ To *quail* before someone is to flinch or give way because you are afraid of him.

quaint   old-fashioned or odd, but in a pleasing way, e.g. Grandma lives in a *quaint* old cottage.

quake   to tremble, e.g. with fear.

Quaker   a member of the Society of Friends, a Christian sect who worship without priests.

quaking   Sheila was *quaking* with cold (or fear) so that her teeth chattered.

qualification   something needed to fit a person for a job, e.g. an examination certificate, or (for a policeman) being tall.

qualified   You are not *qualified* to drive a car if you haven't a licence. ■ A *qualified* chemist, etc., is one who has passed exams, etc., and so is entitled to call himself a chemist.

qualify   To *qualify* as a doctor you have to study a long time and pass exams.

quality   When you talk of the *quality* of a thing you are concerned with how good or bad it is, e.g. This cloth is of poor *quality*; that is a better *quality*.

qualms   an uneasy feeling inside you, caused by fear or conscience, e.g. Mother had *qualms* about letting little Betty hold the baby.

quandary   a situation in which it is difficult to decide what to do.

quantity   What *quantity* of sugar do you like in your tea – a spoonful?

quarantine   If it is thought that a person (or animal) may have been in contact with a disease, he is put in *quarantine* (kept away from others) till all danger of his spreading the disease has passed.

quarrel   The *quarrel* started with the boys shouting at each other, but it ended with a fight.

quarrelled   I know that Susan and Mary have *quarrelled* because they do not speak to each other any more.

quarrelsome   A *quarrelsome* person is one who likes quarrelling.

quarry   The huntsmen's *quarry* is a fox. The detective's *quarry* is a criminal. ■ a place from which stone is taken from the ground for building purposes, etc.

quart   2 pints. 4 *quarts* = 1 gallon.

quarter A *quarter* of an hour is 15 minutes ($\frac{1}{4} \times 60 = 15$). ■ To *quarter* soldiers is to put them in lodgings. ■ To *quarter* anything is to divide it into four. ■ Our soldiers gave the enemy no *quarter* (mercy).

quarterly every three months (quarter of a year), e.g. Our club has *quarterly* meetings.

quarters Four *quarters* make one whole one ($4 \times \frac{1}{4} = 1$). ■ lodgings, e.g. The soldiers' *quarters* were in a farm-house.

quartet a piece of music for four voices or four instruments. ■ The four musicians in a *quartet* either play or sing.

quaver a note (in music) worth half a crotchet.

quaver   quill

quay (pron. key) Ships tie up at a *quay* in order to land their passengers or cargo.

queen When a lady is made *queen* of a country, a crown is placed on her head.

queer strange or odd, e.g. a *queer* smell, a *queer* creature. ■ To feel *queer* is to feel unwell.

quell To *quell* a disturbance or a riot is to put an end to it by force.

quench To *quench* a fire is to put it out.

query a question. ■ To *query* something is to ask questions about it.

quest To go in *quest* of something is to go looking for it.

question Can you answer the *question*, 'Who broke the window?' ■ To *question* someone is to ask him something.

queue (pron. kew) Jane joined the *queue* (line) of people waiting for the bus. ■ To *queue* is to stand in a queue.

quibble to talk a great deal about nothing in order to avoid answering a question.

quick The train is just going; be *quick* or we shall miss it.

quickly Do it *quickly* so that no time is lost.

quicksand sand which is so wet that it sucks people into it.

quiet If we are *quiet* no one will hear us.

quieten To *quieten* anything is to silence it or calm it down.

quietly If we talk *quietly* other people will not hear us.

quill a pen made from a feather; ■ a wing or tail feather of a bird.

quilt a bed cover made by sewing padding between two pieces of material.

quinine a medicine taken to cure colds, malaria, cramp, etc., usually in the form of white tablets which people swallow. (It tastes very bitter.)

quintet a piece of music for five players, or singers; ■ the five people who perform a quintet.

quit to leave, e.g. The owner of our house has given us notice to *quit*.

quite The box is *quite* full; it won't hold another thing.

quits You trod on my toe; so if I tread on your toe we shall be *quits* (i.e. agree that we have each suffered equally, and end the quarrel).

quiver to tremble, e.g. to *quiver* with excitement. ■ An archer keeps his arrows in a *quiver* strapped to his waist.

quivering trembling, e.g. The leaves were *quivering* in the breeze. ■ We knew by her *quivering* voice that Jane was nervous.

quiz a game, often played on radio and television, in which the players answer questions.

radar scanner

quota a share, e.g. We have shared the work out and these jobs are your *quota*.

quotation words you write or say that are an exact copy of someone else's, e.g. Here is a *quotation* from the 23rd Psalm: "The Lord is my shepherd." ■ *Quotation* marks (" ") are put round words which are a quotation.

quote I can *quote* what he said (i.e. I can give his exact words).

R

rabbi a Jewish religious official or teacher.

rabbit a long-eared, fur-covered animal that lives in the ground.

rabble a crowd of rough people, e.g. The *rabble* in the street were shouting and throwing stones.

race The one that goes fastest wins the *race*. ■ The human *race* is made up of all the various peoples who live on the earth.

racing A *racing* car is one specially made for racing. ■ The boys came *racing* home with the good news (i.e. they came at top speed). ■ The horses are *racing* to see which of them is fastest.

rack A luggage *rack* is a special shelf on which to put luggage in a train, coach, etc. ■ an ancient instrument of torture which stretched out people's joints by pulling on their arms and legs.

racket When that teacher is out of the room, the *racket* made by his class disturbs the rest of the school. ■ When playing tennis, you hit the ball with a *racket*.

radar a system for detecting things in the dark or in fog, using radio waves.

radiate Things that *radiate* heat, (or light) send it out in rays, thus the heat doesn't heat the air it passes through, but only the objects that the rays meet. ■ Lines that *radiate* from a point go out from it in all directions.

radiator the front part of a car engine, in which hot water from the engine is cooled. ■ The room is heated by iron *radiators* through which hot water flows.

radio You can listen to sound broadcasts from all over the world on a *radio* (set).

radio-active A *radio-active* substance is one such as radium, which gives off rays that can pass through solid objects.

radish a little plant whose fat, red root is eaten with salad. (It tastes hot.)

radium a radio-active metal which gives off rays used to treat diseases.

radius The *radius* of a circle is the distance from the centre to the edge.

radius   rafters

raffia strips of fibre from palm leaves, used for tying plants, weaving into table mats, etc.

raffle When you *raffle* an article you sell lots of tickets and the person whose ticket has on it the number drawn out of a hat gets the article.

raft The boys made a *raft* by tying logs of wood together, and on this they floated to safety.

raft

rafters The *rafters* of a house are the sloping timbers that support the roof.

ragamuffin a child badly or dirtily dressed.

rage very great anger. ■ To *rage* is to behave in an angry manner, e.g. to shout and stamp.

ragged A *ragged* garment is one that is old and torn.

raging making a great noise and disturbance, e.g. a *raging* storm, a *raging* temper. ■ Little boats cannot put to sea if a storm is *raging*.

raid a sudden attack by soldiers, or aircraft, robbers, police, etc.

raider someone who makes a sudden attack.

rail a bar of wood or metal, e.g. a hand-*rail* beside stairs, a *rail* that a train travels on; ■ (sometimes short for) railway, e.g. We shall travel by *rail*.

railings There are iron *railings* round the place so that people cannot get in except by the gate.

railway Trains travel regularly along the *railway* between London and Edinburgh.

raiment clothing.

rain I hope it will *rain*, for the crops need water. ■ The *rain* now falling is needed to water the crops.

rainbow the arch of colours which you may see if you look at rain on which the sun is shining.

rainfall In our part of the world, the *rainfall* is about 650 mm a year.

rainy On a *rainy* day you need your mackintosh or umbrella.

raise *Raise* your hands above your head. ■ To *raise* a sunken boat is to bring it to the surface again. ■ To *raise* the price of anything is to charge more for it. ■ To *raise* a family is to have children and bring them up.

raisin(s) dried grapes, put in cakes, puddings, etc.

raising The enemy are *raising* their hands above their heads in surrender. ■ Self-*raising* flour is put in cakes, etc., to make them light.

rake a garden tool like a big comb on a long handle. ■ To *rake* anything is to use a rake on it.

rake   ramp

rallies The leader *rallies* (gets together) his men for an attack. ■ At motor *rallies* lots of motorists meet together.

rally To *rally* people is to bring them together for a great united effort. ■ a gathering together, e.g. a Guide *Rally*, a motor *rally*.

ram In a sheep family, the father is a *ram*. ■ To *ram* soil is to bang it down hard so that it is solid. ■ A vehicle, or ship, *rams* another one when it crashes into it.

ramble When you go for a *ramble* you walk just for pleasure, not caring where you go.

rammed Our ship *rammed* the enemy ship (ran straight into it) and sank it.

ramp Cars run up a *ramp* (slope) to get to the deck of the ship.

rampart a strong wall built to protect a place.

ramshackle A *ramshackle* car or building, etc., is one which is rickety and likely to fall to pieces.

ranch Cowboys work on a *ranch*, looking after cattle.

rancid Butter that is *rancid* has gone bad.

random without any special aim or objective, e.g. a *random* shot, a *random* remark, etc.

rang Dick pressed the button and *rang* the bell.

range a cooking stove. ■ The *range* of a rocket or gun, etc., is the distance it can go, or send its missile. ■ A rifle *range* is a place where people practise shooting. ■ The shop keeps a wide *range* of goods (i.e. many sorts and sizes).

rank That officer holds the *rank* of captain. ■ Soldiers stand in *ranks* (lines). ■ *Rank* growth (of plants) is growth that is coarse and there is too much of it.

ransack To *ransack* a place is to search it thoroughly, usually in order to steal things.

ransom The enemy will not release the prisoner until someone has paid them a sum of money as a *ransom*.

rap David gave a *rap* on the door with his knuckles. ■ *Rap* on the door with your knuckles and someone will come.

rapid fast, e.g. the *rapid* growth of a mushroom.

rapidity quickness, e.g. The animal moved with such *rapidity* that we didn't see where it went.

rapidly The snow *rapidly* melted under the hot sun.

rapids a place where a river bed slopes down steeply, causing the stream to be swift and rough.

rapids

rapier a light, thin, pointed sword (for pushing into people, not for cutting them).

rapped Mr. Smith *rapped* on the board with his pointer to call the class to order.

rapping Mr. Smith gets our attention by *rapping* on the board with his pointer.

rapt lost in thought, e.g. Mary was so *rapt* that she had no idea of what was going on around her.

rare A *rare* animal (or plant, etc.) is one that is hardly ever seen.

rarely Snakes are *rarely* (hardly ever) seen in England.

rarity something that you hardly ever come across.

rascal someone, usually a child, who misbehaves, but not seriously.

rash To be *rash* is to do something without stopping to think of the consequences. ■ When you have measles you have a *rash* (lots of spots) on your body.

rasher a slice of bacon or ham.

rasp a very rough file (used, e.g., to rub away the surface of wood).

raspberry a soft, red fruit ■ that grows on *raspberry* canes.

ratable (pron. rate-able) The *ratable* value of a building is the value put on it for the purpose of reckoning the rates.

raspberry   ratchet

ratchet a catch or bar which drops into a toothed wheel to stop it.

rate The car is going at the *rate* of 60 miles per hour. ■ The death-*rate* is the number of people who die out of each 1,000. ■ Things that are first-*rate* are good; third-*rate* things are poor.

ratepayer someone who pays rates.

rates money paid by property owners to the local borough or county council (to pay for such services as education, emptying dustbins, etc.).

rather I would *rather* be well than ill. ■ Jill is *rather* (a little) tired. ■ (Slang) 'Do you like chocolates?' '*Rather!*' (i.e. I certainly do!)

ratio The wages of Jones and Smith are in the *ratio* of 2 to 3 (or 2:3) (i.e. for every £2 Jones gets, Smith gets £3).

ration If there isn't as much of

something (e.g. food) as people would like, you have to *ration* it so that all have a fair share (i.e. you give each person a certain amount per day). ■ The amount thus given to each person is his *ration*.

rattle The *rattle* makes a noise when the baby shakes it. ■ The wind made the doors *rattle* loudly all night. ■ A *rattle*snake is poisonous and makes a rattling noise.

rattling There is someone *rattling* the door (i.e. shaking it to and fro). ■ I know by the sound of *rattling* tea-cups that someone is preparing tea.

raucous A *raucous* voice is harsh and rough, like that of a crow.

rave to talk, shout or scream wildly, like someone very angry or mad.

raven a big, black bird, like a crow.

raven   ravine

ravenous very hungry.

ravine a deep, narrow gap through high land.

raving making wild shouts or screams, like a madman, e.g. The fellow is *raving* mad.

ravishing charming, e.g. That young actress is a *ravishing* creature.

raw uncooked. ■ *Raw* materials are those used in manufacturing something.

ray a narrow beam of light like a thin line, or a similar narrow invisible beam of X-*rays* or of heat.

rayon artificial silk, made from wood pulp, etc.

razor Dad uses a *razor* for shaving the hair off his face.

razor

reach The ladder is not long enough to *reach* to the top of the house. ■ Mother will be glad to see us when we *reach* home.

reached The thirsty travellers were glad when they *reached* the well. ■ Sam *reached* for his gun (i.e. stretched his hand to get it).

* **react** If you touch a hedgehog it will *react* by curling into a ball.

* **reaction** The *reaction* of a person who sits on a pin is to leap into the air.

read You *read* a book in order to find out what it is about.

readable A *readable* book, etc. is one that you enjoy reading.

---

* The 're' usually means 'again' or 'back'.

reader 282 rebuke

reader a person who reads, e.g. Jim is a good *reader*. ■ a book for use in reading lessons.

readily willingly, e.g. Billy *readily* left his work in order to help put out the fire.

readiness You can be sure of John's *readiness* (willingness) to help. ■ Uncle is always expecting a flood, so he keeps a boat near the door in *readiness*.

reading Auntie uses her *reading* glasses when she wants to read. ■ I am *reading* this book in order to find out what it is about.

ready When you are *ready* we will go. ■ James is always *ready* (willing) to help.

real This is a *real* pearl, not an imitation. Fairies are not *real* people.

realistic That wax dummy of a man is so *realistic* that people speak to it.

reality The actor pretends to be a fierce, bold man, but in *reality* he is timid and shy.

realize I did not *realize* (understand) that the dog just wanted to play, or I would not have run away from him.

really Harry is not *really* angry; he's just pretending to be.

realm a kingdom, e.g. The king is liked by everyone in his *realm*.

reap To *reap* grain is to cut it for gathering in. ■ I hope you will *reap* a reward (i.e. get something in return) for your work.

rear the back, e.g. the *rear* of an army, the *rear* end of a train. ■ To *rear* animals is to breed them. ■ If a horse is alarmed it may *rear* up on its hind legs.

* **rearrange** to arrange again, e.g. If you don't like the way I have arranged the flowers in the vase, you can *rearrange* them.

reason The *reason* for my lateness is that I missed my bus. ■ To *reason* with anyone is to use arguments in an attempt to make him believe something.

reasonable A *reasonable* person is one who will listen to advice. ■ A *reasonable* price is a moderate one, not too expensive.

* **reassure** To *reassure* someone is to calm his fears.

rebel (pron. réb-el) a person who fights against, or refuses to obey his king, or his government, teachers, parents, etc. ■ (pron. re-bél) To *rebel* is to act or fight against someone in authority.

rebellion In a *rebellion* people get together to fight against the government.

rebellious A *rebellious* person is one who objects to doing what those in authority tell him to do.

* **rebound** If you throw a rubber ball on to the ground it will *rebound* (into the air again).

* **rebuild** They will *rebuild* the houses destroyed by the floods.

rebuke To *rebuke* anybody is to reprimand him (in slang, tell him off).

* The 're' usually means 'again' or 'back'.

recall *Recall* your messenger (i.e. call him back). ■ Do you *recall* (remember) the day the school caught fire?

recapture The prisoner escaped so the guards set out to *recapture* him.

receipt (pron. re-seet) a signed statement to prove that something has been received. ■ Jane jumped for joy on *receipt* of the letter (i.e. because she received it).

receive I like to *receive* presents on my birthday.

receiver a person who receives stolen goods. ■ The *receiver* of a telephone is the part of the instrument that you hold to your ear.

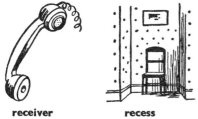

receiver   **recess**

recent A *recent* event is one that has just happened.

recently Someone has stayed here *recently*, for the fire is not yet cold.

receptacle a box or basket, etc., in which to put things, e.g. a waste paper basket is a *receptacle* for waste paper.

reception Jim had an enthusiastic *reception* when he returned home (i.e. he was greeted with enthusiasm). ■ The wedding *reception* was held in the village hall.

receptionist the person, usually a young lady, whose job is to receive people who come into a dentist's surgery, hospital, or hotel, etc.

recess an alcove, e.g. the extra space in a room where the wall goes farther back; ■ a temporary stopping of work, e.g. M.P.'s rest during the Parliamentary *recess*.

recipe (pron. reh-sip-ee) According to Mother's *recipe*, you put 4 eggs and ¼ lb. of butter in the cake.

recipient the person who receives something, e.g. Joan was the *recipient* of the gold medal.

recital At an orchestral *recital* an orchestra plays. The pianist gave a piano *recital*.

recitation To give a *recitation* is, usually, to say a piece of poetry to an audience.

recite To *recite* poetry is to say it aloud to an audience, from memory.

reckless A *reckless* person is one who does things without thinking about what the results might be.

reckon I *reckon* that Jim is our best player (i.e. that is my opinion). ■ When I came to *reckon*, I found I had more money than I had thought.

* **reclaim** To *reclaim* land is to recover it from the sea or swamp and bring it into use.

recline To *recline* in a chair is to lean back in it. ■ To *recline* on a bed is to lie down on it.

---

* The 're' usually means 'again' or 'back'

recognition Denis was presented with a medal in *recognition* of his good work for the school (i.e. as a sign that his good work had been noticed).

recognize To *recognize* a person is to know who he is because you have seen him before.

recoil To *recoil* from something is to spring back from it (in horror or fear). ■ The *recoil* of a gun is the jerk backwards that it gives when fired.

recollect to remember, e.g. Do you *recollect* borrowing 10p from me?

recollection I have no *recollection* (i.e. I do not remember).

recommend To *recommend* a person for a job is to suggest that he is a good person for it.

reconcile To *reconcile* people is to bring them together as friends again, after a quarrel. ■ Pat never liked living in the country, but after a time she became *reconciled* to it (i.e. she could put up with it without being unhappy).

* reconsider Please *reconsider* your answer (i.e. think it over again).

* reconstruct The inventor was able to *reconstruct* his broken machine from the pieces, and soon it was going again.

record (pron. réh-cord) Put a *record* on the record-player and let's have some music. ■ The *record* (best time) for the mile is under four minutes. ■ A criminal's *record* is the list of his crimes. ■ (pron. re-córd) To *record* sounds is

to put them on to a tape or a record so that they can be heard again whenever you wish. ■ To *record* results at a sports meeting, etc., is to write them down officially.

recorder a person who records (results of a sports meeting, etc.); ■ an old English type of flute, now very popular in many schools; ■ a city magistrate.

recover When the police *recover* stolen property they can return it to its owner. ■ To *recover* from an illness is to get well again.

* re-cover To *re-cover* an armchair is to put a new cover on it.

recovery I am glad to hear of Angela's *recovery* from her illness. ■ The owner has offered a reward for the *recovery* of the stolen goods.

recreation play, amusement, e.g. A *recreation* ground is a place on which people may play games, etc.

recruit a soldier who has only just joined the army.

rectangle usually an oblong, but could be any figure with four straight sides and four right angles.

record   rectangle

rectify To *rectify* a mistake is to put it right.

---

* The 're' usually means 'again' or 'back'.

rector   a clergyman in charge of a parish.

rectory   the house provided for a rector.

recuperate   to get well, e.g. The sick child will quickly *recuperate* in hospital.

recur   to happen again, e.g. The trouble will not *recur*.

redden   to become red.

redeem   To *redeem* a thing is to buy it back, or to get it back by some great effort.

redirect   You *redirect* a letter that has come to a wrong address, by writing another address on it.

reduce   To *reduce* pounds to pence you multiply by a hundred. ■ Some fat people try to *reduce* (make less) their weight.

reduction   Usual price £5, sale price £4—a *reduction* of £1.

reed   a plant like giant grass that grows in, or near, water. ■ Oboes and clarinets are *reed* instruments (i.e. they have a piece of cane, called a reed, in the mouthpiece).

reef   a ridge of rocks or sand, etc., in the sea at about water-level. ■ A *reef* knot is a kind of double knot.

reef   **reef knot**

reek   The house *reeks* (smells unpleasantly) of gas.

reel   A cotton *reel* is a wooden roller on which cotton is wound. ■ To *reel* off something (e.g. poetry) is to say it quickly and without hesitation. ■ To *reel* is to stagger because you are dizzy. ■ a Scottish dance.

refer   Do not *refer* to me in your letter or in your speech (i.e. do not mention me). ■ For information about trains you must *refer* to a timetable.

referee   the person in charge of a football match, or of some other contest.

reference   There is a *reference* to Tom in my book (i.e. he is mentioned). ■ In the *reference* library are *reference* books, from which you can get information. You may not take *reference* books out of the library.

referred   I heard about the new school when the mayor *referred* to it in his speech.

referring   I knew the lady was *referring* to Bill when she spoke of a bright young lad.

refine   You *refine* things (such as oil or sugar) to make them more pure.

refined   purified, e.g. Crude oil is brought to Britain to be *refined*. ■ Miss Smythe is a *refined* lady (i.e. she has good taste, good manners, etc.).

reflect   to send back, e.g. A mirror will *reflect* light. A building may *reflect* sounds.

reflection   The sea sparkles because of the *reflection* of sunlight from the water.

reflector   When a light shines on a *reflector*, light comes back from it.

---

* The 're' usually means 'again' or 'back'.

reform to make better, e.g. to *reform* a law, to *reform* a criminal. ■ A *reform* is an improvement, especially in the law.

Reformation The *Reformation*, in the 16th century, was the great religious quarrel that led to the Protestant Churches becoming separate from the Roman Catholic Church.

refrain the lines repeated at the end of each verse of a song or poem (the chorus). ■ Please *refrain* from talking (i.e. do not talk).

* **refresh** A rest and a cool drink will *refresh* you (make you feel fit again). ■ To *refresh* someone's memory is to remind him of something.

refreshment(s) food and drink provided during, or at the end of a meeting, etc.

refrigerator We put food in the *refrigerator* to keep it cool.

refuge a shelter or place of safety, e.g. in the middle of a road.

refugee a person who has had to leave his country because of war, or because of his political or religious opinions.

* **refund** (pron. re-fúnd) If you take those bad eggs back to the shopkeeper he will *refund* your money. ■ (ré-fund) The money so paid back is a *refund*.

refusal The man starved because of his *refusal* to eat the food given him.

refuse (pron. re-fúse) I *refuse* to (won't) eat that nasty stuff. ■

(pron. réf-fuse) Put all the *refuse* (rubbish) in the dust bin.

* **regain** to get back.

regard The boys *regard* (look upon) Brian as a fool. ■ You must *regard* your father's advice (i.e. take notice of it).

regarding Mother gave Linda instructions *regarding* (about) the cake in the oven.

regardless Tim continued to run away, *regardless* of our shouts to him that he should return.

regards good wishes, e.g. Please give my *regards* to your sister.

regatta At a *regatta* there are races for all kinds of boats.

regiment a large body of soldiers under the command of a colonel.

region a large area, e.g. The polar *region* is the large cold area around the pole. The equatorial *region* is the lands around the equator.

register The class *register* contains the names, etc., of all the boys and girls in the class.

registered When you send a letter by *registered* post, ■ details about it are *registered* (written) in a special book at the post office.

registrar the person who keeps the official record of all the births, deaths and marriages in his area.

registration Being late for *registration* means that you arrive after the class register has been called. ■ A car *registration* book contains all the official information about the car.

---

* The 're' usually means 'again' or 'back'.

regret I *regret* (am sorry) that I cannot do what you ask.

regrettable By a *regrettable* accident (i.e. one for which I am very sorry) I shot your cat instead of the rat.

regular To keep *regular* hours is to do things at the same time each day. ■ (slang) A *regular* customer of a shop is one who often buys things there.

regularity His heart beats with the *regularity* of a clock pendulum.

regularly Auntie goes to church *regularly* (i.e. on the same days each week or month).

regulate To *regulate* a clock or watch is to adjust it so that it doesn't go too fast or too slow. ■ The policeman stands at the crossroads to *regulate* the traffic (i.e. to control the flow).

regulation a rule, e.g. There is a *regulation* against railway passengers walking across the lines.

regulator The *regulator* on a clock is a device for making the clock go faster or slower. The *regulator* on a fridge enables you to make the fridge colder or less cold.

rehearsal You have a *rehearsal* of a play or concert so that the players can practise their parts.

rehearse To *rehearse* a play or concert, etc., is to have a practice performance.

reign The king's *reign* over the country lasted many years. ■ Once he is crowned, the king will *reign* until he dies.

reindeer a deer which has long branching antlers (horns) and which lives in cold lands.

reinforce to strengthen, e.g. To *reinforce* an army you send it more soldiers.

reinforced *Reinforced* concrete has metal embedded in it to make it stronger.

reinforcements To strengthen the army many extra men were sent as *reinforcements*.

reins leather ribbons attached to a horse's head to enable the rider or driver to control him.

reject to refuse, e.g. A slot-machine will *reject* bent coins.

rejoice Happy people *rejoice* by dancing, singing, or having a celebration.

rejoicing People are *rejoicing* at the good news by dancing and singing.

rejoin I must leave you now, but I'll *rejoin* (pron. re-join) you later. ■ In the play, I say, 'Come, be mine,' and you *rejoin* (pron. re-joín), 'Never !'

relapse The patient was getting better; then he had a *relapse* and had to go back into hospital.

relate We heard Jim *relate* the story of his escape.

related You are *related* to such people as your parents, brothers, sisters, uncles and cousins. ■ We listened while Jim *related* the story of his adventures.

reindeer   **reins**

relation Mr. Smith is a *relation* (i.e. he is my father, uncle, or cousin, etc.). ■ There is a *relation* (connection) between the length of day and the time of year. ■ We enjoyed the *relation* (telling) of the story.

relative a person such as an uncle or cousin, etc., who is related to you.

relatively The moon is *relatively* close to the earth (i.e. close as compared with other objects in space).

relax to slacken, or to work less. To *relax* muscles is to make them loose and soft. To *relax* discipline is to make it less severe.

relaxation recreation, e.g. After a day's work, Dad's favourite *relaxation* is fishing.

relaxed When he *relaxed* his grip we were able to pull the rope from his grasp.

relay A broadcasting station will sometimes *relay* to its listeners a programme which it has received from another station.

release To *release* a prisoner is to set him free.

relegate To *relegate* something, such as a football team, is to put it in a lower position.

relent Dad is keeping Pat indoors as a punishment, but he may *relent* and let her go out later on.

relentless without pity, e.g. the *relentless* attacks of an enemy.

reliable Jack is a *reliable* boy (i.e. you may depend on him).

reliance You can put no *reliance* on Tom (i.e. you cannot depend on him).

relic something from the past, often kept as a memento, e.g. a piece of some famous person's clothing. Folk dances are a *relic* of a by-gone age.

relief You breathe a sigh of *relief* when you hear that danger has passed. ■ The *relief* of a besieged town is the ending of the siege by a rescuing force. ■ money, etc., given to people in need, e.g. famine *relief*.

relieve To *relieve* pain is to make it less. ■ You *relieve* a sentry or policeman, etc., on duty by taking over his job.

religion The chief *religion* of Europe is Christianity, which is belief in God and Christ.

religious A *religious* person is one who believes in a religion and tries to practise it, e.g. by attending *religious* services, saying prayers, etc.

relish I do not *relish* (like) the idea of a bathe in that icy water.

reluctant unwilling, e.g. I am *reluctant* to get out of bed on cold mornings.

rely You can *rely* on Peter to do whatever he promises.

remain If four of the five go, only one will *remain*.

remainder When you divide 7 by 3 there is a *remainder* of 1 ($7 \div 3$: answer, 2 *remainder* 1).

---

* The 're' usually means 'again' or 'back'.

remark On seeing us, Dad's *remark* was, 'I expect you're hungry.'

remarkable worth noticing.

remarkably You've been *remarkably* quiet (so quiet that it has been noticed).

remedy I know a *remedy* (cure) for headaches. ■ You can *remedy* bad eye-sight by wearing glasses.

remember I *remember* seeing a lion at the zoo years ago.

remind I may forget to do it if you don't *remind* me.

reminder I don't want to forget to do it, so I've tied a knot in my handkerchief, as a *reminder*.

remnant a small piece (especially of cloth) left over after the rest has been used up. ■ Most of the boys went home; the *remnant* assembled in the school hall.

remonstrate Dad went to *remonstrate* with (protest to) the careless driver who ran into us.

remorse To feel *remorse* for something you have done is to be sorry, and wish that you hadn't done it.

remorseless pitiless, e.g. The *remorseless* torturer ignored his victim's shrieks.

remote far away, e.g. a remote star. ■ *Remote* control (of a machine) is control (of it) from a distance by means of radio, etc.

remotely Pam is *remotely* related to Jean (i.e. she is not a near relative).

removal You hire a *removal* van to carry your furniture when you move from one house to another.

remove Please *remove* your bag from the seat so that I can sit down.

render To *render* a piece of music is to play or sing it. ■ To *render* an account (a bill) is to send it in. ■ To *render* (down) fat is to melt it.

rendezvous a meeting place.

* **renew** To *renew* such things as curtains, furniture, etc., is to make them as new or to replace them with new ones. ■ To *renew* a request, etc., is to make it again.

renounce to give up. ■ To *renounce* a treaty or agreement is to state that you won't be bound by it any longer.

renovate to repair or make new, e.g. Instead of buying new furniture we are going to *renovate* the old.

renown fame, e.g. Rome is a city of great *renown*.

renowned famous.

rent The house we live in is not ours; we pay *rent* to live in it. ■ To *rent* a house you make a payment each week (or month, etc.) to the owner. ■ I've made a *rent* (tear) in my coat.

* **reorganize** to organize afresh, e.g. We shall have to *reorganize* the club if the leaders leave.

* **repaid** paid back, e.g. I have *repaid* the money I owed.

* **repay** to pay back (money, or a kindness, etc.).

repeal If the government *repeals* a law, it ceases to be a law.

repeat To *repeat* anything is to say or do it again.

repeatedly You should know, for I have told you *repeatedly* (many times).

repel to drive off (an attack, etc.).

---

* The 're' usually means 'again' or 'back'.

repent to be sorry about something that you have done.

repentance You must show signs of *repentance* (being sorry) if you wish to be forgiven.

repetition the repeating (of something); ■ a piece of poetry or prose to be learnt by heart.

* **replace** You are to *replace* (put back) the picture you took off the wall. ■ John will *replace* (take the place of) Ian in the team.

* **replacement** As Ian is ill, we must find a *replacement* for him in the team.

replica an exact copy.

replied 'Where are you?' asked Joan. 'Indoors,' John *replied*.

reply an answer, e.g. What is your *reply* to the question? ■ to answer, e.g. Please *reply* to my question.

report In your school *report*, teachers tell your parents what progress you are making. ■ The *report* of the gun could be heard miles away. ■ *Report* (go) to Mr. Smith.

reporter a person who finds out about events and writes accounts of them for a newspaper.

repose (used chiefly in poetry) to rest peacefully, e.g. The owl hunts while you *repose* in bed. ■ No sound disturbs her *repose* (rest).

represent Brenda will *represent* the school at the district sports. ■ On my map each dot will *represent* a town.

representative James is our *representative* at the meeting (i.e. James is there on our behalf).

repress To *repress* someone is to prevent him from doing something (e.g. prevent him from expressing happiness, or anger, or just his opinion).

reprieve To *reprieve* someone is to let him off a punishment, perhaps only for the time being.

reprimand To *reprimand* anyone is to rebuke him (slang, tell him off). ■ A *reprimand* is a rebuke (slang, a telling off).

reproach something about which you ought to feel ashamed. ■ To *reproach* a person is to put it to him that he has done something about which he ought to feel ashamed.

reproduce To *reproduce* something is to make a copy of it. ■ When animals or plants *reproduce* they bring forth young ones or seeds.

reptile a creature, such as a snake, crocodile or tortoise, that crawls.

republic a country, such as France or the United States, which has no king or queen.

repulse To *repulse* an enemy attack is to beat it back.

repulsive A *repulsive* creature is one which makes you want to shrink back, because it is so unpleasant.

reputation Colin has the *reputation* of being the worst boy in the class (i.e. that is what people think).

---

* The 're' usually means 'again' or 'back'.

request 291 **resolve**

request Jane came at my *request* (because I asked her). ■ *Request* (ask) those boys to be silent.

require Amongst the things we *require* for the holiday are food, a cooking stove and a tent.

requirements things needed.

rescue Had not Jim dived in to *rescue* him, the boy would have drowned. ■ The boy would have drowned had not Jim gone to the *rescue*.

resemblance There is a *resemblance* between these two boys (i.e. they are alike in some ways).

resemble The boys *resemble* each other in that they both have ginger hair and round faces.

resent I *resent* being told to wash my face when visitors are present (i.e. being told this makes me annoyed).

resentful Joan is *resentful* because no one has asked her to sing (i.e. she feels that she has been badly treated).

resentment To show *resentment* is to show that you have taken offence.

reserve You *reserve* a seat at a theatre, etc., so that even if you are late it will still be kept for you. ■ A nature *reserve* is a piece of land (or water) where creatures are kept safe from hunters.

reservoir a huge tank or a lake, etc., in which a town's water supply is stored.

reside From now on, the headmaster will *reside* (live) at 14 Green Street.

residence The official *residence* of the queen is Buckingham Palace.

resident He is a *resident* here (i.e. he is living here). ■ The school has a *resident* caretaker (i.e. one who lives on the premises).

residential The *residential* part of the town is the part where there are houses (not factories or shops).

resign I intend to *resign* as captain so that Bob can take my place.

resignation I offer my *resignation* as captain so that Bob can take my place. ■ The old woman listened to the bad news with *resignation* (a feeling of helplessness, that made it seem useless to complain).

resigned Eric didn't want to be captain any longer, so he *resigned* to let Bob have the job. ■ The people are *resigned* to their life of hardship (they have come to accept it as their fate).

resin the sticky gum of certain trees and plants (specially hardened to rub on violin bows, and sometimes spelt *rosin*).

resist I am late for school because I cannot *resist* the temptation to stay in bed when I ought to get up.

resistance Our men offered no *resistance* to the enemy (i.e. they made no attempt to fight the enemy).

resolute A *resolute* person will not be put off once he has made up his mind to do something.

resolution Jean made a New Year *resolution* that she would not eat so many sweets. ■ a statement on which people at a meeting vote as an expression of their opinion.

resolve to make up your mind (to do something).

resort The electric lamps went out so we had to *resort* to candles to light the room. ■ Brighton is a well-known holiday *resort*.

resources the various things needed, especially money, e.g. The villagers haven't the *resources* to feed a large number of refugees.

respect To (have) *respect* (for) someone is to think highly of him and look up to him. ■ Your story is wrong in one *respect* (way).

respectable honourable and well thought of, e.g. Mr. Smith is a *respectable* person. ■ fairly good, e.g. John is quite a *respectable* chess-player.

respectful To be *respectful* to someone is to show him that you know he is above you in age, importance, or in knowledge, etc.

respectively The teacher gave John and Joan 7 and 9 marks *respectively* (i.e. John received 7 and Joan 9).

respite a pause that gives you a rest from something unpleasant.

respond How did Jack *respond* to your suggestion? (i.e. what did he say or do in return?).

response I told the man the house was on fire, but he made no *response* (i.e. he neither said nor did anything in reply).

responsibility It is Bill's *responsibility* to see that all the visitors have a chair (i.e. if they don't get a chair it will be Bill's fault.)

responsible Bill was *responsible* for the decorations; so if they are badly done, blame him.

rest After that hard work you will need to lie down and *rest*. ■ You must have a *rest*. ■ Pick out the good apples to use and throw the *rest* in the dust-bin.

restaurant a place where people can go to buy and eat meals.

restful For a *restful* holiday you need a quiet spot where you can just sit or lie in peace.

restive A *restive* horse is one that is difficult to manage because he is jerking about.

restless The sick man had a *restless* night (i.e. he had no rest; or, he was never still).

Restoration the period in history when England returned to having a king again after the rule of Cromwell.

restore You may receive a reward if you *restore* the stolen goods to their owner. ■ to bring back into good condition, e.g. to *restore* a sick person to health, to *restore* a damaged picture.

restrain to hold back, e.g. If I don't *restrain* my dog, he chases the cats.

restrict We *restrict* membership of the club to schoolboys (i.e. no other kinds of people are admitted).

result The *result* of eating too much is that you feel sick.

resume start again. ■ The men *resume* work at 2 o'clock, following their dinner break.

resumption starting again. We all hate the *resumption* of work after a holiday.

resurrect to bring back to life.

resurrection At Easter, Christians celebrate the *resurrection* of Christ from the dead.

retaliate If you tease animals they may *retaliate* by biting you.

retire When his working days are over a man can *retire* and live on his pension. ■ I *retire* (to bed) at 9 o'clock.

retirement After his *retirement*, a man does not have to go to work any more, but lives on his pension.

retort 'I won't have it!' shouted the man. 'It isn't meant for you,' was Tom's *retort*.

* **retrace** To *retrace* your steps is to go back again the way you have come.

retreat We shall never catch up with the enemy if they *retreat* as fast as we advance.

retrieve Tom went to the lost property room to *retrieve* (get back) his hat.

retriever a kind of dog, bred and trained to bring back to a sportsman the birds or small animals that he has shot.

retriever

return Please *return* (to me) the book I lent you. ■ We are going away but we expect to *return* home next week.

* **reunion** All old boys are invited to the *reunion* at school next term.

reveal To *reveal* a secret is to tell it to someone. ■ I will now draw the curtain and *reveal* the picture behind it.

revel Boys *revel* in any excitement (i.e. they enjoy it very much).

revelation something that you are surprised to hear about. ■ (The Book of) *Revelation* is the last book in the Bible.

revelled When detectives came to make inquiries at school, the boys *revelled* in (loved) the excitement.

revelry At our Christmas party, the *revelry* (fun and games, etc.) lasted till midnight.

revenge To have your *revenge* is to pay someone back for a wrong he has done you.

revenue The government's *revenue* is made up chiefly of the money we pay in taxes. ■ A *revenue* officer's job is to prevent smuggling.

reverence very great respect, usually for something religious, e.g. Some people show *reverence* for the name 'Jesus' by bowing their heads.

reverend That clergyman is the *Reverend* P. Brown (usually shortened to *Rev.*).

reverent People who are *reverent* in a church do not shout and play about in it as they might in other buildings.

reverse You put a car in *reverse* (gear) to make it go backwards. ■ When you *reverse* a vehicle you must look behind to see where you are going.

---

* The 're' usually means 'again' or 'back'.

revise To *revise* a piece of work is to look, or read, through it again.

revision When we do *revision* we read through our work again.

revival There is a *revival* of interest in old-time dancing (i.e. people have become interested again).

revive When someone faints you can usually *revive* him by laying him down.

revoke to cancel, take back (permission, or a promise, etc.). ■ Card players *revoke* when they fail to follow suit (e.g. should play a spade and do not, although they have one).

revolt a rebellion; ■ to rise in rebellion, e.g. The tribesmen will *revolt* if you ask them to pay taxes.

revolting horrible, disgusting.

revolution A wheel makes one *revolution* each time it goes completely round. ■ In the French *Revolution*, the people fought and killed those who had ruled them, then set up another kind of government.

revolutionary someone who takes part in a revolution. ■ A *revolutionary* idea is one that involves a complete change of some kind.

revolve to go round as a wheel does, or as the moon goes round the earth.

revolver The cowboy pulled a *revolver* from his holster and shot the cattle thief.

reward There is a *reward* of £100 for the person who returns the lost jewellery to its owner.

rheumatism People who suffer from *rheumatism* have pains in

their joints – especially in wet weather.

rhinoceros a large African animal with tough, thick skin and one or two horns on his nose.

revolver   rhinoceros

rhododendron a big evergreen bush which has large, showy flowers.

rhubarb The thick, red stalks of *rhubarb* are eaten as fruit.

rhyme The last words of two lines of poetry are said to *rhyme* if they end with the same sound, e.g. 'love' and 'dove'.

rhythm *Rhythm* is made by repeating an accent (strong beat) at regular intervals, e.g. LOUD, soft, soft; LOUD, soft, soft; LOUD, soft, soft; etc.

rhythmic A *rhythmic* sound is one that has rhythm.

ribbon Many girls tie their hair with lengths of coloured *ribbon*.

rice a grain grown in hot countries in flooded fields, ■ and eaten in *rice* puddings, etc.

rich A *rich* man has plenty of money.

riches To have *riches* is to be rich.

rickety A *rickety* structure (e.g. a table, chair, building) is one whose joints are so loose that it wobbles about.

ridden I have *ridden* a bicycle, but I have never *ridden* a horse.

riddle a puzzling question, asked for fun. ■ To *riddle* gravel, etc. is to pass it through a sieve to get out the larger pieces.

riddled The wood was *riddled* with holes (i.e. there were holes all over it). ■ The workman *riddled* the cinders (through a sieve) to get out the larger pieces.

ride I can *ride* a bicycle. ■ Shall we *ride* home on the bus?

ridge A *ridge* is formed where two sloping surfaces meet, e.g. at the top of a roof.

rift valley   **rifle**

ridicule To *ridicule* anyone is to make fun of him.

ridiculous If you are asked how much a man weighs, it is *ridiculous* to say, 'Two grammes.'

riding Jim is *riding* along on his bicycle. ■ You go to a *riding* school to learn to ride a horse.

rifle The soldier put his *rifle* to his shoulder and fired a bullet at the enemy. ■ To *rifle* a place is to hunt for the valuables in it and steal them.

rifled The thief *rifled* Dad's desk (i.e. hunted through it for valuables, which he stole).

rift a crack or split, especially one in the earth's surface, e.g. a *rift* valley; ■ a quarrel which separates old friends.

right I write with my *right* hand. ■ That is not the *right* answer; mark it wrong. ■ There is a *right* angle (90°) at each corner of a square.

righteous A *righteous* person is one who is good, honest, etc.

rightful Both girls claim the watch, but Jane is the *rightful* owner (i.e. it is Jane's).

rightly Billy was *rightly* punished for his naughtiness (i.e. he deserved the punishment).

rigid stiff. If a thing (e.g. a person's arm or leg) is *rigid*, it will not bend.

rigmarole talk that goes on and on, but has no meaning.

rim The *rim* of the wheel is the outer part, on which the tyre fits.

rime white frost.

rind You cut the *rind* (skin) off cheese and bacon before eating them.

ring When a lady marries, a *ring* is put on her finger. ■ To *ring* a bell is to cause it to sound. ■ The *ring*leader is the head of a group of wrongdoers.

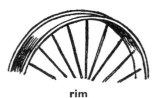

rim

rink a place where you can skate – on ice, or on a floor (for roller skating).

rinse to remove soap, etc., from your hair, or from washing, etc., with lots of clean water.

riot a noisy, dangerous disturbance by crowds in a street.

rip a cut or tear; ■ to cut or tear, e.g. *Rip* the page out of the book.

ripe When crops are *ripe* they are ready to be harvested and eaten.

ripen The crops will not be ready for harvesting until we have had some sunshine to *ripen* them.

ripple a small wave such as that caused by dropping a pebble into a pond.

rippling A breeze is *rippling* the water (making little waves on it).

rise The balloon will *rise* into the sky if you let it go. ■ The price may *rise* from 5p to 10p. ■ Dad hopes for a *rise* (an increase in his wages).

rising We got up at dawn to see the *rising* of the sun. ■ The smoke is *rising* into the sky.

risk If you skate on thin ice there is a *risk* of your falling through. ■ If you go on thin ice you *risk* falling through.

risky Skating on thin ice is a *risky* thing to do (i.e. you may be in danger).

ritual the acts, ceremonies, etc., that are required in a religious service.

rival a person who is competing with you for a job, or for a boy or girl friend, etc.

rivalry There is *rivalry* between two people when they are both striving for something (e.g. a job) that only one of them can have.

river Ships get from London to

the sea by sailing down the *river* Thames.

rivet a metal bolt used to fasten pieces of metal together. (The bolt is held in place by hammering the end till it is rounded like the head.) ■ To *rivet* things is to fasten them with rivets.

rivet   roach

roach a fresh-water fish.

road Many cars, buses and lorries travel along the *road* to the town.

roam I like to *roam* about over the countryside (i.e. to wander around without any special purpose).

roar The *roar* of a lion is a frightening noise.

roast You put meat into the oven to *roast* it for dinner.

rob To *rob* a bank is to steal from it.

robbery The men in prison for *robbery* had stolen some money.

robe a cloak or long garment, especially one such as that worn by a clergyman, or a lawyer, etc.

robin a little bird with a red breast.

robot a machine that is like a human being.

robust A *robust* person is one who is well built and strong (similarly, a *robust* plant or animal).

rock That hill is made of a *rock* called limestone. ■ The *rocks* on the beach are lumps from the cliffs. ■ To *rock* a cradle is to move it gently to and fro.

rockery The *rockery* is the part of the garden where plants grow among rough stones.

rocket The *rocket* sped up into the sky with flames roaring from its tail.

rocky full of rocks. ■ The *Rocky* Mountains are in Canada.

rode Yesterday I *rode* to school on my bicycle.

roe a small kind of deer; ■ the mass of eggs inside a fish.

rogue a dishonest fellow; ■ a naughty, mischievous child.

role What is John's *role* in the play? (i.e. what part does he play?)

roll If you let the ball go it will *roll* down the hill. ■ You make a *roll* of paper, lino, etc., by rolling it over and over, to form a cylinder. ■ To call the *roll* (*roll-call*) is to call out names from a list.

roller A heavy iron *roller* is pulled over grass to level it.

Roman a citizen of the ancient *Roman* Empire, or of the modern city of Rome.

romance a made-up story, especially a love story, or one about adventure.

Romania a European country to the west of the Black Sea (also spelt *Roumania* and *Rumania*).

romantic A *romantic* person is one who likes to imagine things – especially things to do with love or adventure. ■ A *romantic* story is one about love or adventure.

Romany a gipsy.

Rome the capital city of Italy; the centre of the ancient Roman Empire.

romp The children love to *romp* on the grass (i.e. to play vigorously together, chasing, wrestling, etc.).

roof The *roof* covers the top of a building. *Roofs* are made of tiles, or slates, thatch, etc.

rook a black bird related to the crow family; ■ a piece used in the game of chess (also called a castle). ■ To *rook* anyone is to cheat him.

roller   roof   rook   rook in chess

roly-poly a boiled pudding made by coating a slab of pastry with jam and rolling it into a cylinder.

room There is *room* for several people on this seat. ■ We work in a class-*room*, eat in a dining-*room* and sleep in a bed-*room*.

roomy A *roomy* place is one in which there is plenty of space.

roost Many birds *roost* for the night in that tree.

rooster Each morning we are awakened by the *rooster* in the chicken shed calling, 'Cock a-doodle do!'

root The *root* of a plant grows down into the soil. ■ The square *root* of 9 is 3 ($\sqrt{9} = 3$).

rooted I have a *rooted* (firmly fixed) objection to kissing people who have whiskers. ■ Plants that have *rooted* have grown roots.

rope The boat is kept in place by means of a *rope* tied to a post. ■ To *rope* a horse is to tie him up with a rope.

rope   **rosette**

rose a prickly bush and its beautiful, sweet-scented flower. ■ Bob *rose* from the ground where he had been lying. ■ The balloon *rose* into the air.

rosemary an evergreen shrub which has a pleasant smell.

rosette a decoration made of ribbons, etc., to look like a rose.

rosin the hardened gum of certain plants, used to rub on violin bows, etc. (also spelt *resin*).

rosy Susan has *rosy* cheeks (i.e. cheeks the colour of a red rose).

rotate To *rotate* anything is to turn it round as you can turn a wheel. ■ The wheels of a car *rotate* as it moves along.

rotation To deal with things in *rotation* means to take them in the order in which they come, i.e. the first to arrive is dealt with first, and so on. ■ The *rotation* of crops is the growing of crops always in a certain order on a piece of land (e.g. turnips, barley, clover, wheat; then turnips again, and so on).

rotor A helicopter is driven by the *rotor* which rotates above it.

rotor

rotten bad, e.g. You cannot eat a *rotten* apple.

rouge Ladies put *rouge* on their cheeks to make them look red.

rough not smooth, e.g. a *rough* sea, a piece of *rough* wood. ■ A *rough* drawing is one that is not carefully made. ■ A *rough* boy is one who is bad-mannered and violent.

roughly about, e.g. The distance is, *roughly*, five miles. ■ A thing that is *roughly* made is not well finished off.

Roumania a European country to the west of the Black sea (also spelt *Romania* and *Rumania*).

Roumanian a citizen of Roumania, or his language. ■ *Roumanian* things are those from (or of) Roumania.

round A ball is *round* in shape, and so is a circle. ■ If you go right *round* anything you arrive back at your starting point. ■ Each *round* of the boxing match lasts two minutes. ■ a part song in which the voices begin in turn.

roundabout We came home by a *roundabout* way (i.e. not the shortest way). ■ a circular arrangement of roads at a junction; ■ a merry-go-round at a fair.

roundabout   fair roundabout

rounders a game played with a hard ball, and a bat like a thick stick.

rouse When it was time to go we had to *rouse* Peter, who had fallen asleep.

rousing Bob takes a lot of *rousing* (waking) when he is asleep. ■ A *rousing* shout is one likely to startle people.

rout To put an army to *rout* is to cause the soldiers to run away in disorder.

route (pron. root) Our *route* from London to Paris is by way of Dover and Calais.

routine Your *routine* is the round of things that you usually do each day. ■ A *routine* inquiry (or call, etc.) is one made for no reason except that it is the usual thing to do.

rove to wander about without any set idea about where you intend going.

rover someone who wanders about, not making for any particular place; ■ a pirate. ■ A *Rover* (Scout) is a senior Boy Scout.

roving wandering aimlessly. ■ A *roving* commission is a job which makes it necessary for you to move from place to place.

row (rhymes with 'low') a line, e.g. a *row* of plants in a garden. ■ To *row* a boat is to pull it along with oars. ■ (rhymes with 'cow') a disturbing noise; ■ a quarrel.

rowan a tree which bears bunches of scarlet berries (also called mountain ash).

rowdy A *rowdy* person is one who makes a lot of unnecessary noise.

royal The *royal* family consists of the king and queen and their relations. ■ The *Royal* Navy, The *Royal* Society, etc., are organizations that serve the country or its queen (king).

royalist anyone who supports the king or queen, but especially someone who sided with King Charles I against Parliament.

royalty The *royalty* present at the concert included kings, queens, princes and princesses.

rub You *rub* furniture with a cloth to polish it. ■ You can *rub* out pencil marks by rubbing them with a rubber.

rubber a tough, elastic substance made from the juice of *rubber* trees; ■ a small block of rubber used for rubbing out pencil marks.

rubbish We put our *rubbish* in the dust-bin. ■ To talk *rubbish* is to talk nonsense.

rubble After the earthquake all that remained of the buildings were piles of *rubble*.

ruby a precious stone, red in colour; ■ a girl's name (*Ruby*).

ructions (slang) There will be *ructions* (trouble) when Dad hears of this.

rudder A boat or aircraft is steered by movements of the *rudder* (a hinged flap at the rear).

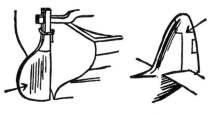

boat rudder   **aircraft rudder**

rude not polite, e.g. It is *rude* to point at people. ■ simple, roughly made, e.g. a *rude* hut, a *rude* carving; ■ sudden, e.g. a *rude* awakening.

rudiments To know the *rudiments* of anything is to know only very little about it.

ruffian A young *ruffian* in the street knocked a man down just because he accidentally brushed against him.

ruffle To *ruffle* feathers (or hair) is to make them untidy.

ruffled Comb your *ruffled* hair and make it tidy. ■ Ian *ruffled* his hair by pushing his fingers through it in all directions.

rug A thick, woollen *rug* covers the floor in front of the fireplace.

Rugby In *Rugby* (football) an oval ball is used and players may pick it up and run with it.

rugged very rough and uneven, e.g. *rugged* mountains, *rugged* bark (on a tree).

ruin to destroy, or spoil completely, e.g. If the rain gets into your exercise books it will *ruin* them. ■ Uncle's *ruin* was brought about by gambling (i.e. gambling spoilt his whole life and made it a failure).

ruins Most of the old building fell down years ago, but people still go to see the *ruins*.

rule To *rule* lines is to draw them straight with the aid of a ruler, etc. ■ Parliament *rules* the country (i.e. its members decide what we all have to do). ■ It is a school *rule* that all boys must wear a school cap.

ruler You use a *ruler* for drawing or measuring lines. ■ The *ruler* of a country is its king or president, etc.

ruling You require something with a straight edge for *ruling* lines on your paper. ■ As we couldn't agree who was right, we asked Dad for a *ruling* (decision).

Rumania a European country to the west of the Black Sea (also spelt *Romania* and *Roumania*).

rumba a native Cuban dance, from which a ballroom dance has grown.

rumble I can hear a *rumble* of thunder in the distance.

rumbling I can hear a *rumbling* noise, like distant thunder.

rummage Auntie had to *rummage* through all the odds and ends in her handbag to find her ticket.

rumour Everyone seems to have heard the *rumour* that Bob has met with an accident, but it isn't true.

rump the tail end of an animal or bird, e.g. *Rump* steak is meat cut from near the animal's tail.

rumpled A handkerchief soon becomes *rumpled* (creased) in your pocket. ■ My hair is *rumpled* when I wake up (i.e. it needs combing).

rung John has *rung* the bell; I heard it. ■ A *rung* of a ladder is one of the short cross-pieces that you step on.

runner In this race, each *runner* has to run a mile. ■ The *runner*-up in a race is the one who comes second. ■ *Runner* bean plants climb up sticks.

running We are *running* to school because we are late. ■ *Running* water is water that is moving along, as in a stream or river.

runway An aircraft runs along a *runway* in order to take off or land at an airport.

rupture to break; ■ a weak place in the wall of the abdomen (belly) through which a piece of intestine has squeezed out.

rural *Rural* things are those connected with the countryside, e.g. a *rural* scene, The *Rural* District Council.

ruse a trick, e.g. Can you think up a *ruse* for getting Jean out of the room for a moment?

rush a plant like giant grass, that grows beside water (it was used ages ago for covering floors and is still used for weaving chair-seats, baskets, etc.) ■ If you *rush* about so wildly you may knock someone over.

russet a reddish-brown colour. ■ A *russet* apple is soft, sweet and reddish-brown in colour.

Russia a country in the east of Europe, and part of the U.S.S.R. (Union of Socialist Soviet Republics).

Russian a citizen of Russia, or the language of Russia; ■ *Russian* music, *Russian* rockets and *Russian* boots are well known.

Russians the people of Russia, e.g. The *Russians* love dancing.

rust If iron is left exposed to damp air it will *rust* away to powder. ■ the yellow-brown surface that forms on iron if it is left in damp air.

rustic a man of the countryside. ■ *Rustic* structures (e.g. arches, summer-houses, bridges) are made not of planks of wood, but of logs, whole or cut down the middle.

rustle As the wind blows you can hear the leaves *rustle* in the trees.

rusty Iron becomes *rusty* (covered with rust) if left in the damp.

rut Each cart wheel makes a *rut* in the mud as it goes along.

ruthless pitiless, e.g. This *ruthless* general burnt down a building, regardless of the women and children in it.

rye a grain (like wheat or barley), grown for breadmaking or cattle food in lands too cold for wheat.

rye

S

Sabbath the day of the week set apart for religious services and rest: Sunday for Christians, Saturday for Jews.

sabotage intentional damage to machinery, etc. ■ To *sabotage* machinery, etc., is to damage it intentionally, e.g. because it belongs to an enemy.

sabre a curved sword for use by horse-soldiers.

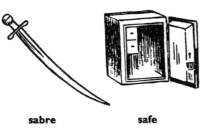

sabre   safe

saccharine If sugar makes you too fat, you can sweeten your drinks with little tablets of *saccharine* instead.

sack a big bag of rough cloth in which coal, potatoes, etc., are carried. ■ To get the *sack* is to lose your job. ■ To *sack* a workman is to stop employing him. ■ Soldiers used to *sack* cities that they had captured (i.e. take all the valuables).

sacred holy, e.g. The cow is a *sacred* animal to Hindus (i.e. their religion requires them to be specially careful not to harm cows).

sacrifice the killing of an animal as an offering to a god; ■ the giving up of something in a good cause.

sacrilege the wrong treatment of holy things, e.g. to hold a boxing match in a church would be *sacrilege*.

sad not happy.

saddle When riding a bicycle or a horse you sit on the *saddle*. ■ To *saddle* a horse you put a saddle on his back.

sadly unhappily, e.g. Pat walked *sadly* home, carrying her injured puppy.

sadness unhappiness.

safe not in danger. ■ You store meat in a *safe* to protect it from flies. ■ People keep their jewels, money, and important papers in a steel *safe* to protect them from robbers and fire.

safeguard Polly wears that lifejacket as a *safeguard* against drowning if she falls into the river.

safely You may *safely* cross the road now that the policeman has held up the traffic.

safety Children can bathe in *safety* in the shallow water of the pool.

safety-pin A *safety-pin* is so shaped that it cannot easily prick you.

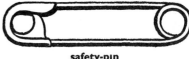

safety-pin

sag A hammock will *sag* in the middle if someone lies in it.

sage a plant with grey-green leaves which are used to flavour food; ■ a very wise man.

sago A *sago* pudding is made of milk and sago. ■ *Sago* looks like tiny balls of jelly when cooked.

said 'Hullo, Mary,' *said* Jack.

sail The ship's *sail* is spread out to catch the wind. ■ Ships can *sail* well in this fresh wind. ■ The liner will *sail* (go) at noon.

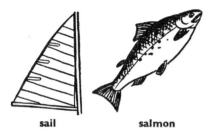

sail   salmon

sailing A *sailing* ship is one that is driven by sails, not by an engine. ■ Ships of all kinds are *sailing* from London every day.

sailor A *sailor* works on a ship. ■ A bad *sailor* is someone who is sea-sick even when the sea is not very rough.

saint (usually shortened to *St* or *S*) holy person, e.g. *St* George, *Saint* Peter.

sake Please do it for my *sake* (i.e. for me).

salad Sometimes for dinner we have with our meat a *salad*, made of such raw green-stuffs as lettuce, water-cress, tomatoes, etc.

salary Dad receives a *salary* of £2,000 a year for his work.

sale If things are for *sale*, you may buy them. ■ When a shop has a *sale*, things are sold at specially low prices.

salesman a man whose job is selling things, especially in a shop.

salient A *salient* point is one that is specially noticeable because it juts out.

saliva the liquid always present in your mouth.

sallow The missing person has dark hair and a *sallow* skin (i.e. his skin is dirty-looking, yellowish-brown).

salmon a fish with pink flesh, and tasty to eat.

saloon a large room in a public house, hotel, ship, etc. ■ A *saloon* car has a covered-in body (i.e. the roof does not fold back).

salt Sea water tastes of *salt*. ■ Vegetables such as potatoes taste better if cooked in *salt* water.

salutary A *salutary* punishment is one that has good results.

salutation a group of words which are used to greet someone, e.g. 'How are you?'

salute Soldiers *salute* by raising their right hands to their foreheads.

salvage to save things from a fire or a shipwreck, etc., e.g. The crew were able to *salvage* some of the cargo of their wrecked ship.

salvation the saving of a person from sin or danger. ■ The *Salvation* Army was formed to bring religion to people in the streets.

same I'm tired of reading the *same* book every day; I'd like to try another one.

sample Many firms give away small quantities of their produce as *samples*, so that people can try them before buying. ■ To *sample* anything is to try it (e.g. eat it) to see what it is like.

sanction My dad will not *sanction* (permit) such a mad scheme. ■ They cannot marry without the court's *sanction* (permission).

sanctuary the holiest part of a church, near the altar; ■ a place of safety.

sand When we go to the seaside Billy loves to dig in the *sand* on the beach.

sandal a simple kind of shoe which is just a sole kept on the foot by straps.

sandal   sandwich

sandwich To make a ham *sandwich* you put a slice of ham between two slices of bread.

sandy A *sandy* beach is one with plenty of sand on it. ■ *Sandy* hair is sand-coloured (pale ginger).

sane sensible, e.g. Jim is not mad; he is as *sane* as any other normal person.

sanitary A thing that is *sanitary* is free from dirt and disease.

sanitation The builders of those old houses didn't bother about *sanitation* (i.e. they didn't put proper drains, lavatories, etc., in them).

sanity being sane, e.g. Bruce behaved in such a strange way that we had doubts about his *sanity*.

sank The ship filled with water and *sank* to the bottom of the sea.

sapphire a precious stone like a blue diamond.

sarcasm an unkind, hurtful remark.

sarcastic To be *sarcastic* is to say unkind things intended to hurt someone.

sardine a small fish, usually sold in a small tin in which many of them are packed tightly together.

sash a broad strip of material worn round the waist or over one shoulder. ■ You slide the window frames up and down to open and shut a *sash* window.

sash   sash window

Satan the devil.

satchel The *satchel* containing your school books has a strap by which you can carry it on your shoulder.

satellite The big *satellite* going round our earth is the moon, but there are also smaller man-made *satellites* which have been put into orbit by rockets.

satin a silk material that is glossy on one side and dull on the other.

satisfaction Bill has the *satisfaction* of knowing that his efforts saved the boy's life.

satisfactory good enough, i.e. neither good nor bad.

satisfied I am *satisfied* with my painting (i.e. it is as good as I could expect it to be). ■ A *satisfied* customer is one who has no complaints.

satisfy To *satisfy* a need is to provide whatever it is that is needed. ■ To *satisfy* a person is to give him all that he wants.

satisfying After a *satisfying* meal you no longer feel hungry.

saturate This heavy rain will *saturate* our clothes (i.e. make them as wet as they can be).

saturated Billy was pulled out of the pond with his clothes *saturated* with water (i.e. as wet as they could be).

Saturday the last day of the week.

Saturn the planet which has a flat ring round it; ■ an ancient Roman god.

sauce Tomato *sauce*, mint *sauce*, etc., are eaten with food to make it more tasty. ■ Billy had the *sauce* (cheek) to ask the lady for his ball back after it had broken her window.

saucepan The potatoes are to be cooked in that *saucepan* of water boiling on the stove.

satellite   Saturn

saucer A tea-cup should stand in a *saucer*.

saucy cheeky. A *saucy* child does not show proper respect for older people.

saunter Children who *saunter* along to school as slowly as that are usually late.

sausage(s) Before you fry the *sausages* for dinner, prick the skins, or they may burst.

sausages   saw

savage an uncivilized human being, who is likely to do cruel things. ■ A *savage* animal is a fierce one.

savagely The criminals *savagely* beat the man about the head with clubs.

save Do not spend your money now; *save* it for another day. ■ Pat dived into the river to *save* a child who was drowning.

savings money that you have saved up, e.g. Bob took his *savings* out of the bank to buy a bicycle.

saviour someone who saves you (from harm, etc.). ■ To Christians, Jesus Christ is The *Saviour*.

savoury A *savoury* smell (or dish, etc.) is one that makes you feel hungry. ■ *Savouries* are foods which are not sweet, e.g. cheese.

savoy a kind of cabbage with crinkled leaves.

saw I *saw* that picture yesterday. ■ You cut wood by forcing a *saw* backwards and forwards through it. ■ To *saw* wood is to cut it with a saw.

sawdust tiny pieces of wood, like powder, made by using a saw.

sawn When you have *sawn* through that piece of wood, put the saw back in its place.

Saxon(s) About the 6th century, England was invaded by the *Saxons* who came from Germany. ■ The *Saxon* invaders settled in England.

saxophone a musical instrument made popular by jazz musicians.

scald If you spill hot liquid on your skin it will *scald* you (i.e. cause a burn).

scale Sing up the *scale* from bottom 'doh' to top 'doh'. ■ The *scale* of the map is 1 inch to the mile. ■ To *scale* a wall is to climb it.

scales You use *scales* for weighing things. ■ The *scales* which cover fish are like tiny pieces of thin bone which overlap.

saxophone   scabbard

scales   fish scales

say I cannot hear what you *say*; speak louder.

saying Just as the speaker was *saying*, 'Down with it!' the ceiling fell on him. ■ a well-known remark or proverb, e.g. One English *saying* is: 'Rain before seven, fine before eleven.'

scab A hard, dry *scab* forms over a sore place as it heals.

scabbard A man carries his sword in a *scabbard* strapped to his side.

scaffold a platform on which criminals were put to death.

scaffolding the structure on which workmen stand while building a house, etc.

scalp the hair and skin of the top of the head. ■ Red Indians used to *scalp* their enemies (i.e. cut off their scalps).

scaly A *scaly* creature is one which has scales, like a fish or a lizard.

scamp a rather unsatisfactory person. ('*Scamp*' is usually used in a playful, kind way, e.g. You lucky *scamp*!) ■ To *scamp* a job is to do it carelessly.

scamper To *scamper* (off) is suddenly to rush away, like a frightened animal.

scampered The animal *scampered* (rushed suddenly) off when Jack threw a stone at it.

scandal gossip about someone's wrong behaviour, e.g. You shouldn't listen to *scandal*. ■ The way that official wastes public money is a *scandal* (i.e. it is so disgraceful that everyone is talking about it).

scandalous disgraceful, shameful.

scant hardly any, e.g. Tom paid *scant* attention to his father's words.

scanty Jane's *scanty* clothing was insufficient to keep her warm.

scapegoat a person who takes the blame for someone else's misbehaviour.

scar Though the wound has healed up, there will always be a *scar* on your skin to show where the injury was.

scarce Strawberries are *scarce* in January (there are hardly any about).

scarcely only just, e.g. The animal is so young that it can *scarcely* walk. I had *scarcely* got into bed when the fire bell rang.

scare to frighten. ■ To give someone a *scare* is to frighten him. ■ During the war there was a *scare* about enemy landings (i.e. many people were afraid of this happening).

scarecrow a dummy made to look like a ragged man, and set up in a field to frighten away birds.

scarf a long strip of material worn round the neck.

scarlet a bright orange-red colour, like the colour of poppies and letter-boxes. ■ The *scarlet* pimpernel is a little wild flower of this colour.

scarred The boxer has a *scarred* face (i.e. there are scars on it).

scarves You know which girls go to our school by the *scarves* they wear round their necks.

scathing A *scathing* remark is one intended to make someone feel foolish.

scatter Mice *scatter* in all directions when a cat appears. ■ To *scatter* seeds is to throw them around over a wide area (i.e. not sow them in rows).

scene In our Christmas play, the *scene* is a stable in Bethlehem.

scenery You go to a beauty spot because of the *scenery* to be seen there (i.e. the trees, lakes, hills, etc.). ■ Painted *scenery* is used by people acting a play to make the stage look like the place where the events are supposed to be happening.

scent smell, e.g. A blind man knows roses by their *scent*. ■ To *scent* something is to become aware of it because of its smell.

scented I love the smell of *scented* soap, *scented* bath cubes, etc.

sceptre the ornamental stick held by kings and queens at their coronation.

schedule Our aircraft arrived on *schedule* (i.e. at the time set out in the timetable).

scarecrow   sceptre

scheme 308 **scorching**

scheme plan, e.g. Joe has a *scheme* for raising the money we need. ■ To *scheme* is to plot or to make plans. ■ The colour *scheme* of a room, etc., is the plan according to which the colours are chosen.

scholar a person who has learnt a great deal, especially from books; ■ a schoolboy or schoolgirl.

scholarship great amount of knowledge, e.g. The professor was famous for his *scholarship.* ■ money, to be spent on his education, that a student may win by passing an exam.

school Children go to *school* to learn.

schooner a sailing ship with at least two masts.

schooner

science People who study *science* learn about nature; i.e. about plants and animals, rocks, chemicals, the stars, etc. (They learn by watching carefully and by doing experiments, etc.)

scientific *Scientific* experiments are carried out by scientists to find out more about the world we live in.

scientifically To do experiments *scientifically* is to carry them out in a thorough way.

scientist a person who knows a great deal about one (or more) of the sciences, especially physics, chemistry, biology or astronomy.

scissors You cut paper, cloth, etc., with a pair of *scissors*.

scissors   toy scooter

scoff Do not *scoff* at (make fun of) the native cures; you may be glad to try them one day.

scold to nag, e.g. If I do that, Mother will *scold* me (in slang, tell me off).

scone a small, soft, plain cake, usually eaten with butter.

scoop The buckets on the dredger *scoop* up mud from the river bottom and dump it in a barge.

scooter a toy on which a child stands with one foot while he pushes himself along with the other foot; ■ a kind of small motorcycle.

scope In that job there is no *scope* for a boy who wants to get on (i.e. a boy has no chance to show what he can do).

scorch to burn the surface, leaving a mark, e.g. The fire will *scorch* your shirt if you hang it so close.

scorching The crops in the fields were burnt by the *scorching* sun.

score twenty (20). ■ At the football match the *score* is 3 goals to 2. ■ To *score* a goal you have to get the ball between those posts.

scorn To treat a suggestion, etc., with *scorn* is to speak of it as too stupid to be taken seriously.

scornful His answer was a *scornful* laugh (i.e. a laugh that showed his scorn).

Scot a native of Scotland.

Scotch *Scotch* whisky, *Scotch* broth, etc., are from Scotland.

scot-free To let someone off *scot-free* is to let him go without punishing or hurting him.

Scotland the country to the north of England.

Scottish *Scottish* things, or *Scottish* people are those from (of) Scotland.

scoundrel a man of bad character, but not necessarily a criminal.

scour To get that saucepan clean you'll have to *scour* it (rub it hard).

scourge To *scourge* someone is to beat him with a whip (in Bible stories, chiefly).

scouring You can clean dirty pans by rubbing them with *scouring* powder.

scout a man sent ahead of the main body of soldiers, travellers, etc., to see that the way is safe. ■ Boys who belong to the Boy *Scouts* try to do a good deed each day.

scowl to screw up your face because you are annoyed, or are thinking deeply.

scramble The boys managed to *scramble* ashore just as the boat sank. ■ You *scramble* an egg by cooking it in a saucepan while stirring in butter, milk, etc.

scrambled You can make *scrambled* egg by cooking it in a saucepan while stirring in butter, milk, etc.

scrambling George is *scrambling* up the rough hillside as fast as he can. ■ Mary is *scrambling* eggs for breakfast (i.e. making scrambled eggs).

scrap There is not a *scrap* of food left; we've eaten it all. ■ A *scrapbook* is a collection of cut-out pictures, stuck in a book. ■ To *scrap* anything is to throw it away because it is of no use. ■ (slang) To *scrap* (■ or to have a *scrap*) is to fight.

scrape To *scrape* potatoes is to scratch off their skins. *Scrape* the mud off your shoes with this knife. ■ To *scrape* through an exam is to pass by only a few marks. ■ I can *scrape* up 50p (i.e. it is difficult to find that much).

scraper Scrape the mud off your shoes on the *scraper* outside the door. ■ You use a *scraper* to scratch wall-paper or paint off a wall.

scratch That cat will *scratch* you with its claws, ■ and the *scratch* may bleed. ■ If a place itches you want to *scratch* it. ■ To start from *scratch* is to start at the very beginning.

scrawl to write untidily; ■ untidy writing.

scream We heard an ear-splitting *scream* from the terrified girl.

screech a harsh scream, e.g. the *screech* of an owl or a parrot.

screen In a cinema the pictures are shown on a big, white *screen*. ■ Nurses stand a *screen* round a hospital bed to prevent people seeing the patient.

screw You get a steel *screw* into a piece of wood by turning it round and round with a screwdriver. ■ To *screw* things together is to fasten them with a screw.

screw   screwdriver

screw-driver a tool for turning a screw by the slot or cross in the head.

scribble to write quickly or carelessly.

scribe a writer, lawyer or teacher (in Bible stories, chiefly).

script handwriting – usually of the kind that is like print.

scripture In *scripture* lessons the class learn about the Bible and religion.

scroll a roll of paper or parchment with writing on it (used before books were made); ■ a decoration in the shape of a scroll, on stone or wood, or in a drawing.

scrub To clean the floor Polly had to *scrub* it (i.e. rub it with soap and water, using a stiff brush).

scrubbing You can clean dirty floors by *scrubbing* them. ■ Use a *scrubbing*-brush for scrubbing floors.

scruff To take anyone by the *scruff* of the neck is to grab him by the back of his neck.

scrupulous very careful not to be dishonest or unfair in any way.

scrutinize The officials at the doors *scrutinize* (look carefully at) all the tickets.

scuffle During the *scuffle* with the thieves a button was torn off the policeman's coat.

scull an oar, used usually with another one, to row a boat. ■ To *scull* is to row a boat.

scullery the room in a house in which the washing-up, etc., is done.

sculptor an artist who makes things such as statues, out of clay or stone.

sculpture A piece of *sculpture* is something such as a statue, carved out of stone, or made in clay, etc.

scum Sometimes the impurities in a liquid rise to the top and form a *scum* on the surface.

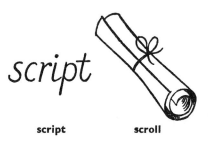

script   scroll

scurry The mice *scurry* away as soon as the cat appears.

scurvy a disease that old-time seamen used to get because they didn't eat fresh vegetables or fruit.

scuttle   We keep small quantities of coal indoors, beside the fire, in a coal-*scuttle*. ■ To *scuttle* a ship is to open holes in it so that it sinks.

scythe   a large, curved blade on a long handle, used, with two hands, for cutting grass, nettles, etc.

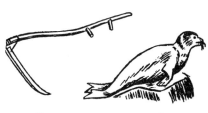

scythe   **seal**

sea   Our ship sailed across the *sea* to another land.

seafarer   a sailor, or anyone who has spent much of his life at sea.

seafaring   A *seafaring* man is a sailor.

sea-gull   a (usually) grey sea-bird with long wings, often seen over land, especially in cold weather.

seal   a large sea animal with a furry skin. ■ To *seal* an envelope, etc., is to stick it down, especially with sealing wax.

seam   the line along which two pieces of material are sewn together.

seaman   a sailor.

seamless   A *seamless* garment is one that has no seams (joins) in it.

seaport   Big ships load or unload at a *seaport* such as Liverpool or Hamburg.

search   I must *search* for that lost money until I find it.

seashore   Holiday-makers love to picnic on the *seashore* where they can see and hear the sea.

seaside   In hot weather we love to go to the *seaside* to bathe and play on the beach.

season   Spring is the first *season* of the year; the other *seasons* are summer, autumn, and winter. ■ To *season* food is to put in it such flavourings as salt and pepper.

seasonable   *Seasonable* weather is weather that is right for the season, e.g. snow is *seasonable* in winter, but not in summer.

seasonal   *Seasonal* weather is the kind of weather that always occurs in the same season of the year.

seasoning   Food tastes better if you add *seasoning* such as salt or pepper.

seat   There wasn't an empty *seat* in the bus so I had to stand. ■ We can *seat* 500 people in our school hall.

seaweed   plants that grow in the sea.

seaworthy   If a boat is *seaworthy* it is safe to go to sea in it.

secluded   The boys found a *secluded* part of the beach where they could undress for bathing (i.e. a place where other people were not likely to come).

second   The *second* day of the week is Monday. ■ Sixty *seconds* make a minute.

secondary   Children over the age of eleven go to *secondary* schools.

second-hand   A *second-hand* car is one that is not new when you buy it.

secondly We're going to Sand-beach for our holidays first because it has a sandy beach, and *secondly* because our friends will be there.

secrecy The work was done with great *secrecy* so that no one would know about it.

secret This is a *secret* between Billy and me, so no one else knows about it. ■ The treasure is kept in a *secret* hiding place, known only to the gang.

secretary The *secretary* of a club is the person who keeps the records and writes the letters.

secretive A *secretive* person is one who does not tell other people anything if he can avoid it.

sect a group of people who have broken away from a church (or some other organization) because they have some special beliefs of their own.

section A *section* of the railway (i.e. part of it) is to be closed. ■ A bamboo cane is divided into *sections* by rings going round it every 30 cm or so.

sector the part of a circle between any two straight lines drawn from the centre to the edge.

sector

secular not religious, e.g. a *secular* song (not a hymn).

secure safe, e.g. Here in this fortress we are *secure* from attack. ■ to get (something that you are pleased to have), e.g. I hope to *secure* front seats at the concert.

securely Be sure that all your doors and windows are *securely* (safely) fastened before you go away on holiday.

security safety, e.g. Spies are a threat to our country's *security*. ■ A *security* man's job is to safeguard property or valuables.

sedate Betty is a *sedate* girl (i.e. she would not behave noisily or wildly).

sediment the tiny solid pieces that settle to the bottom of a liquid when it is still.

seed If you plant a *seed* in suit-able soil it will grow into a new plant.

seedling a young plant grown from a seed.

seedsman If you need seeds to plant in your garden, you buy them from a *seedsman*.

seedy To feel *seedy* is to feel un-well. ■ A *seedy* (looking) person is one who doesn't look respectable.

seek When you play hide and *seek*, one person hides and the others look for him.

seem The conjurer may *seem* to be cutting the girl in halves, but he isn't really.

seen I have *seen* the new girl, so I know what she looks like.

seer a person who can tell you what is going to happen in the future.

seesaw You can make a *seesaw* by putting a plank across a fallen tree-trunk, so that two children, one at each end, can rock up and down on it.

seesaw

seethe to boil or to be in violent movement like a boiling liquid, e.g. The rivers *seethe* as thousands of fish struggle in the fishermen's traps.

seize to take, e.g. Customs officers can *seize* smuggled goods. ■ I shall *seize* the first chance of going up in a rocket.

seldom not often, e.g. Pat *seldom* smiles; she is usually too sad.

select When you *select* a team you pick out the people most suitable for it.

selection We left the *selection* (picking) of the team to the captain. ■ These songs are not a very good *selection*; who picked them?

self Your*self* is you, my*self* is me. ■ In a *self*-service store, the customer takes goods from the shelves for himself.

self-conscious A *self-conscious* person is one who is uncomfortable and nervous in the company of other people (because he thinks about himself too much).

selfish It is *selfish* to want all your own way and not to consider the wishes of other people.

selfishness wanting your own way regardless of the wishes of other people.

self-respect No one who has *self-respect* would lower himself to do anything mean or shameful.

self-same The bird nesting in our garden this year is the *self-same* one that has nested there for the past five years.

sell The salesman offered to *sell* me the watch for £5.

semblance There is no *semblance* of life in the animal (i.e. it seems to be dead).

semicircle a half-circle.

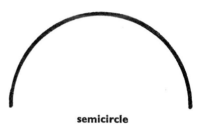

semicircle

semi-conscious half conscious. A person who is *semi-conscious* is not in full possession of his senses.

semolina hard grains of flour, which are cooked in milk, etc., to make *semolina* pudding.

send I will *send* you a post card while I am away on holiday.

sender The *sender* of a letter, etc., is the person who has sent it.

senile old and weak. A person who is *senile* is unable to look after himself.

senior I am 12 and Bob is 14, so he is my *senior* by 2 years. ■ The *senior* partner (in a business, etc.) is the one who is more important.

sensation 'Pins and needles' is a prickly *sensation* in some part of the body.

sensational A *sensational* story is one likely to excite people.

sense There is no *sense* in running for a train that has gone. ■ Auntie has no *sense* of smell so she did not know that the gas was escaping. (People have five *senses*: sight, hearing, smell, taste and touch.)

senseless The rock fell on the man's head and he fell *senseless* to the ground. ■ It is *senseless* to run for a train that has gone.

sensible Philip is a *sensible* boy (i.e. he doesn't do silly things).

sensibly Philip very *sensibly* wrote down the number of the car in which the robbers escaped.

sensitive A *sensitive* person is one who is easily hurt or offended by things that people do or say. ■ A *sensitive* instrument is one that will measure very small quantities, e.g. A balance is a scale so *sensitive* that it can weigh a hair.

sent Have you received the letter I *sent* you last week?

sentence When you write a *sentence*, you must begin with a capital letter and end with a full stop. ■ The criminal is serving a *sentence* of six months in prison.

sentiment feeling, e.g. Jane feels that the boys are rough and noisy, and those are Mary's *sentiments*, too.

sentimental Mother is very *sentimental* (i.e. it is easy to make her cry or laugh, or show sympathy, etc.).

sentinel, sentry a soldier who keeps guard.

separate At the corner the boys *separate* – one goes to the right and the other to the left; ■ i.e. they go their *separate* ways.

separately The headmaster wishes to see the boys *separately* (i.e. one at a time).

separation A Bible parable tells of the *separation* of the sheep from the goats (the sheep go to one place and the goats to another).

September the ninth month of the year.

septic If you get dirt into a wound it becomes *septic* (i.e. poisonous matter forms in it).

sequel The *sequel* to Dad's accident came much later, when he received a bill for the repair of the gate he had hit.

sequence I will give you the *sequence* of events (i.e. tell you, in their correct order, all the things that happened).

serenade In some countries a girl's lover will stand beneath her window playing and singing a *serenade* to her.

serene calm and peaceful.

serf In ancient times, a *serf* was forced to work on his lord's land, almost as a slave.

sergeant The *sergeant* in charge of a group of soldiers (or policemen, etc.) can be recognized by the three stripes on his sleeve.

serial a story that is printed in a paper or a magazine in instalments.

series a number of things that follow each other in some kind of order, e.g. a *series* of crimes.

serious This is no laughing matter, so you must be *serious*.

seriously To take something *seriously* is to give it careful thought, and not treat it as a joke.

sermon In church last Sunday the clergyman preached a *sermon* (i.e. gave a religious talk) about loving our enemies.

serpent a snake.

servant If you are rich you can pay a *servant* to do things for you – especially jobs about the house, such as cleaning or cooking.

serve To *serve* (up) food, etc., is to bring it to people at the table. ■ It *serves* you right (i.e. you deserve the unpleasant thing that has happened to you). ■ Mother likes shops where there are assistants to *serve* her (i.e. get her the things that she wishes to buy).

service Each Sunday Mary goes to the morning *service* at church. ■ The job of the Fire *Service* is to put out fires.

serviceable A *serviceable* garment, etc., is one that will wear well.

serviette You put a *serviette* on your lap during a meal so that if you drop food it won't go on your clothes.

serving The shop assistant is *serving* a customer. ■ A *serving* hatch is a gap in a wall through which food is passed.

session a meeting of a court, etc. The court is in *session* (i.e. its members have assembled).

settee A *settee* is like an easy chair, but wide enough to seat several people at a time.

setting To see the *setting* sun you must look in the west. ■ frame, background, e.g. The trees make a lovely *setting* for the old church.

settle I hope the boys *settle* their quarrel and become friends. ■ We shall not move house again because we've decided to *settle* here. ■ Let the water remain still and the mud will *settle* to the bottom.

settled Dad *settled* the argument about Billy's weight by weighing him. ■ Ivan's grandfather was a Russian who *settled* in England years ago.

settlement a place where settlers in a new country live.

settler a person who settles down (to live) in a new country.

seven (7) one more than six.

seventeen (17) ten and seven.

seventeenth (17th) The *seventeenth* day of the month is the day after the sixteenth. ■ ($\frac{1}{17}$) If you divide anything into 17 equal parts, each part is a *seventeenth*.

seventh (7th) The *seventh* day of the week is Saturday. ■ (7) Seven *sevenths* make one whole one.

seventieth (70th) Sixty-nine boys have arrived; the next will be the *seventieth*. ■ ($\frac{1}{70}$) Seventy *seventieths* make one whole one.

seventy (70) seven tens.

sever You can *sever* a rope, etc. by cutting through it with a knife.

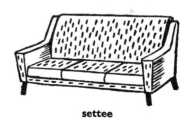

settee

M

several a small number, but more than two, e.g. *Several* boys were injured.

severe John has a *severe* (bad) cold. ■ Don't be *severe* (strict) with Brian; he is only a little boy. ■ A *severe* design is a plain one.

severely The naughty boys were *severely* punished (i.e. it was punishment suited to a serious offence).

severity We cannot play out of doors owing to the *severity* of the weather (i.e. the weather is too cold, or too stormy).

sew (pron. so) Take a needle and cotton and *sew* this button on your coat.

sewage The *sewage* from baths, sinks, lavatories, etc., runs away through a network of pipes under our streets.

sewer a big underground pipe through which sewage runs.

sewing (pron. so-ing) The quickest way to sew is with a *sewing* machine. ■ When you have finished *sewing*, put away your needle and cotton.

sewn (pron. sown) When you have *sewn* the button on your coat, put away the needle and cotton.

sex The *sex* of women and girls is female; men and boys are of the male *sex*.

sextant an instrument used by sailors to find their position at sea.

sexton A church employs a *sexton* to look after the building, and to ring the bell, etc.

sexual to do with sex.

shabby A garment that is *shabby* needs mending, or cleaning, etc. ■ To play a *shabby* trick is to do something deceitful to somebody.

shack a roughly-made hut.

shade It is too hot in the sun; let us sit under these trees in the *shade*. ■ You put a lamp-*shade* over the light so that it doesn't shine in people's eyes. ■ Tom put his hand over his eyes to *shade* them from the bright sun.

shadow When you stand in the sun, your body casts a *shadow* of you on the ground.

shady A *shady* corner, etc., is one that is shaded from the sun (or some other light). ■ A *shady* person is one who seems to be dishonest.

shaft A mine *shaft* is the hole leading down into a mine. ■ A *shaft* of light is a long, narrow beam. ■ The *shaft* of a spear is the long pole which is the handle.

shaggy A *shaggy* dog, horse, etc., is one with long, untidy hair.

shake People *shake* hands as a sign of friendship. ■ You *shake* a medicine bottle to mix up the medicine in it.

shaky People who are old or nervous often have *shaky* hands (i.e. their hands tremble).

shall I (we) *shall* come (i.e. that is what I expect to do). ■ He (you, they) *shall* come (i.e. he will, if necessary, be made to come).

sextant

shallow The depth of water in the swimming baths is 8 ft at the deep end and 3 ft at the *shallow* end.

sham Our dog will *sham* lameness (pretend to be lame) if he wants to be picked up.

shambling The gang of boys are *shambling* along the street (i.e. shuffling along in a lazy way). ■ A person may have a *shambling* walk because he is lame.

shame the unhappy feeling that you have as a result of behaving badly. ■ It is a *shame* to leave the poor old man out there in the snow.

shameful A *shameful* act is one of which you ought to be ashamed.

shamming Dick isn't really asleep; he is *shamming* (pretending to be).

shampoo a special liquid or powder for washing hair. ■ To *shampoo* your hair is to wash it. ■ Having a *shampoo* is washing your hair.

shamrock a kind of clover, the national emblem of Ireland.

shamrock

shan't (short for) shall not. I *shan't* be long (I'll soon be back).

shanty a hut; ■ a song sung by sailors in sailing ships, to help them to do their work of pulling, pumping, etc., in time with each other.

shape A wheel has the same *shape* as the letter 'O'. ■ To *shape* something is to make it, especially to model it in clay, etc.

shapeless A *shapeless* object is one that has no particular shape.

shapely A *shapely* object is one of pleasing shape.

share If you *share* things among a number of people, each of them will have some. ■ The amount that each person thus has is his *share*. ■ When a person buys *shares* in a business, he pays some money in order to own part of it and therefore share in its profits. ■ The plough*share* is the blade of the plough, the part that cuts through the soil.

ploughshare   shark

sharing Mother is *sharing* the cakes among the boys to make sure that every boy gets some.

shark a big, savage fish that feeds on other fish, and sometimes attacks people who are in the water.

sharp a sign (♯) put beside a note in music, to make it a half-note higher. ■ You cannot cut with a knife if it isn't *sharp* ■ Bill is a *sharp* boy (i.e. he is quick to understand things).

sharpen To *sharpen* a knife is to make it sharp by rubbing it on a stone, etc. You *sharpen* a pencil by cutting the end to a point.

sharpener I cannot sharpen a pencil with a knife; I use a pencil *sharpener*.

shatter We saw the glass in the shop window *shatter* into a thousand pieces as the thief threw a brick at it.

shave If Dad didn't *shave* every day he would have a beard. ■ To have a narrow *shave* is to escape death or injury by the skin of your teeth.

shaving Dad looks in his *shaving* mirror ■ while *shaving* the hair off his face.

shawl A lady wears a *shawl* over her shoulders to keep her warm.

shawl   sheaf

sheaf an armful of cut corn tied together by the stalks.

shears a tool which works like a large pair of scissors; used to cut hedges, or the wool off sheep, etc.

shears

sheath a close-fitting cover such as that in which a dagger or sword is kept.

sheathe To *sheathe* a sword or a knife, etc., is to put it in its sheath.

sheaves Each man brought a sheaf of corn, so we had four *sheaves* altogether.

shed Tom keeps his bicycle in a wooden *shed* behind the house. ■ Many trees *shed* their leaves in autumn. ■ To *shed* blood is to cause it to flow. ■ To *shed* tears is to cry.

sheen a shine, like that on polished metal or on the feathers of some birds.

sheep Farmers keep *sheep* for their wool, or kill them for their meat (mutton).

sheep

sheepish A *sheepish* person is one who is uncomfortable and awkward, through shyness.

sheer *Sheer* silk is very thin silk. ■ A *sheer* cliff is quite upright, like the side of a house. ■ *Sheer* nonsense is complete nonsense.

sheet Write your letter on this *sheet* of paper. ■ In bed, we sleep between *sheets* made of cotton or linen.

sheik the chief of an Arab tribe.

shelf The book is on the top *shelf* of the bookcase.

shell the hard outside covering of an egg, or of a crab, snail, tortoise, etc. ■ A big gun fires a *shell* containing explosive.

shelter a place in which to take cover from the weather, e.g. a bus *shelter*; a place that gives protection from bombs, etc. ■ We must *shelter* from the rain or we shall get wet.

shelve To *shelve* a plan, etc., is to put it aside and not do anything about it for the time being.

shelves The *shelves* in the cupboard are to stand things on.

shelves

shepherd a man who looks after sheep.

sherbet a fizzy drink. ■ You can make a kind of sherbet from *sherbet* powder.

sheriff a man whose job is to keep law and order in a place – especially in towns shown in Western films.

sherry a Spanish wine, made from grapes.

shield A knight held a *shield* in front of his body as a protection against the blows aimed at him by his enemies. ■ Dad will *shield* us from danger, so we'll be quite safe.

shift The men on the night *shift* work from 10 p.m. to 6 a.m. ■ *Shift* that bag; it's in the way there.

shifty deceitful, unreliable.

shilling (1s.) old name for our 5p coin.

shimmer to shine with a faint, trembling light.

shin the front of your leg, between knee and ankle.

shine *Shine* your light in that dark corner so that we can see what is there. ■ To put a *shine* on shoes, etc., is to polish them.

shingle small stones. Some seaside beaches consist of nothing but *shingle*.

shining The sun is *shining* from a cloudless sky. ■ You can see by Mary's *shining* face that she is proud and happy.

shinned The boy *shinned* (climbed) up the tree.

shiny The door knob is so *shiny* that you can see your face in it.

ship A *ship* can carry many passengers and tons of goods across miles of sea. ■ To *ship* goods is to put them aboard a ship.

sheriff   shield

shipment The merchant has received a *shipment* of tea (i.e. a quantity of tea has arrived by ship).

shipshape Everything in the school must be *shipshape* when the visitors arrive (i.e. everything must be as it should be).

shipwreck The *shipwreck* was caused by the waves smashing the ship against a rock.

shire a county, e.g. Hamp*shire*. ■ A *shire* horse is a powerful cart horse.

shirk to get out of doing something that you ought to do.

shirker a person who tries to get out of something that he knows he ought to do.

shirt Under his jacket a boy wears a *shirt* made of some thin material.

shirt   shire horse

shiver to shake with cold, or with fear. ■ A *shiver* is a little trembling movement caused by cold or fear.

shivering Jane is *shivering* with cold so that her teeth are chattering.

shivery People often feel *shivery* (inclined to shake) if they are unwell or cold.

shoal a place where the sea is very shallow. ■ Fishermen at sea like to find a *shoal* (crowd) of fish before letting down their nets.

shock You get an electric *shock* if you touch a live wire. ■ To *shock* someone is to say or do something that upsets him very much.

shocking very bad, e.g. *shocking* behaviour.

shod The blacksmith *shod* that horse yesterday (i.e. fitted it with shoes).

shoddy a kind of cloth which is made partly of old rags. ■ A *shoddy* piece of work is not as good as it should be.

shoe Pat took off her left *shoe* because it was hurting her foot. ■ To *shoe* a horse is to put shoes on him.

shoes Let's take off our *shoes* and socks and go for a paddle. ■ A blacksmith *shoes* a horse by nailing iron shoes to its hoofs.

shone Tim *shone* his torch on the cave wall so that we could see the writing on it. ■ The sun *shone* down from the cloudless sky.

shook Dad *shook* hands with the visitor. ■ The bathers *shook* with cold. ■ The nurse *shook* the bottle to mix up the medicine in it.

shoot One way of killing a rat is to *shoot* it with a gun. ■ In spring a new *shoot* (growth) appeared on the tree. ■ When they fire the rocket it will *shoot* straight up into the sky.

shop You go to a *shop* to buy things. ■ To *shop* is to go to shops to buy things. ■ a work-place, e.g. a carpenter's *shop*.

shopkeeper the owner of a shop.

shopping You go *shopping* to buy things. ■ You carry the *shopping* that you have bought, ■ in a *shopping* basket.

shore Row the boat to the *shore* (land). ■ To *shore* a building is to put supports against it to hold it up.

shorn Sheep that have been *shorn* look naked without their wool.

short Dad is a *short* man (i.e. most men are taller than he is). ■ The shopkeeper gave me *short* change (less than I ought to have had).

shortage No one can have as many potatoes as he would like because there is a *shortage* of potatoes.

shorten To *shorten* anything is to make it less in length, or time, etc.

shortening Mary's skirt is too long so Mother is *shortening* it. ■ When making pastry Mother puts *shortening* (fat) in it.

shorthand If you know *shorthand* you can write down words as fast as people say them.

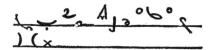

shorthand

shorthanded A hotel, shop, factory, etc., is *shorthanded* when there aren't enough people to do the work.

shortly Brian will return *shortly* (soon).

shortness At the end of the race we were all gasping through *shortness* of breath. ■ I get my knees wet when it rains because of the *shortness* of my mac.

shorts The only time Dad shows his knees is on holiday, when he wears *shorts* instead of his long trousers.

shorts shored-up building

short-sighted A *short-sighted* person cannot see things clearly unless they are close to him.

shot The hunter took aim with his gun and *shot* the animal through the head. ■ Lead *shot* consists of tiny balls of lead which are shot, many at a time, from sporting guns.

should I *should* have been run over if you hadn't pulled me back. ■ *Should* you be up so late at night?

shoulder the part of the body to which the arms are joined. ■ To *shoulder* a load is to put it on your shoulder to carry it.

shouldn't (short for) should not. *Shouldn't* you be in bed by now?

shout If you *shout*, people a long way away can hear what you say. ■ Dick's *shout*, 'Stop thief!' could be heard in the next street.

shove to push.

shovel You use a short-handled *shovel* for putting small quantities of coal on the fire and a long-handled *shovel* for loading sand into a barrow. ■ To *shovel* coal is to move it from one place to another with a shovel.

shovelful the amount of coal, sand, etc., that is contained in a shovel.

shovelfuls Take this shovel and put four *shovelfuls* of sand in that barrow.

shovelling Men spent all day *shovelling* away the snow that blocked the road (i.e. they used shovels to shift it).

show *Show* Mary the picture (i.e. let her see it). ■ I cannot do this sum; please *show* me how to do it. ■ something that people go to see, e.g. The Lord Mayor's *Show*, The Horse *Show*, etc.

shower A *shower* of rain doesn't last long.

showery On a *showery* day there are many short periods of rain.

shown We were *shown* a picture of a boy and asked if we knew him. ■ You were *shown* how to do that sum yesterday.

showy bright and colourful, e.g. a *showy* flower, a *showy* dress.

shrank The woolly *shrank* (got smaller) because it was washed badly. ■ The frightened child *shrank* (withdrew) into a corner.

shred a small piece or strip, e.g. Tom's coat was caught in the machine and torn to *shreds*. ■ To *shred* anything (e.g. suet, cheese, carrots, etc.) is to cut it into shreds.

shredded made or cut in shreds, e.g. *Shredded* Wheat, *shredded* suet.

shrew a mouse-like animal.

shrewd clever – especially at seeing beforehand the results likely to follow from doing something.

shriek We heard a *shriek* of

terror from the girls as they saw the horrible creature.

shrill A *shrill* sound is one that is high and loud.

shrimp a small, tasty sea creature with a hard skin and lots of legs.

shrine a holy place.

shrink Woollen clothes *shrink* (get smaller) if you wash them badly. ■ Why do you *shrink* back in fear?

shrivel to get small and dried up, e.g. Leaves *shrivel* when they die; apples *shrivel* if kept a long time.

shrivelled The plant *shrivelled* (up) and died under the hot sun.

shroud a garment put on a dead person.

Shrove *Shrove* Tuesday (Pancake Day) is the day before Ash Wednesday.

shrub a plant that is woody like a tree, but smaller.

shrubbery a piece of land planted out with shrubs.

shrug to lift up your shoulders as a sign that you don't care.

shrugged Bob *shrugged* his shoulders.

shrunk That woolly has *shrunk* (got smaller) because you washed it badly.

shrew   shrimp

shudder People *shudder* (tremble briefly) because of fear, cold, or disgust, e.g. I *shudder* to think what would happen to us if we fell into the hands of those savages.

shuffle To *shuffle* playing cards is to mix them up ready for play. ■ To *shuffle* your feet is to scrape them about on the floor.

shun To *shun* a person is to avoid meeting him.

shunned Peter is so bad tempered that he is *shunned* by everyone (i.e. everyone keeps out of his way).

shunt A railway engine goes backwards and forwards to *shunt* its trucks on to various different tracks.

shut People *shut* their eyes when they sleep. ■ *Shut* the gate or the cattle will stray from the field. ■ *Shut* your book and put it away.

shutter Many shopkeepers have wooden or metal *shutters* which they fix over their windows at closing time.

shutting 'And that's the end of the story,' said Joan, *shutting* the book as she spoke.

shuttle the part of a weaving machine, which carries the thread from side to side, or a similar part of a sewing machine.

shuttlecock a small light object with a circle of feathers in it, used in the game of badminton.

shy A *shy* person does not like meeting or talking with strangers. ■ A nervous horse will *shy* if you go near it (i.e. he will skip suddenly to one side).

shyness Because of her *shyness* Molly is unhappy at meeting or talking with people she doesn't know well.

sick A *sick* person is one who isn't well. ■ If you eat too much you may be *sick* (bring the food up again from your stomach). ■ I am *sick* (tired) of all this quarrelling.

sickening tiring and saddening. ■ The man's injuries were a *sickening* sight (i.e. they made me feel sick). ■ Brenda is *sickening* for an illness (she is becoming ill).

sickle a small curved blade on a handle, used one-handed for cutting corn, etc.

sickness Nothing but *sickness* (being ill) would keep Pat away from school.

side There is a head on one *side* of the coin. ■ To *side* with someone is to take his part (in a quarrel, etc.). ■ I have a pain in my *side*.

shutter shuttle shuttlecock sickle

side-line the line along the edge of a football pitch, etc. ■ Uncle is a fruit farmer; he keeps hens as a *side-line* (an extra).

sidesman The job of a church *sidesman* is to help the church-wardens by seeing people to their seats, taking up the collection, etc.

sideways A crab walks *sideways* (i.e. not forwards or backwards).

siding a short piece of railway track to one side of the main lines, where trucks may be unloaded or parked. ■ In this quarrel I am *siding* with Peter (i.e. I am agreeing with Peter).

sidle to go sideways, e.g. because you are too shy to walk straight towards someone.

siege The *siege* of a town consisted of surrounding it with an army to prevent food, etc., getting in, and so forcing the people in the town to surrender.

siesta People who live in hot countries have a *siesta* (rest) in the middle of the day.

sieve You shake things like ashes, etc., through a *sieve* to separate the larger pieces from the rest. ■ to shake things through a sieve.

sieve

signet

sift To *sift* ashes, etc., is to shake the material through a sieve to separate out the larger pieces.

sigh to take a deep breath because of tiredness or sadness, etc. ■ You breathe a *sigh* of relief when an expected disaster does not happen. ■ To *sigh* for something is to want it very badly.

sighing Are you *sighing* (taking deep breaths) because you are sad? ■

sight A person who has lost his *sight* is not able to see. ■ That garden is the most beautiful *sight* I have ever seen. ■ The first sailor to *sight* land called out, 'Land ho !'

sightseer someone who goes around seeing such things as famous buildings.

sign You *sign* your name at the bottom of a letter. ■ This *sign*, +, means add. ■ Dad nodded his head as a *sign* of agreement.

signal Traffic *signals* tell drivers when to stop and go. ■ A driver should *signal* his intention to turn by putting out his arm or by using his car indicator.

signaller A *signaller's* job in the army or navy was to send messages by lights, flags, etc.

signature You write your *signature* at the end of a letter, etc., as proof that it is from you.

signet a ring made with a flat surface (usually with initials, etc., cut into it) for pressing on to sealing wax to seal letters, etc.

significance What is the *significance* of that striped band round a policeman's sleeve? (i.e. what does it tell you?).

signify The striped band round

a policeman's sleeve is to *signify* (tell people) that he is on duty.

silence There is *silence* when no noise can be heard. ■ To *silence* anyone (anything) is to stop him (it) making a noise.

silent A place is *silent* when there is no noise there. ■ Be *silent*, Billy!

silhouette the dark outline of something seen against a light background.

silhouette

silk a fine, soft, shiny material, made from threads spun by silkworms.

silkworm a caterpillar that spins threads of silk.

silky A *silky* material is one that is like silk.

sill The window *sill* is the large stone or wooden base to the window frame.

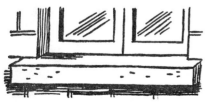

sill

silliness He showed his *silliness* by swimming too far out to sea (i.e. he did not think how dangerous and unwise it was).

silly unwise and thoughtless, e.g. Peter left his ice-cream on the radiator, a *silly* thing to do!

silt the mud, sand, etc., left by rivers, e.g. left on land when flood waters have dried up.

silver a precious, white, shiny metal used to make coins, ornaments, etc.

silver-plated *Silver-plated* articles are made of cheaper metal covered with a layer of silver.

similar like, e.g. Wheat is *similar* to barley.

similarity There is a *similarity* (likeness) between wheat and barley.

similarly The girls are *similarly* dressed, e.g. they are all wearing blouses and skirts of the same colours.

simmer to boil very gently.

simple Anyone can understand a *simple* problem. ■ The poor old man is *simple* (weak-minded).

simpleton a very silly person, a half-wit.

simplicity You mustn't take advantage of the old man's *simplicity* (i.e. the fact that he is simple).

simplify To *simplify* anything is to make it easier to understand.

simply It is easy to cook an egg: you *simply* boil it in water for four minutes.

simultaneously Thunder and lightning happen *simultaneously* (i.e. at the same moment).

sin something done, said, or thought which is wrong in the sight of God.

since Much has happened *since* the war (i.e. from the war up to now).

sincere A person who is *sincere* really means what he says, and is not deceitful.

sincerely I usually end letters to people I know with the words, 'Yours *sincerely*,' followed by my signature.

sincerity You have doubts about a person's *sincerity* if he laughs while saying, 'I'm sorry' (i.e. you doubt if he means what he says).

sinew a cord in the body which joins a muscle to a bone.

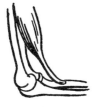

sinew   siphon

sinful A *sinful* person is one who has done wrong in the sight of God (not necessarily the same thing as breaking the law).

sing When people *sing* a song I like to hear both the words and music.

singe To *singe* hair (or feathers) is to burn the ends. ■ To *singe* cloth is to burn the surface, e.g. when ironing with an over-hot iron.

singeing That iron is too hot, for it is *singeing* the material you are ironing.

singer I like the song, but not the *singer* who is singing it.

singing When you are *singing*, people should be able to hear both the words and the music.

single A *single* man (or woman) is one who is not married. ■ A *single* bed is for one person only. ■ I haven't a *single* sweet left (i.e. not one).

singly The boys came forward *singly* (one at a time) to receive their prizes.

singular odd, unusual, e.g. A *singular* thing happened this morning. ■ The *singular* of the word 'boys' is 'boy'.

sinister wicked, evil, e.g. The bad man of the story is the *sinister* Mr. Woo.

sink A ship will *sink* if very much water gets into it. ■ We do the washing up in the kitchen *sink*.

sinner a person who has done wrong.

sip To *sip* a liquid is to drink it a little at a time, as you would very hot tea. ■ To take a *sip* is to take one such little drop.

siphon When you press the lever on a soda-water *siphon*, the fizzy liquid gushes out of a pipe.

sipped The tea was too hot to drink so I *sipped* it a little at a time.

siren an imaginary woman who, in ancient stories, so attracted sailors by her singing, that they ran their ships on to rocks. ■ During the war, air raid *sirens* made loud wailing noises to warn people of air raids.

sirloin A *sirloin* of beef is a tasty joint cut from between a bullock's ribs and hips.

sister Your *sister* is a girl who has the same parents as you. ■ A hospital *sister* is a nurse who is in charge of other nurses.

sit to rest on your bottom.

site The *site* of a building or town is the ground on which it stands. ■ A building *site* is (usually) ground on which a building is to be built.

sitting The bird is *sitting* on her eggs to hatch them. ■ Dick is *sitting* at the table having his dinner. ■ The house has three rooms downstairs, kitchen, dining-room and *sitting*-room.

situated The house is *situated* in Wood Street between the church and the café.

situation Describe the *situation* of your school (i.e. explain exactly where it is). ■ The explorers are in a dangerous *situation* (i.e. dangerous circumstances).

six (6) one more than five.

sixpence a small silver coin, once worth 6 old pennies, now worth $2\frac{1}{2}$p.

sixteen (16) ten and six.

sixteenth (16th) Fifteen boys have arrived, so the next will be the *sixteenth*. ■ ($\frac{1}{16}$) Sixteen *sixteenths* make a whole one.

sixth (6th) The *sixth* day of the week is Friday. ■ ($\frac{1}{6}$) Six *sixths* make one whole one.

sixtieth (60th) On his *sixtieth* birthday Grandad will have lived for sixty years. ■ ($\frac{1}{60}$) Sixty *sixtieths* make one whole one.

sixty (60) *Sixty* minutes make an hour.

size Jack takes *size* 10 in shoes. ■ Things that are the same *size* are as big as each other. ■ a sticky liquid painted on walls before papering them.

sizzle You can hear things such as sausages and bacon *sizzle* in the pan while they are frying.

sizzling You can hear the bacon *sizzling* in the frying pan. ■ (It is making a *sizzling* noise.)

skate to glide over ice ■ on *skates* (or over the floor on roller-*skates*); ■ a large flat-fish.

skates

skating People are *skating* on the ice. ■ A *skating* rink is a place where you may go to skate.

skein Hold out this *skein* (loop) of wool on your hands so that Mother can wind it off into a ball.

skein

skeleton When a body is dug up after many years, all the flesh has gone leaving only a *skeleton* (i.e. the bones).

sketch a rough drawing. ■ To *sketch* is to make a rough drawing.

skewer The butcher puts a *skewer* through a joint of meat to hold it together.

ski to glide down snow-covered slopes ■ on long, narrow boards called *skis*.

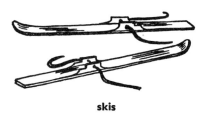

skis

skid When roads are slippery cars sometimes *skid* (slide). ■ The car went into a *skid* (slide) when the driver tried to stop it on the slippery road.

skies In Britain the *skies* are often cloudy.

skiff a light-weight rowing boat.

skiing Before you can go *skiing* on those snowy mountain slopes you will need some skis.

skilful A *skilful* person is one who is very good at doing something, e.g. a *skilful* artist, driver, mechanic.

skill You get the *skill* needed for doing something tricky (e.g. driving a racing car) by lots of careful practice.

skilled A *skilled* man is one who has been trained to do a particular job.

skim When you *skim* milk you take the thin layer of cream off the surface.

skimp to provide insufficient money, food, or material (for a dress, etc.).

skin There is a thin *skin* covering all parts of your body. ■ To *skin* an animal is to remove its skin. ■ We escaped by the *skin* of our teeth (i.e. we only just managed to escape).

skinned The hunter *skinned* the animal and hung the skin up to dry. ■ A thin-*skinned* person is one who easily takes offence.

skinny very thin (person or animal).

skip jump, e.g. Girls like to *skip* (i.e. to jump over a rope as they swing it under them).

skipper the captain of a ship or an aircraft, or of a football team, cricket team, etc.

skipping When you want to skip you use a *skipping* rope.

skirmish a fight between small numbers of soldiers.

skirt At school each girl wears a navy blue *skirt* and a white blouse. ■ To *skirt* a place is to go along the edge of it.

skirt

skittle *Skittles* is a game  in which nine *skittle* pins are set up to be knocked down by rolling a *skittle* ball at them – in a *skittle* alley.

skulk to hide, with the idea of misbehaving, or of avoiding your duty.

skull the bone of the head. A pirate's flag had a *skull* and cross bones on it.

skull   skyscraper

skunk a small, furry American animal which gives off a very nasty strong smell when attacked.

sky The sun shone out of the clear blue *sky*.

skylark a small brown bird that sings while soaring high into the sky.

skylight a window in the roof.

skyline the line along which the land or the buildings, etc., on it appears to meet the sky.

skyscraper a very tall building.

slab A *slab* of stone is usually a big rectangular piece that is not very thick.

slack A rope is *slack* if it hasn't been pulled tight.  A *slack* person is one who does things carelessly.  Shopkeepers consider that trade is *slack* when they have only a few customers.

slacken To *slacken* a rope is to make it loose.

slackness laziness, especially laziness in the form of doing a job without sufficient care.

slacks trousers – of the kind worn by girls or women.

slag the stone-like waste that comes from blast furnaces, etc.

slain The soldiers *slain* in the battle were buried that night.

slake To *slake* your thirst you have a drink.

slam Do not *slam* the door; shut it gently.

slammed Instead of shutting the door gently, he *slammed* it.

slang language that people often use although it isn't considered very good English, e.g. 'Dad is hopping mad' is *slang* for 'Dad is very angry'.

slant to slope or lean. Don't run the path straight down the garden; *slant* it a little towards one corner.

slanting A *slanting* line is one that goes off at an angle to other lines.

slap hit with the palm of the hand.

slapped Jean raised her hand and *slapped* the boy on the face.

slash To *slash* anything is to make long cuts at it or in it (with a knife or whip, etc.).  a sweeping stroke made with a knife, etc., or the cut made by such a stroke.

slate a grey rock which easily splits into thin, flat pieces, and is used to cover roofs, etc.

slaughter to kill many people or animals at once;  to kill animals for food.  The Bible tells of the *slaughter* of babies by King Herod.

slave someone who belongs to another person and, usually, works for him without payment. ■ To *slave* is to work hard, as a slave might.

slavery When *slavery* was stopped in the British Colonies, all the slave-owners had to set their slaves free.

slay St George's task was to *slay* the dragon and rescue the maiden.

sled, sledge a vehicle like a cart, but fitted with runners instead of wheels so that it can travel easily over snow (also called a *sleigh*). ■ A *sledge* hammer is a heavy, long-handled hammer.

sled (sledge, sleigh)

sleek shiny, smooth and soft, like the fur of a cat.

sleep I go to bed at night and *sleep* till someone wakes me next morning. ■ If you are tired, lie down, shut your eyes and have a *sleep*.

sleeper a person who is asleep; ■ a large rectangular block of wood or iron to which railway lines are fastened; ■ a railway carriage fitted with bunks in which people can sleep.

sleepy If you feel *sleepy*, go to bed.

sleet a mixture of rain and snow.

sleeve The *sleeve* of a garment is the part that covers the arm.

sleigh a vehicle fitted with runners so that it will slide over snow (also called a *sled* or *sledge*).

sleight-of-hand conjuring (tricks) worked by skill and quickness with the hands.

slender thin, e.g. a *slender* spire, a *slender* tree, a *slender* girl.

slept The tired boy got into bed and *slept* till we woke him the next morning.

sleuth a detective.

slew St George *slew* (killed) the dragon.

slice For my tea I had a *slice* of bread and butter and a *slice* of cake. ■ To *slice* bread is to cut it into thin, flat pieces.

slid Dick got downstairs quickest because he *slid* down the banisters.

slide It is fun to *slide* on the ice.

sliding Dick got downstairs quickly by *sliding* down the banisters. ■ You open *sliding* doors by pushing them to one side (they slide along in grooves).

slight It is only a *slight* injury, not at all serious. ■ A person who is *slight* in build is thin. ■ To *slight* someone is to give him cause for taking offence.

slightly Dad was only *slightly* injured so he didn't have to go to hospital.

slim To *slim* is to eat special things, etc., in order to become less fat. ■ Only a *slim* girl could crawl through that tiny hole.

slime thick, slippery mud; ■ the wet, slippery substance covering fish, etc.

slimy covered with slime, e.g. The fish is so *slimy* that I cannot keep hold of it.

sling Bob's broken arm is supported in a *sling* tied round his neck.

sling

slink When my dog knows that he has done wrong he will *slink* away with his tail between his legs.

slip If you tread on a banana skin you may *slip* and break a leg. ■ a small, careless mistake, e.g. You've made a *slip* in this sum.

slipped The old lady *slipped* on the ice and fell down.

slippers When indoors, Dad takes off his shoes and puts on a pair of soft, warm *slippers*.

slippery The ice has made the streets so *slippery* that people slip when they try to walk.

slipshod A *slipshod* piece of work is a job that has been done very carelessly.

slit a long cut or a long, narrow hole. ■ To *slit* material is to make a long cut in it, or to cut it into long strips.

slither to slip about.

sliver a thin piece of wood, torn or knocked off a larger piece; a splinter.

slog to hit very hard, but without much skill (in cricket, boxing, etc.). ■ To *slog* away at your work is to keep at it doggedly.

slogan a short catch-phrase used by advertisers, politicians, etc., e.g. 'Go well. Go Shell'.

slop If you don't carry that bucketful of water carefully, the water will *slop* over the edge. ■ The invalid cannot take solid foods, only *slops*. ■ *Slops* are also the waste liquids from bedrooms, kitchens, etc.

slope A surface that is not level must *slope* up or down. ■ We love to freewheel down that *slope* on our bicycles.

sloppy The paths are *sloppy* (wet) after all that rain. ■ That is a *sloppy* (careless) piece of work. ■ *Sloppy* talk or behaviour is that which is sentimental and babyish.

slot To get chocolate, etc., from a *slot* machine, ■ you simply put a coin in the *slot*.

sloth a bear-like South American animal which hangs upside down from branches and moves very slowly.

sloth

slothful very lazy.

slouch to walk or stand in a lazy, untidy manner.

slovenly A *slovenly* person is one who is too lazy to take trouble over his work or appearance. (He produces *slovenly* work.)

slow 4 m.p.h. is *slow* for a car. ■ If your watch is an hour *slow*, it will show 2 o'clock when the time is really 3 o'clock.

slowly Snails and tortoises move *slowly*.

slug a slimy creature like a snail without a shell, that eats garden plants.

slug   sluice

sluggish slow-moving, e.g. a *sluggish* river.

sluice a door fitted across a stream, which can be raised or lowered to stop the flow of water, or to let only the required amount through.

slum Those poor people live in a *slum* where the houses are old, dirty and crowded too closely together.

slumber sleep.

slump When there is a *slump* in a country it is difficult to do trade, and many people are out of work.

slung Bob's camera was *slung* round his neck by a strap.

slur To *slur* words (or speech) is to talk with your words running into each other so that they are not clear. ■ A *slur* on your reputation is something that spoils an otherwise good reputation. ■ a curved line over (musical) notes to show that they are to be sounded as a group and not separately.

slurred When a person is drunk, his speech is so *slurred* that you cannot understand what he is saying.

slush Snow turns into *slush* when it begins to melt.

slut a lazy, dirty, untidy woman.

sly A *sly* person is one who gets up to crafty tricks behind your back.

smack Mother will *smack* your bottom if you're naughty. ■ Sally gave him a *smack* on the face which hurt her hand. ■ a small fishing boat.

small The mouse is a *small* animal (i.e. most animals are bigger).

smallpox a dangerous disease which causes lots of tiny sores to appear on your body.

smart James looks *smart* in his new clothes, with his clean face and well-brushed hair. ■ You can get warm on cold days by walking at a *smart* pace. ■ Colin is a *smart* boy (he quickly understands things). ■ A sore place will *smart* (sting) if you get salt in it.

smarten Those untidy children must *smarten* (up) their appearance before the visitors come (i.e. they must look more clean and tidy).

smash In *smash* and grab raids ■ thieves *smash* shop windows by throwing bricks at them. ■ In that car *smash* both cars were badly damaged.

smashing (slang) very good indeed, e.g. a *smashing* holiday.

smear If the baby gets jam on his fingers he will *smear* it over his face, on the walls, and on anything else he can touch.

smell I'm holding my nose because I don't like this *smell* of onions. ■ If you don't want to *smell* the onions, hold your nose.

smelly Billy-goats are *smelly* creatures (i.e. they have a strong smell which is not pleasant).

smelt I have never *smelt* anything as sweet as the scent of these roses. ■ You *smelt* ore in a hot furnace to get the metal out of it. ■ a tasty fish, like a small salmon.

smile You can see by the *smile* on Mary's face that she is very pleased to see us.

smiling You can see by Mary's *smiling* face that she is very happy.

smirk a silly smile, e.g. one that is not caused by real amusement or pleasure.

smite to hit (hard) – used chiefly in the Bible, e.g. Shall I *smite* the enemy?

smith a man who makes things of metal, e.g. a black*smith* (iron), a tin*smith*, a silver*smith*, a gold*smith*.

smock a shirt-like outer garment, usually decorated with embroidery, etc.

smog fog that has been made dark, thick and poisonous through mixing with smoke, etc., in the air.

smoke The *smoke* from the fire goes up the chimney. ■ Dad does not *smoke* cigarettes, but he does *smoke* a pipe.

smoker someone who smokes tobacco (in a pipe or in cigarettes).

smoking Dad is *smoking* his pipe. ■ A *smoking* carriage in a train is one in which people are allowed to smoke.

smoky Coal burns with a *smoky* flame (i.e. smoke appears with the flame).

smooth completely level and even like a good lawn, or free of roughness, like silk. ■ To *smooth* anything is to make it smooth.

smoothly Dick's plan was carried out *smoothly* (i.e. nothing went wrong). ■ The engine in a Rolls Royce runs *smoothly* (i.e. without jerks or bumps).

smother To *smother* a person is to kill him by putting something over his face that stops his breathing. ■ To *smother* a fire is to put it out by covering it, e.g. with a wet blanket.

smoulder When fires *smoulder* they burn slowly and without bursting into flame.

smudge There is a *smudge* on your face where you touched it with your dirty finger. ■ You *smudge* ink writing if you rub your arm over it before it is dry.

smug self-satisfied, e.g. People are *smug* when they think that what they have done is very good.

smock

smuggle People secretly *smuggle* goods into the country to avoid paying customs duty (tax) on them.

smuggler someone who smuggles goods into the country to avoid paying customs duty (tax) on them.

smut a small particle of soot, e.g. The *smuts* floating about the room have come from that smoky fire. ■ dirty (sexy) talk.

snack There isn't time for a proper meal so we'll get a *snack* (to eat) at the coffee stall.

snag It's a good plan; the *snag* is that we haven't enough money to carry it out.

snail a small, slimy, crawling creature that eats plants, and lives in a shell which it carries about on its back.

snail **snake**

snake a long, thin creature without arms or legs.

snap A dry stick will *snap* if you try to bend it. ■ To *snap* your fingers is to click one against another. ■ I will take a *snap* of you with this camera. ■ A bad-tempered dog may *snap* at you (i.e. try a quick bite). ■ a card game in which you call, '*Snap*,' when you see two similar cards.

snappy bad-tempered: ■ 'Look *snappy*!' and 'Make it *snappy*!' mean 'Hurry up!'

snapshot (usually shortened to *snap*) I'll take a *snapshot* of you with my new camera.

snare To trap animals a hunter fixes a *snare*, usually made of cord, across the path they are likely to take.

snarl Dogs *snarl* (show their teeth and growl) when they are angry.

snatch We saw the thief *snatch* the money and rush off.

sneak To *sneak* into a place is to enter so as not to be noticed. ■ A *sneak* is a person who tells tales that get others into trouble.

sneer an insulting smile; ■ to make an insulting smile.

sneeze When you have a cold you *sneeze*, 'Ah-tishoo !'

sniff If your nose needs wiping, don't *sniff*; blow it on your handkerchief.

snigger half-stifled laughter. ■ You *snigger* when you are amused but cannot laugh out loud.

snip Ask the barber to *snip* off that bit of hair with his scissors.

snippet A *snippet* of cloth, etc., is a small piece cut off.

snivel To *snivel* is to cry and run at the nose.

snob a person who looks down on people who are poor or humble, and thinks highly of those who are rich or have titles.

snobbery There is no *snobbery* in our family (i.e. we do not prefer rich or titled people to poor and humble folk).

snobbish A *snobbish* person is one who is a snob.

snooze Dad settled down in the deck chair for a *snooze* (short sleep). ■ After dinner Dad likes to *snooze* in his chair (have a short sleep).

snore If you sleep on your back with your mouth open you're likely to *snore* (breathe with loud noises).

snort to make a noise by blowing out air through your nose – as a sign of anger or indignation.

snout the nose and mouth of an animal, especially the pig.

snow When it is too cold for rain, white flakes of *snow* fall from the clouds. ■ I hope it will *snow* so that we can play snowballs.

snowdrop a small, white winter flower.

snowflake one of the separate little pieces in which snow falls. If you magnify a *snowflake* you will see that it is a beautiful pattern of ice-crystals.

snowflake   **snowplough**

snowplough a device fixed in front of trains, lorries, etc., to push snow off the track or road.

snowy The flower is *snowy* white (i.e. white as snow).

snub To *snub* someone is to make him feel that he, or an idea of his, is not welcome. ■ A *snub* nose is one that is short and turned up at the end.

snubbed made to feel unwelcome, e.g. Jane *snubbed* Brian by turning her back on him and walking away.

snuffle to breathe noisily and with difficulty, as if you have a cold.

snug The baby should feel *snug* (comfortable) in that warm, soft bed.

snuggle A nervous little girl will *snuggle* close to her mother for comfort and protection.

soak You will have to *soak* the wallpaper before you can scrape it off (i.e. make it wet through). ■ You *soak* the dirty linen in cold water for hours before you wash it.

soap You'll need *soap* and hot water to get those dirty hands clean.

soapsuds the mass of bubbles made by stirring up soap in hot water.

soapy *Soapy* water is water that has soap in it.

soar I saw a lark rise from the ground and *soar* high into the sky.

sob a deep breath that you take in as part of the act of crying. ■ To *sob* is to take such a deep breath while crying.

sobbing Janet was crying and *sobbing* (taking in great deep breaths).

sober Anyone who is not drunk is *sober*.

sociable A *sociable* person is one who likes to mix in a friendly way with other people.

social a gathering where people meet to talk, dance, play games, eat, etc.

socialism the political idea that people's private interests should take second place to the interests of the nation as a whole; a belief in working together rather than competing.

socialist a politician who believes in socialism.

society a group of people, formed for some special purpose, e.g. The *Society* of Friends, The *Royal Society* for the Prevention of Cruelty to Animals, The School Debating *Society*.

socket a hollow into which something fits, e.g. your eye fits in your eye-*socket*.

socks I wear a pair of *socks* on my feet. ■ Give him *socks*! (Hit him hard and often).

sod A *sod* of grass is a small lump pulled up complete with roots.

soda a chemical, usually in the form of white crystals, which is used in water to make it soft, or for removing grease.

soda-water a colourless fizzy drink, usually sold in a siphon.

sodden soaked, e.g. The carpet was *sodden* with water from the burst pipe.

sofa a seat like a very wide armchair, to seat two or three people.

Sofia the capital city of Bulgaria.

soft not loud, e.g. a *soft* voice. ■ When you touch *soft* things, your fingers sink into them. ■ *Soft* water makes a lather with soap very easily.

soften You can *soften* crusts by soaking them in water.

softly If we tread *softly* no one will hear us.

soggy soaked with liquid, e.g. Crops won't grow in *soggy* soil. The toast is *soggy* because I spilt tea on it.

soil Plants get their food from the *soil* in which they grow. ■ To *soil* things (e.g. hands, clothing, etc.) is to make them dirty.

soiled That *soiled* linen must be washed. ■ If you've *soiled* your hands in doing that job, you must wash them.

solar The *solar* system is the system of planets, etc., of which our sun is the centre.

solder a special metal used hot (melted) on metal things to join them, or to mend holes, etc. ■ To *solder* (metal) things is to use solder on them.

soldier A *soldier* joins the army to fight for his country.

sole only, e.g. My *sole* complaint is that the party ended too soon. ■ When walking you put the *sole* of your foot (or shoe) on the ground after the heel. ■ a kind of flat fish.

solely At parties Tubby is interested *solely* in the food (i.e. he is not interested in anything else).

solemn serious and important, e.g. A religious service is a *solemn* ceremony.

solicitor a lawyer, whose job is to give people advice about the law and help those who are accused of crimes, etc.

solid When water becomes ice it changes from a liquid to a *solid*. ■ That spoon is *solid* silver (silver all the way through). ■ not hollow.

solidify Water will *solidify* into ice if you freeze it.

solitary There was but one *solitary* boy among all those girls. ■ The old lady lives a *solitary* life alone in that house, miles from the nearest neighbour.

solitude If I were wrecked on a desert island I should hate the *solitude* (the state of being alone).

solo A *solo* is performed by one person only – e.g. a piano *solo*.

soloist A *soloist* at a concert, etc., is a person who plays or sings by himself.

solos In the concert there were solo items by Jean, Janet and John – three *solos* altogether.

soluble Salt is *soluble* in water (i.e. if you stir salt into water it disappears).

solution I know the *solution* (answer) to the problem. ■ You make a salt *solution* by stirring salt into water until it disappears.

solve To *solve* a problem is to work out the answer to it.

solvent a liquid into which substances will dissolve, e.g. water (salt, sugar, soda, etc., will dissolve in it). ■ A person who is *solvent* is one who has enough money to pay all his debts.

some There are *some* boys at the door. I had *some* jam for tea.

somebody *Somebody*, I don't know who, has taken my pen.

someone I saw *someone* pass, but I don't know who it was.

somersault To turn a *somersault* is to go head over heels.

something I have *something* for you, but I won't tell you what it is.

sometimes *Sometimes* I walk to school; at other times I go by bus.

son A boy is the *son* of his father and mother.

song I like both the words and the music of that *song* you sang.

songster The blackbird is a good *songster* (i.e. it sings well).

sonny Dad calls all little boys, 'Sonny'.

soon in a short time, e.g. We'll *soon* be home.

sooner The shopkeeper returned *sooner* than the thieves had expected and he caught them robbing his shop. ■ I would *sooner* walk home than ride in that unsafe old car.

soot a black powder deposited on the inside of chimneys by smoke.

soothe To *soothe* pain is to make it less. ■ To *soothe* a person who is angry or excited is to calm him down.

soothing This *soothing* ointment will make the sore place hurt less. ■ Dad is *soothing* the angry motorist (i.e. calming him down).

soprano A lady or child with a *soprano* voice sings high notes. ■ If the singer sings only high notes she is a *soprano*.

sorcerer a magician, e.g. In one fairy story, the *sorcerer* turns an old man into a frog.

somersault

sorceress a female magician, e.g. One famous *sorceress* turned some sailors into pigs.

sordid A *sordid* story is one about the unpleasant side of life, e.g. greed, poverty, wickedness, etc.

sore A *sore* arm, or leg, etc., feels painful, or hurts when it is touched. ■ I have a *sore* (place) on my leg where that dog bit me.

soreness Your feet and legs feel sore after a long walk, but the *soreness* soon goes if you have a hot bath.

sorrow sadness.

sorrowful sad, e.g. Mother is *sorrowful* because I have been so wicked.

sorry I am *sorry* that I broke your pen (I wish I hadn't). ■ I am *sorry* for the people who are starving (I wish they had enough to eat).

sort 'What *sort* of dog is yours?' 'A poodle.' ■ When postmen *sort* letters they put them into different bags according to the towns to which they have to go.

sought The king *sought* everywhere for the missing princess, but he never found her.

soul There isn't a *soul* on the beach (i.e. not a single person). ■ the part of you which, according to some religions, lives on when your body dies.

sound I hear the *sound* of voices. ■ To *sound* a trumpet, gong, etc., is to cause it to make its noise. ■ Don't cut off that branch; it is a *sound* one (i.e. not diseased). ■ To *sound* water is to measure its depth, e.g. to see if it is deep enough to float a ship.

soup We started our meal with *soup*, which looked just like gravy.

sour Unripe apples, oranges, etc., taste *sour* (not sweet).

source The *source* of a river is the spring at which it begins.

south In Europe and Asia the sun is in the *south* at midday. On most maps the *south* is at the bottom.

southerly A *southerly* wind blows from the south to the north.

southern The *southern* parts of a country, etc., are those farthest south.

souvenir When Uncle Bill went abroad to live, he left me his watch as a *souvenir* (something to remember him by).

sovereign the king or queen of a country; ■ a British gold coin worth £1 (no longer in use).

Soviet Union (short for) The Union of Socialist Soviet Republics, the U.S.S.R., often known simply as Russia.

sow (to rhyme with 'cow') At the farm we saw a *sow* with her little baby pigs. ■ (to rhyme with 'low') If you *sow* the seed in the ground it will grow into a plant.

sown The seeds that I have *sown* in the garden should start growing soon.

spa a place where people go to drink (as medicine) water which comes up out of the ground.

space There isn't enough *space* for all that furniture in this little room. ■ Many rockets have been launched into *space*. ■ *Space* the chairs so that there is room for people to walk between them.

spaced The posts are to be *spaced* ten feet apart.

spacious A *spacious* hall is one in which there is plenty of room.

spade Dad uses a *spade* to dig the garden.

spaniel

spaghetti an Italian food consisting of long, brittle strings of flour paste, which go soft when cooked.

Spain a country in the south west of Europe.

span Bob can *span* 8 inches (i.e. it is 8 inches from tip of thumb to tip of little finger when they are stretched as far apart as possible). ■ In years to come a bridge will *span* this river.

spangle(s) little pieces of sparkling material, put on dresses, etc., to make them glitter.

Spaniard a native of Spain.

spaniel a dog with big, drooping ears and long, silky hair.

Spanish *Spanish* things are those from Spain, e.g. *Spanish* onions, The *Spanish* Armada. ■ the language spoken by Spaniards.

spank If you're naughty, Mother will *spank* you (slap your bottom).

spanner You use a *spanner* for turning a nut on a bolt.

spar a thick pole.

spare We carry a *spare* wheel in the car in case one of the other wheels becomes faulty, e.g. because of a puncture. ■ Can you *spare* (do without) one of your sandwiches for this hungry boy?

spares spare parts, used to replace parts of a machine, etc., that become faulty.

sparing Cook is very *sparing* with the sugar (i.e. she doesn't give us much).

spark A tiny *spark* flew out of the fire and set fire to the hearth-rug.

sparkle to send out little glittering lights, like a diamond, e.g. The waves *sparkle* in the moonlight.

sparkling giving out little lights, e.g. You can see the diamonds *sparkling* under the bright lights. ■ In her ring was a *sparkling* diamond.

sparrow a small, rather colourless bird, often seen around houses.

spasm a sudden jerking or tightening of muscles, e.g. a *spasm* of coughing.

spat As Billy didn't like the sweet he *spat* it out (of his mouth).

spatter As the cars go through the puddles they *spatter* people with muddy water.

spawn the eggs of a frog, fish, etc.; ■ to deposit (lay) spawn.

spanner   spawn

speak If you *speak* clearly I shall know what you are saying.

speaker someone who speaks, especially one who speaks at a public meeting, etc. ■ The *Speaker* is the man in charge of the proceedings in the House of Commons (Parliament).

spear a long pole with a sharp spike on the end, used as a weapon in ancient times, and still used by some primitive tribes. ■ To *spear* anything is to stab it with a spear.

spear

special I don't wear my best clothes every day, only on *special* occasions. ■ This is no ordinary torch; it is a *special* kind which will work under water.

specialist someone who has made a special study of one part of a subject, especially a doctor who is expert on one particular kind of illness.

specialize Some doctors *specialize* in one type of illness (i.e. they devote most of their studies to this one type of illness).

species kind or sort, e.g. That strange animal belongs to a *species* that I haven't seen before.

specify Dad just said he wanted a big box; he didn't *specify* the exact measurements.

specimen a sample, e.g. The police want a *specimen* of my handwriting to compare with the handwriting of the mysterious letter.

speck a tiny piece, e.g. A *speck* of dust on a camera lens can spoil a picture.

speckled anything that is *speckled* has coloured spots on it.

spectacle An erupting volcano is a wonderful *spectacle* (sight).

spectacles glasses. People wear *spectacles* so that they can see better.

spectacular The men gave a *spectacular* display of horse riding (i.e. it was exciting to watch).

spectator a person who watches such sports as football, cricket, etc.

spectre a ghost.

speculate To *speculate* on something is to wonder about it.

sped The car *sped* past us at 80 m.p.h.

speech When the mayor makes a *speech* people listen to what he says. ■ When a man is drunk his *speech* is slurred (i.e. he speaks indistinctly).

speechless Pat said nothing; she was *speechless* with surprise.

speed On this road the *speed* of cars must not exceed 30 m.p.h. (50 km). ■ Some cars *speed* along the road at 80 m.p.h. (130 km).

speedily quickly.

speedometer Robert's *speedometer* shows that his car is going at 45 m.p.h. (72 km per hour).

spectacles   speedometer

speedway a track, usually of cinders, for motor-cycle racing. ■ Motor-cycle racing on a cinder track is called *speedway* racing.

speedy A *speedy* reply is one that comes without delay.

spell Does she *spell* her name ANN or ANNE? ■ The witch put a *spell* (charm) on the prince so that he could not move from the spot.

spellbound To be *spellbound* is to behave as if under a witch's spell (e.g. due to the powers of a great speaker, actor, etc.).

spelling You've made a *spelling* mistake (i.e. you've spelt a word wrongly).

spelt You have *spelt* Ann's name ANNE instead of ANN.

spend On what did you *spend* your money? ■ How do you *spend* your time?

spent Tim *spent* his money on ice cream. ■ Bob *spent* several hours on the job.

sphere A *sphere* is shaped like a ball.

spider The *spider* is sitting in its web eating a fly it has caught.

spied Our look-out *spied* a man hiding in some bushes.

spies people who try to get information, or who keep watch on other people, secretly – especially *spies* employed by one country to find out another country's secrets. ■ He *spies* (keeps watch) on us.

spike a sharp point, e.g. on the bottom of a running shoe.

spill If you carry a full glass of water carelessly you will *spill* some of the water on to the floor. ■ While Joe was out cycling he had a *spill* (i.e. he fell off).

spilt Sally *spilt* her drink on the floor and had to wipe it up.

spin To *spin* strands of cotton or wool, etc., is to twist them into thread. ■ To *spin* a top is to set it going round and round on its base.

spinach a vegetable with dark green, cabbage-like leaves.

spindle the pin on which a part in a machine, etc. turns.

sphere

spider

spindle

spherical A *spherical* object is one that is ball-shaped.

spice a scented flavouring such as cloves, nutmeg, pepper, etc.

spine the bones running down the centre of your back (your backbone); ■ a sharp spike such as those on some plants or on the backs of certain fish.

spinster an unmarried woman, e.g. Miss Smith is a *spinster*.

spiral A *spiral* staircase is one that winds round and round as it goes up, like the thread on a screw.

spiral staircase   spire

spire a tall, pointed top to a tower, usually on a church.

spirit a ghost; ■ a drink such as gin, brandy, etc. ■ A person's *spirit* is his soul, or ■ his determination not to give in (his courage).

spirited A *spirited* horse is a lively one. ■ Our soldiers launched a *spirited* attack (they attacked courageously).

spiritless Our team gave a *spiritless* performance (i.e. they didn't try very hard).

spiritual *Spiritual* things are those connected with religion. ■ (Negro) *spirituals* are religious songs of the American negroes.

spit If the sweet is nasty, *spit* it out (of your mouth). ■ a rod on which meat is turned round and round while roasting.

spite When you do anything just for *spite*, you do it in order to annoy or upset someone.

spiteful A *spiteful* person is one who likes to injure or upset people.

splash Billy fell into the water with a *splash*. ■ Do not *splash* water on the bath-room walls while you are bathing.

splendid The guards in their smart, colourful uniforms were a *splendid* sight.

splendour I love the *splendour* of a royal procession (i.e. I like it because it is a showy and dignified spectacle).

splice to join, especially to join a rope by weaving the ends together.

splint a length of wood to which a broken bone is fastened while it mends, e.g Tom has a *splint* on his broken arm.

splinter When I handled that piece of rough wood I got a *splinter* (a little sharp piece) in my finger.

split You can *split* a block of wood by forcing a chopper through it.

splutter to make a spitting noise, e.g. We heard Bob *splutter* as he tasted the nasty stuff.

spoil You *spoil* a cake if you put salt in it instead of sugar. ■ To *spoil* someone is to do too much for him, to be more kind than is good for him.

spoiled, spoilt A *spoilt* child is one who has too much done for him. ■ Our picnic was *spoilt* by the thunderstorm.

spoke What did Dick say when he *spoke* to you?

spokesman someone who speaks on behalf of a group of people.

sponge a lump of material full of tiny holes, that people use when bathing, or when washing the car, etc.; ■ a light, soft cake, (similarly full of tiny holes); e.g. a jam *sponge*. ■ To *sponge* a piece of cloth, etc., is to wipe it clean with a sponge. ■ The man ought to be ashamed to *sponge* on those poor old people for his meals (i.e. it is shameful that he should get meals from them).

sponging You can remove that stain from your coat by *sponging* it with clean water.

sponsor The *sponsor* of a radio or TV. show is the advertiser who pays for it.

spook a ghost.

spooky ghostly, e.g. I'd hate to be alone at night in that *spooky* castle.

spool The film used in a camera is wound on a *spool*. The cotton is put into a sewing machine wound on a *spool*.

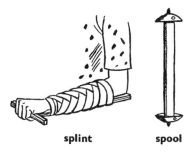

splint   **spool**

spoon You stir your tea with a tea*spoon*, eat your pudding with a dessert*spoon* and serve up the vegetables with a table*spoon*.

spoonful I like one *spoonful* of sugar in my tea.

sport Which *sport* do you like best, football, cricket, athletics, or swimming?

sports My favourite *sports* are swimming and cricket. ■ On *sports* day we have competitions in running, jumping, etc.

sportsman Jack is a good *sportsman* (he likes fair play). ■ A *sportsman* is a man who likes some such game as cricket, football, etc.

spot a small mark, e.g. You have a *spot* on your face. ■ a place, e.g. That's the *spot* where I found the watch. ■ To *spot* something is to see it, e.g. See if you can *spot* Jim among those boys.

spotless a *spotless* garment is one that is completely clean.

spotted A *spotted* dog, handkerchief, etc., is one with spots on it. ■ I *spotted* (saw) Jim as soon as he came into the hall.

spotty Fred has a very *spotty* face (i.e. there are lots of spots on it).

spout Tea is poured out of a teapot through the *spout*.

sprain To *sprain* your ankle is to twist it (by falling, etc.) so that it is painful.

sprang The cat crouched low for a moment and then *sprang* on the mouse.

sprat a sea fish like a very small herring.

sprawl Ian loves to *sprawl* on the floor (i.e. to lie with arms and legs spread out).

sprawling The run-away thief tripped over Tom's outstretched leg and fell *sprawling* on the pavement (i.e. with arms and legs spread out). ■ A *sprawling* town, etc., is one that is spreading out in all directions.

spray   When you *spray* a liquid, ■ you force it out of a *spray* in tiny drops, like mist. ■ A *spray* is a small piece of a plant with leaves or flowers on it.

spread   I like to *spread* butter on my bread before I eat it. ■ I hope your cold does not *spread* to the rest of us.

spree   To go on the *spree* is to set out with the intention of having a jolly good time.

sprig   A *sprig* of holly, etc., is a small branch.

sprightly   gay, lively and full of spirits.

spring   The four seasons of the year are *spring*, summer, autumn and winter. ■ a piece of coiled steel used to work clocks, toys, etc.; ■ a place where water comes out of the ground. ■ A *spring* tide is an extra big one. ■ Soldiers *spring* to attention when the order is given. ■ A ship may *spring* a leak (i.e. water may get in through a hole).

sprinkle   To scatter small drops or pieces, e.g. to *sprinkle* salt over your food, to *sprinkle* water on the garden.

sprinkling   For *sprinkling* water on the garden you need a hose that gives a fine spray. ■ A *sprinkling* of people, etc., is a few widely scattered.

sprint   to run at full speed for a short distance; ■ a race run over a short distance, e.g. 100 yards.

sprite   a fairy.

sprout   In spring the trees begin to *sprout* (grow green shoots). ■ (Brussels) *sprouts* are like lots of tiny cabbages all on one stalk.

spruce   smart, e.g. You must look *spruce* for Jane's party. ■ *Spruce* (fir) trees grow in many parts of the world.

sprung   Why has the cat *sprung* up on to the wall? ■ The ship has *sprung* a leak and is filling with water.

spry   lively, e.g. Grandad's a *spry* old man.

spun   The spider has *spun* a web. ■ The old lady has *spun* yards of thread on her spinning wheel.

spur   Horsemen used the *spurs* on their heels to prick their horses into action. ■ To *spur* someone (on) is to urge him to make a greater effort.

    spruce   **spur**

spurn   To *spurn* help is to refuse it because you think it beneath your dignity to accept it.

spurt   I made a *spurt* at the end of the race and just managed to pass the boy ahead of me.

sputnik   a Russian satellite, put in orbit round the earth.

spy   That boy came here to *spy* on (watch) us. ■ a person who secretly keeps watch on others or who tries to get secret information.

squabble   to quarrel (over some small matter); ■ an unimportant quarrel.

squad   a small group of soldiers or policemen, etc.

squadron   a group of aircraft, ships, etc. ■ A *Squadron* Leader is an Air Force officer.

squalid   dirty and unpleasant, e.g. a *squalid* house, a *squalid* story.

squall   a sudden severe storm, especially one at sea.

squally   A *squally* wind is one that is not steady, but blows as a number of hard gusts, separated by periods of lighter winds.

squander   Do not *squander* (waste) your money on that rubbish.

square   Anything that is *square* has four equal sides and four equal angles (each 90°). ■ The *square* of three is nine ($3^2 = 9$). ■ Trafalgar *Square* is an open space in London where there are fountains and Nelson's Column.

square

squared   *Squared* paper has squares ruled all over it.

squash   If you tread on an orange you *squash* it and the juice runs out. ■ Orange *squash* is a drink made of crushed oranges, etc.

squat   When you squat you bend your knees and sit on your heels. e.g. There are no chairs so we shall have to *squat* on the floor.

squatter   someone who settles on land that isn't his.

squatting   The tribesmen are *squatting* on the ground (i.e. with knees bent, sitting on their heels).

squaw   a Red Indian woman.

squawk   The hen gave a loud *squawk* as the fox grabbed it.

squeak   A door hinge will *squeak* if you don't oil it. ■ The baby bird gave a feeble *squeak* as Mary picked it up.

squeaky   Colin has a *squeaky* voice (i.e. small and high-pitched).

squeal   a high pitched noise like that made by a hurt pig. ■ Most creatures *squeal* loudly if they're hurt, especially pigs.

squeamish   To be *squeamish* is to be easily made to feel sick – by unpleasant sights, etc. ■ To be *squeamish* is also to have the kind of conscience that won't allow you to do dishonest things.

squeeze   You *squeeze* a lemon to get the juice out of it.

squib   a small firework that explodes with a loud bang.

squint   To have a *squint* is to be cross-eyed. ■ People *squint* when they try to see something while a bright light is shining in their eyes.

squire   in olden times, a man who was a knight's attendant. ■ The *squire* (of a village) is the man who owns most of the land in the district.

squirm   to wriggle, e.g. An eel or a worm will *squirm* if you pick it up.

squirrel   an attractive red or grey furry animal with a bushy tail, that lives in trees.

squirt If you turn on the tap, water will *squirt* out of that hole in the hose.

stab To *stab* anyone is to thrust a dagger or knife into his body. ■ It was this *stab* in the back that killed the man.

stable A horse lives in a *stable*. ■ To *stable* a horse is to put him in a stable. ■ firm and not likely to wobble about, e.g. You may safely climb those steps; they are quite *stable*.

stack a pile, e.g. a *stack* of wood, a hay*stack*. ■ A chimney *stack* is a group of chimneys.

stadium Important football matches are played at Wembley *Stadium*.

staff the five lines on which music is written. ■ The school *staff* are the teachers. ■ A flag *staff* is the pole to which the flag is fastened.

stag a male deer.

stage We shall act our play on the school *stage*. ■ You have to pay extra on the bus if you travel past your fare *stage*. ■ Before buses and trains were invented people travelled by *stage*coach.

stagecoach

stagger I saw the injured man *stagger* away like someone drunk.

stagnant *Stagnant* water is water that is not flowing (e.g. in a pond).

staid A *staid* person is one who is unlikely to do anything wild or surprising.

stain The coffee I spilt made a *stain* on the table cloth. ■ You will *stain* your hanky if you let the blood get on it.

stained *Stained* glass is used to make coloured pictures in church windows. ■ I *stained* the floor to give the wood a darker colour.

stainless *Stainless* steel stays bright under circumstances that would cause other steel to become rusty or dirty.

stair(s) You walk up the *stairs* to get to the room above this. ■ The stairs are covered with a *stair*-carpet.

staircase a flight of stairs.

stake a stick pointed for pushing or hammering into the ground; ■ the post to which people to be burnt to death were fastened.

stalactite an icicle-like rock hanging from the roof of a cave.

stalactites   **stalagmites**

stalagmite a rock like a stalactite, but rising up from the floor of a cave.

stale That bread is *stale*; we've had it for days.

stalk A flower is joined to a plant by its *stalk*. ■ When hunters *stalk* animals, they are trying to get as near as possible without frightening the animals away. ■ Those proud boys *stalk* around the school as if they owned the place.

stall Each cow has her own *stall* in the milking shed. ■ There is a *stall* in the market where fruit is sold. ■ The car engine may *stall* (stop) as we go up this hill. ■ In a theatre, the *stalls* are the seats near the front, downstairs.

stallion a male horse.

stalwart big, strong and brave, e.g. a *stalwart* soldier.

stamen On each *stamen* in a flower is a yellow dust called pollen.

stall   stamens

stamina Brian hasn't the *stamina* to run a mile (i.e. he hasn't the strength to keep up the effort long enough).

stammer When I *stammer*, I say, 'P-p-p-p-please g-g-g-go,' instead of, 'Please go.'

stamp To *stamp* your foot is to bang it on the floor (e.g. in anger). ■ You must stick a 3p *stamp* on a letter before you post it.

stampede When a herd of cattle *stampede* they all rush madly away.

stanch I will put something over the wound to *stanch* the blood (i.e. to stop it flowing) (also spelt *staunch*).

stand *Stand* up and let the lady have your seat. ■ *Stand* the vase on the table. ■ What does that sign *stand* for? (i.e. what does it mean?) ■ We sat in the (grand)*stand* to watch the football match.

standard a flag, e.g. The Royal *Standard* is the queen's own flag. ■ We beat that team because their play was not up to our *standard*.

standstill Work in the factory has come to a *standstill* because of the strike.

staple The *staple* diet of eastern people is rice (i.e. rice is their chief food). □ a U-shaped nail used to fasten down wire, etc.

star Venus is not the only bright *star* in the sky. ■ an important performer in the cinema, on TV., etc., e.g. a film *star*.

starboard the right hand side, as you look forward, of a ship or an aircraft.

starch You soak linen, etc., in *starch* so that it becomes stiff when you iron it. ■ a food-substance present in bread, potatoes, etc.

starchy *Starchy* foods are those such as bread and potatoes, which contain starch.

stare To *stare* at something is to look at it hard for some time.

staring What are you *staring* (looking long and hard) at? ■ The children don't like the man's *staring* eyes (eyes that are wide open and looking hard at them).

stark completely, e.g. *stark* naked, *stark* mad.

N

starling a small, dark, speckled bird which often roosts in large numbers in towns.

starring The actress is now *starring* in an Italian film (i.e. she is the star in it).

starry On a *starry* night there are lots of stars to be seen in the sky.

start We *start* work each day at 9 a.m. ■ The unexpected noise made me *start* (jump).

startle To *startle* someone is to give him a sudden fright.

startling very surprising and alarming, e.g. the *startling* effect of a sudden loud bang.

starvation People who have no food eventually die of *starvation*.

starve People who do not eat food *starve* to death.

state Betty was in a nervous *state* while waiting to go on stage to sing her solo. ■ I heard the official *state* that no children are to be admitted. ■ a nation, e.g. The United *States* of America.

stately grand and important-looking, e.g. a *stately* building, a *stately* person.

statement The prisoner made a *statement* (said something).

statesman a great politician (Churchill, for example).

station You go to the railway *station* to catch a train. ■ The police *station* is the headquarters of the police. ■ The police will *station* a man on the opposite side of the road where he can watch the bank.

stationary A *stationary* vehicle is one that is not moving.

stationer someone who sells writing paper, pens, ink, etc.

stationery You go to a stationer's shop to buy *stationery* (i.e. paper, pens, ink, etc.).

statue In the park there is a *statue* of a king, made of stone – or metal.

starling   statue

stature To be short of *stature* is to be short in height.

staunch A *staunch* friend is one whose help you can be sure of. ■ to stop the flow, e.g. *staunch* the blood (also spelt *stanch*).

stave To *stave* off a blow, or trouble, is to keep it off, with an effort. ■ one of the short cross-pieces on which you step when climbing a ladder.

stay I am lonely; please *stay* (keep near) with me. ■ Pat is coming to *stay* (live) with us during the holidays. ■ a support, especially a rope fixed to a ship's mast to hold it in place.

steadfast A *steadfast* friend is one who will remain friendly to you whatever happens.

steadily The police car *steadily* overhauled the stolen one (it was gaining on the stolen car all the time).

steady A table or chair, shelf, etc., that is *steady* will not wobble about when you use it. ■ Paul will *steady* the ladder (keep it from wobbling) while you climb. ■ not changing, e.g. a *steady* wind, a *steady* speed.

steak a thick slice of meat, cut for frying, grilling, etc., e.g. a beef *steak.*

steal To *steal* something is to take it without its owner's permission. ■ We'll *steal* away during the night and no one will know we've gone.

stealing The man was sent to prison for *stealing* goods from a shop.

stealth To do something by *stealth* is to do it secretly.

steam When a kettle boils, *steam* comes out of the spout. ■ *Steam* engines work by steam. ■ To *steam* fish, etc., is to cook it in steam.

steamer a ship driven by steam engines; ■ a special pan in which food can be cooked by steam.

steed a horse.

steel the metal used for making knives, swords, etc.

steep Our old car cannot get up *steep* hills. ■ to soak, e.g. Mother likes to *steep* very dirty clothes in cold water for a time before washing them.

steeple Above the church tower is a tall, pointed *steeple.*

steeplejack   stencil

steeplejack a man who climbs steeples and other high structures in order to clean or repair them.

steer You *steer* a car in the direction in which you wish to go by turning the steering wheel. ■ a young bullock (or bull).

stem the main stalk of a plant, tree, etc. ■ To *stem* a stream is to stop the flow of water.

stencil a thin sheet of card or metal, etc., in which shapes (letters or drawings) are cut out, so that copies can easily be made, e.g. by dabbing paint through the holes on to paper placed under them.

step *Step* forward one pace. ■ Wait on the top *step* of the stairs. ■ I know someone came; I heard a foot*step.*

stepped Betty *stepped* on the wet cement and left a footprint.

steps I shall take *steps* (action) to see that the criminal does not escape. ■ A pair of *steps* is a short ladder with flat ■ *steps* on which to tread, and a hinged support.

sterilize To *sterilize* anything (especially equipment used in hospital) is to kill the germs on it, usually by boiling.

sterling The pound *sterling* is the British £1.

stern Mr. Smith is a *stern* teacher (he stands no nonsense). ■ The *stern* of a ship is the back end.

stevedore a workman who loads and unloads ships.

stew To *stew* food you put it in a little water and cook it slowly in a closed container. ■ We had *stew* for dinner today (i.e. meat, etc., that had been stewed).

steward the man who waits on passengers in a ship, aircraft, etc.

stewardess the woman who waits on passengers in a ship, aircraft, etc.

stick a long, thin piece of wood, e.g. a walking *stick*. ■ You can *stick* the broken pieces together with glue. ■ If you *stick* a pin into yourself it hurts. ■ Windows sometimes *stick* so that you can't open them.

stickleback a small fresh-water fish with spines on its back.

sticky Glue is a *sticky* substance; so is jam.

sties (plural of *sty*) sore places on the edges of your eyelids. ■ Pigs live in *sties*.

stiff Things that are *stiff* will not easily bend.

stiffen To *stiffen* something is to make it stiff.

stiffening Our soldiers are meeting with *stiffening* resistance (i.e. the enemy soldiers are resisting harder). ■ The washing is *stiffening* as it freezes on the line.

stiff-necked The king was described as *stiff-necked* because he could not be persuaded to change his mind.

stifle We tried to *stifle* our laughter by holding handkerchiefs over our mouths.

stifling I can hardly breathe in the *stifling* atmosphere of this room (i.e. the room is too hot and stuffy).

stile You are expected to cross the fence between the two fields by climbing over the *stile*.

still Keep *still* (don't move). ■ Though we are late, we can *still* arrive in time if we hurry. ■ I have only an old car; *still* it is better than nothing.

stilts poles with which you can walk with your feet high above the ground.

stimulant a drink (usually), given to a person to make him more lively – brandy, for example.

stimulate to make lively, to stir into activity.

sting If you hurt the bee it may *sting* you. ■ The *sting* of a bee or wasp is the sharp, poisonous point in its tail end.

stingy mean, e.g. A *stingy* person will not give anything away if he can help it.

stink Pat held her nose because of the horrible *stink* of rotten fish. ■ Things such as bad eggs or fish *stink* (i.e. have a nasty smell).

stint The farmer provided milk without *stint* (i.e. lots of milk).

stipulate Some manufacturers *stipulate* the price at which their goods are to be sold by shopkeepers (i.e. state the price at which shopkeepers **must** sell the goods.

stir I *stir* my tea with a spoon, to mix in the sugar and milk.

stirred I *stirred* my tea with a spoon, to mix in the sugar and milk.

stirring I need the spoon for *stirring* my tea. ■ A *stirring* song, or speech, etc., is one that excites people.

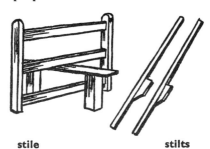

stile   stilts

stirrups When riding, you put your feet in the *stirrups* that hang one on each side of the horse.

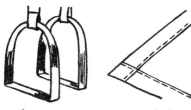

stirrups   stitches

stitch In neat sewing every *stitch* is of the same size. ■ The button has come off my coat; please *stitch* it on again for me.

stoat a small, long, thin, fierce, furry animal.

stock We have a big *stock* of books, ■ which are kept in the *stock* room till they are needed. ■ You can't buy jam at that shop; they don't *stock* it. ■ a garden flower with a sweet smell.

stockade a strong wooden wall of stakes, put round a place to keep out enemies.

Stockholm the capital city of Sweden.

stockings A lady's *stockings* cover the whole of her legs and feet.

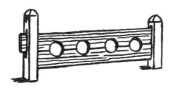

stocks

stocks In olden times wrong-doers were punished by having their legs fastened in the *stocks*.

stock-still To stand *stock-still* is to stand without any movement at all.

stocky A *stocky* person is one who is broad and strong, but short.

stoke To *stoke* a fire is to keep it supplied with fuel.

stoker a man who looks after a fire (or furnace) and keeps it supplied with fuel.

stole A thief *stole* goods from the shop. ■ a strip of material, like a long scarf, worn by clergymen. A shorter, wider kind of *stole* is worn indoors by ladies.

stolen Those boys are thieves; they have *stolen* our money.

stolid A *stolid* person is one who is not easily excited.

stomach the bag inside the middle of your body into which food goes when you swallow it. ■ The word *stomach* is also used to mean the lower part of the front of the body (the belly).

stomach-ache a pain in the stomach.

stone a small piece of rock; ■ the hard seed in the middle of a plum, peach, etc. ■ A diamond is a precious *stone*. ■ To *stone* anyone is to throw stones at him. ■ To *stone* fruit is to take the stones out of it. ■ 14 pounds(weight) = one *stone*.

stony *Stony* ground is ground covered with stones. ■ A *stony* stare is the kind of stare you direct at someone you do not recognize.

stood Tom *stood* up to let the lady have his seat. ■ Jane *stood* the vase on the table. ■ Bob asked what the sign *stood* for (meant).

stooge a person to be made fun of, especially a comedian's partner.

stool a small, low seat without a back.

stool   stork

stoop A tall man has to *stoop* to get through a low door-way.

stop *Stop* the bus; I want to get off. ■ *Stop* talking (be quiet). ■ You must always put a (full)*stop* at the end of a sentence.

stoppage The water won't run out of the sink because of a *stoppage* in the pipe.

stopped The baby *stopped* crying when I gave him a sweet. ■ All the vehicles *stopped* as the traffic lights changed to red.

stopper That glass *stopper* fits into the top of the vinegar bottle.

storage *Storage* (space) is space in which you can store things.

store To *store* things is to keep them till they are wanted. ■ The *store* of apples in the shed will last us through the winter. ■ a shop, especially a big shop where you can buy practically anything.

storey floor, e.g. There was a fire in the top *storey* of the building.

storeys floors, e.g. A building with 100 *storeys* is a sky-scraper.

stories That book contains many good *stories*.

stork a big, long-legged, white bird.

storm During a *storm* the wind blows very hard and there is a great deal of heavy rain. ■ To *storm* a fortress is to attack by going straight at it.

story Auntie told them the *story* of Cinderella.

stout brave, e.g. a *stout* warrior; ■ fat, e.g. Uncle Jack is rather *stout*. ■ a kind of beer.

stove a fireplace in which the fire is completely covered.

stow They *stow* (pack) the luggage in the tail of the aircraft.

stowaway someone who travels free in a ship or aircraft, etc., by hiding until it is too late to send him back home.

straddle To *straddle* something is to stand, or sit, with one leg on each side of it.

straggle to dawdle along in an untidy group; ■ to lag behind the main party in an untidy group.

straight A *straight* line has no bends or corners in it. ■ I don't trust the man; he's not *straight* (honest). ■ That picture is crooked; please put it *straight*.

straighten To *straighten* anything (e.g. your tie) is to put it straight.

strain You *strain* gravy through a sieve to get the lumps out. ■ If you read in a bad light you may *strain* your eyes. ■ The *strain* on the rope was too great and it broke. ■ The horses *strain* at the heavy carts that they are pulling up the hill.

strainer To prevent the tea leaves from getting into your cup you pour the tea through a *strainer*.

strait a narrow stretch of water connecting two seas, e.g. The *Strait* of Dover.

strand A *strand* of rope is one of the strings in it. ■ a stretch of land beside water; ■ to run aground, especially to run a ship aground.

stranded run aground, e.g. a *stranded* ship, a *stranded* whale; ■ left in an awkward situation, e.g. I was *stranded* in the strange town without money or friends.

strange A *strange* thing, place or person is one that you do not know.

strangely Brian is acting *strangely* (i.e. in a way not usual with him).

stranger None of us knows the boy; he is a *stranger* here. ■ Your story is strange, but mine is *stranger* (more strange).

strangle To *strangle* anything is to kill it by squeezing its throat.

strap a strip of tough material such as leather used for holding things together. ■ *Strap* the parcel on to the back of your bicycle (i.e. fasten it with straps).

strapping A *strapping* boy or girl is a well-built, lively one ■ To give someone a *strapping* is to beat him with a strap.

strategy careful planning, especially planning the movements of armies in a war.

straw the dried stalks of wheat, barley, etc., or one such stalk.

strawberry a soft, pulpy, sweet, red fruit which has its seeds on the outside.

stray To *stray* is to wander off the right path. ■ A *stray* (dog, etc.) is one which cannot find its way home, or which has no home.

streak a narrow band, e.g. There is a *streak* of fat running through this slice of bacon.

streaky In *streaky* bacon there are streaks of fat and of lean.

stream The *stream* runs down from the hill and flows into the sea. ■ At four o'clock children *stream* out of the school gates. ■ The banners *stream* (float out) in the wind.

streamer a ribbon fixed at one end only, so that it streams out in the wind.

streamlet a little stream.

streamlined Cars, boats, aircraft, etc., are *streamlined* so that they offer less resistance to the air or water that they travel through.

street There are many houses in the *street* in which I live.

strength Billy hasn't the *strength* to carry such a heavy load.

strengthen To *strengthen* anything is to make it stronger.

strenuous You feel very tired after doing *strenuous* work.

stress To *stress* something is to call special attention to it. ■ It is in times of *stress* that you most need a friend (i.e. when you're worried and anxious). ■ When you say, 'dinner,' you put the *stress* on the sound 'din' (i.e. you make 'din' the loud part of the word).

strap   strawberry

stretch If you *stretch* a piece of elastic it becomes much longer. ■ The *stretch* of water between Britain and Europe is called the North Sea.

stretcher Two ambulance men carried the injured girl away on a *stretcher*.

stretcher

strict Mr. Smith is a *strict* teacher; he allows no nonsense in his room.

stride a step, e.g. With one *stride* Jim was across the stream. ■ To *stride* along is to walk with big steps.

strident A *strident* sound is one that is unpleasant and loud, e.g. a *strident* voice.

strife fighting, quarrelling. e.g. From the room we heard blows being struck, angry voices, and other sounds of *strife*.

strike to hit. ■ *Strike* a match and light the fire. ■ At midnight the clock will *strike* twelve times. ■ The workmen will *strike* (stop work) if they're not given more pay. ■ The workmen may call a *strike* (stop work). ■ Miners dig in those hills hoping to *strike* (find) gold.

striking There is a *striking* resemblance between Jane and Mary (i.e. they're so much alike that everyone notices it).

string I need some *string* to tie up this parcel. ■ There are four *strings* on a violin. ■ Mary has a *string* of beads round her neck. ■ To *string* beads is to put them on a string.

stringent There are *stringent* (strict) rules against cheating in an exam.

strings The group of orchestral instruments played with bows (violins, violas, 'cellos and basses) are known as the *strings*.

strip It didn't take Tom a moment to *strip* and put on his bathing trunks. ■ The tin is sealed with a *strip* of sticky tape round the lid.

stripe A zebra's body is marked with *stripes*. ■ A soldier with three *stripes* on his sleeve is a sergeant.

strive to try very hard, e.g. I shall *strive* to be a useful member of the team.

strode walked with big steps, e.g. Mr. Smith *strode* away angrily.

stroke Bill cut through the rope with one *stroke* of his axe. ■ Tom has had a *stroke* of luck; he has won £50. ■ Pat crossed out the mistake with a *stroke* of her pen. ■ To *stroke* an animal is to pass your hand gently along it.

stroking Joan is *stroking* the cat (smoothing its fur with her hand).

stroll a slow, leisurely walk. ■ To *stroll* is to walk in a slow, leisurely way.

strong A *strong* man can lift heavy weights. ■ There is more taste in *strong* tea than in weak tea.

stronghold a fortress.

strove tried very hard, e.g. Tom *strove* to be a useful member of the team.

struck I *struck* a match to light the fire. ■ The clock *struck* twelve.

structure something such as a building or a bridge, which has been constructed; ■ the way in which a thing or (body) is constructed.

struggle In the *struggle* to arrest the thief the policeman's coat was torn. ■ We had to *struggle* against strong winds all the way home.

strum Peter would sit and dreamily *strum* his guitar.

strummed We sat round while Peter idly *strummed* his guitar.

strumming After gently *strumming* his guitar for a time, Peter at length began to play a definite tune.

strung I picked up the beads from the broken necklace and *strung* them on another string.

strut a length of wood or metal put into a structure to make it stronger. ■ Those conceited boys *strut* about as if they owned the place (i.e. they walk proudly and stiffly).

strutted The victorious soldiers *strutted* (walked proudly) through the streets of the enemy city.

stub The *stub* of a pencil or a cigar, etc., is the little useless piece left over when the rest has worn or burnt away. ■ To *stub* your toe is to kick it against something as you walk.

stubble the short bits of corn stalks left standing in a field after the harvest.

stubborn The donkey is a *stubborn* creature (it is difficult to make him do anything).

stuck Mary *stuck* the broken pieces together with glue. ■ Pat *stuck* a needle into her finger and made it bleed. ■ We can't open the window because it has *stuck*.

stud A collar *stud* fits into two button-holes to fasten a shirt. ■ a nail with a big, round head (used in the soles of climbers' boots, etc.). ■ A *stud* farm is a place where horses are kept for breeding.

student A college *student* goes to college to learn.

studio People such as painters, photographers, etc., work in a *studio*.

studious A *studious* person is one who wants to learn and who therefore studies hard.

study the room in which a student or a writer does his work. ■ To *study* is to get knowledge, especially from books. ■ To *study* a problem is to think about it very carefully.

stuff The *stuff* that girls put on their faces is called powder. ■ What kind of *stuff* do they use to make swimming trunks? ■ Put all that *stuff* in the dust bin. ■ *Stuff* some newspaper into that crack to stop the draught. ■ To *stuff* a turkey is to fill its inside with stuffing before cooking it.

stuffed Jim *stuffed* rags into the hole to stop the draught. ■ Cook *stuffed* the turkey (with stuffing).

stuffing Before cooking a turkey, Cook fills its inside with *stuffing* made of breadcrumbs, onion, etc.

stuffy A small room with several people in it soon becomes *stuffy* if you don't open a window.

stumble to trip and almost fall, e.g. because you catch your foot in something.

stump The tree was cut down, leaving a short *stump* standing up from the ground. ■ In cricket the batsman hopes the ball will not hit the three *stumps* behind him. ■ The wicket keeper will sometimes *stump* a batsman (get him out by touching the ball on the stumps when he is out of position).

stump   **stumps**

stumpy short and thick.

stun The robbers *stun* the guard by banging him on the head and escape before he wakes up again.

stung The angry wasp settled on my hand and *stung* me.

stunt It was thought that smoking would *stunt* boys' growth (i.e. stop them growing). ■ (slang) a piece of showmanship used by advertisers, etc., e.g. The story about the missing film star is just a *stunt* to get her name into the newspapers.

stunted A *stunted* plant is one whose growth has been slowed down or stopped, e.g. by cold winds.

stupefy You *stupefy* someone when you give him a drug (or do anything else) that makes him less alert and intelligent.

stupendous amazing (usually because of bigness), e.g. a *stupendous* building.

stupid A *stupid* person is one who is slow to understand things, or who cannot understand at all.

stupidity Old Joe can't carry out even the simplest instructions because of his *stupidity* (i.e. because he is stupid).

stupor For days after he had received the blow on the head the man was in a *stupor* (i.e. he wasn't properly aware of where he was or what he was doing).

sturdy A *sturdy* child is one who is strong and well-built.

stutter to stammer. When I *stutter*, I say, 'P-p-p-please g-g-g-go,' instead of, 'Please go.'

sty a sore place on the edge of your eyelid; ■ a pig's house.

style way of speaking, writing, painting, building, etc.; e.g. the Norman *style* of architecture, a painting in the *style* of Picasso. ■ Auntie dresses in the latest *style* (fashion).

stylish up-to-date, fashionable.

sub (short for) subscription, ■ submarine, ■ substitute, (etc.).

subconscious You are not fully aware of what goes on in the *subconscious* part of your mind.

subdue An army was sent to *subdue* the rebellious tribes (i.e. to make them behave).

subject (pron. súb-ject) Every British person is a *subject* of the queen. ■ The *subject* of the composition is, 'Holidays at home.' ■ The teacher says I can go early, *subject* to the headmaster's approval. ■ (pron. sub-ject) Scientists *subject* space men to all kinds of tests before they send them up in rockets.

submarine In a modern *submarine* you can travel under the sea for months without coming to the surface.

submarine

submerge Submarines can *submerge* (go below the surface of the water) very quickly. ■ The rising flood waters will soon *submerge* (cover) the village.

submit All boys who were in the room when the watch was stolen must *submit* to being seached (i.e. must allow someone to search them).

subscribe Boys who wish to *subscribe* to the present for Mr. Smith should bring their money to me.

subscription money you pay in order to belong to a club, etc.; e.g. Members of our club pay a *subscription* of 5p a week.

subside When the flood waters *subside* you will see the green fields again.

substance Almost anything can be called a *substance*, e.g. water is a wet *substance*, oil is a greasy *substance*, glue is a sticky *substance*, etc. ■ The *substance* of a talk, etc., is the really important idea in it.

substantial We require a *substantial* (solidly made) building to house our telescope. ■ The thing

was not a ghost, but something much more *substantial* – our friend Billy.

substitute When a member of the team is injured, a *substitute* plays in his place. ■ While Mary is not looking we'll *substitute* a toy cat for her real one (i.e. put a toy in place of the cat).

subterranean underground, e.g. a *subterranean* stream.

subtle (pron. sut'l) difficult to grasp, e.g. Bob doesn't see the joke; it is too *subtle* for him.

subtract When you *subtract* 3 from 7, the answer is 4.

subtraction In *subtraction* sums you take numbers away from other numbers.

suburb a district which is close to a big city and is considered to be part of it, e.g. Richmond is a *suburb* of London.

suburban *Suburban* trains go to the suburbs; *suburban* houses, shops, etc., are those in the suburbs.

subway Instead of crossing over the busy road, people can walk under it through the *subway*.

succeed If you *succeed* in winning the race you will get the trophy. ■ When the Queen dies, the Prince of Wales will *succeed* to the throne.

success Your efforts have met with *success* when they have the results you hoped for.

successful A *successful* operation is one that has the desired results.

succession A *succession* of cars passed us one after another. ■ The Prince of Wales is next in *succession* to the Queen (i.e. he is the next ruler after the present Queen).

successive It rained on four *successive* days (i.e. four days following each other).

successor Bob's *successor* as form captain is Tom (i.e. Tom follows Bob as form captain).

succumb to give way, e.g. to *succumb* to temptation, to enemies, etc.

such Did you ever see *such* lovely apples as these? ■ Pat was in *such* a temper that she didn't know what she was saying.

suck I usually *suck* the milk out of the bottle through a straw. ■ You mustn't *suck* sweets in class.

suckle Cows *suckle* their calves (i.e. the calves suck milk from the cows).

suction Vacuum cleaners take up dirt by *suction* (i.e. they suck it up).

sudden The *sudden* storm took everyone by surprise.

suddenly We were all enjoying the party, when *suddenly* (without warning), the lights went out.

suds the mass of bubbles you get by stirring soapy water about.

suède rough kid-skin, used to make *suède* shoes, *suède* gloves, etc.

suet beef or mutton fat, used to make *suet* puddings, etc.

suffer to be in pain, e.g. The animal did not *suffer* – he died instantly. ■ to allow, e.g. Our captain will *suffer* no interference with his plans.

suffered The injured man *suffered* great pain.

sufferer The doctor gave the *sufferer* drugs to ease the pain.

suffering Mary is *suffering* from a serious illness.

sufficient I don't need any more food; there is *sufficient* here.

suffocate to choke, and perhaps kill people, by stopping their breathing, e.g. Thick smoke in a burning house may *suffocate* the people in it.

sugar You put *sugar* in food or drink to make it sweet.

suggest I *suggest* that we go by train (that is the idea that I put forward).

suggestion Mary's *suggestion* (idea) is that the boys should act a play.

suicide The man committed *suicide* by shooting himself in the head. ■ A *suicide* is someone who has killed himself.

suit George is wearing a new *suit* (of clothes). ■ That dress doesn't *suit* Mary (i.e. she doesn't look nice in it). ■ In playing cards there are four *suits*, spades, hearts, diamonds and clubs.

suitable A pipe isn't a *suitable* gift for a lady.

suite a set (of things), e.g. a *suite* of furniture, a *suite* of rooms, *Suite* in D (a set of pieces of music).

suitor A girl's *suitor* is a man who is trying to persuade her to marry him.

sulk If Pat doesn't get her own way she will *sulk* (be quietly bad-tempered and generally disagreeable).

sulky disagreeable; Pat is *sulky* because she can't get her own way.

sullen A *sullen* look on someone's face is a resentful and disagreeable look.

sulphur a pale yellow substance which causes a choking feeling if you smell it burning (used to make gunpowder, matches, etc.).

sultan a ruler or prince of a Mohammedan country.

sultana a sultan's wife; ■ a dried grape, ■ used in *sultana* cakes.

sultry On a *sultry* day people sweat and feel uncomfortable because the air is hot, damp and still.

sum In arithmetic lessons we do *sums*. ■ The *sum* of 3 and 4 is 7. ■ You owe me the *sum* of 55p.

summary a short account which gives the chief facts of a story, etc.

summer We have our holidays in *summer* because the weather is warmest and the days longest then.

summit This is the *summit* of the mountain; we can't get any higher.

summit

summon If he attacks you, *summon* (call) a policeman. ■ To *summon* a person is to cause him to be called to a court of law, where he will be accused of having done something wrong.

summons When the magistrates (judges) require a person to come to a law court, they send out a *summons* (an official order).

sumptuous A *sumptuous* meal, flat, etc., is one on which a great deal of money has been spent.

Sunday the first day of the week.

sundial On a *sundial* you tell the time by the position of the sun's shadow.

sundial

sundry several, e.g. There are *sundry* packages here for you.

sung The choir have *sung* their songs.

sunk The ship has *sunk* to the bottom of the sea.

sunken They are going to raise the *sunken* ship to the surface again.

sunrise At *sunrise*, day begins.

sunset After *sunset*, night begins.

sunstroke an illness caused by being in very hot sunshine.

super (short for) superintendent (police); ■ (slang) extremely good, or the highest possible quality, etc., e.g. Uncle has a *super* car.

superb remarkably good, e.g. a *superb* voice, a *superb* picture, a *superb* view, etc.

superficial on the surface only, e.g. A *superficial* injury is not serious.

superfluous more than is wanted, e.g. *superfluous* hair, *superfluous* fat.

superhuman A *superhuman* effort is one that is greater than can normally be expected of a human being.

superintendent someone whose job is to see that others do their work properly, e.g. A police *superintendent* is an officer of high rank.

superior better in some way, e.g. This new radio is *superior* to our old one. ■ A sergeant is a corporal's *superior*.

superman It would require a *superman* to move that great rock (i.e. it is more than any earthly man could do).

supermarket When you shop at a *supermarket* you help yourself to goods set out on long rows of shelves, and pay as you leave the shop.

supernatural *Supernatural* events are those for which there is no earthly explanation, i.e. they are miracles, or are brought about by ghosts, magic, etc.

superstitious *Superstitious* people are those who believe in luck and they will not, e.g. walk under ladders, use the number 13, travel on a Friday, etc.

supervise A foreman's job is to *supervise* the men while they work, to see that they do the job properly and don't waste time.

supper We go to bed immediately after we have eaten our *supper*.

supple Anything that is *supple* will easily bend about, e.g. a cane, or a dancer's body.

supplement an extra part added to a book, newspaper, etc. News-papers and magazines often include a free *supplement*.

supply We can *supply* all the children with pencils and rulers. ■ There is a good *supply* of books in the cupboard so we are unlikely to run short.

support If you don't put a *support* under that roof it will fall down. ■ Bill had to *support* Jill or she would have fallen to the floor.

supporter Tom is a regular *supporter* of our football team; he sees every match.

suppose I *suppose* we'll have fish for dinner, as it's Friday.

supposed It's midnight, so you're *supposed* to be asleep.

suppress To *suppress* a book, or a sneeze, etc., is to stop it coming out. ■ To *suppress* a rebellion is to put an end to it.

supreme highest of all, in rank, importance, etc. The *supreme* being is God.

sure If you are *sure* the answer is right, there is no need to check it.

surely *Surely* you don't need an hour to dress? (i.e. Are you sure this is so?)

surf foaming water produced by waves breaking on a beach.

surf

surface The bubbles rise to the *surface* of the water. ■ Submarines *surface* to get air and sunlight.

surgeon a doctor who treats illnesses by cutting into the body, or cutting parts of it away.

surgery If you want to see your doctor or your dentist, you go to his *surgery*. ■ A surgeon is an expert in *surgery* (treating illnesses by cutting parts of the body).

surly A person who is *surly* says very little, and what he does say is rude and ill-mannered.

surname Bill Smith's *surname* is Smith.

surplice A choir-boy usually wears a white *surplice* over a long black robe.

surplice

surplus To have a *surplus* of anything is to have some left over when you have taken all that you need.

surprise something unexpected, e.g. Don't tell Joan what I've bought her; I want it to be a *surprise*. ■ Let's *surprise* Mother by repainting the room while she's away.

surprising Colin brought his pet monkey to school, with *surprising* (unexpected) results.

surrender When soldiers *surrender* they stop fighting and agree to do as the enemy tells them.

surround If the police *surround* the house, the people in it will not be able to get away in any direction.

surroundings A person's *surroundings* are the things all around him.

survey to look over, e.g. Experts came to *survey* the burnt-out ruin. ■ To *survey* a district or an estate is to measure it up and make plans of it.

surveyor a man whose job is measuring up and making plans of estates or districts.

survive to remain alive, e.g. Did anyone *survive* the earthquake?

survivor When the ship sank Jack was the only *survivor* (everyone else aboard was drowned).

susceptible Ian is very *susceptible* to flattery (i.e. you can get him to do almost anything if you flatter him).

suspect The police don't know who committed the crime, but they *suspect* Jones (i.e. they think he may have done it). ■ a person who is suspected.

suspend To *suspend* a workman, or a footballer, etc., is to order him not to carry out his usual duties for the time being. ■ *Suspend* the balloons from the ceiling on a string.

suspenders Some people keep up their socks or stockings by fastening them to *suspenders*.

suspense To keep someone in *suspense* is to keep him waiting for news that he is very anxious to have.

suspension A *suspension* bridge is made by fixing great cables across the gap and hanging the bridge from them.

suspicion If it is believed that a person has done something wrong, but there is no proof, the person is said to be under *suspicion*.

suspicious 'Where have you been?' asked the farmer with a *suspicious* glance at the boy's pocketful of apples.

sustenance food.

swagger to walk in a boastful, cocky way.

swallow When you *swallow* food it goes down into your stomach. ■ a fast flying bird with a forked tail, which visits Britain during the summer.

swarthy A *swarthy* man has a dark, but not black, skin.

swat To *swat* a fly is to squash it (by hitting it with something).

sway The snakes *sway* from side to side as the snake-charmer plays his pipe.

swear to use bad language; ■ to make a solemn promise, in particular to make a promise in the presence of a lawyer.

sweat Jimmy was so hot that his face was wet with *sweat*. ■ When you *sweat* (through heat or fear), drops of moisture form on your skin.

sweater a thick, woolly, outer garment that covers the top half of the body.

suspension bridge

swallow   **swan**

swam Pat jumped into the swimming pool and *swam* to the other end.

swamp an area of very wet land – a marsh.

swan a beautiful, big, white, long-necked bird, often seen on rivers and lakes.

swarm There are thousands of bees in the *swarm* that has settled in the tree. ■ When bees *swarm*, hundreds of them come together in a great mass.

Swede a citizen of Sweden.

swede A *swede* is a big, round, yellowish, turnip.

Sweden a country in north west Europe between Norway and the Baltic Sea.

Swedish the language spoken in Sweden. ■ *Swedish* things are those from Sweden, e.g. *Swedish* furniture.

sweep Take a brush and *sweep* away that dirt. ■ The *sweep* comes and pushes brushes up the chimney to remove the soot.

sweeping These special brooms are for *sweeping* up the leaves. ■ *Sweeping* changes are those that affect many people or many things (similarly a *sweeping* criticism, a *sweeping* statement, etc.).

sweepstake a gamble on a race (many people take part and one of them wins all the money subscribed).

sweet To make tea *sweet* you put sugar in it. ■ *Sweet* sounds are those that are tuneful and pleasing. ■ You may not suck *sweets* in school. ■ The meat course at dinner is followed by a *sweet*, usually a pudding, or stewed fruit.

sweeten Mother puts sugar in food to *sweeten* it.

sweater   swede

sweetheart Jill is Jack's *sweetheart*. Jack and Jill are *sweethearts* (i.e. they're in love).

swell When you blow air into balloons they *swell* up. ■ As the racing cars get nearer, the quiet sounds *swell* into a great roar of noise. ■ the big, smooth waves that continue on the sea after a storm has died down.

swelling The balloon is *swelling* up as the air goes into it. ■ The quiet sounds are *swelling* into a great loud noise. ■ My injured ankle is better now that the *swelling* has gone down (i.e. it is no longer fatter than it should be).

swelter While the ship's passengers sun-bathe on deck, the stokers *swelter* in the engine-room (i.e. the stokers are too hot).

swept When you have *swept* up that dirt, put the brush away. ■ The small boy was *swept* away by the tide and drowned.

swerve Cyclists who *swerve* to avoid dogs may fall off their bicycles.

swift John is a *swift* runner (he runs fast). ■ a bird like a swallow.

swill pig-food in the form of a liquid that contains all kinds of waste, etc.; ■ to drink in a vulgar, greedy way.

swim We shall have to *swim* across the river if it's too deep for wading. ■ I go to the swimming baths to have a *swim*.

swimmer a person who swims.

swimming The fish are *swimming* round the pond. ■ We go to the *swimming* baths to have a swim.

swindle Don't let that dishonest salesman *swindle* you out of your change. ■ The competition was a *swindle* (i.e. it was not fairly run).

swine pig, or pigs.

swing Grandfather clocks have pendulums which *swing* from side to side. ■ Children love to have a *swing* ■ on the *swing* in the park.

swipe I love to see a batsman *swipe* the cricket ball right out of the ground. ■ With a mighty *swipe* the batsman sent the ball out of the ground. ■ (slang) to steal.

swirl Pull out the plug and watch the water *swirl* round and round as it runs out of the bath.

Swiss a citizen of Switzerland. ■ *Swiss* watches, etc., are made in Switzerland.

switch I can't see; please *switch* on the electric light. ■ If you press that *switch*, the light will come on.

Switzerland a small, mountainous, European country, surrounded by Germany, France, Italy and Austria.

swivel a joint connecting two parts of something in such a way that one part can turn while the other remains still; ■ I saw the headmaster *swivel* round in his chair so as to face his visitor.

swollen My twisted ankle has *swollen* up to twice its usual size.

swoop The eagles *swoop* down from the sky and grab any small creature they see. ■ The thieves took everything we had at one *swoop*.

swop Will you *swop* (exchange) your knife for this pen?

sword A knight of olden times fought with a long, sharp *sword*, which he carried strapped to his waist.

swore The man *swore* when the hammer hit his thumb (he used bad language). ■ The witness in the law-court *swore* that he had seen the prisoner take the jewels.

sworn I have *sworn* (promised) never to tell the secret to anyone.

swum John has *swum* four lengths of the swimming baths.

swung The children *swung* backwards and forwards on their swing. ■ Jack *swung* the axe and with one blow split open the door.

sycamore a big, broad-leafed tree.

syllable The middle *syllable* of the word 'lem-on-ade' is 'on'.

syllabus the outline of what has to be taught in a subject, e.g. According to the geography *syllabus* we are going to learn about Europe next year.

symbol a sign that stands for something, e.g. this *symbol*, +, means 'add'.

symbolize The crosses (xxxx) that some people make at the end of a letter *symbolize* (mean) kisses.

symmetrical An object or a drawing, etc., is *symmetrical* if its two halves balance, if the proportions are pleasing, or if it is a design made by regularly repeating the same shape.

sympathetic A *sympathetic* person is one who shares your feelings, i.e. one who is sorry when you are sorry and glad when you are happy.

sympathize To *sympathize* with someone is to share his feelings, but especially to be sorry for someone who has suffered some misfortune.

sympathy I have no *sympathy* for people who are ill because they've eaten too much (i.e. I'm not sorry for them).

sycamore

symphony a piece of music for a complete orchestra, and written according to a special plan.

symptom The only *symptom* of illness that Billy has is a pain in his stomach.

synagogue a Jewish place of worship.

synopsis At the beginning of each instalment of a serial story there is a *synopsis* of the story so far, which tells you, briefly, what has happened.

synthetic man-made, not natural, e.g. *Synthetic* fibres do not come from sheep nor from the cotton plant; they are made by chemists.

syringe Doctors squirt liquids into people's bodies with a *syringe.* ■ Gardeners use a *syringe* to spray chemicals on to plants.

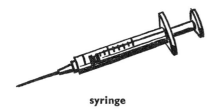

syringe

syrup a thick, sweet, sticky liquid – especially that produced in the manufacture of sugar.

system A railway *system* consists of all the parts of a railway. ■ The solar *system* consists of the sun and its planets. ■ The digestive *system* is made up of all the parts of the body that help in digesting food.

systematic To do things in a *systematic* way is to do them according to a plan, and not haphazardly.

tab a small strip of cloth, e.g. a name *tab* (on which your name is marked), sewn on clothes. ■ To keep *tabs* on someone is to keep an eye on him.

tabby a female cat; ■ a cat whose fur is grey or brownish, with dark streaks.

tabernacle a place of worship, especially a tent used by the Israelites in the wilderness.

tabernacle

table Your dinner is on the *table*; come and eat it. ■ On a bus time *table* the times of the buses are set out in order of days and times.

tableau People in a *tableau* stand still and silent on a stage, dressed and grouped to look like an incident in a story, etc., e.g. the shepherds with Mary and Joseph round the manger.

tablespoon Mother uses a *tablespoon* to serve out the vegetables at dinner.

tablespoonful the amount contained in a tablespoon when it is full.

tablet In order to wash you need water and a *tablet* of soap. ■ Doctors sometimes give medicine in the form of a *tablet* which you put in your mouth, either to swallow or to suck.

taboo In our club bad language is *taboo* (not allowed).

tabulate To *tabulate* facts, figures, etc., is to write (or print) them in columns.

tack a small, sharp nail; ■ to nail with tacks; ■ a long stitch used to fasten material for the time being; ■ to stitch with tacks. ■ A sailing ship *tacks* when it zig-zags to make the best use of the wind.

tackle the things needed for doing something, e.g. Bring your fishing *tackle* and we'll go fishing. ■ To *tackle* a problem is to set about it vigorously. ■ In football, players *tackle* an opponent in order to get the ball away from him.

tacky sticky, e.g. Partly dry paint and glue are *tacky*.

tact ability to say or do things in such a way that you do not offend anyone.

tactful A *tactful* person is one who has tact.

tactics Before each match our players meet to decide on their *tactics* (plans for outwitting the opponents).

tadpole a baby frog or toad, consisting only of a round head and a tail.

tail A dog wags his *tail* when he's pleased. ■ A coin has two sides, a head and a *tail*.

tailor a man who makes clothes.

taint That dirty saucepan will *taint* our food (i.e. make it impure). ■ There is a *taint* of madness in the family (i.e. a slight tendency to madness).

take *Take* (drink) your medicine. ■ *Take* your hand out of your pocket. ■ I will *take* a photo with my camera. ■ You mustn't *take* things from a shop without paying for them.

takings At the end of the day the shopkeeper added up his *takings* and found they came to £125.

talcum I put *talcum* powder on my body after bathing.

tale a story.

talent Percy has a *talent* for music (i.e. he is specially clever at it).

talented A *talented* person is one who is unusually clever at something.

talk If they *talk*, try to remember every word they say. ■ The speaker gave the school a *talk* on road safety.

talkative A *talkative* person is one who loves talking.

tall One advantage of being *tall* is that you can see over the heads of others in a crowd.

tally The books in the library should *tally* with this list (i.e. all the books named in the list should be in the library).

talon the claw of a bird such as the eagle or hawk.

tambourine a musical instrument like the top of a drum with jingling metal discs fixed into the rim.

tadpole   **tambourine**

tame That wild animal is now so *tame* that it will eat out of your hand. ■ To *tame* wild animals is to make them tame.

tameness Everyone remarked on the *tameness* of the lion (i.e. it was not as wild as they expected).

tamer An animal-*tamer* is someone who tames animals. ■ That animal is *tamer* (less wild) than this one.

tamper Don't *tamper* with that gun; you might accidentally cause it to go off.

tan To *tan* skins is to make them into leather. ■ You can get a *tan* by exposing your skin to the sun. ■ The hot sun will *tan* you (make you brown).

tandem a bicycle on which two people pedal, one behind the other.

tandem

tang a strong taste or flavour, e.g. I don't like that tea; it has a smoky *tang* (or a nasty *tang*).

tangent A *tangent* to a circle is a line that touches it, but doesn't cut it. ■ To fly off at a *tangent* is suddenly to leave the subject that you're talking about and start on another that is entirely different.

tangerine a small kind of orange.

tangible easy to see, touch, or understand, e.g. There is no *tangible* evidence that John is guilty.

tangle The kitten has been playing with the ball of wool and so it is in a *tangle* (the strands are muddled and knotted together).

tank There is a *tank* of water in the roof of the house. ■ The kind of *tank* used in war carries a big gun and travels on caterpillar tracks.

water tank   **tank**

tankard

tankard Uncle drinks his beer from a metal *tankard*.

tanker a ship fitted with special tanks for carrying oil in large quantities.

tanned You can become *tanned* (brown) by lying in the sun.

tanner a man who makes skins into leather.

tannery a place where skins are made into leather.

tantalize To *tantalize* anyone is to tease him by raising his hopes of getting something which he can never get.

tantrum To go into a *tantrum* is to get into a temper.

tap to knock lightly. ■ To get water you turn on the *tap*. ■ In *tap* dancing you beat a rhythm with your feet while you dance.

tape a long, narrow strip of material, especially a length that is marked in inches, etc., for measuring,  i.e. a *tape*-measure. ■ A *tape*-recorder records sounds on special magnetic tape.

taped (slang) To have anyone *taped* is to understand what sort of person he really is.

taper a long, stiff, wax-covered string, used to take a light from a fire, etc., to light something else. ■ Things that *taper* get smaller at one end.

taper   **tassel**

tapestry material into which pictures have been woven (for hanging on a wall, etc.).

tapioca little balls of a starchy food obtained from a tropical plant and ■ used to make *tapioca* pudding, etc.

tapped Mother *tapped* on the window to attract Dad's attention.

tar a thick, black, strong-smelling liquid obtained from coal. ■ To *tar* something is to paint it with tar.

target When people practise shooting they aim at a special round *target* which is marked with coloured rings. ■ Last year we raised £50 for the R.S.P.C.A. This year's *target* is £75 (we aim to get £75).

tariff a price list, e.g. in a restaurant; ■ customs duty, payable on goods brought into a country from abroad.

tarmac tar-covered stones, used for making roads, paths, etc. ■ the part of an aircraft landing-ground that is made of tarmac.

tarnish When polished metal is exposed to dirt, etc., it becomes *tarnished* (dull and stained); ■ the *tarnish* can be removed by polishing the article.

tarpaulin a sheet of tough material made waterproof by coating it with tar.

tarry (pron. tar-y) covered with tar; ■ (pron. to rhyme with 'carry') to stay, e.g. We mustn't *tarry* or we'll be late.

tart Fruit stewed without sugar is *tart* (i.e. it tastes sharp). ■ I like fruit *tart* for dinner (i.e. pastry crust baked over fruit).

tartan cloth with woven coloured stripes crossing at right angles, as used to make Highland kilts.

tartar a hard substance which forms on people's teeth. ■ A person who is fierce and violent may be called a *Tartar*.

task Your *task*, John, is to weed the garden.

Tasmania the island to the south of Australia.

tassel a bunch of threads gathered together to hang down as an ornament, e.g. on the end of a dressing-gown cord.

taste If you drink sea water you can *taste* the salt in it. ■ A person who has good *taste* is one who has a liking for things that are of high quality.

tasteless Pure water is a *tasteless* liquid (i.e. it has no flavour).

tasty You enjoy eating things that are *tasty* – even when you are not hungry.

tattered ragged.

tatters The strong wind has blown our flag into *tatters* (rags).

tattoo To *tattoo* a person is to make a picture, etc., on his skin by pricking it and putting dye into the holes. ■ To beat a *tattoo* is to tap quickly many times.

taught The teacher *taught* Jane to read.

taunt a jeering remark intended to hurt someone; ■ to jeer (at someone).

taut A rope is *taut* when it has been pulled tight.

tavern an inn or public house.

tawdry showy, but cheap and vulgar, e.g. The stage costumes that had seemed so splendid looked *tawdry* when we saw them close up.

tawny brownish yellow, the colour of a lion, or of the *tawny* owl.

tax The government must *tax* people to get money for running the country. ■ Most people pay income *tax* on the money they earn. ■ That heavy work will *tax* your strength (you will have difficulty in finding enough strength to do it).

taxi We hired a *taxi* to take us home from the station. ■ Aircraft *taxi* to their hangars across the landing ground.

taxies After the aircraft has landed, it *taxies* across the landing ground to its hanger.

taxis Three *taxis* will be required to carry us all home from the station.

tea To make *tea,* ■ you put dry *tea* leaves in a pot and pour boiling water on them.

teach If you want to learn to swim, the instructor will *teach* you.

teacher The *teacher* in charge of your class will explain anything that you don't understand.

teak a hard, dark, heavy wood that doesn't easily rot. ■ The *teak* tree grows in tropical forests.

team There are eleven players in a football *team.* ■ The plough was pulled by a *team* of horses (2 or 3 horses harnessed together).

tear (pron. taire) *Tear* the paper to pieces. ■ There is a *tear* in my coat where I caught it on a nail. ■ At 4 o'clock the boys grab their hats and *tear* off (hurry away). ■ (pron. teer) Mary felt so sad that a *tear* came into her eye.

tearfully (pron. teer-fully) The little boy *tearfully* explained that he was lost (i.e. he cried as he spoke).

tease To *tease* anyone is to play-fully to say or do things intended to make him cross.

teaspoon I use a *teaspoon* to stir my tea.

teaspoonful I put one *teaspoonful* of sugar in my tea.

taxi

teaspoonfuls George puts several *teaspoonfuls* of sugar in his tea.

technical At a *technical* college students learn such subjects as engineering, building, etc.

tedious A *tedious* job is one that is long and boring.

teem The rivers here *teem* with fish (i.e. they're full of fish).

teens A person in his *teens* is from 13 to 19 years old.

teeth We use our *teeth* for biting and chewing. ■ A comb also has *teeth*.

teething A baby likes things to chew when he is *teething* (i.e. when his teeth are just beginning to grow through his gums).

telegram When you send a *telegram*, your message is sent from one post office to another by electricity.

telegraph the apparatus used for sending telegrams from one post office to another.

telephone You can pick up a *telephone* and talk into it to someone miles away.

telescope In order to see objects that are a long way away, such as stars, you look through a *telescope*.

telescope

televise They are going to *televise* the football match so we shall all be able to see it on our TV. sets.

television (TV. for short) When you look into a *television* set you see pictures of things that are happening miles away.

tell *Tell* me what John said.

temper What sort of *temper* is he in? (i.e. is he pleased, or angry, sad, or amused, etc.) ■ To lose your *temper*, or to get into a *temper*, is to become very angry. ■ To *temper* steel, etc., is to make it hard (by alternately heating and cooling it).

temperamental A *temperamental* person is one who easily changes from one mood to another, e.g. is one moment very angry, the next moment laughing.

temperate A *temperate* climate is one that is neither very hot nor very cold.

temperature On a hot day the *temperature* is high (say, 30° Celsius); on a cold day the *temperature* is low (say 0° C).

tempest a severe storm.

tempestuous very stormy, e.g. No ship could put to sea in such *tempestuous* weather.

temple a building in which people worship, or a building dedicated to a god.

temporarily The telephone is *temporarily* out of order (i.e. it will soon be all right again).

temporary A *temporary* postman, etc., is one who has the job only for the time being (not for long).

tempt persuade, e.g. The devil is said to *tempt* people to do wrong. ■ Don't *tempt* Mary to stay later than she should.

temptation He couldn't resist the *temptation* to steal the jewel (i.e. he couldn't stop himself wanting to steal it).

tempting Those chocolates are very *tempting* (so attractive that I feel I must have one).

tenacious Things that are *tenacious* hold fast, e.g. glue, a person's grip on you, a dog's grip on your trousers, etc.

tenant A *tenant* pays rent to the landlord who owns the house in which he lives.

tend People *tend* (are inclined) to get fat as they grow older. ■ Nurses *tend* the sick.

tendency Motorists have a *tendency* to take that corner too quickly, so a warning notice has been put up.

tender To make tough meat *tender* enough to eat you must cook it for a long time. ■ If you have a *tender* heart you easily feel sorry for people who are in trouble.

tenderly The father *tenderly* picked up his injured child.

tennis a game in which players hit ■ a soft *tennis* ball backwards and forwards over a net with a *tennis* racket.

tenor a man singer who sings high notes.

tense 'I say,' is in the present *tense*; 'I said,' is in the past *tense*. ■ strained, e.g. You feel *tense* when you're nervous, or when you expect trouble is about to break out.

tension When the *tension* (pull) in a rope becomes too great, the rope snaps.

tent At camp we sleep in a canvas *tent*.

tent

tentacle a long, thin feeler that some creatures have, e.g. An octopus has eight *tentacles*.

tenth (10th) The *tenth* of the month is the day after the ninth. ■ ($\frac{1}{10}$) Ten *tenths* make one whole one.

tepid slightly warm.

term The Christmas *term* at school ends at Christmas time; the Easter *term* ends at Easter. '

terminal the end (of something), especially a screw on electrical apparatus, to which a wire can be fixed.

terminus the station at the end of a railway line.

termite a tropical ant-like insect that does enormous damage to woodwork (of houses, etc.).

terms conditions, e.g. The hire purchase *terms* are £1 deposit and 52 weekly instalments of 75p.

terrace a row of houses all joined to each other; ■ a flat area of raised ground. ■ Terraced hillsides are those cut into a series of *terraces* (steps), so that crops can be grown.

terraced hillside

terrestrial A *terrestrial* globe is one that represents the earth. ■ *Terrestrial* animals are those that live on the earth (i.e. not in water nor in the air).

terrible Being lost in that forest was a *terrible* experience (i.e. one that made me very frightened).

terribly (slang) very, e.g. I'm *terribly* sorry.

terrier a small, lively kind of dog, e.g. a fox *terrier*.

terrific terrible.

terrify to frighten very much, e.g. Low-flying aircraft *terrify* wild animals.

territory a large area of land, e.g. Uncle was the only white man in the whole *territory*.

terror very great fear, e.g. The boys fled in *terror* from the horrible monster.

terrorize The bully would *terrorize* all the smaller boys (i.e. frighten them into doing what he told them).

test Motorists take a *test* so that the examiner can see how well they drive. Your teacher gives you a *test* to see if you have learnt your work.

testament The Old *Testament* is the first part of the Bible; the New *Testament* is the second part.

testify The witnesses *testify* (give evidence) in the law court.

testimonial When applying for a job, people need a *testimonial* from their previous employer (i.e. a letter giving his opinion of their character, ability, etc.).

tether To *tether* an animal is to tie it to something (e.g. a post) by a rope.

text a short quotation from the Bible, e.g. The clergyman preached a sermon on the *text*, 'Love your enemies.'

textbook any one of the books that you study during your lessons, e.g. a history *textbook*.

textile(s) Woven materials such as cotton, wool, silk, nylon, etc., are all *textiles*.

texture the quality (of a cloth), i.e. its roughness, smoothness, thickness, etc.

than John is a year older *than* Jean.

thank It is polite to say, '*Thank* you,' when you are given something.

thankful You say, 'Thank you,' to show that you are *thankful*.

thanks I must send my *thanks* to all those who gave me presents. ■ *Thanks* very much for the present.

thanksgiving In the autumn we have a service of *thanksgiving* for the harvest (i.e. we thank God for the harvest).

that This is the house *that* Jack built. ■ *That* man (i.e. the one over there) is my uncle.

thatch To *thatch* a building is to put on it a roof of straw or rushes, etc. ■ The *thatch* (straw roof) keeps the rain out of the building.

thatch

thaw When the temperature rises above freezing point, the ice will *thaw* and turn into water again.

theatre You go to a *theatre* to see a play acted. ■ The surgeon performs operations on people in the operating *theatre* of the hospital.

theatrical A *theatrical* performance is one usually given on the stage of a theatre.

theft A person who has stolen something is guilty of *theft*. ■ The police charged the man with the *theft* of the watch (i.e. they accused him of having stolen it).

The Hague the capital city of The Netherlands (Holland).

their The children leave *their* coats in the cloakroom.

theirs We boys know our coats from the girls' coats, because ours have belts and *theirs* haven't.

them Peel the potatoes and put *them* in the saucepan.

theme the subject about which a person talks, thinks, or writes; ■ the subject of a piece of music.

themselves There is no need to pass the food to the boys; they can help *themselves*. No adults would go camping with the boys, so they went by *themselves*.

then There was a flash of lightning; *then* (a few seconds later) a roll of thunder.

thence (an old-fashioned word, found chiefly in the Bible) from that place.

theoretical Eric has only a *theoretical* knowledge of cars (i.e. though he knows lots about them he hasn't actually driven one, or made or repaired one).

theory Dad had a *theory* (idea) that people with big noses catch colds more often than other people.

there I looked in the drawer and *there* saw my lost pen.

therefore The rain is pouring down; it will *therefore* be necessary for us to wear macs.

there's (short for) there is, e.g. *There's* a hole in your sock.

thermometer The *thermometer* shows that the temperature is 15° C.

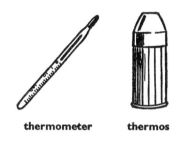

thermometer   thermos

thermos (flask) You put tea or coffee, etc., into a *thermos (flask)* to keep it hot.

these What shall I do with *these* flowers that I have brought you?

they John and Peter are my friends; *they* will help me.

they'll (short for) they will, Peter and John are my friends; *they'll* help me.

they're (short for) they are, Don't eat those cakes; *they're* for the visitors.

they've (short for) they have, Help me to look for the rabbits; *they've* escaped from their hutch.

thick You can cut many thin slices of bread from a loaf, but not many *thick* ones. ■ *Thick* soup is not watery; it is more like paste.

thicken To *thicken* gravy is to make it less watery by mixing flour paste into it. ■ I hope the fog doesn't *thicken* (get thicker).

thicket a group of trees, shrubs, etc., growing close together.

thickness The length of the board is 5 ft., its breadth 6 inches and its *thickness* 1 inch.

thief That is the *thief* who stole my watch.

thieves The police have caught some of the *thieves* who stole our money.

thievish Several gold rings have been stolen by those *thievish* jackdaws.

thigh the top part of the leg, down to the knee.

thimble When I sew, I wear a *thimble* on my finger so that I do not prick it when pressing the needle through the material.

thimble   thistle

thin not thick, e.g. You can cut many slices of bread from a loaf if they are *thin* ones. ■ *Thin* soup is a rather watery liquid.

thing(**s**) A tin opener is a useful *thing* to have in a kitchen. ■ You can pack your *things* (belongings) in this bag.

think I *think* that dogs should be kept on leads in busy streets. ■ You cannot do a difficult sum unless you *think* about it first.

thinly We have only a little butter, so you must spread it on the bread *thinly*.

thinness It is dangerous to skate on the pond because of the *thinness* of the ice.

thin-skinned A *thin-skinned* person is one who easily takes offence.

third (3rd) The *third* of the month is the day after the second. ■ ($\frac{1}{3}$) Three *thirds* make one whole one.

thirst You drink to quench your *thirst*.

thirsty When you are *thirsty* you need something to drink.

thirteen (13) ten and three.

thirteenth (13th) The *thirteenth* of the month is the day after the twelfth. ■ ($\frac{1}{13}$) Thirteen *thirteenths* make a whole one.

thirtieth (30th) The last day of June is the *thirtieth*. ■ ($\frac{1}{30}$) Thirty *thirtieths* make a whole one.

thirty (30) three tens.

this *This* house (here) is ours. ■ Dad gave me *this* (i.e. the thing I am showing you).

thistle a prickly weed, the Scottish national emblem.

thither (an old-fashioned word) Hearing that our friend was in London, we went *thither* to see him.

thorn a short, hard, sharp growth, on such bushes as roses, gooseberries, etc.

thorough We'll give the room a *thorough* (complete) clean. ■ He is a *thorough* nuisance (i.e. as bad a nuisance as it is possible to be).

thoroughbred A *thoroughbred* horse, etc., is one whose ancestors are known to be of high quality.

thoroughfare A notice, 'No *thoroughfare*,' means that people are not allowed to go along that road, path, etc.

thoroughly You mustn't wear that wet coat again until it is *thoroughly* dry (i.e. not the least bit wet).

thoroughness The machine cleaned the milk bottles with such *thoroughness* that not a speck of dirt remained on them.

those These clothes (here) are ours; *those* (over there) belong to someone else.

though Betty is a good reader *though* she is only five years old.

thought David *thought* hard for a moment, then gave the answer to the problem. ■ I *thought* Pat danced very well (i.e. that was my opinion).

thoughtful Susan is in a *thoughtful* mood (i.e. she is thinking). ■ Brian is a *thoughtful* (considerate) boy.

thoughtless That was a *thoughtless* action (i.e. had you stopped to think, you wouldn't have done it).

thousand (1,000) ten hundreds.

thousandth (1,000th) The *thousandth* page is the one that follows page 999. ■ ($\frac{1}{1000}$) A millimetre is a *thousandth* of a metre (i.e. 1,000 millimetres = 1 metre).

thrash To *thrash* a person is to beat him with a stick or a whip.

thrashing The master gave the naughty boy a *thrashing* with the cane. ■ Why are you *thrashing* (beating) that boy?

thread The *thread* on a screw is the spiral ridge that goes round and along it. ■ To sew a button on, you need a needle and *thread*. ■ To *thread* a needle is to put thread through the hole in the needle.

screw thread

threadbare Cloth that is *threadbare* has had the surface fluff worn off so that the bare threads can be seen.

threat something said or done that warns you of trouble or punishment, etc., to come.

threaten To *threaten* is to make a threat.

three (3) one more than two.

thresh To *thresh* corn is to beat the grain out of it.

threshing *Threshing* corn is beating the grain out of it. ■ Farmers use a *threshing* machine for threshing corn.

threshold the slab of timber or stone that forms the floor in a doorway. ■ You could say on December 31st: 'We stand on the *threshold* of a new year'.

threw Jack *threw* the ball high into the air and caught it again.

thrifty A *thrifty* person does not waste his money, but saves as much as possible.

thrill You experience a *thrill* as the aircraft dives towards the ground (i.e. you find it exciting).

thriller a book or play in which exciting things happen, especially murders.

thrilling A *thrilling* book (or a *thrilling* experience, etc.) is one that makes you feel excited.

thrive Babies *thrive* on milk (i.e. they grow strong and healthy).

throat Jane has a sore *throat* which hurts every time she swallows something.

throb to beat, like your heart or your pulse.

throes Mother is in the *throes* of packing for the holidays (she is struggling with the job).

throne a special, official chair for a king, a queen, or a bishop, etc.

throng Crowds of people *throng* round the great man wherever he goes. ■ I couldn't get near enough to see the great man because of the *throng*.

throttle When you press a car accelerator, it opens the engine *throttle*, and so makes it go faster. ■ To *throttle* anyone is to choke him, e.g. by squeezing his neck.

through A bird flew into the room *through* the open window. ■ To read a book *through* is to read it from cover to cover.

throughout Grandad slept *throughout* the programme so he didn't see any of it.

throw Pick up the ball and *throw* it over the wall.

thrown Some boy has *thrown* a stone and broken my window.

thrush a song bird with a speckled breast.

thrust to push hard or with determination, e.g. The knight *thrust* his sword into the dragon's body.

thud A great rock fell on to the soft ground with a dull *thud*.

thug a ruffian, a bully who beats people up and robs them.

thumb You have four fingers and a *thumb* on each hand.

thump When I get excited over an argument, I sometimes *thump* the table with my fist.

thunder During a storm there are usually flashes of lightning and the rumbling noise of *thunder*.

Thursday the fifth day of the week.

thus You should hold your cricket bat *thus* (like this). ■ We arrived late at the concert and *thus* missed the first item on the programme.

thwart The good fairy is able to *thwart* the evil plans of the witch (i.e. prevent the evil plans from working).

thy (an old-fashioned or poetical word) your, e.g. 'Our Father which art in heaven, hallowed be *Thy* name.'

thyme (pron. time) a plant with sweet-smelling leaves, used to flavour food.

tick If you can hear your watch *tick* you know it is going. ■ The teacher puts a *tick* (√) against sums that are correct. ■ (slang) To *tick* someone off is to tell him off.

ticket When you travel by train or bus, etc., or go to an entertainment, you buy a *ticket*, which you can show to people to prove that you have paid.

tickle If you *tickle* my ribs I cannot help laughing.

ticklish Joyce is very *ticklish*; you have only to touch her ribs and she goes into fits of laughter. ■ A *ticklish* job is one over which you have to be very careful.

tidal A *tidal* river is one in which the water flows up from the sea until high tide, then flows out to the sea until low tide.

tide the rise and fall of the water level in the seas due to the pull of the moon and sun. High *tide* is when the water level is high.

tidings news.

tidy When a room, etc., is *tidy*, everything is in its proper place and there is no litter lying around. ■ To *tidy* a room is to make it tidy.

tie *Tie* the ends of the string together in a knot or in a bow. ■ Men wear a collar with a *tie* (neck-*tie*) round it. ■ The race ended in a *tie*, Paul and Peter finishing together.

tied Pat *tied* her hair ribbon in a bow. ■ Tom and Bob *tied* for first place in the competition, so the prize was shared between them.

tier Each *tier* of the wedding cake is smaller than the one below it. ■ a row of seats as in a theatre, placed slightly higher than the row in front.

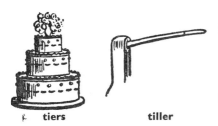

tiers **tiller**

tiff a little quarrel – not a serious one.

tiger a big, striped, cat-like wild animal.

tight Hold *tight* or you will fall over when the bus goes round the corner. ■ This coat is so *tight* that I can hardly move my arms or breathe when I'm wearing it.

tighten to make more tight, e.g. to *tighten* your grasp on [some-thing, or to *tighten* your belt.

tightly Mother held little Billy's hand *tightly* so that he could not run away.

tights a close-fitting garment like knickers and stockings all in one.

tile A roof *tile* is made of baked clay or of slate. ■ To *tile* a room (e.g. a bathroom) is to cover the walls with *tiles* (squares of hard, shiny clay, or of a plastic material, etc.).

till I'll wait *till* 4 o'clock. ■ A shopkeeper puts the money he takes in a *till* (a special drawer in the counter, etc.). ■ To *till* the soil is to cultivate it, as a farmer does.

tiller a handle fixed to the top of a boat's rudder.

tilt You *tilt* a jug in order to pour the milk out of it.

timber Builders use *timber* (wood) to make the floors, doors, cupboards, etc., in a house.

time The *time* was 4 o'clock. ■ We had a good *time* at the party. ■ There were no cars in olden *times*. ■ To *time* a race, etc., is to see how long it takes.

timetable You look at a railway *timetable* to find the times of the trains. ■ The school *timetable* shows the times when we have the various lessons.

timid a timid creature is one that takes fright very easily.

tin a shiny, white metal. ■ You use a *tin*-opener ■ to open a *tin* of fruit or meat, etc. ■ To *tin* food is to put it in a tin (made air-tight so that the food keeps for a long time).

tinder dry material that you can light with a spark.

tinge That blue paint has a *tinge* of green in it (i.e. it is a slightly greenish blue).

tingle The frost makes my fingers and toes *tingle* (sting).

tinker a man who mends pots, pans, kettles, etc.

tinkle The little bells round the cows' necks *tinkle* as they walk. ■ I like to hear the *tinkle* of cow-bells.

tinned Food is *tinned* (sealed into tins) to preserve it. ■ You can't use *tinned* food if you haven't a tin-opener.

tinny The little chapel bell makes a *tinny* sound (as if someone were beating on a tin).

tinsel shiny strips of metal hung over Christmas trees, etc., to make them glitter.

tint Autumn *tints* are the colours seen in autumn leaves.

tiny very small.

tip-toe If we walk on *tip-toe* no one will hear us.

tip-toeing The late-comers are *tip-toeing* to their rooms so as not to make a noise.

tire The boys will soon *tire* (have enough) of weeding the garden. ■ Each car wheel has a rubber *tire* on it (more often spelt *tyre*).

tired Jane was so *tired* that she fell asleep as soon as her head touched the pillow. ■ When we are *tired* of walking we shall get on a bus.

tireless A *tireless* person is one who seems never to get tired.

tiresome A *tiresome* person is one who soon makes people cross.

tissue *Tissue* paper is very soft, thin paper, used for wrapping or packing things, etc.

titbit a particularly nice little piece (of food, etc.).

title The *title* of the book is 'Treasure Island'. ■ Peter Brown's uncle has a *title*; he is called Lord Brown, Sir Paul Brown, or something of that kind.

titled Lord Tilney, Sir Edward Jones, the Earl of Staines, Lady Hilgay, etc., are all *titled* people.

titter a short, quiet laugh; ■ to make a short, quiet laugh.

toad a frog-like animal that breeds in water and lives on land. ■ A *toad*-in-the-hole is sausages or pieces of meat, baked in batter.

toad   toadstool

toadstool a mushroom-like growth, often see on lawns, etc.

toast You make *toast* by browning slices of bread in front of a fire or under a grill, etc. ■ To *toast* bread is to make it into toast. ■ To *toast* a person is to drink to his health.

tobacco   People smoke *tobacco* in cigarettes, cigars or pipes.

tobacconist   If you want to buy tobacco you go to a *tobacconist's* (shop).

toboggan   It's fun to slide down snow-covered slopes sitting (or lying) on a *toboggan.*

today   We have a holiday *today* (this day).

toddle   My little brother is not old enough to walk, but he can *toddle* a few steps. (He is a toddler.)

toddler   a very young child, but not a baby.

toe   Your big *toe* is showing through the hole in your sock. ■ John kicked a stone and damaged the *toe* of his shoe.

toffee   a kind of sweet which is hard when you buy it, but it becomes soft and sticks to your teeth when you chew it.

together   Betty and Brian often walk home *together.* ■ Play the two notes *together* (at the same time).

toil   hard work. ■ To *toil* is to work hard for a long time.

toilet   Jane hasn't completed her *toilet* (i.e. she's still dressing). ■ a lavatory, W.C., convenience.

token   When Mr. Smith retired we presented him with a watch as a *token* of our affection for him.

Tokyo   the capital city of Japan.

told   Dad *told* the man to go away.

tolerable   I find this weather quite *tolerable* (i.e. I can put up with it).

tolerate   Dad will not *tolerate* (allow) swearing in the house. ■ I can *tolerate* (put up with) jazz, though I don't like it.

toll   To *toll* a bell is to ring it slowly as for a funeral. ■ a payment made for travelling on certain roads or bridges.

tomahawk   an axe used by Red Indians for fighting.

tomahawk   tongs

tomato   a red fruit, usually eaten with salad.

tomatoes   Many *tomatoes* are used to make tomato sauce.

tomb   a grave.

tombstone   The man's name is cut into the *tombstone* placed over his grave.

tomorrow   If today is Monday, *tomorrow* will be Tuesday.

ton   A *ton* of coal is usually delivered in 20 hundredweight (cwt.) bags.

tone   The *tone* of a school is its standard of behaviour. ■ The curtains do not *tone* with the wallpaper (i.e. the colours do not look well together). ■ In music, the note B is a *tone* higher than the note A.

tongs   The *tongs* in the sugar-basin are for picking up the sugar lumps.

tongue   The doctor told Paul to open his mouth and put out his *tongue*. 'Hold your *tongue*' means 'Be quiet.'

tonic   a medicine, etc., that makes sick people feel well again.

o

tonight If you don't sleep *tonight* you'll be tired tomorrow.

tonsillitis an illness in which the tonsils become swollen and painful.

tonsils two little growths, one on each side of the hole in the back of your mouth.

too Dad can't get through that little hole because he is *too* fat. ■ You can come, and Betty can come *too* (also).

took I *took* a photo with Tom's camera. ■ Bob *took* an apple from the dish. ■ Janet *took* care of the baby while Mother went shopping.

tool something such as a saw, chisel, drill, etc., used when doing a job.

tooth Open your mouth and the dentist will pull out that bad *tooth*. ■ Tom broke a *tooth* out of the comb as he pulled it through his tangled hair.

toothache a pain in a tooth.

topic On what *topic* (subject) were you talking? (i.e. What were you talking about?)

topical A *topical* event, etc., is one that is in the news.

topple If you shake the table that vase will *topple* (wobble about and fall).

topsy-turvy upside-down.

torch When night came Jim took a *torch* from his pocket and shone it on the path so that we could see where to go.

tore Tom *tore* the paper into little pieces. ■ Sandra *tore* her dress on a nail sticking out of the chair. ■ The naughty boy saw the policeman and *tore* off down the street at top speed.

torment Do not *torment* the animal (i.e. don't cause it pain). ■ The injured man was in *torment* (great pain).

torn I have *torn* the paper into pieces.

tornado a very severe storm in which winds whirl round with great force.

torpedo a big, cigar-shaped weapon which travels just beneath the surface of the water and explodes on hitting a ship. ■ To *torpedo* a ship is to fire a torpedo at it.

torpedo   **tortoise**

torrent After heavy rain the quiet mountain stream becomes a *torrent* that rushes madly down the valley. ■ The rain fell in *torrents* (very heavily).

torrential *Torrential* rain is very heavy rain.

tortoise a slow-moving, scaly, land creature, completely covered with a thick shell out of which he pushes his head and legs when necessary.

torture To *torture* someone is to hurt him so that he suffers great pain. ■ In olden times people were tortured with instruments of *torture* to make them tell secrets.

toss To *toss* a coin is to spin it up into the air (usually to guess which of the sides – head or tail – will be uppermost when it falls.)

tossed The referee *tossed* a coin to decide which team should kick off. ■ The ship was *tossed* about by the stormy sea.

total To find the *total* you add up all the numbers. e.g. The *total* of 2, 6 and 5 is 13.

totally wholly, completely, e.g. You are *totally* wrong if you think that chalk is like cheese.

totter to stand or to walk about as if you were likely to fall over at any moment – like a drunken man.

touch If you *touch* the wet paint you'll get some on you.

touching sad, e.g. a *touching* story, a *touching* letter, etc.

touchy A *touchy* person is one who easily takes offence.

tough This meat is so *tough* that I can't chew it. ■ A long walk in bad weather won't hurt Jack; he's very *tough*.

tour During the holiday we shall *tour* Scotland (i.e. travel around in the country). ■ During our *tour* of Scotland we hope to visit all the important towns.

tourist a person who travels for pleasure.

tournament a sporting competition in which many players take part, e.g. a tennis *tournament*; ■ (in olden times) a mock battle between small numbers of knights in armour.

tow Tie your car to ours and we'll *tow* you home ■ (or, we will give you a *tow* home).

towards As people come *towards* you they appear to get bigger.

towel After washing, you dry yourself on a *towel*.

tower The highest part of the church is its big, square *tower*. ■ The new buildings *tower* above the old ones (i.e. they are very much higher than the old ones).

tower   tractor

town More people live in a *town* than in a village.

trace To *trace* a drawing or a map, etc., is to copy it on to a piece of transparent paper put over it. ■ The police can find no *trace* (sign) of the missing man.

tracing a copy of a drawing, etc., made ■ on (transparent) *tracing* paper placed over it. ■ The police had difficulty in *tracing* the missing man (i.e. in following up clues leading to him).

track Trains travel along the railway *track*. ■ It is easy to follow the *track* left by the car tyre in the mud. ■ Police used dogs to *track* the criminal (they followed his scent).

tractor To pull his plough, etc., the farmer uses a powerful motor *tractor* with big wheels.

trad. (short for) traditional jazz, i.e. jazz in the old style.

trade To *trade* is to buy and sell things. ■ *Trade* is good when there is much buying and selling. ■ Uncle is a carpenter by *trade*.

trader a person who earns his living by buying and selling things.

tradesman a shopkeeper.

tradition the passing down of ideas, etc., from generation to generation.

traditional A *traditional* song is one that has been passed down to us by generations of people who have sung it through the ages (i.e. not because it was written down).

traffic Road *traffic* is increasing as more cars, coaches, lorries, and buses come into use.

tragedy an impressive play about some great event, or a sad play; ■ any happening that is very sad.

tragic Mrs. Smith will be a long while recovering from the *tragic* death of her husband (i.e. he died under specially sad circumstances).

trail We could follow the dog by the *trail* of blood from his cut paw. ■ To *trail* anything is to pull it behind you along the ground.

trailer pieces from a coming film, shown (at a cinema) to advertise it. ■ The farmer takes his produce to market in the *trailer* pulled by his car.

train If you want to do well at sports you must *train* for them (i.e. put in lots of practice). ■ A railway *train* runs along lines. ■ The *train* of a dress is the long end that trails along the ground.

trainer the man in charge of the training of a boxer, or of a football team, etc.

training Our team are *training* for an important match. ■ Their *training* consists of exercises, running, practice games, etc.

traitor The *traitor* was shot for giving away his country's secrets to an enemy.

tramp a beggar who walks around the countryside; ■ to walk, e.g. The car broke down and we had to *tramp* all the way home. ■ Don't *tramp* about so noisily; you'll wake everyone up.

trample Boys come into the garden to look for a ball and *trample* on my flowers and ruin them.

trance When people go into a *trance* they don't seem to know what is going on around them, though they are apparently awake.

transfer Football clubs who *transfer* players to other clubs ■ are paid a *transfer* fee. ■ a small picture which can be removed (by soaking) from the paper on which you buy it and put on any object that you wish to decorate.

transfix Mary was *transfixed* with horror (rooted to the spot).

transformer an apparatus used to change the voltage of electricity, e.g. from the 240 volts in your house to the 12 volts needed for your electric train set.

transfusion When doctors give a person a blood *transfusion*, they put blood from another person into his body.

translate Can you *translate* French (language) into English?

translation 'If you please,' is a *translation* of the French, 'S'il vous plaît.'

transmit The broadcasting stations *transmit* radio and TV. programmes to all parts of the country.

transmitter That B.B.C. *transmitter* sends out broadcast radio programmes.

transparent If a thing is *transparent* you can see through it.

transplant To *transplant* seedlings, etc., is to take them out of the soil and plant them again elsewhere.

transport You can *transport* goods (or people) from one place to another by train, or by lorry, bus, ship, etc.

trap We caught the mouse in a *trap* baited with cheese. ■ To *trap* any creature is to catch it in a trap, or by a trick. ■ You get into the cellar through a *trap*-door in the kitchen floor.

trapeze bar(s) supported by ropes so that they swing freely; ■ *Trapeze* artists at the circus can swing from one trapeze to another.

trapeze artist

trapper a man who hunts animals by setting traps for them.

trappings ornaments, decorations – especially those put on a horse for some special occasion.

trash rubbish.

travel We shall *travel* from London to Newcastle by coach or train.

travelled Last year we *travelled* to Italy by boat and train. ■ A much *travelled* man is one who has done a great deal of travelling.

traveller someone who travels.

travelling *Travelling* by coach makes Jane sick. ■ A *travelling* salesman is one who travels from place to place selling his goods.

trawler a ship that catches fish by pulling a wide-mouthed net along the sea-bottom.

tray You can carry all the things we need for tea on a *tray*. ■ Ash-*trays* are for cigarette ash.

treacherous A *treacherous* person is one whom you trust, but who harms you secretly. ■ Ships steer clear of the *treacherous* Goodwin Sands (i.e. the sands are likely to trap ships).

treacle a thick, dark, sweet and sticky liquid obtained during the manufacture of sugar.

tread the flat surface of a stair, on which you put your foot. ■ Look where you're walking or you'll *tread* in that puddle.

treadle A machine such as a sewing machine, potter's wheel, etc., sometimes has a *treadle* so that you can work it with your foot.

treason It is *treason* to give away your country's secrets to an enemy – or to help your country's enemy in any other way.

treasure The buried *treasure* consisted of a box full of gold and precious stones. ■ I shall *treasure* this gift because it was given me by someone I love (i.e. I shall value it highly).

treasurer The *treasurer* of a town, a club, or a society, etc., is the person who looks after the money matters, takes in the fees, pays the bills, etc.

treat The natives *treat* travellers well (i.e. they are pleasant to them). ■ Doctors *treat* people for illnesses by giving them medicine, etc. ■ Uncle took us to the circus as a *treat* (to please us).

treatment I have no complaint about my *treatment* (i.e. the way in which I was treated). ■ The best *treatment* for tiredness is rest.

treaty The two countries signed a *treaty* in which they agreed to help each other.

treble To *treble* anything is to make it three times as big. ■ A boy who sings high notes is a *treble*. ■ Boys who have high voices sing the *treble* part (of a song, hymn, etc.).

tree The apple *tree* produced no fruit so we sawed it up for firewood.

trellis The roses grow up a *trellis* made of wooden strips nailed across each other.

trellis

tremble to shake with fear or excitement, etc.

trembling The frightened boys were *trembling* so much that their teeth chattered and their knees knocked together.

tremendous There was a *tremendous* explosion as the aircraft hit the ground (i.e. the explosion was severe and frightening).

trench a ditch – either a small one dug in the course of digging a garden, or a big one to provide soldiers with shelter from bullets, etc.

trend The present *trend* in women's fashions is towards trousers (i.e. more and more women are wearing trousers).

trespass To *trespass* is to go on to another person's property without permission. ■ (old-fashioned use, in the Bible, etc.) to sin.

trespasser someone who goes on to another person's property without permission.

tresses the hair of a woman's head.

trestle a framework to support a table top, or on which a carpenter puts wood while he saws it, etc.

trial The prisoner was put on *trial* (i.e. brought into court where a judge heard the evidence for and against him). ■ Mother finds Tommy a great *trial* (i.e. he is a lot of trouble to her).

triangle a flat shape made up of three straight lines, of equal or differing lengths

trestle   **triangle**

tribal A *tribal* custom is one observed by a tribe.

tribe a group of people ruled by a chief. The ancient Israelites were made up of twelve *tribes*.

tribulation great suffering.

tributary A *tributary* of a river is a smaller stream that flows into it.

tribute money paid to a conqueror, etc., e.g. the Jews paid *tribute* to the Romans (Caesar). ■ Many people paid *tribute* to (praised) Donald's courage.

trick I didn't mean to give Tom the money; he got it from me by a *trick*. ■ My favourite conjuring *trick* is bringing a rabbit out of an empty hat. ■ People who try to *trick* you out of your money are dishonest. ■ the cards played in one round of a game.

trickery behaviour intended to deceive someone.

trickle Only a *trickle* of water came from the tap so it took a long time to fill the cup.

tricky That man is a *tricky* (crafty) fellow. ■ Making an unexploded bomb safe is a *tricky* job (if you don't do it properly, there may be a disaster).

tricycle a cycle with three wheels.

tricycle   trident

trident a fork with three prongs, like that held by the sea-god, Neptune.

tried The prisoner was taken to court to be *tried* by a judge. ■ John *tried* to put out the fire (i.e. he did his best).

trier someone who tries, e.g. Johnny doesn't always succeed, but he's a good *trier*.

trifle a little, e.g. Spare a *trifle* (a little money) for the carol-singers. Dad seems a *trifle* angry. ■ To *trifle* with someone (or something) is to refuse to take him (it) seriously. ■ You make *trifle* by soaking cake, etc., in wine and covering it with jelly, fruit, cream, etc.

trifling A *trifling* matter is one that is of no importance.

trigger To fire a gun you press the *trigger* with your finger.

trill the sound of two quickly alternating notes, or a similar sound made by a bird, etc.

trim neat and tidy, e.g. a *trim* garden; ■ to make neat and tidy, e.g. *Trim* the edges of the lawn. ■ to decorate, e.g. I'll *trim* the hat with ribbon. ■ The car is in good *trim* (condition).

trimming The *trimming* on a dress is the lace, ribbon, etc., put on as decoration. ■ Dad is *trimming* the edges of the lawn with the shears.

trinket a cheap ornament, piece of imitation jewellery, etc.

trio a piece of music for three performers; ■ a group of three people who play music or sing together.

trip I saw Pat *trip* over the step and fall down. ■ I enjoyed our *trip* to the seaside. ■ to dance or walk lightly.

tripe   part of a bullock's stomach, cooked as food (*tripe* and onions). ■ anything that is of poor quality, e.g. a poor book.

triple   made up of three parts, e.g. *triple* time (in music).

triplet   a set of three musical notes played in the time of one. ■ *Triplets* are a set of three babies born at the same time to the same mother.

tripod   a three-legged stand to support a camera, etc.

tripod   **trombone**

tripped   The dancers *tripped* daintily across the stage. ■ David *tripped* over the rope and fell flat on his face.

tripper   someone who goes on a trip, especially on a day trip to the seaside, etc.

triumph   To *triumph* over an opponent is to defeat him. ■ Our team returned home in *triumph* (pleased with themselves for having won).

triumphant   Brian returned *triumphant* (pleased because he had won.)

trivial   of little value, unimportant, e.g. The loss of a pencil is too *trivial* a matter to report to the police.

trod   Tom *trod* in the puddle and got his foot wet.

trodden   Someone has *trodden* in this wet cement; I can see the footprints.

trolley   A tea *trolley* (or *trolley*-table) is like a tray fitted with four long legs and wheels. ■ A *trolley* bus is driven by electricity from two overhead wires.

trombone   a musical instrument rather like a trumpet, but with a longer tube which slides in and out.

troops   soldiers.

trophy   a cup or a shield, etc., kept as a reward for winning a sports competition, etc.

tropical   *Tropical* things are those that have some connection with the tropics, e.g. *tropical* diseases, *tropical* plants.

tropics   the hottest part of the earth, between the *Tropic* of Cancer (north of the equator) and the *Tropic* of Capricorn (south of the equator).

trot   to run at a gentle pace. ■ When horses *trot* they go at a pace between a walk and a gallop.

trouble   It's no *trouble* (i.e. I don't mind doing it). ■ Peter caused us a lot of *trouble* (i.e. he caused us extra work and worry). ■ May I *trouble* you for a match, please? (a courteous ·vay of asking).

troublesome   A *troublesome* person is one who causes trouble.

trough   (pron. troff) the low part between two waves. ■ Pigs feed from a *trough* (a long narrow, container).

trounce   To *trounce* an opponent is to beat him by a big margin (e.g. by 10 goals to 0 in a football match).

troupe At the circus we were entertained by a *troupe* of acrobats.

trousers A man wears *trousers* over the lower part of his body.

trout a fresh-water fish which people enjoy fishing for, and eating.

trowel a small spade-like tool used by bricklayers for spreading mortar on the bricks; a garden *trowel* is similar except that the blade is not flat.

garden trowel

truant a child who is absent from school without permission. ■ To play *truant* is to be absent from school without permission.

truce a stopping of fighting for a time, e.g. The armies agreed to a *truce* while the leaders met to talk over their quarrel.

truck A railway *truck* carries about 10 tons (of coal, etc.). ■ I advise you to have no *truck* with that man (i.e. have nothing to do with him).

trudge to walk, usually to walk heavy-footed like someone who is very tired.

true It is *true* (i.e. it actually happened). ■ A *true* friend is one who will always stand by you when in need.

truly truthfully. ■ You can end letters to people you don't know very well with the words, 'Yours *truly*,' (followed by your name).

trump To *trump* up a story is to invent it. ■ a playing-card of the suit chosen to be of higher value than the other three suits for that game. ■ To *trump* (at cards) is to play a trump (winning card).

trumpet a brass musical wind-instrument.

truncheon a short, thick stick carried by policemen as a weapon.

trundle The market salesmen *trundle* their barrows noisily along the street.

trunk the part of a tree just above the ground, between roots and branches; ■ a big box with a hinged lid, in which clothes, etc., can be packed for travelling. ■ An elephant has a tail at one end and a *trunk* at the other. ■ A (telephone) *trunk* call is one to a place some distance away. ■ If the head, arms and legs are cut from a body, only the *trunk* is left.

trunks Boys usually wear bathing *trunks* for swimming.

truss a bundle of hay or straw. ■ To *truss* a fowl is to tie it up ready for cooking.

trust To *trust* someone is to be sure that you can depend on his honesty.

trustworthy A *trustworthy* person is one you can depend on.

trusty (an old-fashioned word) You could rely on a *trusty* sword, a *trusty* steed, a *trusty* servant, etc.

truth Bob speaks the *truth* (i.e. what he says is true).

truthful A *truthful* person is one who tells the truth, not lies.

try Let's *try* the TV to see if it is working. ■ No matter how hard I *try*, I cannot run as fast as Peter. ■ The job of judges in law courts is to *try* prisoners (to decide whether or not they are guilty).

trying   I am *trying* (attempting) to mend my bicycle. ■ A *trying* person is one who is hard to put up with.

tub   a container like half a barrel, used to plant shrubs in, etc.

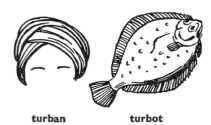

turban   turbot

tuba   a big, brass instrument that plays very low notes.

tube   To get the toothpaste out of the *tube* you squeeze it. ■ London's *tube* railways run through huge pipes built under the ground.

tuck   a fold sewn into a garment to take up unwanted material. ■ A *tuck* shop is a shop where sweets, etc., can be bought. ■ *Tuck* your shirt into the top of your trousers.

Tuesday   the third day of the week.

tuft   a bunch, e.g. a *tuft* of grass, a *tuft* of hair.

tuition   teaching, e.g. At this school the *tuition* is free, but you pay for the books you need.

tulip   a colourful, bell-shaped flower that grows from a bulb.

tumble   a fall. ■ There is a gate at the top of the stairs so that the baby can't *tumble* down them.

tumbler   a big drinking-glass for water, beer, orange squash, etc. ■ a kind of acrobat who does cartwheels, somersaults, etc.

tummy   childish name for the abdomen or stomach, ■ e.g. *tummy*-ache.

tumult   a din, a crowd's loud and disorderly noise.

tune   I know the words of the song, but not the *tune* to which they are sung. ■ You are not singing in *tune* (i.e. your notes are a little too low or too high). ■ To *tune* a violin, etc., is to adjust its strings so that they produce the right notes. ■ To *tune* a radio set is to adjust its controls so that you can hear the programme you require.

tuneful   That is *tuneful* music (i.e. it has a pleasant melody).

tunic   a short jacket that is part of a uniform. ■ Gym *tunics* are the school uniform in many girls' schools.

tunnel   Traffic crosses the river by going through a *tunnel* built under it. ■ To *tunnel* is to dig a tunnel.

turban   an Indian head-covering made by winding a scarf round and round.

turbine   a machine worked by water or steam power.

turbot   a large and very tasty kind of flat fish.

tureen   a deep dish with a lid, in which gravy is put on the dinner table.

turf   the top layer of soil containing growing grass, e.g. Dad cut *turf* from the field and laid it on our garden to make a lawn.

Turk   a citizen of Turkey.

Turkey   a country partly in Europe, but chiefly in Asia Minor, south of the Black Sea.

turkey a big bird which people like to eat, especially on Christmas Day.

Turkish the language spoken in Turkey. ■ *Turkish* things are those from Turkey, e.g. *Turkish* carpets, *Turkish* baths, *Turkish* delight.

turn Don't stand with your back towards me; *turn* and face me. ■ The sails of the windmill *turn* when the wind blows. ■ The witch can *turn* a man into a toad. ■ The next *turn* in the show is a song-and-dance act.

turning To get to our school you take the first *turning* on the right. ■ The tomatoes are *turning* red as they ripen. ■ I'm *turning* round to see who is behind me.

turnip the swollen root of a plant, boiled and eaten as a vegetable.

turnover The shopkeeper's *turnover* is £200 a week (that is the amount of money he takes each week – not all of it is profit). ■ An apple *turnover* is a fold of pastry with apple in it.

turnstile a little gate in the entrance to a sports ground, etc., which goes round as you walk through it and so lets in only one person at a time.

turpentine a thin, colourless, strong-smelling liquid obtained from pine trees, and used to make paint, etc.

turret a small tower on a building. ■ The gun-*turret* of a tank, etc., is the moving part on the top, which contains the gun.

turtle a sea animal like a big tortoise. ■ When anything (e.g. a ship) turns *turtle* it turns upside down.

tusk On each side of an elephant's trunk is a big, bony *tusk* (a very big tooth).

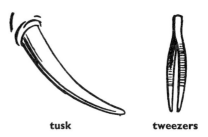

tusk   tweezers

tussle When the boys met in the doorway there was a *tussle* to decide which of them would let the other through.

tutor As there were no schools near by, Dad had to pay a *tutor* to come to the house to teach us.

twain (an old-fashioned word) two, e.g. The lightning flash split the rock in *twain*.

twang You hear a *twang* as the archer releases the taut bow-string.

tweak To *tweak* anyone's nose or ear, etc., is to give it a pull and a twist.

tweed a thick, rough, woollen cloth often used to make sports jackets and overcoats.

tweezers small nippers, such as those used to pull out splinters, or used by ladies to pull hairs from their eyebrows.

twelfth (12th) The *twelfth* of the month is the day after the eleventh. ■ ($\frac{1}{12}$) A month is a *twelfth* of a year. (i.e. 12 months = 1 year).

twelve (12) ten and two.

twentieth (20th) The *twentieth* of the month is the day after the 19th. ■ ($\frac{1}{20}$) A hundredweight is a *twentieth* of a ton (i.e. 20 cwts. = 1 ton).

twenty (20) two tens.

twice *Twice* three is six. ■ I told you *twice*, once yesterday, and again this morning.

twig a very small branch of a tree or bush.

twilight Just after the sun has set, and again just before sunrise, is a period of *twilight*, when it is neither light nor dark.

twin This engine has *twin* cylinders (i.e. two cylinders exactly alike). ■ Peter and Paul are *twins* (i.e. brothers born at the same time).

twine string. ■ Plants such as runner beans *twine* round other things for support.

twinge a sudden, sharp, shooting pain, e.g. a *twinge* of toothache.

twinkle to sparkle, like a star. ■ I know by the *twinkle* in his eye that Brian is amused.

twirl Dancers can *twirl* round and round on one toe.

twist You *twist* strands of wool together to make a cord. ■ To *twist* your ankle is to injure it painfully through bending it hard in a wrong direction. ■ a dance, popular in the early 1960's.

twitch A sudden pain made the man's face *twitch* (suddenly jerk).

twitter the tuneless repeated squeaking made by birds such as sparrows. ■ Sparrows don't sing; they *twitter*, tunelessly.

two (2) We have *two* eyes, *two* ears, *two* hands and *two* feet.

tying Why are you *tying* the string in a bow when I asked you to tie it in a knot?

type That boy is not my *type* (not the sort of boy I like). ■ Words in books, etc., are printed with metal *type* which is inked and pressed on the paper. ■ You can *type* (print) your own letters with a *type*writer.

typewriter a small machine on which people can type (print) letters, etc., by pressing keys.

typewriter

typhoon a particularly violent kind of storm well known in the China seas.

typical David is a *typical* English schoolboy (i.e. he has all the qualities, abilities, faults, etc., that you would expect an English schoolboy to have).

typist someone who types (on a typewriter).

tyrant a cruel ruler (or master) who allows his people no freedom.

tyre The rubber *tyre* on a car or bicycle wheel has air inside it (also spelt *tire*).

tyre

udder the milk bag that hangs under a cow.

ugly unpleasant to look at, e.g. Witches were *ugly* creatures. I hate to see *ugly* buildings.

U.K. (short for) United Kingdom (i.e. England, Scotland, Wales and Northern Ireland).

ukulele a kind of guitar with four strings.

ukulele   umbrella

ulcer a big sore from which nasty matter runs.

ultimately After many attempts I *ultimately* succeeded in getting the bird back into its cage.

ultimatum To give someone an *ultimatum* is to make a proposal to him that he must agree to or there will be trouble.

umbrella You hold an *umbrella* over your head to keep off the rain.

umpire The job of the *umpire*, in games such as cricket, is to supervise the game and see that the rules are kept.

* **unable** I am *unable* to cycle to school because my bicycle is broken.

unaccompanied An *unaccompanied* song is one in which there is no instrument playing with the singer.

unaided This is my own *unaided* work (i.e. no one helped me).

unaltered Although it is raining, our plans for the day's outing remain *unaltered* (i.e. we are still going to do what was planned).

unanimous A *unanimous* decision is one with which everyone present agrees.

unarmed An *unarmed* person is one who is not carrying any weapons.

unassuming An *unassuming* person is one who would rather not have attention drawn to his bravery, his cleverness, or his success, etc.

unavoidable Noise is *unavoidable* when you learn to play a drum (i.e. you can't learn without making a noise).

unawares The enemy came on us *unawares* (i.e. took us by surprise).

---

* 'un' in front of a word can cause the word to have the opposite meaning. Thus, 'untidy' means 'not tidy'. Such words are included here only if: (1) they are very common; (2) the word is better known in its 'un' form than without the 'un'; (3) the 'un' does not merely give the word the opposite meaning, but alters the meaning. For other 'un' words, remove the 'un' and look up the part of the word that you have left.

unbearable I find the noise of road drills *unbearable* (I can't stand them). Derek is *unbearable* (I can't stand him).

uncanny mysterious, strange, and rather frightening, e.g. *uncanny* noises or movements in a dark, old house.

unceasing never ending.

uncertain not sure.

uncle Your *uncle* is the brother of your father or your mother, or he is your aunt's husband.

uncomfortable I am very *uncomfortable* lying on this hard, cold floor. ■ Jane felt most *uncomfortable* (ill at ease) while her mother talked to the teacher about her.

uncommon The golden eagle is an *uncommon* bird in England (i.e. you hardly ever see one).

unconscious I didn't know anything about the pulling out of my tooth because the dentist gave me gas that made me *unconscious*.

uncouth An *uncouth* person is one who lacks politeness and good manners.

undaunted neither discouraged nor afraid, e.g. The explorers went forward *undaunted* by the dangers around them.

undecided I am *undecided* about which book to choose (i.e. I can't make up my mind).

under Tom is lying on the floor *under* the table. ■ He earns *under* (less than) £20 a week. ■ The men work *under* a foreman. ■ This packet of butter is *under* weight (i.e. weighs less than it should).

undercarriage The *undercarriage* on which the aircraft runs along the ground is raised when the

aircraft is properly in the air, and lowered again just before it lands.

underclothes garments such as vests, pants, etc., which are worn next to the skin.

undergo I hope that I shall never again have to *undergo* such an unpleasant experience.

underground The *underground* railway runs through tunnels built under the ground.

undergrowth vegetation growing under trees.

underhand An *underhand* action is one done on the sly (i.e. it is unpleasantly secret).

underline To *underline* a word, etc., is to put a line under it.

underneath *Underneath* this carpet is a wooden floor.

underrate To *underrate* a person is to think that he is less able than he is.

understand Do you *understand* what I mean? ■ To *understand* another language is to know what it means. ■ I *understand* (I have heard) that Jane is to have a party.

understandable It is *understandable* that John should want to be like the other boys (i.e. we know why this is so).

understood The motorist *understood* that the red light meant that he had to stop, so he put on his brakes.

undercarriage

understudy An actor, etc., has an *understudy* to take over his part if ever he is unable to appear himself.

undertake I will *undertake* (agree to do) all the camp cooking.

undertaker a man who supplies the coffin and sees to all the arrangements for a funeral.

undertone To talk in an *undertone* is to talk very quietly.

undertook I *undertook* (agreed to do) all the camp cooking.

underwear underclothes.

undesirable not wanted.

undid The parcel fell apart when I *undid* the string. ■ Mary tidied the room but the boys who came in later *undid* her good work (i.e. the boys made the room untidy again).

undies (slang) female underclothes.

undisturbed If I wish to remain *undisturbed* I lock my door.

undo You have to *undo* the lace before you can take off your shoe. ■ To *undo* a piece of work, etc., is to ruin what has been done.

undoing Dick is *undoing* his belt because it is too tight. ■ The prisoner's greediness was his *undoing* (i.e. the cause of his downfall).

undone I can't take off the shoe until I have *undone* the lace. ■ Are there any jobs I have left *undone*?

undoubtedly You are *undoubtedly* right (i.e. there is no doubt about it).

undress Before swimming, you *undress* and put on a swimming costume.

undressed I cannot come to the door while I am *undressed* (naked). ■ The boys *undressed* and put on their swimming trunks.

undue more than the proper amount, e.g. Brian spends an *undue* amount of money on sweets.

unduly The price of apples is *unduly* high (i.e. higher than it ought to be).

unearth While searching in the attic you may *unearth* (find) all kinds of long-lost things. ■ While digging in the ruins you may *unearth* a skeleton (dig it out of the earth).

unearthly An *unearthly* noise (or sight, etc.) is one so strange that it doesn't seem to be of this world.

uneasy There was an *uneasy* silence as each person waited nervously for the other to speak first.

unemployed An *unemployed* person is one who hasn't a job.

uneven The car bumped over the *uneven* surface of the road.

uneventful It's been an *uneventful* day. We had an *uneventful* journey (i.e. nothing of special interest happened).

unexpected We had some *unexpected* visitors (i.e. we didn't know they were coming).

unfold To *unfold* a tale is to tell it. ■ To *unfold* a letter (or a newspaper, etc.) is to open it flat so that you can read it.

unfortunate unlucky, e.g. It was *unfortunate* that Larry broke his leg on the first day of the holiday and so missed all the fun.

ungainly The crocodile is an *ungainly* animal (i.e. clumsy in his movements).

unicorn an imaginary animal, like a horse with a single horn on his head.

uniform The children attending our school wear school *uniform*. ■ Police, soldiers, sailors, etc., all wear *uniform* (i.e. special clothes so that we know what their job is). ■ The eggs are *uniform* in size (i.e. all of the same size).

uninhabited An *uninhabited* island is one on which no one lives.

union a joining together, e.g. the *union* of two states to form one country. ■ Workers join a trade *union* because it protects their interests, gets them increases in wages, etc. ■ The *Union* Jack is the flag of the United Kingdom.

unison When people sing in *unison* they all sing the same tune at the same time – i.e. they don't sing in parts.

unit one (1); ■ a single thing or person, e.g. The degree Celsius is the *unit* in which we measure temperature. The *unit* in which we measure the distances between places is the kilometre.

unite To *unite* things or people is to join them together. ■ People *unite* when they join together.

United States the country in North America between Canada and Mexico.

unity the number one (1), e.g. You add $\frac{1}{4}$ to $\frac{3}{4}$ to make *unity*. ■ People are working for the *unity* of all the Churches (i.e. to unite them all into one Church).

universal concerning everyone or everything, e.g. a *universal* complaint, a *universal* fear, etc.

universe The *universe* is all the things that exist in space – the earth, sun, stars, galaxies, etc.

university A *university* such as those at Oxford, Cambridge, London, etc., is made up of colleges where people go to study after leaving school.

unjust It is *unjust* to punish a person who has done nothing wrong.

unkempt untidy, especially hair in need of combing, e.g. I can see by Pat's *unkempt* appearance that she has just got out of bed.

unkind An *unkind* person is one who does or says things that make other people unhappy.

unless The bath will overflow *unless* you turn off the tap.

unlikely The boys are always hungry so it is *unlikely* that they will forget to come in to dinner.

unmistakable In the mud were the *unmistakable* marks of car tyres (i.e. they certainly were car tyre marks).

unnatural An *unnatural* mother is one who does not show her children the love, etc., that she should. ■ The boy's leg was bent into an *unnatural* shape so we knew it was broken.

unnecessary It is *unnecessary* to wear your glasses when you are asleep (i.e. you have no need of them at that time).

unnerve To *unnerve* anyone is to cause him to be afraid.

U.N.O. (short for) United Nations Organization.

unpleasant nasty, not pleasing, e.g. an *unpleasant* smell, an *unpleasant* taste.

unpopular Clive is an *unpopular* boy; hardly anyone likes him.

unravel To *unravel* a tangled piece of string, etc., is to get the knots and tangles out of it.

unreasonable An *unreasonable* person is one who expects more from people than they are able to do or give.

unreliable An *unreliable* car may break down on the road. You cannot depend on an *unreliable* person.

unrest There is *unrest* among the people (i.e. they are ill at ease, discontented, beginning to grumble, etc.).

unrivalled The boys sitting in the tree had an *unrivalled* view of the procession (i.e. no one else had such a good view).

unruffled Mary sat calmly in her seat, quite *unruffled* (not upset) by the rude remarks of the boys.

unruly An *unruly* horse or person is one who doesn't do as he is told.

unsatisfactory not as good as expected, e.g. an *unsatisfactory* school report, an *unsatisfactory* explanation, etc.

unscathed The driver stepped *unscathed* (not at all injured) from the wrecked car.

unscrupulous An *unscrupulous* person will not hesitate to use dishonest means to get what he wants.

unsightly ugly, e.g. an *unsightly* advertisement in the countryside.

unskilled *Unskilled* workers are those who do jobs for which they have not required any special training.

unsociable An *unsociable* person is one who does not like mixing with other people.

unsuccessful Jack made an *unsuccessful* attempt to stop the thief (i.e. the thief got away).

unsuspecting You can play the trick only on an *unsuspecting* person (i.e. someone who isn't thinking of the possibility of a trick).

unthinkable I know Brian wouldn't do such a wicked thing; it's *unthinkable* (I cannot think it is possible).

untie *Untie* the lace and take off your shoe.

untied Bob's shoe lace became *untied* and he tripped over the loose ends. ■ Jack *untied* the lace and took off his shoe.

until Wait here *until* I come back.

unto (an old-fashioned word) to, e.g. Come *unto* me.

untold not told, e.g. His adventures remained *untold* because he was too modest to speak of them. ■ That disease is the cause of *untold* suffering (i.e. more suffering than can ever be known).

untrustworthy not honest, e.g. Don't let him have charge of the money; he's *untrustworthy*. You cannot rely on what he says; he's *untrustworthy*.

untruth a lie.

unusual It is *unusual* for a girl to play football (i.e. you don't often see it).

unwell Mary is *unwell* so I've sent her to bed and called the doctor.

unwieldy An *unwieldy* thing is one that is difficult to manage because it is too big, too heavy, or of an awkward shape.

unwise foolish.

uphill Riding a bicycle *uphill* is harder than riding along a level road. ■ An *uphill* task is one that is very difficult.

uphold If the teacher makes a rule I can be sure that my dad will *uphold* it (support it).

upholster To *upholster* chairs, etc., is to put springs, padding and cloth over the seats, backs or arms to make them soft and springy.

upkeep Dad spends a great deal of money on the *upkeep* of this house (i.e. keeping it repaired, painted, etc.).

upland high land.

upon on, e.g. The parachutist fell *upon* a haystack. ■ Once *upon* a time there were three bears.

upper Your top teeth are those in your *upper* jaw. ■ The sole and heel of the shoe are made of stiff leather, but the *upper* is made of softer material.

uppermost Tom is on the *uppermost* branch of the tree; he can't get any higher. ■ The thought that is *uppermost* in your mind is the one you are most aware of.

upright To see if a post is *upright* you hang a weight on a string beside it. ■ An *upright* person is one who is completely honest and fair.

uproar the loud disorderly noise made by an excited crowd – e.g. because of delight or anger.

uproot To *uproot* a plant is to pull it up by the roots.

upset Mary is so *upset* by the loss of her kitten that she is crying. ■ In reaching across the table Tom *upset* a cup of tea over the cakes.

upshot result, e.g. We couldn't agree about the plans for the party and the *upshot* was that we had no party at all.

upstairs The bedrooms are *upstairs* (on the floor above). ■ We go *upstairs* to bed (i.e. we climb the stairs).

upwards I climbed steadily *upwards* till I reached the top of the ladder.

uranium a very heavy white metal. Atomic energy is obtained by splitting atoms of *uranium*.

Uranus a small planet, farther from the sun than the earth, Mercury, Mars, Venus, Jupiter or Saturn.

urban An *urban* district is a town. *Urban* things are those in a town, or to do with a town.

urchin a small, mischievous boy.

urge Riders sometimes *urge* their horses on with whips. ■ I *urge* you to stop (do please stop, I beg you). ■ To have an *urge* to do something is to feel very strongly that you simply must do it.

urgent Anything that is *urgent* must be attended to immediately.

urn When tea or coffee is required for a large number of people, it is often made in a big metal *urn* with a tap at the bottom. ■ a container for the ashes of a dead person.

U.S.A. the United States of America, the country in North America between Canada and Mexico.

usable Though it is rather old, the boat is *usable* (i.e. it can be used).

usage The damage to this book has been caused by rough *usage* (i.e. it has not been handled with care).

use (pron. to rhyme with 'juice') What is the *use* of that? (i.e. What is it for?) As a result of the accident Joe lost the *use* of his arm (i.e. he couldn't do anything with his arm). ■ (pron. to rhyme with 'fuse') You *use* a handkerchief for blowing your nose.

used When I was younger I *used* to be afraid of dogs, but I'm not now.

useful A pocket knife is a *useful* thing (there are many jobs you can do with it).

useless Shoes are *useless* to a person with no feet.

user The last *user* of this washbasin didn't empty out the water.

usher the door keeper in a law court, etc.; ■ a person who shows people to their seats in a hall, etc.

U.S.S.R. (short for) the Union of Socialist Soviet Republics, the state of which Russia is a part, but which is sometimes called Russia.

usual It is *usual* for people to sit when they eat.

usually People *usually* eat sitting down (i.e. they don't often stand up when eating).

utensil Kitchen *utensils* are the pots, pans, etc., used in the kitchen.

utmost To do your *utmost* is to do all that you possibly can.

utter complete, e.g. That is *utter* nonsense. ■ In spite of the pain he was in, Ian didn't *utter* a sound.

utterly Nothing remains of the building; it was *utterly* destroyed.

vacancy an empty place, e.g. Janet is going to work in Dad's office when they have a *vacancy* for her.

vacant empty, e.g. a *vacant* house.

vacate To *vacate* a house, or a seat, etc., is to go away and leave it empty.

vacation holiday, e.g. No one goes to the school during the *vacation*.

vaccinate Doctors *vaccinate* us so that we don't catch smallpox. (They do it by making a scratch on an arm or leg, and putting a special liquid into it.)

vaccination This *vaccination* scar on my arm shows where I was vaccinated ■ *Vaccination* (being vaccinated) takes only a moment.

vacuum a space that contains nothing, not even air. ■ You can keep liquids hot in a *vacuum* flask. You can suck up dust with a *vacuum* cleaner.

vagabond a tramp.

vague not clear or distinct, e.g. That *vague* description would fit anyone. I have only a *vague* idea of what he said.

vain A *vain* person is one who has too high an opinion of himself. ■ Our efforts to put out the fire were in *vain*, for the building was burnt to the ground.

vale a valley.

valentine a special card with amusing or loving greetings sent to a member of the opposite sex on Saint Valentine's Day (14th February); ■ the sweetheart to whom a valentine is sent.

valiant brave.

valley The river flows along a *valley* between two hills.

valour (a rather old-fashioned word) courage – especially in battle.

valuable A *valuable* article is one worth a great deal of money.

value The *value* of this watch is £15 so I'll not sell it for less. ■ If you want to know what the ring is worth, get a jeweller to *value* it for you. ■ People *value* such things as freedom, the love of friends, etc. (i.e. they attach great importance to such things).

valve a device through which air, or water, electricity, etc., can flow in one direction only.

van Goods are delivered to people in a motor *van*. On the railway, luggage is carried in the luggage *van*, and the guard travels in the guard's *van*. ■ The *van* of an army is the group of soldiers in the front.

vandal a person who destroys something beautiful for no apparent reason.

vane On top of the steeple is a weather *vane* to show which way the wind is blowing.

vane

vase

vanilla a flavouring used in ice-cream, custard, etc.

vanish When things *vanish* they disappear from sight – slowly, or suddenly.

vanity a wrong kind of pride in your own ability, or your deeds, good looks, etc.

vanquish (not often used nowadays, except by writers) to conquer.

vapour water in the air in the form of a gas. ■ When you heat a liquid it changes into a *vapour* (becomes a gas).

variation There has been no *variation* in the temperature (i.e. it has stayed the same). ■ In music, a *variation* on a tune is a different way of playing the tune.

varied People who have a *varied* diet eat all kinds of different things.

variety In a *variety* show there are many different kinds of acts. ■ A gardener has produced a new *variety* (kind) of rose.

various There are *various* ways of cooking an egg – frying, boiling, poaching, scrambling, etc.

varnish a substance that looks like treacle, with which you paint things to give them a hard, shiny surface. ■ To *varnish* anything is to coat it with varnish.

vary You can *vary* the loudness of the radio by turning this knob to right or left.

vase The *vase* stands on the table as a decoration; it looks even nicer with flowers in it.

vaseline grease obtained from petroleum and used as an ointment.

vassal a very humble servant. ■ A *vassal* state is one having to take orders from a more important state.

vast of very great size, e.g. a *vast* forest, a *vast* palace.

vat a very big tub – especially of the kind used in factories to contain liquids during manufacturing processes.

vault a cellar, especially an underground place where the dead are buried, or wine stored. ■ When you *vault* over anything you rest your hands on it to help you over.

veal meat from a calf, e.g. *veal* and ham pie.

veer When the wind *veers* it changes direction clockwise, e.g. starting as a north wind, it would become in turn, N.E., E., S.E. and then S.

vegetable a plant, especially one such as a cabbage, potato, carrot, etc., which is grown for food. ■ *Vegetable* oils, *vegetable* dyes, etc., are those obtained from vegetables.

vegetarian someone who eats only vegetable foods, not meat.

vegetation No *vegetation* can grow in that dry land (i.e. no plant life of any kind).

vehicle any such thing as a car, lorry, cart, van, bus, etc., that is used to carry goods or people over land.

veil the part of a woman's head-covering that hides her face (worn, e.g., by eastern women and

veil

nuns). ■ To *veil* anything is to hide it.

vein a blood vessel; strictly, one of the kind through which blood flows back to the heart.

velocity The *velocity* of the bullet is greater than the speed of sound.

velvet a silk or cotton material with thick, carpet-like pile on one side.

vendor someone who sells something, e.g. The *vendor* wants £16,000 for the house.

vengeance revenge.

venison deer-meat, e.g. They killed a deer to provide them with *venison* for supper.

venomous poisonous, e.g. a *venomous* snake.

vent an air hole, such as that under the sleeve of a macintosh. ■ Tom gave *vent* to his anger by shouting and kicking the door. ■ It is silly to *vent* your anger on a door.

ventilate To *ventilate* a room is to keep it supplied with fresh air. ■ When you *ventilate* a grievance you tell people about it.

ventilation The *ventilation* in the room was so bad that people fainted from lack of fresh air.

ventilator a device through which a room is kept supplied with fresh air, e.g. a special kind of brick with holes in it.

ventriloquist A *ventriloquist* can talk without moving his mouth, so that his voice seems to come from the dummy that he holds.

venture to dare, e.g. Tom did not *venture* to ask the gunman his business. ■ Only a brave man would undertake such a *venture* (dangerous journey, task, etc.).

venturesome A *venturesome* person is one who likes to do things that are dangerous.

Venus the planet that is often seen as a bright evening or morning star; ■ the goddess of love to the ancient Romans.

veranda, verandah a low platform with a roof, joined to the side of a house.

veranda

verb a word such as 'swim', 'run', 'think', 'wonder', etc., that tells of something that you do; or that tells of the state of being something, e.g. 'be', 'was', 'am', 'live', etc.

verbal Dad didn't write; he sent a *verbal* (spoken) message.

verdict After hearing the evidence, the *verdict* of the jury was 'Not guilty'.

verge Angela is on the *verge* of tears (almost crying). ■ There is usually a grass *verge* beside a country road.

verger a church caretaker – he also assists the clergymen with the arrangements for funerals, weddings, etc.

verify To *verify* anything is to find out whether it is true.

vermilion a bright red (colour).

vermin harmful creatures such as rats, mice, fleas, lice, bugs, etc.

verminous People (or places) that are *verminous* have vermin on them (or in them).

versatile A *versatile* person is one who is good at a number of different things.

verse You repeat the tune for each *verse* of a hymn, or song. ■ poetry, e.g. Shakespeare's plays are in *verse*.

version Bob's *version* of what happened is not the same as the story told by Peter. ■ There have been several translations of the Bible, including the Authorized *Version* and the Revised *Version*.

versus Today's football match is The School *versus* The Old Boys (or, in shortened form, The School *v.* The Old Boys).

vertical A *vertical* line is one that is upright, i.e. at right angles to the horizon, or to some other fixed line. A *vertical* take-off aircraft rises straight up into the air.

very You are the *very* person I am looking for. ■ A hundred years is a long time; 500 years is a *very* long time.

vessel A blood *vessel* is a vein or an artery. ■ Liners, ships, boats, tugs, tankers, etc., are *vessels* that sail on the sea. ■ Cups, basins, pots, bottles, casks, etc., are *vessels* that hold liquids.

vest a garment worn over the top part of the body, next to the skin; ■ a waistcoat.

vestibule a small hall in the entrance to a building.

vestige Baby lay on the rug without a *vestige* of clothing (i.e. not even a little clothing).

vestments garments, specially the special clothes worn by clergymen for important services.

vestry The clergy and choir put on their special robes in the church *vestry*.

vet. (short for) veterinary surgeon. If my dog is ill I take it to a *vet*. (animal doctor).

veteran a person who has had many years of experience, but especially an old soldier. ■ A *veteran* car is a very old car.

veterinary You take sick animals to a *veterinary* surgeon for treatment.

veto To *veto* anything is to forbid it (i.e. say that it shall not be done).

vex To *vex* someone is to make him cross.

vexed Auntie was *vexed* (upset and annoyed) because Joan was rude to her.

via We go to Paris *via* (through) London, Dover and Calais.

viaduct a structure like a long bridge with many arches, on which a road or railway crosses a valley, etc.

viaduct

vibrate If you pluck, or bow, the string of a musical instrument, it will *vibrate* (tremble) and give out a note.

vibration It is the *vibration* (trembling) of the string of the instrument that makes the note.

vicar the clergyman in charge of a parish.

vicarage the official house provided for a vicar.

vice a very bad habit or fault, e.g. drunkenness. ■ To hold a thing firm while he works on it, a workman puts it between the jaws of a *vice* and screws them together.

vice

vice-captain The *vice-captain* does the captain's job when the captain is absent or unfit.

vicinity There are no shops in the *vicinity* of (near) our house.

vicious A *vicious* person or animal is one who has very bad habits or faults – especially one who is bad-tempered.

victim an innocent person who suffers as a result of an accident or crime, etc.

victimize To *victimize* someone is to make him the victim of some crime, or swindle, etc.

victor the winner (of a battle or a race, etc.).

victorious To be *victorious* is to win.

victory If we win this match, it will be our first *victory* this year.

Vienna the capital city of Austria.

view You get a lovely *view* of the countryside if you look out of this window. ■ In my *view*, school holidays are too long. ■ We will go and *view* the house before we buy it.

vigilant watchful, e.g. The shop-keeper has to be *vigilant* in case naughty boys steal things off his counter.

vigorous After that *vigorous* exercise you will feel very tired.

vigour strength and energy, e.g. Uncle set about the job with *vigour* (of body or mind).

Vikings sea raiders from across the North Sea, who made many attacks on Britain 1,000 years ago.

vile wicked and detestable, e.g. I could not be so *vile* as to betray a friend for money. ■ (slang) very bad indeed, e.g. a *vile* TV pro-gramme, *vile* weather.

villa a big country house.

village There are fewer houses in a *village* than there are in a town.

villain The *villain*, especially in a pantomime or a play, is the bad man.

vindicate To *vindicate* anyone is to prove that, after all, he was right.

vine a climbing plant on which grapes grow.

vinegar a sour, pleasant-smelling liquid, used for pickling onions, etc., and eaten with such foods as tinned fish, salad, etc.

vineyard Large quantities of grapes are grown in French *vine-yards*.

viola a flower like a pansy; ■ a musical instrument like a violin, but a little bigger.

violence The wind blew with such *violence* that trees were up-rooted. ■ As the man would not leave the house when Dad told

him, we had to use *violence* to put him out.

violent A *violent* explosion, etc., is one of very great force. ■ A *violent* death is not a natural death, but one caused by an accident or murder.

violet a tiny, sweet-scented, bluish-mauve flower. ■ *Violet* is the colour of a violet.

violet   violin

violin a small, stringed musical instrument which you hold under your chin and play with a bow.

violinist The *violinist* took up his violin and began to play.

violoncello ('*cello* for short) an instrument like a big violin, but with a spike in the bottom, on which it stands while you play it.

viper a poisonous kind of snake, such as the adder.

virgin a girl who has not had sexual experience.

virtue goodness.

virtuous A *virtuous* person doesn't commit sins or crimes.

viscount a nobleman more im-portant than a baron, but less important than an earl.

visibility On a clear day when *visibility* is good, you can see for miles. *Visibility* is very poor in fog.

visible The stars are *visible* on any cloudless night.

vision People wear glasses to improve their *vision*. ■ something seen by people (especially holy people) in a dream, etc.

visit Auntie lives in London so I'm going there to *visit* her. ■ Auntie paid us a *visit*, but she didn't stay with us long.

visitor That boy doesn't attend this school; he's just a *visitor* here.

visual *Visual* aids are pictures that help you to understand something.

vital very important, e.g. A piece of *vital* information is information of special importance.

vitality To be full of *vitality* is to be energetic and very much alive.

vitally It is *vitally* (extremely) important that this message should be delivered.

vitamin a substance present in small quantities in certain foods, and of vital importance to health, e.g. Fresh greenstuffs contain *vitamin* C.

vivid Night was made like day for an instant by a *vivid* flash of lightning. ■ very clear, e.g. a *vivid* description, a *vivid* imagination.

vixen a female fox.

viz. (short for) namely, e.g. Great Britain consists of three countries, *viz.* England, Scotland and Wales.

vocabulary a list of words, e.g. All the French words used in our French book are listed in the *vocabulary* at the end of the book.

vocal You make sounds when air from your lungs causes the *vocal* cords in your throat to vibrate. *Vocal* music is music that is sung.

vocalist a singer.

voice Mary spoke in a quiet *voice*. What a lovely *voice* that singer has! ■ To *voice* an opinion, etc., is to talk about it.

void an empty space, e.g. Nothing can fill the *void* left by Father's death.

volcano When a *volcano* erupts, masses of lava, steam, ash, etc., from deep inside the earth are hurled into the air.

vole a small, mouse-like animal.

volley Soldiers fire a *volley* when a number of them shoot at the same time. ■ In tennis, etc., to *volley* is to hit the ball back before it touches the ground.

volt the unit used to measure the force of an electric current. Your house electric lights probably work at 240 *volts* and your bicycle lamp at about 3 *volts*.

volume The *volume* of a block 2 cm × 3 cm × 4 cm is 24 ccs. ■ There are thousands of *volumes* (books) in the library. ■ *Volumes* of smoke poured from the factory chimney.

voluntary This club is a *voluntary* organization (you don't have to join). ■ The church organist plays a *voluntary* while people are arriving for the service.

volunteer Who will *volunteer* (offer) to do the washing up? ■ A *volunteer* is someone who volunteers.

vomit to be sick (i.e. to bring up food, etc., from your stomach). ■ the stuff brought up from your stomach when you are sick.

voracious A *voracious* animal or person is one who is very hungry and greedy.

vote In an election you *vote* for a person by putting a cross against his name on the voting paper. ■ I gave Brown my *vote* (i.e. I voted for Brown).

voter a person who has a right to vote.

voting People are not *voting* for Brown because they do not want him to be elected. ■ You vote for a person by putting a cross against his name on the *voting* paper.

vouch I can *vouch* for the truth of Jack's story (i.e. I assure you that it is true).

voucher a printed paper to prove your right to a sum of money, or to a gift, etc., e.g. gift *vouchers* (which people send each other at Christmas), luncheon *vouchers* (which people hand over in exchange for lunch in a restaurant).

vow To make a *vow* is to promise solemnly. ■ At their marriage ceremony people *vow* to be faithful to each other.

vowel any one of the letters, a, e, i, o, u.

voyage To *voyage* is to travel by ship. ■ The ship set out on a long *voyage*.

vulgar rude, e.g. a *vulgar* person, *vulgar* language. ■ Don't be *vulgar* (i.e. behave decently). ◪ A *vulgar* fraction is one such as $\frac{3}{4}$, $\frac{7}{8}$, etc., made up of numbers above and below a line.

vulture a big, bald-headed bird, noted for eating dead animals.

wad a lump of some soft substance, used to block a hole, etc. ■ A *wad* of notes is a bundle of paper money.

wadding cotton wool, etc., used when packing breakable articles.

waddle to walk like a duck, i.e. slowly and rolling from side to side.

waddling A duck came *waddling* across the farm towards us.

wade to walk with difficulty through water, or mud, snow, etc., that is quite deep.

wafer a very thin, sweet biscuit, especially one of the kind that is sold with ice cream.

wag A dog will *wag* his tail from side to side if he is happy. ■ Joe is a *wag* (i.e. he likes making jokes).

wage(s) When Dad started work his *wages* were £5 a week. ■ The king raised an army with which to *wage* war on his enemies.

waggle to wag.

waggon, wagon The settlers travelled out west in a covered *wagon* drawn by horses. ■ The engine is pulling a train made up of coal *wagons*.

wagtail I know that little bird is a *wagtail* by the way it keeps moving its long tail up and down.

vulture   wagtail

waif a child (or animal) that has been left with neither home nor parents.

wail to cry – especially with a long-continued cry caused by very great sorrow.

waist Tom wears a belt round his *waist* to hold up his trousers.

waistcoat a garment like a short jacket without sleeves, which is worn under a jacket.

waistcoat　　　　wallet

wait I shall *wait* here till Mary comes. ■ To *wait* at table is to bring on the food, etc., for people to eat.

waiter You sit at a hotel or restaurant table while a *waiter* brings you the food and drink that you require.

waitress a girl who waits on the customers in a café or restaurant, etc.

waits people who go round carol singing at Christmas time. ■ If I am not ready, Joe *waits* for me.

wake If Billy is asleep, *wake* him (up) and tell him it's time to get dressed.

wakeful If the sentry is *wakeful*, the enemy cannot creep up and take him by surprise.

waken Dad oversleeps unless he has an alarm clock to *waken* him each morning.

waking Brian spends all his *waking* hours thinking about his invention (i.e. he stops thinking about it only when he is asleep).

Wales the country joined to the west side of England.

walk If I *walk* too far my feet get sore. ■ Let's go for a *walk* through the woods.

wall There is a brick *wall* round the garden to keep people out. I like to hang pictures on the *walls* of my room.

wallet Dad keeps his paper money, his driving licence, etc., in a leather *wallet* in his jacket pocket.

wallflower a sweet-smelling garden flower that blooms in the spring; ■ a girl who sits out by the wall of a dance-hall because she hasn't a partner.

wallow The hippopotamus loves to *wallow* (roll about) in mud.

walnut a tasty nut in a crinkled shell, ■ that grows on the *walnut* tree; ■ the wood of the walnut tree, used to make furniture, etc.

walrus a sea animal like a seal with tusks, found near the North Pole.

wallflower　　　　walrus

waltz If a band plays a *waltz* ■ I like to dance a *waltz* to the music. ■ *Waltz* time is three beats in a bar.

wan People look *wan* (pale) when they are ill or very tired.

wand The fairy touched the man with the *wand* that she held in her hand and he turned into a frog.

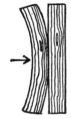

wardrobe   **warped wood**

wander to move from place to place without any definite idea of where you intend to go.

wane to become smaller and less powerful, as a full moon does.

want To be in *want* is to be very poor. ■ Our car was useless for *want* of petrol. ■ I don't *want* to go to bed (I'd rather stay up).

wanton playful. ■ *Wanton* destruction is destruction for which there seems to be no reason.

war In the last great *war*, Germany, Italy and Japan fought against the United States, the Soviet Union and Britain.

warble Some birds *warble* rather than sing (i.e. they make a pleasant, quiet, continuous, vibrating sound).

warbler a bird that warbles, e.g. the reed *warbler* or the blackcap.

ward There are a number of beds in each *ward* of the hospital. ■ To *ward* off an attack, etc., is to keep it off.

warden a guardian or a governor. ■ During the war, air raid *wardens* helped people during air raids. ■ A church*warden* is a church official.

warder The job of a prison *warder* is to look after the prisoners.

wardrobe a big cupboard in which to keep clothes. ■ A person's *wardrobe* is his stock of clothes.

warehouse a building in which goods (of all kinds) are stored.

warfare The soldiers are glad when the *warfare* between the countries is ended and they can go back home.

warily The animal crept *warily* out of its hole (i.e. it was keeping a careful look-out for enemies).

warlike A *warlike* person is one who likes wars.

warm I like my bath water to be neither hot nor cold, but pleasantly *warm*. ■ *Warm* clothes are of the kind that keep you warm on cold days.

warmly When you greet a person *warmly* you let him know that you are very pleased to see him.

warmth It is pleasant to feel the *warmth* of the spring sunshine.

warn I must *warn* you against bathing on this dangerous beach.

warning A man gave us this *warning*, 'If you bathe on this beach you may be drowned.' ■ While he was *warning* us, someone was drowned.

warped Wood often becomes *warped* (twisted) as it gets old and dry.

warrant Janet has done nothing to *warrant* such unkind treatment (i.e. she does not deserve it). ■

There is a *warrant* for his arrest (an official document giving the police authority to arrest him). ■ The manufacturers *warrant* that all the washing machines they supply are properly tested (they give a promise to this effect).

warren A (rabbit) *warren* is a piece of ground in which many rabbits live together.

warrior a soldier, usually an experienced or famous one.

Warsaw the capital city of Poland.

wart a small, hard, painless lump on the skin – usually of the finger.

wary To be *wary* is to be cautious, especially to be keeping a careful look out for danger.

wash You *wash* dirty hands with soap and water. ■ If you don't hold tight a big wave might *wash* you off the ship. ■ The *wash* made by passing ships causes little boats to bob about violently. ■ That dirty shirt needs a good *wash*.

washable A thing that is *washable* is not spoilt by being washed.

washer a washing machine; ■ a flat ring of rubber, or leather, etc., inside a tap, which shuts off the water when you turn the tap off; a flat ring of metal put, for example, under a nut before you screw it down.

washer   wasp

washing Tom is *washing* his dirty hands (with soap and water). ■ Mother uses a *washing* machine for washing dirty linen.

Washington the capital city of the United States (i.e. where the government buildings are).

wasn't (short for) was not, e.g. It *wasn't* George who scored the goal; it was Fred.

wasp a flying insect like a big, thin bee, with black and yellow stripes and a poisonous sting.

wastage It is a pity there is so much *wastage* of food when millions of people are starving and need the food that is thrown away.

waste To *waste* anything is not to make good use of it, to use more than necessary, or to throw it away unused. ■ The *waste* left on the dinner plates is thrown in the dustbin.

wasteful A *wasteful* person is one who wastes things.

watch When I want to know the time, I look at my wrist-*watch*. ■ To be on the *watch* is to be looking out for something. ■ If you *watch* carefully you'll see how the trick is done.

watchman In many workplaces a (night) *watchman* is employed to keep an eye on things while the workers are away.

water We use *water* for drinking and washing. ■ Take this can of water and *water* the garden with it.

water-closet (usually shortened to *W.C.*) a lavatory, i.e. a place where waste is passed out from the body, and washed away with water from a tank above.

watercolour paint that you mix with water, not oil. ■ A *watercolour* is a picture painted with watercolours.

watercress a hot-tasting plant that grows in water and is eaten in salad.

wave A great *wave* swept up the beach and washed away Billy's sandcastle. ■ As visitors leave, people *wave* their hands or handkerchiefs and shout, 'Goodbye.'

watercress

waterfall

wave

waterfall A *waterfall* is made by a stream tumbling over a precipice.

waterlogged A *waterlogged* boat is one so full of water that it is hardly afloat.

watermark The *watermark* in paper cannot be seen unless you hold the paper up to the light, when it can be seen as a mark lighter in colour than the paper.

waterproof Water will not go through anything that is *waterproof*. ■ A *waterproof* is a coat that keeps out the rain.

watertight A thing (such as a roof, a boat or a container) that is *watertight* will not let water in or out.

watery Soup that is *watery* has too much water in it. ■ You often have *watery* eyes when you have a cold, or if you have been crying.

watt the unit in which the amount of electricity used is measured, e.g. a big electric fire takes 3,000 *watts*; a 100-*watt* lamp is a bright one.

waver to begin to give way, e.g. The soldiers were seen to *waver* as the enemy attack became fiercer.

wavy *Wavy* things have an up and down surface like waves on the sea, e.g. a *wavy* line, or *wavy* hair.

wax the yellowish stuff of which bees make their honeycomb, or some other substance that is like beeswax. ■ To *wax* is to become bigger as a new moon does in growing.

way The *way* to cook an egg is to put it in boiling water for four minutes. ■ The *way* to school is along London Road.

waylay To *waylay* anyone is to wait till he is near, and then suddenly appear (with the idea of talking to him, or robbing him).

wayside the side of the road.

W.C. (short for) water-closet (lavatory).

weak The invalid is so *weak* that he can't even sit up in bed. ■ *Weak* tea is almost tasteless and colourless (because there is too much water in it).

weaken To *weaken* anything is to make it weaker.

weakling a weak, unhealthy person or animal.

weakness This stormy sea will break through the sea-wall wherever there is a *weakness*. ■ Auntie has a *weakness* for tea (i.e. she is very fond of it).

weal If you beat anyone with a whip or a stick, it makes a *weal* (line of raised flesh) on his body.

wealth To have great *wealth* is to possess a great deal of money, property, or other valuables.

wealthy rich.

weapon something such as a gun, sword, spear, knife, etc., that is used for fighting.

wear I shall *wear* my new clothes today. ■ Walking on this rough ground will soon *wear* holes in your shoes.

weary Tom was so *weary* after all that hard work that he fell asleep before he could get into bed. ■ I won't *weary* (bore) you with the details of the story.

weasel a small, thin, wiry, furry animal which eats other small animals.

weasel

weather The farmers want rainy *weather*, but the holiday-makers want sunny *weather*. ■ To *weather* a storm, etc., is to come through it safely.

weave You use a loom to *weave* threads into cloth.

web-footed *Web-footed* creatures such as ducks have skin joining their toes (so that they can swim better).

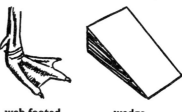

web-footed   **wedge**

wedding At their *wedding* Mr. Brown and Miss Smith will become Mr. and Mrs. Brown.

wedge a V-shaped piece of solid wood or metal. ■ You *wedge* a door open by pushing a wedge under it.

wedged Susan was *wedged* in the corner so tightly that she couldn't move.

Wednesday the fourth day of the week.

weed any wild plant that is not wanted in the garden or on a farm. ■ To *weed* the garden is to remove the weeds from it.

weedy A *weedy* garden is one full of weeds. ■ A *weedy* person is one who is thin and weak-looking.

week There are seven days in a *week*.

weekly each week, or once a week, e.g. *weekly* payments, *weekly* newspapers.

weep to cry, i.e. to shed tears.

weevil a little beetle that damages food and crops, especially grain.

weigh *Weigh* the parcel on the scales. ■ Tell me how many kilogrammes it *weighs*.

weight To find the *weight* of a thing you weigh it–on scales usually. ■ a piece of metal of known weight, used when weighing things on scales.

weir a barrier put across a stream. (The water level on one side of the *weir* is raised, so making a little waterfall.)

weir

weird People think the house is haunted because of the *weird* (strange) noises that come from inside it.

welcome Mother went out to *welcome* the guests (i.e. to let them know she was glad to see them). ■ You are sure of a *welcome* at our house (i.e. you may be sure that we shall be glad to see you). ■ You are *welcome* to the apples (i.e. I shall be pleased for you to take them).

weld To *weld* two pieces of metal is to join them together by heating, hammering, etc., so that they become as one piece.

welfare When people inquire about your *welfare* they want to know whether or not you're healthy and happy. ■ A *welfare* state is one in which people who are sick, old, or unemployed, etc., are looked after.

well a deep hole made in the earth to obtain water, oil, etc. ■ 'Are you ill?' 'No, I am quite *well*, thank you.' ■ You did *well* to get such high marks in the examination.

Wellingtons rubber boots that reach almost to your knees.

Wellingtons

Welsh the people of Wales; ■ the language of Wales.

wench a girl or a young woman.

went Last year we *went* to Scotland for our holidays.

wept cried (i.e. shed tears).

were The boys *were* in school yesterday, and they *were* working hard.

west The sun rises in the east and sets in the *west*.

westerly A *westerly* wind is one that blows from the west to the east.

western The *western* part of a country, etc., is the part that is farthest west. ■ A *western* is a book or a film about cowboys, Indians, gunmen, etc., in the west of the U.S.A. years ago.

West Indies islands west of the Atlantic Ocean between North and South America.

westward To get from London to New York the fastest you travel *westward* (i.e. to the west).

whack The men driving the cattle to market *whack* them with sticks if they go the wrong way.

whale a very big sea animal, hunted for its oil.

whale

wharf

wharf a platform beside which ships are tied up for loading or unloading.

what *What* do you want? ■ I do not know *what* to do.

whatever I will do *whatever* (anything) you ask me. ■ We are going to the seaside *whatever* the weather (if the weather is good or bad). ■ We have none *whatever* (i.e. none at all).

wheat a grass-like plant, the seeds of which are ground to make flour.

wheat

wneel

wheel Jim rode into a tree and bent the front *wheel* of his bicycle.

P

■ You'll have to walk and *wheel* the bicycle if you cannot ride it.

wheelbarrow a small hand-cart with one wheel.

wheelbarrow

wheeze to breathe noisily like someone with a cold in his chest.

when I shall be glad *when* Christmas comes. ■ *When* shall I come – at 6 o'clock?

whenever We will start *whenever* you like.

where *Where* are you going? ■ You may go *where* you like.

wherever My dog follows me *wherever* I go.

whet To *whet* a tool (e.g. a knife) is to sharpen it ■ on a *whet*-stone. ■ To *whet* someone's appetite is to make him more hungry (e.g. by giving him a little of something to taste).

whether I don't know *whether* I can come to your party. I can't decide *whether* to go swimming or (whether) to play cricket.

which You may have *which* apple you like. ■ *Which* of the boys is Jim? ■ The train *which* is in platform 7 leaves in a minute.

whiff Let's go outside for a *whiff* (breath) of fresh air. ■ I got a *whiff* (smell) of the turkey when the oven door was opened.

while A thief broke into our house *while* we were out shopping. ■ I have been here a long *while*. ■ *While* we waited we talked, read, or played cards, ■ to *while* away the time.

whim a sudden wish – usually for something that you don't really want very much.

whimper the quiet cry of an unhappy child or dog. ■ To *whimper* is to cry quietly.

whine When dogs *whine*, they make a long sad sound. ■ As soon as anything goes wrong, Ian begins to *whine* (i.e. to complain and grumble).

whinny the sound made by a horse. ■ I heard the horse *whinny*.

whip a stick with a cord on it. ■ To *whip* someone is to beat him with a whip. ■ To *whip* an egg, or cream, etc., is to beat it up in a basin, etc., with a fork or a machine.

whip   whirlpool

whipped Mary *whipped* the cream till it became stiff. ■ The guard took a whip and *whipped* the prisoner till he cried out in pain. ■ *Whipped* cream is cream that has been beaten till it is stiff.

whir (whirr) a noise such as that made by the wheels of a machine turning quickly and quietly, or by the rapid movement of birds' wings. ■ Ciné cameras *whirr* as they take moving pictures.

whirl The dancers *whirl* round and round till they're dizzy. ■ Cowboys *whirl* their ropes round and round above their heads before throwing them.

whirlpool The water in a *whirlpool* spins round and round.

whirlwind The wind in a *whirlwind* goes round and round with great force.

whirred Dad pulled the knob and the car self-starter *whirred* (i.e. made a quiet noise of rapidly turning wheels).

whirring You hear a *whirring* noise from a machine as its wheels spin round quickly but quietly.

whisk You use an egg-*whisk* for beating (whisking) eggs. ■ Horses *whisk* their tails to brush away flies.

whiskers stiff hair, e.g. above a cat's mouth, or on a man's face.

whisper If you speak in a *whisper*, only a person very near can hear you. ■ If you don't want other people to hear your message, *whisper* it in my ear.

whispered Mary *whispered* the words in my ear so that no one else could hear what she said.

whistle a small instrument for making a loud, high-pitched noise – used by football referees, policemen, etc. ■ You *whistle* by making a tiny hole with your lips and blowing through it.

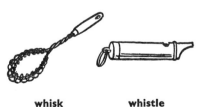

whisk   whistle

whistling A *whistling* kettle will whistle loudly when it boils. ■ Tom is *whistling* a tune (i.e. by blowing through a hole between his lips).

Whit *Whit* Sunday is the 7th Sunday after Easter. *Whit* Monday was the holiday that followed *Whit* Sunday.

white the colour of snow, milk, etc. ■ The *white* of an egg is the clear part that becomes white when you cook it.

whiteness The *whiteness* of the mountain-top is due to the covering of snow on it.

whitewash a mixture of lime and water, painted on walls to make them white. ■ To *whitewash* anything is to paint it with whitewash. ■ To *whitewash* a person is to cover up or excuse his faults.

whither (an old-fashioned word) where, e.g. *Whither* are you going?

whiting Sea fishermen catch many *whiting* for people to eat. A *whiting* is like a small cod-fish.

whiz, whizz A gun was fired and Dick heard the bullet *whiz* past his ear.

*****who** *Who* has borrowed my pen? ■ You are the boy *who* broke the window.

*****whoever** The boys who did the damage must be punished *whoever* they are.

*****whole** *Whole* numbers are those without fractions, e.g. 2, 5, 17, etc. ■ The greedy boy put a *whole* cake in his mouth at once. ■ The snake swallowed the rat *whole* (i.e. not in pieces). ■ Joan dropped a tray of cups and couldn't find one

whole (unbroken) one among the pieces.

*****wholesale** To sell things *wholesale* is to sell them in large quantities, e.g. to a shopkeeper.

*****wholesome** good for you, e.g. *wholesome* food, *wholesome* entertainment.

*****wholly** (pron. hóle-y) I do not *wholly* agree with you (i.e. I agree with only some of your ideas).

*****whom** John is the boy to *whom* I gave the money.

*****whoop** a loud shout of joy or excitement; ■ the noise of a deep breath being taken in with great difficulty, especially by someone with whooping-cough (also spelt, and pron., *hoop*).

*****whooping-cough** a disease which causes people to cough violently and then gasp for breath.

*****whose** *Whose* books are these? ■ These are the boys *whose* photographs were in the newspaper.

why *Why* are you hiding? ■ I will tell you *why* Tom is laughing.

wick the strip of material that goes up the middle of a candle or an oil lamp (the oil soaks up it and burns at the top).

wick

wicked *Wicked* people are those who do things that are very wrong.

wicker   A *wicker* basket or chair, etc., is one made by weaving together the stems of plants.

wicker basket   **wicket gate**

wicket   In cricket, the *wicket* is the three stumps with two bails fitted across the top of them, ■ or it may be the pitch (e.g. a sticky *wicket*, a fast *wicket*, etc.). ■ A *wicket* gate is a small one, especially one for use when a big gate near by is not open.

wide   If a door is *wide* open you cannot open it any further. ■ The stream is too *wide* for me to jump across. ■ In cricket, a *wide* is a ball beyond the batsman's reach.

widow   a woman whose husband has died.

widower   a man whose wife has died.

width   The *width* of my ruler is 30 mm; its length is 300 mm.

wield   To *wield* a sword is to fight with it; ■ to *wield* an axe is to chop with it; ■ to *wield* power over a country, etc., is to rule it.

wife   Mr. Smith's *wife* is the lady he married, Mrs. Smith.

wigwam   a Red Indian's tent.

wild   A *wild* animal is one such as a lion, or wolf, etc., that has not been caught and taught things by men. ■ *Wild* flowers are those that grow in the countryside (i.e. not grown on farms nor in gardens). ■ Billy is a *wild* boy (i.e. he is not under control.)

wilderness   a desert; ■ a part of a garden in which plants are allowed to grow wild.

wildly   Billy got into a temper and hit out *wildly* in all directions.

wilds   The *wilds* of a country are the uncivilized parts.

wilful   intentional, not accidental, e.g. *wilful* disobedience, *wilful* murder. ■ A *wilful* person is one who does what he likes, regardless of the wishes or advice of others.

will   a document in which a person says who is to have his property after his death. ■ The boys *will* be there tomorrow. ■ I *will* (am determined to) make a noise if I want to. ■ You need a strong *will* to stop yourself from doing things that you like doing.

willing   I am *willing* to go (i.e. I don't mind going). ■ Bob is a *willing* boy (i.e. he doesn't mind doing things for people).

willingly   I will *willingly* do the shopping (i.e. I don't mind doing it).

willow   the wood from willow trees, used to make cricket bats, etc. ■ *Willow* trees usually grow near water.

wigwam   **willow trees**

wilt Plants *wilt* if you take them out of the soil and leave them in the sun.

wily A *wily* person is one who is crafty and up to all kinds of cunning tricks.

wince When the doctor pushes a needle into my arm I *wince* (i.e. I make a little movement because of the pain).

winch a device for hoisting things, e.g. by turning a handle which winds a rope on to a drum.

windscreen The driver of a vehicle sees the road ahead of him through a *windscreen* made of special tough glass.

windy A *windy* day is one on which there is a fairly strong wind blowing.

wine a drink containing alcohol, and made from the juice of grapes or other fruits.

wing A bird flies by flapping its *wings*. ■ To make the school bigger, a new *wing* has been built on to it.

    winch   **window**

    windscreen   **winkle**

wind (pron. to rhyme with 'tinned') The *wind* blew so hard that trees were uprooted. ■ A *wind* instrument is one such as a trumpet or clarinet, which the player blows. ■ (pron. to rhyme with 'kind') To *wind* up a clock you turn a key, which tightens a spring. ■ You *wind* wool into a ball; machines *wind* cotton on to reels. ■ Rivers *wind* when their courses are not straight but full of curves and bends.

window Light gets into a room through the glass in the *window*.

window-pane a piece of glass fixed into a window-frame.

window-sill the big slab of stone or wood on which a window stands.

wink To *wink* at someone is to shut one eye at him. ■ To *wink* at something is to pretend not to see it. ■ I didn't sleep a *wink* (i.e. not at all).

winkle a small sea snail that is good to eat.

winner The *winner* is the one who beats all the others in a race or a competition, etc.

winning Tom was in the *winning* team (i.e. the team who won). ■ George has a *winning* (charming) smile.

winter The weather is colder in *winter* than in summer.

wintry *Wintry* weather is cold, unpleasant weather.

wipe You *wipe* your nose on your handkerchief.

wire metal made long and thin, like string. Electricity travels along *wire*. ■ To *wire* a house is to put the necessary electric wires in it. ■ To send a *wire* is to send a telegram.

wireless a radio (set). On a *wireless* set you can hear sound broadcasts from all parts of the world.

wiry A *wiry* person is one who is tough and doesn't easily tire.

wisdom knowledge and the ability to use it well.

wise A *wise* person is one who has much knowledge and the ability to use it well.

wisely Tom spends his money *wisely* (i.e. as a wise person would).

wish I *wish* you a happy Christmas. ■ I *wish* the sun would shine. ■ If a fairy gave me one *wish*, I would ask for happiness.

wisp a small amount, e.g. a *wisp* of hay (a handful), a *wisp* of smoke (a thin spiral).

wistful thoughtful. *Wistful* eyes, or voice, etc., usually show that the person is wishing for something, e.g. The hungry boy looked *wistful* as he passed the cakes in the shop window.

witch People used to think that a *witch* was an old woman who rode on a broomstick and could work magic.

witch

witchcraft the use of magic.

with Tom goes to school *with* Mary. ■ Dad dug the hole *with* a spade.

withdraw I wish to *withdraw* (take back) my offer to lend you the money. ■ The general decided to *withdraw* his soldiers (i.e. to remove them from their positions).

wither In autumn the leaves *wither* (dry up) and fall off the trees.

withered A *withered* arm or leg, etc., is one that has become small and weak through disease.

within Library books have to be returned *within* a week (i.e. before a week has passed). ■ Foreign ships may not fish *within* three miles of the coast.

without I am wet because I was caught in the rain *without* my mac. ■ Don't go *without* saying goodbye to Mother.

witness someone who sees something happen, but especially someone called to a law court to tell what he has seen, as evidence.

witticism an amusing remark.

witty humorous, e.g. A *witty* remark is one that amuses people.

wives When women marry men they become the *wives* of the men.

wizard a man who works magic.

wizened The lady was old and *wizened* (small and wrinkled as if dried up).

woad a blue dye with which primitive people used to paint themselves.

wobble to rock about from side to side, e.g. like a jelly when you jerk the dish containing it.

wobbly A *wobbly* chair, etc., is one that is not firm (e.g. it moves about under you unless you sit completely still).

woe very great sadness. ■ Mrs. Jones told us all her *woes* (troubles).

woebegone sad-looking.

woeful sad (usually used in a slightly humorous way, e.g. Dad apologized for his *woeful* ignorance of pop music).

woke At the sound of the alarm clock the boys *woke* and sat up in bed.

wolf a fierce, dog-like wild animal.

wolf   woodpecker

wolves fierce, dog-like wild animals.

woman When a girl grows up she becomes a *woman*.

women When girls grow up they become *women*.

wonder It is a *wonder* that you weren't killed when you fell over that high cliff. ■ I *wonder* (I would like to know) whether Janet knows I am here.

wondered Mary *wondered* (tried to think) what it would be like to travel in space.

wonderful We had a *wonderful* holiday (i.e. it was even better than we had expected). ■ Uncle has invented a *wonderful* machine (i.e. one that does greater things than you would expect).

won't (short for) will not, e.g. I *won't* be long.

woo To *woo* a girl is to try to win her love so that she will marry you.

wood an area of land on which trees grow close together. ■ This table is made of *wood* cut from an oak tree.

wooden *Wooden* articles are those made of wood. ■ A *wooden* person is one who is stiff and awkward (as if made of wood).

woodpecker a handsome bird which makes a hole in a tree for its nest and is often seen clinging to the trunk of a tree pecking insects out of the bark.

wooed Jack *wooed* Joan (i.e. he tried to win her love so that she would marry him).

wool The *wool* used to make clothes, etc., grows on sheep.

woollen A *woollen* garment is one made of wool.

woolly a garment made of wool, especially a pullover or a sweater. ■ A *woolly* toy, etc., is one made of sheepskin with the wool on it.

word This sentence contains five *words*. ■ Don't move till I give the *word* (i.e. the order). ■ I give you my *word* (i.e. I promise). ■ Tell me how to *word* the message (i.e. what words to use).

wore It was cold yesterday so I *wore* my overcoat.

work Most people have to *work* to earn a living. ■ How does this machine *work* (go)? ■ Can you *work* out (discover) the answer to this problem?

worker someone who works, but especially a man who works for someone else, in a factory, or a mine, etc.

working A *working* man is one who works for his living, especially one who works with his hands. ■ A *working* model (e.g. of a train) is one in which the parts move like those in the real thing. ■ A *working* day is the number of hours per day that a man works.

workmanship the skill of a workman, especially one who makes such things as furniture, jewellery, etc.

works a factory. ■ The machine stopped because someone dropped a spanner in the *works*. ■ The clock *works* again now that Dad has mended it.

workshop a place where men work with tools, e.g. a carpenter's *workshop*.

world The *world* is made up of five continents, Europe, Asia, Africa, America and Australia, and a great area of sea. ■ There are many unexplored *worlds* out in space.

worldly A *worldly* person is one who is interested only in the pleasures of this life (he is not, for example, interested in religion, or life after death).

worm a small, slimy, snake-like creature found in the soil.

worn I have *worn* a hole in the sole of my shoe through walking so much. ■ I haven't *worn* my coat today because the sun was shining.

worried Mother is *worried* (anxious) if I am late home. ■ The farmer is angry because our dog *worried* his sheep (i.e. the dog bit the sheep and pulled them about).

worry Mother will *worry* if I am home late (i.e. she will fear that something has happened to me). ■ Don't *worry* me when I'm busy (i.e. don't try to get my attention). ■ Don't let your dog *worry* the sheep (i.e. chase and bite them). ■ Jill is a *worry* to her mother (i.e. she causes her mother to worry about her).

worrying I shall not stop *worrying* about Jill till I know that she is safe.

worse They are both bad boys, but Simon is *worse* than Peter. ■ The sick man is not better; he is *worse* (i.e. more ill then he was).

worship A church is a place of *worship*, ■ i.e. a place where people go to *worship* God. ■ People call the mayor, 'Your *Worship*.'

worst Of all the bad boys I know, Simon is the *worst* (the others are less bad). This is the *worst* weather we've had for years.

worth If an article is *worth* £1, then £1 is the fair price for it. ■ This book is *worth* reading (i.e. it is not a waste of time to read it). ■ I've bought a shilling's *worth* of sweets.

worm

worthless A *worthless* article is one that has no value, i.e. no one would give you anything for it.

worthy To be *worthy* of something is to deserve it. ■ A *worthy* person is one who is well thought of by all who know him.

would Jimmy *would* have drowned if Tom hadn't rescued him.

wouldn't (short for) would not, e.g. Jane *wouldn't* do as she was told.

wound (pron. woond) an injury – usually a deep gash in the flesh. ■ To *wound* a person is to injure his body (e.g. by shooting him), or to hurt his feelings (e.g. by saying something unkind). ■ (pron. to rhyme with 'sound') My watch is still going because I *wound* it up last night. ■ Mary *wound* the wool into a ball before she started to knit with it.

wove We watched as the woman *wove* the threads into cloth on her loom.

wrangle a noisy quarrel or argument; ■ to quarrel or argue noisily.

wrap I like to *wrap* Christmas presents in pretty paper. ■ Joan likes to *wrap* a scarf round her neck when she is cold. ■ a scarf or shawl, etc., put round the neck for warmth.

wrapped The vase was *wrapped* in cotton wool so that it would not get broken in the post. ■ Joan *wrapped* her scarf round her neck to keep her warm.

wrapper the cover or paper, etc., in which something is wrapped.

wrapping Mary removed the *wrapping* from the parcel to see what was inside it. ■ I love *wrapping* up Christmas parcels in pretty paper.

wrath (an old-fashioned word) anger.

wreath The woman put a *wreath* (a ring of flowers) on her husband's grave.

wreath   wren

wreck From the cliffs you can see the *wreck* of the ship which was smashed on the rocks during the storm. ■ Is that stupid driver trying to *wreck* his car (i.e. smash it up)?

wreckage The *wreckage* of the crashed aircraft was strewn over the mountain side.

wren a very small European bird.

wrench to pull or twist hard, e.g. Dad had to *wrench* open the door. ■ a hard pull or twist, e.g. I gave my ankle a painful *wrench*. ■ a tool with which to grip nuts in order to turn them.

---

* The 'w' is not sounded in words that begin with 'wr'.

***wrestle** The policeman had to *wrestle* (struggle) with the criminal in order to get the handcuffs on him. ■ When people *wrestle* for sport, they try to hold and throw each other.

wrestler a man who likes to wrestle for sport.

wrestling a sport in which two men struggle to hold and throw each other. ■ Seeing a policeman *wrestling* (struggling) with a criminal, Dad went for help.

wretch a person who does disgraceful things; ■ a miserable person, e.g. I feel sorry for that poor *wretch* who begs in the street.

wretched miserable, e.g. I saw the *wretched* boy being led away in tears. ■ We had *wretched* (bad) weather during the holiday.

wriggle To *wriggle* is to twist about like a worm.

wriggling Why are you *wriggling* about in your seat? (i.e. Why don't you sit still?) ■ Jane screamed when Tom put a live, *wriggling* worm into her hand.

wring Mother likes to *wring* the washing with her hands to get out as much water as possible.

wrinkle a crease in the skin, e.g. Janet has a *wrinkle* beside each eye when she laughs. ■ When you *wrinkle* your brows you make little creases come into the skin.

wrist You wear a *wrist*-watch; ■ it is strapped round your *wrist*.

write *Write* your name on this piece of paper.

writhe To *writhe* is to twist about (usually in pain). We saw the injured man *writhe* in agony.

writing Pat is *writing* her name on her examination paper. ■ You write letters to people on *writing* paper.

written Read what I have *written* on this paper. ■ *Written* instructions, etc., are those set down on paper in writing.

wrong It is *wrong* to steal, to hurt people, to cause unhappiness, etc. ■ To *wrong* anyone is to think, say, or do something that is not fair to him.

wrote Mary *wrote* the boy's name in her diary some time ago.

wrung I have *wrung* as much water as possible out of the washing (i.e. by twisting and squeezing it).

wry A *wry* neck, nose, or mouth, etc., is one that is twisted to one side.

Xmas (short for) Christmas.

x-rays invisible rays used to take ■ *x-ray* photographs of bones, etc., inside the body.

xylophone a musical instrument consisting of a frame across the top of which lie strips of wood, which are played with little wooden hammers.

wrist   **xylophone**

* The 'w' is not sounded in words that begin with 'wr'.

yacht a boat (not a row boat) used for pleasure, but especially a fast sailing boat.

yacht   yew

yachting sailing about in a yacht.

yap the high-pitched bark of a fussy little dog. ■ I don't let my dog *yap* if it annoys the neighbours.

yapping We were awakened by the *yapping* of the little dog next door.

yard 1 *yard* is nearly a metre in length. ■ Behind the house is a back *yard* where Mother hangs out the washing and Dad keeps pigeons.

yarn thread, especially the kind that is spun from wool and used for weaving or knitting; ■ a tale, e.g. To spin a *yarn* is to tell a story.

yawn People open their mouths wide in a *yawn* when they are tired or bored. ■ People *yawn* when they are tired or bored.

ye (an old-fashioned word) you.

yea (an old-fashioned word) yes.

year 1 *year* = 12 months. (A *year* is the time the earth takes to go round the sun.)

yearly A *yearly* event is one that happens once in every year.

yearn To *yearn* for something is to feel a great longing for it, e.g. to *yearn* for home, or for affection.

yeast a soft, yellowish, living substance used for brewing beer, making bread rise, etc.

yell Billy was kicked on the shin and let out a *yell* that could be heard in the next street. ■ You will have to *yell* to make your voice heard above all this noise.

yellow the colour of gold and buttercups.

yelp I heard a *yelp* of pain from the dog as I trod on its foot.

yeoman a farmer who has his own small farm.

yesterday If today is Monday, *yesterday* was Sunday.

yet We can't start *yet*, for Jane hasn't arrived. ■ I gave him all he asked for, *yet* he is still not satisfied.

yew an evergreen tree with tiny leaves and poisonous red berries.

yield A cow will *yield* several gallons of milk each day. ■ Tom tried to make Janet change her mind, but she would not *yield*.

yoke a wooden frame put round the necks of oxen so that they pull together on a plough, or cart, etc. ■ the shoulder or waist piece of a shirt or skirt, etc., from which the rest of the garment hangs.

ox yoke   dress yoke

yokel a humble, simple country-man.

yolk the yellow part of an egg.

yonder (an old-fashioned word) over there, e.g. On *yonder* hill is the man we seek. '*Yonder* peasant, who is he?'

you *You* are your father's child. ■ Are all *you* boys in the same form?

you'll (short for) you will. If you don't hurry, *you'll* be late for school.

young A *young* person is one who is not grown up. ■ Most animals look after their *young* (i.e. their babies).

younger Bill is 10 and Tom is 8, so Tom is two years *younger* than Bill.

youngest Colin was born after his brothers and sisters, so that he is the *youngest* in the family.

youngster a boy or a girl, but especially a lively boy.

your Open *your* mouth and put out *your* tongue.

you're (short for) you are, e.g. Look where *you're* going.

yours I like my book better than I like *yours*. I usually end letters with the words, '*Yours* sincerely,' followed by my name.

yourself You can't blame any-one else for breaking the pen when you did it *yourself*.

youth a young man, older than a child, but not a grown-up. ■ Grandad was a keen sportsman in his *youth* (i.e. when he was young).

youthful young, e.g. Our *youthful* visitor is Pamela's boy-friend.

you've (short for) you have, e.g. *You've* dropped your handkerchief.

Yugoslav one of the people of Yugoslavia. ■ *Yugoslav* things are those from Yugoslavia (also spelt *Jugoslav*).

Yugoslavia a country in south-east Europe, east of Italy (also spelt *Jugoslavia*).

yule-tide Christmas-time.

Z

zeal enthusiasm, e.g. You can see by the *zeal* with which the boys are setting about the job that they are keen on doing it.

zealous A *zealous* person is one who is full of enthusiasm.

zebra an animal like a horse with a striped coat. ■ A *zebra* crossing is a path across a road, marked with stripes so that drivers know that they have to stop their vehicles there to let people cross.

zebra   zebra crossing

zero nought (o), e.g. five, four, three, two, one, *zero*. Ice begins to form when the temperature falls to *zero* (o°).

zest The boys joined in the party with *zest* (i.e. with great en-thusiasm and enjoyment).

zigzag A *zigzag* line is made up of a series of sharp turns to right and left.

zigzag

zinc a white metal which doesn't rust and is therefore used for coating sheet-iron, making the edges of roofs water-tight, etc.

zip   a noise such as that made by cloth suddenly tearing. ■ A *zip* fastener is used to join the two edges of a garment, or a bag. (The special metal, or plastic, edges are fastened by sliding a clip along them.)

zither   a musical instrument consisting of strings stretched over a flat box and played by plucking.

zone   an area of the earth's surface, e.g. the temperate *zone*.

zoo   a zoological garden.

zoological   A *zoological* garden is one such as that in Regent's Park, London, where people can go to see wild animals in cages and enclosures.

zoologist   a scientist who studies animals.

zoology   the scientific study of animals.

Zulu   A *Zulu* is a member of a tribe of native South Africans.

zip   zither